THEOLOGY IN CONFLICT

SUPPLEMENTS TO
NOVUM TESTAMENTUM

EDITORIAL STAFF

C. K. Barrett, Durham
A. F. J. Klijn, Haren — J. Smit Sibinga, Amsterdam

Editorial Secretary: H. J. de Jonge, Leiden

VOLUME LIII

LEIDEN / E. J. BRILL / 1980

THEOLOGY IN CONFLICT

Studies in Paul's Understanding of God in Romans

BY

HALVOR MOXNES

LEIDEN / E. J. BRILL / 1980

ISBN 90 04 06140 1

To Nils Alstrup Dahl

and

Birgit Rosencrantz Dahl

CONTENTS

PREFACE

This study was started under Professor Nils A. Dahl at Yale University Divinity School in 1973-74, and as a small token of gratitude it is dedicated to him and to Mrs. Birgit Dahl. Professor Dahl was a stimulating and patient supervisor who shared his great knowledge generously with me and gave direction and structure to my work, and Mrs. Dahl followed my work with energetic support. I also want to express my gratitude to my professors at the Faculty of Theology at the Oslo University, above all to Professor Jacob Jervell, who first taught me how to read the New Testament, and who followed my work on this study to its completion with constructive criticism and encouragement. Furthermore, I am grateful to New Testament scholars at Yale, Duke, Tübingen and Cambridge for their interest in my work, in particular I will mention Dr. W. D. Davies at Duke University who shared his thorough knowledge of Paul and Judaism with me.

Thanks are also due to the various libraries I have used. First I must mention the Royal University Library in Oslo and its branch at the Faculty of Theology, further, the University and Divinity Schools Libraries at Yale, Duke, Tübingen and Cambridge and the Tyndale Biblical Research Library in Cambridge and the British Library in London.

This study could not have been undertaken without a fellowship in theology from the Oslo University. I am further greatly indebted to Yale University Divinity School for generously awarding me a Research Fellowship for two years, and to the Department of Religion at Duke University, Durham, N.C., for the opportunity to spend a term as visiting scholar there. Two travel grants from the Norwegian Research Council for Science and the Humanities made my studies in the United States possible.

I have written this study in English, but cannot claim that it is idiomatic. I am grateful to my Cambridge friends, Dr. Claude Schneider, Dr. Brian McNeil and Dr. Gerald Bray who have read and corrected the manuscript, and who have made valuable suggestions which have greatly improved the style. Further, I wish to express my gratitude to Mrs. Perdita Robinson, who with great skill and much needed patience typed the manuscript, and to Mr. Vernon Robinson who helped edit it. Cand. theol. Leif

J. Hvidsten and stud. theol. Oluf Volkckmar and Knut Erling Johansen helped prepare the index.

Finally, I am indebted to Prof. W. C. van Unnik, who, shortly before he died, accepted this study for inclusion in the Supplements to Novum Testamentum, and to the Norwegian Research Council for Sciences and the Humanities for a substantial grant towards the publication costs of this book.

ACKNOWLEDGMENTS

Biblical quotations are taken from *The New Oxford Annotated Bible with the Apocrypha* (RSV), Oxford, 1973; quotations from the pseudepigrapha from *The Apocrypha and Pseudepigrapha of the Old Testament*. II. The Pseudigrapha. Ed. by R. H. Charles, Oxford, 1913; quotations from Philo from the translations by F. H. Colson, G. H. Whitaker and R. Marcus in the Loeb Classical Library.

ABBREVIATIONS

The abbreviations of periodicals, reference works and serials follow the style sheet in *Journal for Biblical Literature* 95 (1976) 339-46, with some additions. This style sheet is also followed for abbreviations for biblical, apocryphal, pseudepigraphal, Rabbinic and Qumran references. Abbreviations for the works of Philo are taken from *Studia Philonica* I (1972) 92, for the works of the Fathers of the Early Church from G. W. Lampe, *A Patristic Greek Lexicon*. Oxford. 1973.

AB	Anchor Bible
ALGHJ	Arbeiten zur Literatur und Geschichte des hellenistischen Judentums
AnBib	Analecta Biblica
ATANT	Abhandlungen zur Theologie des Alten und Neuen Testaments
Bauer	W. Bauer, Griechisch-Deutsches Wörterbuch zu den Schriften des Neuen Testaments und der übrigen urchristlichen Literatur. 5th edition. Berlin. 1963
BDF	F. Blass and A. Debrunner, *A Greek Grammar of the New Testament and Other Early Christian Literature*. Transl. and rev. by R. W. Funk. Chicago. 1961
BETL	Bibliotheca ephemeridum theologicarum lovaniensium
BEvT	Beiträge zur evangelischen Theologie
BHT	Beiträge zur historischen Theologie
Bib	*Biblica*
Billerbeck	H. Strack and P. Billerbeck, *Kommentar zum Neuen Testament aus Talmud und Midrasch*, 6 vols. Munich. 1922-1961
BWANT	Beiträge zur Wissenschaft vom Alten und Neuen Testament
BZ	*Biblische Zeitschrift*
BZAW	Beihefte zur Zeitschrift für die alttestamentliche Wissenschaft
BZNW	Beihefte zur Zeitschrift für die neutestamentliche Wissenschaft
CBQ	*Catholic Biblical Quarterly*
ConBNT	Coniectanea biblica. New Testament series
DBSup	Dictionnaire de la bible. Supplément. 1ff. Paris. 1928ff
EHS.T	Europäische Hochschulschriften. Reihe 23: Theologie
EvT	*Evangelische Theologie*
FRLANT	Forschungen zur Religion und Literatur des Alten und Neuen Testaments
GCS	Die griechischen christlichen Schriftsteller der ersten drei Jahrhunderte
HNT	Handbuch zum Neuen Testament
HTKNT	Herders theologischer Kommentar zum Neuen Testament
HTR	*Harvard Theological Review*
HUCA	*Hebrew Union College Annual*
IDBSup	Interpreter's Dictionary of the Bible. Supplementary volume. Nashville. 1976
JBL	*Journal of Biblical Literature*
JQR	*Jewish Quarterly Review*
JSJ	*Journal for the Study of Judaism in the Persian, Hellenistic and Roman Period*

MeyerK	H. A. W. Meyer, Kritisch-exegetischer Kommentar über das Neue Testament
MGWJ	*Monatsschrift für Geschichte und Wissenschaft des Judentums*
NorTT	*Norsk Teologisk Tidsskrift*
NovT	*Novum Testamentum*
NovTSup	Novum Testamentum, Supplements
NTAbh	Neutestamentliche Abhandlungen
NTD	Das Neue Testament Deutsch
NTS	*New Testament Studies*
PG	Patrologiae cursus completus. Accurante J.-P. Migne. Series Graeca
PL	Patrologiae cursus completus. Series Latina
QD	Quaestiones disputatae
RB	*Revue biblique*
RHPR	*Revue d'histoire et de philosophie religieuses*
SANT	Studien zum Alten und Neuen Testament
SBL	Society of Biblical Literature
SBS	Stuttgarter Bibelstudien
SBT	Studies in Biblical Theology
SEÅ	*Svensk exegetisk årsskrift*
SJLA	Studies in Judaism in Late Antiquity
SNTSMS	Society for New Testament Studies Monograph Series
SP	*Studia philonica*
SPB	Studia postbiblica
ST	*Studia theologica*
TBü	Theologische Bücherei
TLZ	*Theologische Literaturzeitung*
TRu	*Theologische Rundschau*
TU	Texte und Untersuchungen
TWNT	*Theologisches Wörterbuch zum Neuen Testament.* 9 vols. Eds. G. Kittel and G. Friedrich. Stuttgart. 1933-73
TZ	*Theologische Zeitschrift*
VF	*Verkündigung und Forschung*
WA	Martin Luther, Kritische Gesamtausgabe (Weimar edition)
WMANT	Wissenschaftliche Monographien zum Alten und Neuen Testament
WUNT	Wissenschaftliche Untersuchungen zum Neuen Testament
ZNW	*Zeitschrift für die neutestamentliche Wissenschaft*
ZTK	*Zeitschrift für Theologie und Kirche*

INTRODUCTION

This study of Paul's understanding of God in his letter to the Romans has been undertaken in light of the renewed interest in recent years about the quest for God. Only a few years ago this question was seldom raised; in fact, so rarely was it broached that in 1975, Professor Nils A. Dahl provocatively, but not unjustly, characterized it as "the neglected factor in New Testament theology".[1]

Studies in the theology of the New Testament—in its narrow sense—are few and far between. This is all the more remarkable, in that there are quite a number of studies about the concept of God in the periods before and directly after the New Testament (i.e. Judaism on the one hand, the Early Church on the other).[2]

---

[1] The title of a paper read to the faculty conference at the Yale University Divinity School, September 1975, printed in *Reflection* 73/1 (Yale Divinity School, 1975) 5-8. The word "theology" has a wide range of implications. In this passage, Dahl uses it to mean "the discipline of study of the NT". That is different from "theology" as "the general content of the NT", as well as from "theo-logy", which Dahl employs for "the doctrine of God". Since we are primarily interested in Paul's use of language, we shall use "theology" in its narrower sense as "language about God", but always in its bearing upon the issues that Paul is discussing. So that we shall always keep this larger context in mind, we will not make any formal distinction between "theo-logy" and "theology".

[2] A look at the *Internationale Zeitschriftenschau für Bibelwissenschaft und Grenzgebiete* confirms this. Only from vol. 16 (1969-70) is there a separate entry for "God in NT". *Elenchus* has had a separate section on "God. NT" since vol. 40 (1959), but the comparison between the OT and the NT is made difficult since the NT section includes a variety of themes, as well as many entries on "God" in systematic theology. A good introduction with many bibliographical references to earlier works on the OT concept of God is W. H. Schmidt, *Alttestamentlicher Glaube und seine Umwelt. Zur Geschichte des alttestamentlichen Gottesverständnis* (Neukirchen, 1968). On God in Rabbinic Judaism the classical study is A. Marmorstein, *The Old Rabbinic Doctrine of God* 2 vols. (London, 1927, 1937). For bibliography, see J. Maier, *Geschichte der jüdischen Religion* (Berlin, 1972) 39-40. On God in the theology of the Early Church, see G. L. Prestige, *God in Patristic Thought* (2nd edition, London, 1952); R. A. Morris, *God and the World in Early Christian Theology*, (London, 1966); W. Pannenberg, "Die Aufnahme des philosopischen Gottesbegriffs als dogmatisches Problem der früchristlichen Theologie", *Zeitschrift für Kirchengeschichte* 70 (1959) 1-45. For an extensive bibliography covering also writers other than Tertullian, see J. Moingt, *Théologie trinitaire de Tertullien* 1 (Aubier, 1966) 29-48.

A few books about the theology of the New Testament are still
written after the traditional model of a textbook in systematic
theology. Here "God" is discussed as one among other themes.[3]
This approach is methodologically unsatisfactory in that it tends
to emphasize God's "essence and attributes", and thus it isolates
statements about God from their context. Other studies are more
satisfactory in this regard, especially in their discussion of the
teaching of Jesus in the Gospels. Most frequently Jesus' understanding of God is examined in the broader context of his proclamation of the coming kingdom.[4] Apart from that, this subject has
been mostly explored in short articles, some of which have been of
great importance.[5]

Paul has fared slightly better than other New Testament authors,
in that recently a number of articles have addressed themselves to
the question of God in his writings.[6] When this question has been
raised, most often it has focused upon the relationship between
theology and Christology. This is also the subject of the only full-
scale monograph published on Paul's theology so far, *Per Christum*

---

[3] E.g., A. Richardson (*An Introduction to the Theology of the New Testament*
(London, 1959) 62-83) deals with different "aspects" of God, his power, glory,
wrath etc. Similarly, K. H. Schelkle, *Theologie des Neuen Testaments* 2
(Düsseldorf, 1973) 251-322. Schelkle discusses the NT teaching about God in
a volume on christology. It is this context for the presentation of theology
which distinguishes his approach from that of traditional Catholic dogmatic
theology.

[4] A section on Jesus's proclamation of the Kingdom is often followed by
one dealing with his preaching of God; so R. Bultmann, *Theologie des Neuen
Testaments* (6th edition, Tübingen, 1968) 2-26; also W. G. Kümmel, *Die
Theologie des Neuen Testaments* (NTD Ergänzungsr. 3, Göttingen, 1969)
29-52. Less satisfactory in this regard is H. Conzelmann (*Grundriss der
Theologie des Neuen Testaments* (2nd edition, Munich, 1968) 118-46) who
divides the material into "Der Gottesgedanke", "Das Reich Gottes", and
"Die Forderung Gottes".

[5] Notice especially W. G. Kümmel, "Die Gottesverkündigung Jesu und
der Gottesgedanke des Spätjudentums", *Judaica* 1 (1945) 40-68; U. Luz,
"Einige Erwägungen zur Auslegung Gottes in der ethischen Verkündigung
Jesu", *Evangelisch-Katholischer Kommentar zum Neuen Testament*, Vorarbeiten 2 (Neukirchen, 1970) 119-30, 133-35; J. Becker, "Das Gottesbild Jesu
und die älteste Auslegung von Ostern", *Jesus Christus in Historie und Theologie, Festschrift für H. Conzelmann* (ed. G. Strecker, Tübingen, 1975) 105-26;
R. Schäfer, *Jesus und der Gottesglaube* (Tübingen, 1970).

[6] C. H. Giblin, "Three Monotheistic texts in Paul", *CBQ* 37 (1975) 527-47;
C. Demke, " 'Ein Gott und viele Herren'. Die Verkündigung des einen Gott
in den Briefen des Paulus", *EvT* 36 (1976) 473-84; W. Schrage, "Theologie
und Christologie bei Paulus und Jesus auf dem Hintergrund des modernen
Gottesfrage", *EvT* 36 (1976) 121-54.

in Deum by Wilhelm Thüsing.[7] A recent dissertation by Antoinette C. Wire, "Pauline Theology as an Understanding of God: The Explicit and the Implicit",[8] represents a significant step forwards. Here she is able to show how the context modifies Paul's explicit statements about God. Our knowledge of Paul's background in the Jewish tradition has been greatly enhanced by studies of appellations of God found in the New Testament letters. By far the most comprehensive of these is the almost monograph-size article by Gerhard Delling, "Partizipiale Gottesprädikationen in den Briefen des Neuen Testaments".[9] However, he makes only brief, although suggestive, remarks about the theological interpretation of this material.

These signs that the situation is changing in New Testament studies reflect a more visible shift of emphasis in other areas, notably in systematic theology.[10] After the question about God was seemingly made obsolete by the "Death of God"—debate of the 1960's, it underwent a remarkable revival, and has once again emerged as a primary focus of interest for theological discussion.

---

[7] *Studien zur Verhältnis von Christozentrik und Theozentrik in den paulinischen Hauptbriefen* (NTAbh NF 1, Münster, 1965). Even this theme has not been widely discussed; Thüsing refers primarily to W. Bousset, *Kyrios Christos* (Göttingen, 1913), and E. Rohde, "Gottesglaube und Kyriosglaube bei Paulus", *ZNW* 22 (1923) 43-57. See also Thüsing, "Neutestamentliche Zugangswege zu einen transzendental-dialogischen Christologie", K. Rahner and W. Thüsing, *Christologie — systematisch und exegetisch* (QD 55, Freiburg, 1972) 81-233; a shorter version is published as "Das Gottesbild des Neuen Testaments". *Die Frage nach Gott* (ed. J. Ratzinger, QD 56, Freiburg, 1972) 59-86. Although useful, Thüsing's work suffers from over-systematization of the biblical material. In *Per Christum ad Deum* he investigates Paul's use of prepositions governing "Christ", "God", without paying attention to the various contexts, genres, etc. where these phrases are found.

[8] Unpublished Ph.D. dissertation, Claremont, 1974.

[9] *ST* 17 (1963) 1-59; also "Geprägte partizipiale Gottesaussagen in der apostolischen Verkündigung", in his *Studien zum Neuen Testament und zum hellenistischen Judentum* (ed. F. Hahn, T. Holtz and N. Walter, Göttingen, 1970) 401-16; "Zusammengesetzte Gottes und Christusbezeichnungen in den Paulusbriefen", *ibid.* 417-24.

[10] For surveys of recent literature, including the "Death of God" debate, see R. Grass, "Die Gottesfrage in der gegenwärtigen Theologie", *TRu* 35 (1970) 231-69; H.-G. Geyer, "Gottes Sein als Thema der Theologie", *VF* 11 (1966) 3-37; B. Klappert, "Tendenzen der Gotteslehre in der Gegenwart", *EvT* 35 (1975) 189-208. For more references to English and American works, see F. Duane Lindsay, "Current American Theism—a Bibliographical Survey", *Bibliotheca Sacra* 126 (1969) 232-39; and K. Ward, "Recent Thinking on Christian Beliefs. 2. The Concept of God", *Expository Times* 88 (1976) 68-71.

It will suffice to mention a few indications of this: within the last few years various groups (e.g., the conference of German Catholic theologians, Lutheran theologians associated with the journal *Kerygma und Dogma*, and a group of French and Swiss Protestant professors) have arranged seminars and discussions of this question.[11] Significantly enough, this new quest is again more concerned with "God himself" than with his relation to mankind.[12] Thus there is a turning away from the anthropological concern that dominated so many theological studies in the last generation. This concern was voiced most influentially by Bultmann when he coined a phrase that became almost a theological axiom: "Es zeigt sich also: will man von Gott reden, so muss man offenbar *von sich selbst reden*" (his italics).[13] There is no doubt that Bultmann here is close to the way in which the Bible—as well as the Protestant Reformation—spoke of God, always with a view to his acts towards men. It is this perspective that risks being lost when the attention is focused on "God himself".

However, although Bultmann insisted that God and man be always spoken of together, the outcome was a rather one-sided concentration on man. This is evident in the section on Paul in his *Theologie des Neuen Testaments*, where he says in an introductory chapter: "Jeder Satz über Gott ist zugleich ein Satz über den Menschen und umgekehrt. Deshalb und in diesem Sinne ist *die paulinische Theologie zugleich Anthropologie*" (his italics).[14] This almost reads like a programme for the study of Paul, however, Bultmann never carried it out. He himself emphasized the former part of this statement, to the almost complete neglect of the latter. This was not because of oversight; rather, it was a result of his concern that God must not be conceptualized, for only so could his freedom vis-à-vis man be preserved. One should not think of faith in terms of acceptance of an idea of God, but rather as an

---

[11] The German Catholic contributions are published in *Die Frage nach Gott* (see n. 7), the Lutheran in several articles in *Kerygma und Dogma* 19/1 (1973) by E. Schlink, W. Joest *et al*. The French-Swiss group published its studies in *RHPR* 56/4 (1976) 467-544, under the title "Rendre compte de Dieu".

[12] Especially Schlink, *Kerygma und Dogma* 19 (1973) 8 and Ratzinger, *Die Frage nach Gott*, 5; more balanced is H.-G. Fritzsche, "Gott 'an sich' oder als 'Ausdruck für . . .'?" *TLZ* 100 (1975) 561-72.

[13] "Welchen Sinn hat es, von Gott zu Reden?", *Glauben und Verstehen* 1 (2nd edition, Tübingen, 1954) 28.

[14] *Theologie*, 192.

existential encounter with God, outside man's control.[15] Bultmann
here grasped a characteristic element in the way the New Testament—in particular Paul—described the encounter between God
and man. But Bultmann's insistence that God's freedom vis-à-vis
man could be preserved only by not conceptualizing him is less
self-evident.[16] For the authors of the New Testament, God's freedom
was not expressed through silence but through speech—they used
concepts of God expressed in words as their arguments. Consequently, we shall have to study what they actually said about
God. We cannot just continue where Bultmann left off, turn his
question around and start from the "vice versa" of his famous
statement, because we cannot without modification accept Bultmann's equation of "assertion about God" and "assertion about
man". The New Testament writers did not speak about "man" in
general. Rather, they addressed themselves to the question of
Israel and the church, that is, certain groups of people in a certain
space and a specific time. Therefore we must raise the questions,
both literary and historical, anew.[17]

First: how can we proceed from isolated statements about God
to an assessment of the place and function of theology within
Paul's thinking as a whole? And second: what was the function of
theology in the historical situation of Paul and his audience?
Studies of individual phrases or appellations for God, helpful and
necessary as they are, often manifest characteristics of a dogmatic
approach. Statements about God are isolated from their context
within the letter and treated as dogmatic expressions. Together
with this, there is often a tendency to study Paul's theology
primarily as a starting point for the subsequent development of
Christian doctrine.[18] Over against this, we will offer a different

---

[15] Wire, "Pauline Theology", 3.

[16] See the criticism by N. A. Dahl, "Die Theologie des Neuen Testaments",
TRu 22 (1954) 43-44.

[17] For the following, compare the viewpoints in L. E. Keck, "On the
Ethos of Early Christians", *Journal of the American Academy of Religion* 42
(1974) 435-52, and the study on Mark by H. L. Kee, *Community of the New
Age* (London, 1977).

[18] Notice the criticism of Bultmann by Keck, "Ethos", 439: "How much
different would Bultmann's *New Testament Theology* have turned out had
he probed each writer's (and not merely Paul's and John's) theology as both
growing out of and responding to the theological and moral issues they
perceived to be at stake in their communities? if their theologies had been
related more clearly to the social realities of the early Christian communities?"

approach, studying not the isolated statements as dogmatic sayings, but rather as they function within the wider literary context of Paul's argumentation. In doing this, we will follow Professor Dahl's proposals for the study of New Testament "theo-logy", in the article mentioned above: "The elementary, but all too neglected task is to make a careful, analytic description of words and phrases and of their use within sentences and larger units of speech (e.g. narratives, kerygmatic, credal and hymnic texts, maxims, doctrinal and paraenetic topoi, etc)". On the basis of such preliminary studies one may proceed to more general descriptions: "One option for the comprehensive survey would be to represent the form and function of theological language within the context of the New Testament writings, arranged according to their literary genre...".[19]

The *historical* question that corresponds to this approach concerns the function of statements about God in the religious, social and political situation of Paul and his audience. To what situation in the Early Church does the rhetorical situation of the letters correspond? It is the underlying assumption of this study that there is a close correspondence between the theological language used and a real situation in the Early Church. The centre of ancient religions was not an "idea" or a "concept" of God. Rather, religious life centred around the experience of interaction between God and man.[20] This implies that that the question about God was not primarily a theoretical one; rather, it was practical in nature. It did not deal with abstract ideas of faith, but with God's intervention in human life. Likewise, Israel's religion cannot be properly described as the development of the concept of God "an sich", it was always related to the pressing problems of Israel as a social, religious and political entity.[21] The Jews were frequently confronted in the face of suffering and oppression with the question of God's relationship with Israel. As a result, expressions of faith in God were, more than anything else, statements about God and Israel.

This mode of thinking was carried on by Jews who became Christians. For them also, the question of God and the identity of his people were inextricably bound up with one another.[22] Paul

---

[19] "Neglected Factor", 6.

[20] Cf. C. Westermann, *Die Verheissungen an die Väter* (FRLANT 116, Göttingen, 1976) 94.

[21] Cf. J. Maier, *Geschichte*, 39 and 162-63.

[22] Kee (*Community*, 107) argues that the question of identity takes precedence over that of theology: "The central feature is, therefore, the

was no exception to this.[23] The Christian church did not suddenly emerge as a totally new entity with a structure of its own. We are becoming more aware of how slow and gradual was the process in which small Christian groups were cut off from the mainstream of Jewish communities and developed a new set of group-commitments. Recent studies in the Gospels and in Acts have shown how this process provoked discussion and theological reflection that almost monotonously focused on the claim to be the true Israel.[24] In this first period of the church the Christians had to defend their identity vis-à-vis non-Christian Jews. Moreover, they had to express this identity in Jewish terms, that is, on the basis of common presuppositions. It was on this common ground that Paul also argued when he gave a theological defence for his missionary practice of including non-Jews in the Christian communities without circumcision.

Against this background, the traditional question of the relation between theo-logy and Christology takes on a new meaning. In this initial period, it was not a question of the belief in Jesus as God being a threat to Jewish monotheism. With more justification one could argue that it was the identity both of God and of his people that was at stake. From the life and teaching of Jesus sprang a new group within Judaism. Its members proclaimed that God had vindicated Jesus—and thereby the movement he started—by raising him from the dead.[25] Furthermore, this movement continued to bring into their fellowship groups that had earlier been excluded from Israel. This affected the very centre of Jewish understanding of God's acts towards his people. The rise of the Christians as a group with their own identity, separate from the synagoge, produced in the New Testament writings a re-examination of the relationship between God and Israel. We must understand this process in terms

---

community as the people of God. For this group, messianic titles and other theological questions are clearly secondary to the primary issue of its own identity".

[23] See N. A. Dahl, Das Volk Gottes (Skrifter utgitt av Det Norske Videnskapsakademi i Oslo, II. Hist.-Fil. Klasse 1941/2, Oslo, 1941) 209.

[24] E.g. for Matthew, W. Trilling, Das wahre Israel (SANT 10, 3rd revised edition, Munich, 1964); for Luke-Acts, J. Jervell, Luke and the People of God (Minneapolis, 1972); G. Lohfink, Die Sammlung Israels (SANT 39, Munich, 1975).

[25] The notion that God vindicated Jesus by raising him from the dead is combined in Acts with the belief that God created the church; both are acts of God (5:35-39; 13:40-41; 15:16-18; 20:28); cf. Lohfink, Sammlung 85-92.

of a struggle for identity in a period of crisis, first of all for Christians Jews, but to some extent also for non-Christian ones.[26] When Jewish communities were confronted with Christian missionary preaching and practice (especially in its Hellenistic-Christian or Pauline form) they recognized that this represented a threat to their conception of world-order. In the conflict over the right to be called the true Israel or descendants of Abraham it was the creation and preservation of their "symbolic universe" that was at stake.[27]

This outline of the situation in which the theological reflection of the first Christian generations took place, although brief, has emphasized the necessity of seeing the interchange between theological reflection and situation as a dialectical relationship.

It is as a witness to this transitional stage in the relationship between Jewish and Christian groups that we will focus upon Paul's understanding of God in his letter to the Romans.[28] Here Paul mentions God more frequently than Christ, and thus he keeps close to a Jewish way of speaking about God. Moreover, the most significant use of predications of God is found in chapter 4 where Paul appropriates the tradition about Abraham. Our study divides into two parts. The first part deals with the function of Paul's statements about God in the literary context of Romans in general. It seemed necessary at this point to give first a survey of Paul's literary usage, as a basis for further studies. Therefore many suggestions about links to the historical situation could not be pursued. In this first part of our study we will argue that Paul, together

---

[26] Keck, "Ethos", 451: "NT theology itself could no longer be written independently of sociology and ethics, for it would become clear that the theologies of the NT are wrought in the matrix of an ethos undergoing diverse crises". Keck describes "ethos" by saying that it "refers to the lifestyle of a group or a society", 440.

[27] For the use of the concepts "symbolic universe" and "social world" see P. Berger, *The Sacred Canopy: Elements of a Sociological theory of Religion* (New York, 1967). For the use of these terms on the NT scene, see G. Theissen, "Theorethische Probleme religionssoziologischer Forschung und die Analyse des Urchristentums", *Neue Zeitschrift für systematische Theologie* 16 (1974) 35-56; J. Gager, *Kingdom and Community. The Social world of Early Christianity* (Englewood Cliffs, N.J., 1975); J. Z. Smith, "The Social Description of Early Christianity", *Religious Studies Review* 1 (1975) 19-25; J. H. Schütz, "Ethos of early Christianity", *IDBSup* (1976) 289-93.

[28] It follows that the conflict between a Christian and various Hellenistic concepts of God is not part of the problem we shall study here; cf. G. Schneider, "Urchristliche Gottesverkündigung in hellenistischer Umwelt", *BZ* 13 (1969) 59-75.

with other New Testament authors, gave expression to the historical conflicts over the law, mission, group identity etc. in the form of a controversy over the understanding of God. That is, Paul theologized the conflict. Furthermore, when he used theology as an argument for his position, he pointed out the consequences of this theological self-understanding for the co-existence and unity of his audience. From this perspective, Paul's understanding of God is important not only as an example of a particular stage within the history of Christian doctrine, but even more as a reflection of a specific situation among a group of Christians.

We are here confronted with a major problem, however, in our attempt to understand Paul's theology: what does his frequent use of traditional expressions tell us about his concept of God? Moreover, we must consider that he used these expressions as arguments against Jews (Christian Jews included) who held the same convictions about God. A mere assembling of expressions and statements of faith cannot answer these questions, a study of the qualifying influence of the context becomes imperative. A study of theological statements in their context would bring to light an implicit theology which we may describe as Paul's understanding of God. In the second part of our study, we attempt to locate the centre of his theology, i.e. his basis when he interprets and modifies traditional statements about God. This we will do by a closer study of Rom 4:13-22. The main theme in this passage is God's promise to Abraham that he would become the father of many nations. The tradition that Paul interprets here combines the interest in the steadfastness of God's promise with the quest for the identity of his people. Thus it corresponds with our previous description of the Sitz im Leben for the question about God in Judaism and early Christianity. At the centre of this text stands the traditional predication of God used in 4:17: "who gives life to the dead and calls into existence the things that do not exist". It is here that we shall seek the centre of Paul's understanding of God through a study of the literary pattern of his argument in 4:13-22.

PART ONE

PAUL'S USE OF GOD-LANGUAGE IN ROMANS [1]

In this study we are first of all concerned with the *function* of language about God in Romans. For what purpose did Paul use it and what did he want to express by it?

To answer these questions we must examine the actual usage, frequency and form of Paul's statements about God. This is the task of our first chapter. There is less use of explicit Christian terminology in Romans than in Paul's other letters. Instead he emphasizes "God" throughout the letter, but especially in chapters 1-4 and 9-11.

This initial observation prompts us to ask what is the function of these statements about God in their literary context. In our next chapter this is studied with special attention to Romans 1-4 and 9-11. We focus upon passages that reflect controversies between Paul and his opponents. Here traditional statements about God took on a controversial meaning when Paul invoked them as arguments for his position.

In chapter three of our study we will show that Paul and his opponents not only had recourse to theological language as argument in their controversy, but went even further and expressed their conflict as an irreconcilable disagreement over the understanding of God. This final stage of their controversy was characterized by charges of blasphemy.

However, God-language was not only used as an extreme form of criticism of rival groups. It could also be employed to express group-identity. It is to this usage that we turn in our last chapter. In Romans, statements about God are frequently followed by

---

[1] For the use of the term "God-language" to describe language about God, cf. the following books: L. B. Gilkey, *Naming the Whirlwind; the Renewal of God-Language* (Indianapolis, Ind., 1967); J. Macquarrie, *God-Talk: An Examination of the Language and Logic of Theology* (London, 1967). Another explanation of the terminology used in this study is necessary here. In the following discussion we speak of "non-Jews" instead of "Gentiles", thereby attempting to find a term which expresses more clearly to modern readers the conflicts involved in the relationship between the three groups we are dealing with: non-Christian Jews, Christian Jews and Christians who were not Jews.

expressions like "for Jew and Greek". This emphasis on his gospel's being "universal", for everybody, was related to the controversy over Paul's missionary activity. Paul not only argues that non-Jews be included in the Christian community—he was also concerned that it should remain a community for Jews. Thus he tried to end a separation between Jews and non-Jews that traditionally had been justified with theological arguments. In Romans, Paul used the same type of argument—but he turned it against tradition. He employed God-language to create a new identity for a community consisting of Jewish and non-Jewish Christians.

CHAPTER ONE

FORMULAIC EXPRESSIONS IN ROMANS

An introduction to Paul's understanding of God

Why should we choose Romans for a study of Paul's understanding of God? Was not God always the centre of his theology? As a general rule, this question is to be answered in the affirmative, but since his preaching of God has for too long been dealt with only in general terms, it is appropriate to look at this question more closely. A study of Paul's letters shows how his theology was directed in each case towards a specific "letter-situation". Such a study makes us realize how unique was the position of Romans among Paul's letters. Through the titles of their commentaries several scholars have suggested that Paul here focused on God in a special way. Among these, *Gottes Gerechtigkeit* by Adolf Schlatter is probably the best-known. Here, the title itself conveys a programme for the understanding of Romans.[1]

It is in support of such a "God-centred" reading that we will point to Paul's frequent use of θεός in this letter. Statistics are by themselves no answer to theological questions, but at times they may indicate significant evidence that might otherwise be overlooked. The word θεός occurs more often in Romans than in any other New Testament document, except for Acts.[2] However, it is the comparison with other Pauline letters that is our primary interest. In Romans θεός occurs more frequently than in any other of his letters, except for the short 1 Thessalonians: a total of 153 times.[3] This represents an average of 4.5 times on each page of

---

[1] (Stuttgart 1935). Other examples are R. Baulès, *L'évangile puissance de Dieu* (Lectio Divina 53, Paris, 1968): J. Jervell, *Gud og hans fiender, Forsök på å tolke Romerbrevet* (Oslo, 1973).

[2] Acts has 166, but on 93pp. in the Nestle-text over against the 35pp. of Romans; cf. R. Morgenthaler, *Statistik des neutestamentlichen Wortschatzes* (Zürich, 1958) 105. L. Morris ("The Theme of Romans", *Apostolic History and the Gospel, Biblical and Historical Essays presented to F. F. Bruce* (ed. W. W. Gasque and R. P. Martin, Exeter, 1970) 249-63) is a notable exception to the traditional neglect of this statistical evidence. He makes this evidence his starting point for an interpretation that focuses upon "God" as the central theme of the letter.

[3] Cf. Morgenthaler, *Statistik*, 105, 1968. For the comparison we have followed the text of Nestle, 25th edition, Stuttgart, 1963.

Nestle's Greek text; or, to put it another way, θεός occurs once in every 46 words. This compares with 105 times in 1 Corinthians, an average of 3.3 per page; 79 and 3.7 in 2 Corinthians; 31 and 3.0 in Galatians; 24 and 3.0 in Philippians and 36 and 5.1 in 1 Thessalonians.[4] In the shorter letters, however, such statistics are less trustworthy indicators.

That Paul mentions God more frequently in Romans than in any other of his major letters is in itself noteworthy. But it is only when it is compared to the occurrences of "Christ", "Jesus Christ", etc. that the full profile of Paul's theology in Romans becomes visible. Contrary to the heavy concentration of θεός, "Christ" is mentioned less frequently than in Paul's other letters. "Christ" and other names for Jesus occur 87 times, or ca. 2.5 times on each page of Nestle's Greek text. This ratio between the occurrences of "God" and of "Christ Jesus" is highly unusual in Paul's correspondence: in other letters there is either a near parity between the two or a marked prefence for "Christ Jesus".[5] Admittedly, this study of word frequency does not give a complete picture of this situation. Nevertheless, it reveals that Romans occupies a special position among Paul's letters. His use of κύριος in quotations from Scripture confirms this.[6] Romans, again, has by far the largest

---

[4] θεός occurs in 1 Corinthians once in every 65 words, in 2 Corinthians once in 64, in Galatians once in 72, in Philippians once in 68 and in 1 Thessalonians once in 41. The numbers for Ephesians and Colossians are: Ephesians 31; 2.8 per p.; once in every 78 words; Colossians 21; 2.8 per p.; once in every 75 words; Morgenthaler, *Statistik*, 164.

[5]

Letter	pp. of text	"God"	per p.	"Christ", etc.	per p.
Rom	35	153	4.5	87	2.5
1 Cor	31.5	105	3.3	106	3.3
2 Cor	21.5	79	3.7	76	3.5
Gal	10.5	31	3	40	4
Phil	8	24	3	47	6
1 Thess	7	36	5.1	31	4.4
Eph	11	31	2.8	65	6
Col	7.5	21	2.8	35	4.7

[6] κύριος refers to God   κύριος refers to Jesus Christ

Rom 4:8; 9:28, 29; 10:16; 11:3, 34;   10:13
       12:19; 14:11; 15:11.
1 Cor 3:20; 14:21   1:31; 10:21, 22, (26)
2 Cor 6:17, 18   3:16, 18; 10:17

The list is compiled from W. Kramer, *Christos, Kyrios, Gottessohn* (ATANT 44, Zürich, 1963) 154-58; cf. also L. Cerfaux, " 'Kyrios' dans les citations pauliniennes de l'Ancien Testament", *Receuil L. Cerfaux* I (BETL 6-7/1, Gembloux, 1954) 173-88.

number of this, ten in all, nine referring to God. In 1 and 2 Cor, where κύριος occurs less frequently in quotations (six and five times respectively) at least half of these verses apply to Christ. A closer comparison would also require a thorough study of other pertinent questions, e.g. of how often God is the subject in a passive construction.[7] Moreover, the actual function of θεός within the sentence must also be considered, whether it is used as subject or in some other position as object or complement.

Paul spoke of God in both ways. Some sentences describe God's acts towards Israel, the world, or mankind in the past, present or future tense. Here God is the subject, e.g. in Rom 11:32: "For God has consigned all men to disobedience, that he may have mercy upon all", or in passive form in 3:21: "But now the righteousness of God has been manifested apart from Law". In other instances "man", "the believers" etc. is the grammatical subject, and Paul focuses upon their life before God, as in the exhortation in 6:11: "So you also must consider yourselves dead to sin and alive to God in Christ Jesus". An analysis of which of these two modes of speech predominates in a particular text may give us a clearer understanding of the intention behind that passage.[8] A full understanding of Paul's theology in a letter must consider all statements he made about God, both direct and indirect. In Romans, however, this would result in a verse-by-verse commentary on the text.

Instead we have chosen to concentrate upon the smaller units which Dahl called "words and phrases". In themselves they are only parts of sentences or larger periods, giving descriptions of God or "general statements" about him. To select the material in this way is the most adequate method for our purpose. When we break down Paul's statements about God to their smallest units, we can analyse more precisely their function within the larger literary context. Furthermore, many of these smaller units share a traditional formulaic way of speaking of God. Thus, they represent a common basis for Paul and his contemporaries, Jews and non-Jewish Christians alike. Such descriptions were part of a common religious vocabulary that had developed over the centuries, formed and reinforced by liturgical and other religious experiences. Some

---

[7] Cf. ἐγείρω in 4:25; 6:4, 9; 7:4; 8:34.

[8] Thüsing (Per Christum in Deum, 3-4) is aware of this, but sees it too much in terms of prepositional usage and expresses the difference in rather dogmatic language.

expressions had reached the stage of a rather fixed terminology, others were more fluid, and open for development. They shared a common idea or motif rather than a fixed formal structure.

Against this background, it becomes difficult to draw a strict line for what material should be included and what should be left out. A limitation to any one group on the basis of formal similarity (e.g. to participial predications of God) will be arbitrary, since there is no necessary correspondence between the participial form as such and its function in a literary context. Other forms (e.g., a relative clause) may, in some cases, exercise the same function as the participial formula.[9] We shall therefore have to include a larger number of forms, starting with those of a fixed formal structure and then proceeding to those where an original formula has been freely adapted or where there was always more unity in motif than in form. Nevertheless, we intend to limit the selection to expressions that can in some way be distinguished on formal grounds. This does not imply that Paul and his audience perceived these statements to be different from what he said about God in ordinary discourse, where traditional motifs and concepts were also present. As a cross-section of Paul's use of traditional "God-language", however, the number of expressions collected this way is large enough to be representative.

In recent years we have witnessed an increasing interest in a form-critical study of the New Testament letters,[10] together with a continuation of more traditional studies of early Christian liturgical forms, "confessions" and "faith-formulas".[11] These studies help us to identify traditional material in Paul's expressions about God. We need not be too concerned that so far no consensus has been reached on the history of development of these various formulae, since there is considerable agreement about the content of this traditional material. Typically Christian predications form only a small part of the large group of traditional statements about God in

---

[9] *BDF* 412. See the list of formulaic material by E. Norden, "Formelhafter Partizipial- und Relativstil in den Schriften des Neuen Testaments", *Agnostos Theos* (4th edition, Darmstadt, 1956) 380-87.

[10] A convenient introduction which summarizes much of the discussion and also gives many bibliographical references is available in W. G. Doty, *Letters in Primitive Christianity* (Philadelphia, 1973); see also N. A. Dahl, "Letter", *IDBSup* (1976) 540-41.

[11] See the review-article by M. Rese, "Formeln und Lieder im Neuen Testament", *VF* 15 (1970) 75-97; also n. 12.

Romans. Most of them have their origin in the Old Testament or in intertestamental Judaism, with Diaspora-Judaism often serving as a vehicle for the introduction of Greek, especially Stoic, concepts. Many descriptions of God have their origin in liturgical language in hymns or prayers, and they are often found in the same position within a letter, e.g. in doxologies or benedictions (eulogies).[12] Whereas benedictions are frequently found in the letter-opening, doxologies are typical elements from the letter-closing, and both may occur at the conclusion of a chapter or at other divisions in a letter. Another common element in both is a description of God, usually in the form of a participial predication, a genitive construction or some other form. Paul sums up chapters 9-11, maybe even chapters 1-11, in the large doxology in 11:33-36:

"O the depth of the riches and wisdom and knowledge of God! How unsearchable are his judgments and how inscrutable his ways!"
34. "For who has known the mind of the Lord, or who has been his counsellor?"
35. "Or who has given a gift to him that he might be repaid?"
36. For from him and through him and to him are all things. To him be glory for ever. Amen."

Ὦ βάθος πλούτου καὶ σοφίας καὶ γνώσεως θεοῦ ὡς ἀνεξεραύνητα τὰ κρίματα αὐτοῦ καὶ ἀνεξιχνίαστοι αἱ ὁδοὶ αὐτοῦ (33).
ὅτι ἐξ αὐτοῦ καὶ δι᾽ αὐτοῦ καὶ εἰς αὐτὸν τὰ πάντα αὐτῷ ἡ δόξα εἰς τοὺς αἰῶνας. ἀμήν. (36).

This hymn combines motifs from the Old Testament and intertestamental Judaism with Hellenistic motifs in a carefully built structure; we notice especially the elaborate use of prepositions in v. 36.[13] Compared to this, the benediction in 1:25 is very simple, attached to a single participle:

---

[12] R. Deichgräber, *Gotteshymnus und Christushymnus der frühen Christenheit* (Studien zur Umwelt des Neuen Testaments 5, Göttingen, 1967) 25-43; cf. further J. M. Robinson, "Die Hodajot-Formel im Gebet und Hymnus des Frühchristentums", *Apophoreta, Festschrift für E. Haenchen* (ed. W. Eltester and F. H. Kettler, BZNW 30, Berlin, 1964) 194-235; R. Jewett, "The Form and Function of the Homiletic Benediction", *Anglican Theological Journal* 51 (1969) 18-34. For the use of benedictions and doxologies within the NT letters, see Doty, *Letters*, 31-33, 39-40.
[13] Deichgräber, *Gotteshymnus*, 61-64.

they ... worshipped and served the creature rather than the Creator, who is blessed for ever! Amen

ἐσεβάσθησαν καὶ ἐλάτρευσαν τῇ κτίσει παρὰ τὸν κτίσαντα, ὅς ἐστιν εὐλογητὸς εἰς τοὺς αἰῶνας. ἀμήν.

There has been much discussion whether the benediction in 9:5 was attributed to God or to Christ, who is mentioned in the previous verse:

God who is over all is blessed forever. Amen.[14]

ὁ ὢν ἐπὶ πάντων θεὸς εὐλογητὸς εἰς τοὺς αἰῶνας, ἀμήν.

Most scholars hold the doxology in 16:25-27 where God is described as ὁ δυνάμενος to be a later addition to the letter.[15]

As part of a larger study Reinhard Deichgräber offers a list of predications of God in the New Testament, especially in the letters.[16] He emphasizes the hymnic character of these predications. The most important group, as he sees it, is made up of names for God (as "God", "Father", "Lord") modified through a genitive construction, e.g. "God of mercy". Deichgräber points to non-Rabbinic Judaism as a possible milieu where this usage originated, and where such predications were frequently found in the introduction to prayers. This is also the case in many instances in Romans, in particular the wish-prayers towards the end of the letter, 15:5, 13, 33 and 16:20.[17]

15:5   May the God of steadfastness and encouragement grant you to live in such harmony with one another, in accord with Christ Jesus.[18]

ὁ δὲ θεὸς τῆς ὑπομονῆς καὶ τῆς παρακλήσεως δῴη ὑμῖν τὸ αὐτὸ φρονεῖν ἐν ἀλλήλοις κατὰ Χριστὸν Ἰησοῦν.

---

[14] The most recent study of this passage is O. Kuss, "Zu Römer 9:5", *Rechtfertigung. Festschrift für E. Käsemann* (ed. J. Friedrich, W. Pöhlmann and P. Stuhlmacher, Tübingen, 1976) 291-303. After a careful discussion he concludes that the benediction should be attributed to *God*.

[15] W. G. Kümmel, *Einleitung in das Neue Testament* (13th edition, Heidelberg, 1964) 225-26.

[16] "Hymnische Gottesprädikate", *Gotteshymnus*, 87-105.

[17] For the interpretation of these passages, see G. P. Wiles, *Paul's Intercessory Prayers* (SNTSMS 24, Cambridge, 1974).

[18] The appellation ὁ δὲ θεὸς τῆς ὑπομονῆς is not found in Jewish texts, whereas τῆς παρακλήσεως corresponds to בעל נחמות, b. *Ketub.* 8b; Deichgräber, *Gotteshymnus*, 94; cf. 2 Cor 1:3-7.

15:13 May the God of hope fill you with all joy and peace in believing, so that by the power of the Holy Spirit you may abound in hope.[19]

ὁ δὲ θεὸς τῆς ἐλπίδος πληρώσαι ὑμᾶς πάσης χαρᾶς καὶ εἰρήνης ἐν τῷ πιστεύειν, εἰς τὸ περισσεύειν ὑμᾶς ἐν τῇ ἐλπίδι ἐν δυνάμει πνεύματος ἁγίου.

15:33 The God of peace be with you all. Amen.[20]

ὁ δὲ θεὸς τῆς εἰρήνης μετὰ πάντων ὑμῶν. ἀμήν.

16:20 then the God of peace will soon crush Satan under your feet.

ὁ δὲ θεὸς τῆς εἰρήνης συντρίψει τὸν Σατανᾶν ὑπὸ τοὺς πόδας ὑμῶν ἐν τάχει.

Paul supports his exhortation in 12:1-2 with a similar predication:

I appeal to you therefore, brethren, by the mercies of God, to present your bodies . . . [21]

Παρακαλῶ οὖν ὑμᾶς, ἀδελφοί, διὰ τῶν οἰκτιρμῶν τοῦ θεοῦ, παραστῆσαι τὰ σώματα ὑμῶν . . .

This similarity in function between the genitive of quality (15:5, 13, 33) and the subjective genitive (12:1) suggests the inclusion at this point of a larger group of saying where certain "powers" or "qualities" are attributed to God. We move from formulaic expressions to deal more with motifs. In several instances it is noticeable how Paul "Christianized" these predications. Most of them are well known and only some examples are given here: the power of God, δύναμις θεοῦ (1:16, 20; 9:17); the righteousness of God, δικαιοσύνη θεοῦ (e.g. 1:17; 3:21, 26) the faithfulness of God, πίστις

[19] This designation itself is not found in Jewish texts; cf. Deichgräber, Gotteshymnus, 95 although hope in God is a motif frequently expressed in the Psalms; cf. LXX 4:5; 5:11; 7:1 etc. The conclusion to the quotation from Isa 11:10 in Rom 15:12: ἐπ' αὐτῷ ἔθνη ἐλπιοῦσιν, serves as an introduction to the predication in v. 13.

[20] Also found in 1 Cor 14:33; 2 Cor 13:11; Phil 4:9; 1 Thess 5:23; Hebr 13:20; 2 Thess 3:16. This predication corresponds to the Pauline greeting in the opening of his letters; Rom 1:7; 1 Cor 1:3; 2 Cor 1:2; etc.; see G. Delling, "Die Bezeichnung 'Gott des Friedens' und ähnliche Wendungen in den Paulusbriefen", Jesus und Paulus. Festschrift für W. G. Kümmel (ed. E. E. Ellis and E. Grässer, Göttingen, 1975) 76-84.

[21] This is a subjective genitive with "God" as nomen regens, whereas ὁ πατὴρ τῶν οἰκτιρμῶν in 2 Cor 1:3 is a genitive of quality with the abstract noun as nomen regens, as in Rom 15:5, 13, 33. The genitive expression "God of mercies" is found in the Qumran documents, 1 QH 10:14; 11:29, etc. Cf. Deichgräber, Gotteshymnus, 93-94, and C. J. Bjerkelund, Parakalo (Oslo, 1967) 163-64, 217-18.

τοῦ θεοῦ (3:3).[22] Adjectives attributing characteristic features to God are in the same category, e.g. that God is immortal, ἀφθάρτος.[23] Above all, God is *one*: in 3:30 Paul explicitly refers to this concept that was fundamental both to Judaism and Stoicism.[24]

From the early Christian tradition came expressions describing God as the father of Jesus, e.g. in 15:6, or as "our Father", e.g. in 1:7. These and similar expressions are frequently found in Paul's letters, most often in the benedictions in the opening of the letter.[25]

Another large group of expressions of faith in God is made up by participial predications with common features that make them easily identifiable. Here a participle either in the present or in the aorist tense serves as an attributive to θεός or a similar name for God. It can also be found in substantival use without θεός, thus in itself functioning as a name.[26] As Gerhard Delling points out, however, in his magisterial study of participle designations for God in the New Testament letters, the fact that a participial construction is used does not in itself imply that this was a fixed formula. Rather, it may well be a result of the syntactical structure of the sentence.[27] Consequently, we shall first list those participial predications that may be regarded as coined phrases.

1:25   ... they ... worshipped and served the creation rather than the Creator.

ἐσεβάσθησαν καὶ ἐλάτρευσαν τῇ κτίσει παρὰ τὸν κτίσαντα.[28]

4:5   And to one who does not work but trusts him who justifies the ungodly, his faith is reckoned as righteousness

πιστεύοντι δὲ ἐπὶ τὸν δικαιοῦντα τὸν ἀσεβῆ.[29]

---

[22] Cf. also the expressions in 2:4; 3:26; 11:22.

[23] The contrast between τοῦ ἀφθάρτου θεοῦ and φθαρτοῦ ἀνθρώπου, 1:23, is typical for Hellenistic religion; see G. Harder, "φθείρω", *TWNT* 9 (1973) 94-106.

[24] Also in 1 Cor 8:6 and Gal 3:20. For the historical background, cf. E. Peterson, 'Εἷς θεός (Göttingen, 1926); see further p. 40, n. 30.

[25] Cf. n. 20.

[26] Delling ("Gottesprädikationen", 27-8) distinguishes between the use of the present participle to describe God's character ("Wesensmerkmale Gottes"), and the use of the aorist participle to record God's act of salvation ("das entscheidende Heilshandeln Gottes"); e.g. Rom 5:8; cf. *BDF* 412, 413.

[27] Delling, "Gottesprädikationen", 27-35, esp. 27 n. 5; further 51-52.

[28] ὁ κτίσας is in the NT used for "creator", Col 3:10; Eph 3:9. Both in the LXX and in later Jewish texts as well as in early Christian literature outside the NT (e.g. Hermas, Justin), ὁ ποιήσας is more common; it is also found in Acts 4:24; Hebr 3:2; Rev 14:7.

[29] Most commentators suggest that this phrase was coined by Paul himself; *contra* A. Kolenkow, "The Ascription of Romans 4:5", *HTR* 60 (1967) 228-30.

4:17   in the presence of the God in whom he believed, who gives life to the dead and calls into existence the things that do not exist

κατέναντι οὗ ἐπίστευσεν θεοῦ τοῦ ζῳοποιοῦντος τοὺς νεκροὺς καὶ καλοῦντος τὰ μὴ ὄντα ὡς ὄντα.[30]

4:24   It will be reckoned to us who believe in him that raised from the dead Jesus our Lord

οἷς μέλλει λογίζεσθαι, τοῖς πιστεύουσιν ἐπὶ τὸν ἐγείραντα Ἰησοῦν τὸν κύριον ἡμῶν ἐκ νεκρῶν.[31]

8:27   And he who searches the hearts of men knows what is the mind of the Spirit

ὁ δὲ ἐραυνῶν τὰς καρδίας οἶδεν τί τὸ φρόνημα τοῦ πνεύματος.[32]

9:11-12   ... in order that God's purpose of election might continue, not because of works but because of him who called

ἵνα ἡ κατ᾽ ἐκλογὴν πρόθεσις τοῦ θεοῦ μένῃ, οὐκ ἐξ ἔργων ἀλλ᾽ ἐκ τοῦ καλοῦντος.[33]

9:16   So it depends not upon man's will or exertion, but upon God who shows mercy

ἄρα οὖν οὐ τοῦ θέλοντος οὐδὲ τοῦ τρέχοντος, ἀλλὰ τοῦ ἐλεῶντος θεοῦ.[34]

Both in 9:12 and 9:16 there is a strong connection in terminology between the participial predications καλῶν and ἐλεῶν, and their context. Bultmann remarks that "Paulus von Gottes ἔλεος bezeichnenderweise nur in den heilsgeschichtlichen Aussagen R 9;

---

[30] See below, 233-239.

[31] Cf. Delling, "Gottesprädikationen", 32-36 and below, 270.

[32] Also in Rev 2:23; cf. Rom 2:16. Although the verb ἐρευνάω is rarely used in the OT in this meaning (but cf. Prov 20:27) the motif is well-known throughout the OT, e.g. 2 Sam 16:7; Jer 17:9-10; Ps 7:10. Cf. G. Delling, "ἐρευνάω", *TWNT* 2 (1935) 653-54.

[33] Although there are parallels in the OT, e.g. Isa 45:3, ὁ καλῶν or ὁ καλέσας takes on new importance in the NT and becomes in most instances a distinctively Christian predication of God. It is used of his relationship with the Christians, who are for their part described as "called", 1 Cor 1:9; Gal 5:13; Delling, "Gottesprädikationen", 28-31. Paul uses this predication frequently in Galatians: 1:6, 15; 5:8; see also 1 Thess 2:12; 5:24. In Romans, Paul uses both the participle, 4:17, and the finite form of the verb, 8:30; 9:7, 24, 25, 26 (9:7, 25, 26 in quotations from the OT).

[34] In the LXX a genitive construction with the noun ἔλεος is more common than the participle, e.g. Ps 12:6; 20:8; 22:6. So also in the NT, cf. Luke 1:58; Eph 2:4; 1 Pet 1:3. Notice the combination with οἰκτιρμοί in 1 Clem 9:1; cf. Rom 12:1.

11; 15 redet".[35] Consequently, this example shows that there was
no strict line between an already fixed formula applied to a suitable
context and one that received its formulaic character more directly
from its particular context. Moreover, hymnic or liturgical forms
were very much part of Paul's vocabulary and could easily blend
into his style.

Some participles had their background in a traditional motif
without necessarily being formulae, e.g. in 3:26:

it was to prove at the present time that he himself is righteous
and that he justifies him who has faith in Jesus

πρὸς τὴν ἔνδειξιν τῆς δικαιοσύνης αὐτοῦ ἐν τῷ νῦν καιρῷ, εἰς τὸ εἶναι
αὐτὸν δίκαιον καὶ δικαιοῦντα τὸν ἐκ πίστεως 'Ιησοῦ.

So also in 8:33, where, however, the use of the participle puts a
strong emphasis upon the statement: [36]

Who shall bring any charges against God's elect?
It is God who justifies,

τίς ἐγκαλέσει κατὰ ἐκλεκτῶν θεοῦ;
θεὸς ὁ δικαιῶν.

In other instances the use of a participial form appears to be less
significant, as in 3:5 and 8:20 where it does not seem to carry more
weight than an ordinary clause.[37]

3:5   But if our wickedness serves to show the justice of God, what
shall we say? That God is unjust to inflict wrath on us?

μὴ ἄδικος ὁ θεὸς ὁ ἐπιφέρων τὴν ὀργήν;

8:20   . . . for the creation was subject to futility, not of its own will
but by the will of him who subjected it in hope;

τῇ γὰρ ματαιότητι ἡ κτίσις ὑπετάγη, οὐχ ἑκοῦσα ἀλλὰ διὰ τὸν ὑπο-
τάξαντα, ἐφ' ἐλπίδι.

Since a sentence could be constructed in different ways, the
same idea or motif could accordingly be expressed by various
means. Paul could use a genitive construction, a participial predication or an adjective. At other times he employed a subordinate
clause, most often a relative clause, or even a main clause. The

---

[35] "ἔλεος", TWNT 2 (1935) 480. The passages are 9:15, 16, 18, 23; 11:30-
32; 15:9.
[36] Delling, "Gottesprädikationen", 27 n. 8; see also 2 Cor 5:5a; Phil 2:13.
[37] Delling, "Gottesprädikationen", 27 n. 8.

similarity in function between the participle and the adjective in Romans is best illustrated by Paul's use of δυνατός. In doxologies God is frequently praised as him "who is able to . . . ". There is an example of this in Rom 16:25:

Now to him who is able to strengthen you . . . [38]

Τῷ δὲ δυναμένῳ ὑμᾶς στηρίξαι.

However, this is part of a later addition to Romans in 16:25-27. Instead of the expression with a participle, Paul uses δυνατός followed by an infinitive, e.g. in 4:21:

fully convinced that God was able to do what he had promised

πληροφορηθεὶς ὅτι ὃ ἐπήγγελται δυνατός ἐστιν καὶ ποιῆσαι.

and in 11:23:

and even the others, if they do not persist in their unbelief, will be grafted in, for God has the power to graft them in again [39]

ἐὰν μὴ ἐπιμένωσιν τῇ ἀπιστίᾳ, ἐγκεντρισθήσονται· δυνατὸς γάρ ἐστιν ὁ θεὸς πάλιν ἐγκεντρίσαι αὐτούς.

The one form that is most easily interchangeable with the participial predication is the relative clause.[40] In Rom 3:30 εἷς ὁ θεός is followed by a finite form of δικαιόω in a relative clause that functions much in the same way as the participle forms in 3:26b and 8:33. Several relative clauses or other subordinate clauses also contain old formulaic material, as is the case in the expressions of early Christian faith in 8:3 and 32. In 2:5-6 the relative clause is used attributively to θεός:

. . . when God's righteous judgment will be revealed.
For he will render to every man according to his work.[41]

. . . ἐν ἡμέρᾳ ὀργῆς καὶ ἀποκαλύψεως δικαιοκρισίας τοῦ θεοῦ, ὃς ἀποδώσει ἑκάστῳ κατὰ τὰ ἔργα αὐτοῦ.

---

[38] In doxologies in Eph 3:20-21; Jude 24-25; *Mart Pol.* 20:2; other examples are Heb 5:7; Jas 4:12; Herm. *Mand.* XII 6:3; cf. Deichgräber, *Gotteshymnus*, 29, and Delling, "Gottesprädikationen", 15, 26-27.

[39] See Rom 14:4; here δυναται (strong mss. evidence for δυνατός) is used in an example from daily life about the relationship between slave and master; however, it is the implicit assumption in 14:4c that the master actually is the Lord (Christ).

[40] Cf. Acts 4:25 with 14:15, and 1 Thess 5:24 with 1 Cor 10:13; further examples in Delling, "Gottesprädikationen", 42-45.

[41] This is a quotation from Ps 62:13; see also Prov 24:12; Sir LXX 35:22; *Pss. Sol.* 2:16. That God will judge men according to their deeds is a central motif in the OT, e.g. Isa 3:10-19; Jer 17:10; Hos 10:2. Similarly in the NT, e.g. Matt 16:27; 2 Tim 4:14; Rev 2:23; 20:12; 22:12.

In 8:32 the relative clause introduces the passage:

He who did not spare his own Son but gave him up for us all,

ὅς γε τοῦ ἰδίου υἱοῦ οὐκ ἐφείσατο, ἀλλὰ ὑπὲρ ἡμῶν πάντων παρέδωκεν αὐτόν,

will he not also give us all things with him?

A similar idea of God's sending his own son is contained in 8:3, in a participial clause with the adverbial use of the participle. This is possibly a fragment of a pre-Pauline tradition that is more fully represented in Gal 4:4.[42]

8:3   For God has done what the law, weakened by the flesh, could not do: sending his own Son in the likeness of sinful flesh and for sin, he condemned sin in the flesh.

τὸ γὰρ ἀδύνατον τοῦ νόμου, ἐν ᾧ ἠσθένει διὰ τῆς σαρκός, ὁ θεὸς τὸν ἑαυτοῦ υἱὸν πέμψας ἐν ὁμοιώματι σαρκὸς ἁμαρτίας καὶ περὶ ἁμαρτίας κατέκρινεν τὴν ἁμαρτίαν ἐν τῇ σαρκί.

It is possible that Paul also knew the substantival use of the participle as a designation for God, which is typical of the Johannine usage of πέμπω, for example.[43] Paul employs the same grammatical variety in his use of forms to describe other aspects of God's salvation through Jesus Christ, e.g. that he raised Jesus from the dead. In 4:24 he expresses this by means of a participial predication, in 10:9 by a ὅτι-clause,[44] also introduced by πιστεύω:

If you confess with your lips that Jesus is Lord and believe in your heart that God raised him from the dead

ὅτι ἐὰν ὁμολογήσῃς ἐν τῷ στόματί σου κύριον Ἰησοῦν, καὶ πιστεύσῃς ἐν τῇ καρδίᾳ σου ὅτι ὁ θεὸς αὐτὸν ἤγειρεν ἐκ νεκρῶν.

There is still another group of statements that may reasonably be included here: aphorisms and maxims that stood within a long Jewish tradition. Being main clauses, they do not share the formal characteristics of the earlier examples. Nevertheless their axiomatic form makes them stick out from their context. Their function is similar to that of the participial predications or the relative clauses.

---

[42] E. Schweizer, "υἱός", *TWNT* 8 (1969) 385-86.
[43] 4:34; 5:23, 24, 30, 37; etc. See J. P. Miranda, *Der Vater, der mich gesandt hat* (EHS.T 7, Frankfurt, 1972) 29-32.
[44] See below, 270.

They give "general" descriptions of God, best understood as an explanation or a supplement that does not directly continue the process of thought within the larger period. In 2:6 Paul used a relative clause to express this purpose when he said, "For he will render to every man according to his work". In 2:11 a main clause functions in the same way:

For God shows no partiality.[45]

οὐ γάρ ἐστιν προσωπολημψία παρὰ τῷ θεῷ.

Similarly in 11:29, a main clause serves as an explanation to what Paul had already said:

For the gifts and call of God are irrevocable.[46]

ἀμεταμέλητα γὰρ τὰ χαρίσματα καὶ ἡ κλῆσις τοῦ θεοῦ.

Even acknowledging that we are now dealing with beliefs more than with formulae for beliefs, we find that in the short section 3:1-8 references to commonly accepted conceptions abound.[47] In chapters 1-3, Paul frequently referred to the well known concept of God as judge: here it is found in v. 6:

For then how could God judge the world?[48]

ἐπεὶ πῶς κρινεῖ ὁ θεὸς τὸν κόσμον;

Moreover, in 3:3 Paul introduces a question that refers to, and presupposes, a certain understanding of God—that he is characterized by his faithfulness (πίστις τοῦ θεοῦ). Similar rhetorical questions are frequently used to introduce passages where Paul was engaged in dialogues, real or fictitious:[49]

3:3   Does their faithlessness nullify the faithfulness of God?

μὴ ἡ ἀπιστία αὐτῶν τὴν πίστιν τοῦ θεοῦ καταργήσει;

---

[45] Although the noun προσωπολημψία is found first in the NT it probably was used in Hellenistic Judaism. The motif itself is common in the OT, used of God as judge, cf. in the LXX e.g., Deut 10:17; Sir 35:13; Wis 6:7; further Jub 5:16; 33:18. In the NT it is found in various contexts; reflecting traditional usage in the "Haustafeln", in Eph 6:9 and Col 3:25; further Acts 10:34; Gal 2:6; 1 Pet 1:17; *Barn.* 19:7; E. Lohse, "προσωπολημψία", *TWNT* 6 (1959) 780-81.

[46] The closest parallel is Ps LXX 109:4, also quoted in Heb 7:21; cf. C. Spicq, "᾽Αμεταμέλητος dans Rom 11:29", *RB* 67 (1960) 210-19.

[47] πίστις, 3:3; δικαιοσύνη, 3:5; ἀλήθεια, 3:7, see 3:4; δόξα, 3:7.

[48] Cf. the recent study of Paul's understanding of God as judge, by C. J. Roetzel, *Judgment in the Community* (Leiden, 1972).

[49] *BDF* 496.1.

9:6   But it is not as though the word of God has failed.

Οὐχ οἷον δὲ ὅτι ἐκπέπτωκεν ὁ λόγος τοῦ θεοῦ.

9:14   What shall we say then? Is there injustice on God's part?

Τί οὖν ἐροῦμεν; μὴ ἀδικία παρὰ τῷ θεῷ;

11:1   I ask, then has God rejected his people?

Λέγω οὖν, μὴ ἀπώσατο ὁ θεὸς τὸν λαὸν αὐτοῦ;

Starting with formulaic expressions about God and enlarging our search to include other statements with a similar form and function, we have assembled a collection of expressions that embody both Old Testament and inter-testamental Jewish as well as early Christian tradition. A few comments about this material are in order.

First of all, we have noticed that these statements about God are not evenly distributed throughout the letter. There is a strong concentration of them in chapters 1-4 and 9 and 11, whereas chapters 5-8 and 12-14 have only a few. Chapter 8, especially the last part of the chapter, is a notable exception.[50] Likewise chapter 15 has several statements in the wish-prayers in the concluding part of the letter, where we would expect to find such forms. Consequently, apart from chapter 8, most formulaic statements about God in the body of the letter are found in the section 1:16-4:25 and chapters 9-11. Moreover, in these chapters θεός occurs more frequently than in the rest of the letter.[51] And when God is actually spoken of in chapters 5-8 and 12-14, it is mostly in a predominantly Christ-centred context.[52] θεός is therefore here often used in the

---

[50] 8:31, 33, 39, cf. 32. Paul argues in a similar way in chapter 8, especially 8:31-39, and in chapter 11. In both instances it is God's acts in the past which give reassurance for the future, and Paul concludes with a hymnic confession to God. A similar, but more christologically centred section in 5:1-11 introduces chapters 5-8; see N. A. Dahl, "Two Notes on Romans 5", ST 5 (1952) 37-42.

[51] In chapters 1-4 and 9-11 (ca. 15pp) θεός occurs 71 times, in chapters 5-8 and 12-14 (13, 5pp) 55 times. In addition, seven out of the ten OT quotations with κύριος used of God are found in chapters 1-4 and 9-11. The epistolary parts 1:1-16 and 15:1-16:27 are not included in this comparison.

[52] See R. Scroggs, "Paul as Rhetorician: Two Homilies in Romans 1-11", Jews, Greeks and Christians, Essays in Honour of W. D. Davies (ed. E. Hamerton-Kelly and R. Scroggs, SJLA 21, Leiden 1976) 282-83. Chapters 5-8 can be divided into nine subsections sharing one main theme: God's victory in Christ over death, cf. chapter 8, n. 156. In chapters 5-8 "Christ" etc. occurs 28 times, whereas it occurs only 12 times in chapters 1-4 and 9-11; Scroggs, 276. The paraenesis in chapters 12-14 also has explicit references to Christ; cf. 12:5; 13:14; 14:9, 15, 18.

dative, in passages where Paul's primary concern is *man's relation to God.*[53] It is also worth noticing that of the predications of God in chapter 8, several are in themselves distinctively Christian, speaking of God's acts towards Christ or through him. In chapters 1-4 and 9-11 only a few statements are qualified in this way.[54] This indicates that not only are there differences in terminology at this point between Romans and other of Paul's letters, as we noticed initially, but there are differences within various parts of Romans as well.

Thus our findings support the observations of Robin Scroggs concerning the difference in character between Romans 1-4 and 9-11 on the one hand and 5-8 on the other:

> One of the striking features throughout chapters 1-4, 9-11 (and in distinction from chapters 5-8) is the sparseness of explicit Christian language and content. It is God who is emphasized in these chapters, one might even say the "Jewish God", while the figure of Christ remains in the background.[55]

Although we will argue that there is more thematic unity between chapters 1-4, 9-11 on the one hand, and 5-8 on the other than Scroggs supposes,[56] he has convincingly pointed out a difference in style, situation and audience for these two parts. In chapters 5-8 (and certainly also in 12-15) Paul addressed Christians—be they Jews or non-Jews—and he spoke to them on the basis of their being "in Christ". The common ground for his exhortations and paraenesis was their new life in Christ. In chapters 1-4 and 9-11 on the other hand, Paul is directly involved in a dialogue with Jews— Christian or non-Christian—and his use of Jewish instead of typically Christian terms for God is related to this situation. Here he meets his dialogue-partners on the common ground of their faith in the God of Israel. They also shared the conviction that Israel was the people of God, and it was an urgent concern of Paul's to explain how this should be understood in the light of the new situation that had arisen after the coming of Christ. Partly because Paul was concerned with the history of Israel before Christ, but also because he discussed the contemporary situation of the non-believing (i.e. non-Christian) Israel, it is God, more than Christ,

---

[53] Notice especially 6:10, 11, 13, 17, 22; also 5:10, 11; 7:4; 8:8.
[54] 8:3, 11, 32, 33a (by its parallel with 33b); in chapters 1-4 and 9-11 only 1:7; 1:16; 3:26; 4:24; 10:9.
[55] "Rhetorician", 276.
[56] See below, 276 n. 152, 155.

who is the central figure. Paul could even speak of God's δικαιοσύνη without explicit mention of Christ.

We have already noticed that many of the formulaic expressions about God had a terminology which has been formed by the context. Thus they are closely related to Paul's argument in those particular passages and express not only traditional beliefs but also his own intentions. These intentions become more visible when we realize that there is an underlying thematic unity to Paul's use of statements about God. Many of them are constructed with some form or other of δικαιόω or δίκαιος:

3:4   Ὅπως ἄν δικαιωθῇς ἐν τοῖς λόγοις σου
3:5   μὴ ἄδικος ὁ θεὸς ὁ ἐπιφέρων τὴν ὀργήν
3:26   εἰς τὸ εἶναι αὐτὸν δίκαιον καὶ δικαιοῦντα τὸν ἐκ πίστεως Ἰησοῦ
3:30   ὃς δικαιώσει περιτομὴν ἐκ πίστεως καὶ . . .
4:5   πιστεύοντι δὲ ἐπὶ τὸν δικαιοῦντα τὸν ἀσεβῆ
8:33   θεὸς ὁ δικαιῶν
9:14   μὴ ἀδικία παρὰ τῷ θεῷ;

Romans is the only one of Paul's letters with such a widespread use of δικαιόω/δίκαιος in predications of God.[57] This usage is obviously related to the main theme of the letter—Paul's exposition of salvation resulting from δικαιοσύνη θεοῦ as he first set it out in 1:16-17. His statements about God tend to cluster around passages where the theme from 1:16-17 is repeated. A typical example is 3:21-26 where he sums up the intention behind God's salvation through Jesus in 3:26. Paul repeats the same point in 3:30 and gives it its most polemical expression in the participial predication in 4:5. Similarly, the various issues under discussion in 3:1-8 converged on the question of God's righteousness in 3:4 and 5. Apart from 8:33, predications with δικαιόω and δίκαιος are primarily found in chapters 3 and 4. However, the question in 9:14: "Is there injustice on God's part?" points to a rhetorical situation similar to that in 3:1-8. But when Paul describes God's salvific acts in chapters 9 and 11, καλέω and ἐλεέω take the place of δικαιόω.[58] Paul here used the terminology of his scriptural quotations (9:7, 15) in

---

[57] The closest parallels are the ὅτι-clauses in Gal 3:8, 11. However, in Galatians ὁ καλῶν has a thematic function similar to ὁ δικαιῶν in Romans, occurring in passages where Paul argues for his apostolate and his gospel, 1:6, 15; 5:8; cf. also 5:13.

[58] See nn. 35, 37. Notice also that καλέω/κλῆσις is closely linked to ἡ ἐκλογή; see 9:11; 11:5, 7, 28, 29.

his predications of God in 9:12 and 16 in order to find a common basis of communication with his Jewish readers.

This survey has shown that there is a close correlation between Paul's use of traditional or formulaic statements about God and the purpose of his argument in the texts where they occur. "Tradition" was not something outside of Paul's own theology; rather it was a resource that he shared with his fellow-Jews and fellow-Chiistians.[59] We tend to misconstrue the situation when at a distance of two thousand years, we classify statements as "traditional" or "formulaic", thereby implying that they were set apart in a special way. It was their *content* more than any particular form that mattered to Paul. However, their formal structure was not unimportant to him. In some instances, particularly in Romans 4, we find a very elaborate use of participial predications. From what we have said so far, it should also be clear that we cannot single out formulaic expressions about God as the foundations for Paul's theology or as the formative element in it.[60] But given that these statements about God represented a common basis on which Jews (Christian as well as non-Christian) and non-Jewish Christians could meet—what was their function in the construction of Paul's argument?

It is to this problem that we now turn.

---

[59] G. Eichholz, "Verkündigung und Tradition", *Tradition und Interpretation* (TBü 29, Munich, 1965) 30; K. Wegenast, *Das Verständnis der Tradition bei Paulus und in den Deuteropaulinen* (WMANT 8, Neukirchen, 1962) 91-92.

[60] See the discussion in Rese, "Formeln", 93-95.

CHAPTER TWO

PAUL'S USE OF GOD-LANGUAGE IN CONTROVERSY IN ROMANS 1-4 AND 9-11

When we ask what function statements about God have in their literary context, we must always bear in mind that we are studying *a letter*. The primary intention of a letter is to be a means of *contact and communication* between author and recipients. Paul's letters are probably closer to the official letter of his time than to the private. He seeks to inform, to exhort, to convince and to discipline—in short, to perform the same function as he would were he preaching in person.[1] What Paul says about God is related not only to the general purpose of the letter but also to the specific intention of the individual passage where a statement is found. This is true also of general expressions about the "nature" of God, as E. Stauffer points out: "Vor allem aber: nirgends stehen solche Gottesaussagen allein und um ihrer selbst willen da. Sie sind stets verbunden mit Dank oder Bitte, Botschaft oder Forderung: Es geht dem NT nicht um eine Lehre von der Persöhnlichkeit Gottes, sondern um die geschichtliche Bezeugung und Durchsetzung des Gotteswillens."[2] Stauffer's comments were made concerning the New Testament in general; with modifications they apply also to the Pauline letters.

In some cases there is a conventional usage of general statements about God, especially in the opening or closing sections of the letter, or in other formulaic parts such as a thanksgiving or a doxology. In the doxology in 11:33-36, the description of God as the creator is an incentive to praise him; likewise in wish-prayers and blessings, e.g. in 15:5, where God is described as "the God of steadfastness and encouragement", this expression is related both to the act that God will perform and to the effect Paul hopes this will have upon his readers.[3] In the opening and closing of the letter the

---

[1] The apostolic presence is an important theme in Paul's letters; see R. Funk, "The Apostolic *parousia*; Form and Significance", *Christian History and Interpretation: Studies presented to J. Knox* (ed. W. R. Farmer, C. F. D. Moule and R. R. Niebuhr, Cambridge, 1967) 249-68; but cf. the critical response by T. Y. Mullins, "Visit Talk in New Testament letters", *CBQ* 35 (1973) 350-58.

[2] "θεός", *TWNT* 3 (1938) 112.

[3] Wiles, *Prayers*, 79-83 and Delling, "Gott des Friedens", 82.

almost stereotyped use of "God our father" and "the God and father of our Lord Jesus Christ" has a formulaic, liturgical character. These expressions do not primarily give *information* about God; based on their common faith in God, their purpose is to establish a link between author and recipients.[4] It is therefore Paul's use of statements about God in the body of the letter that most clearly reflects his own intentions. It is here that he spells out his concern in each particular letter. In Romans, 1:16-15:33 form the body of the letter; within this main section we shall concentrate upon chapters 1-4 and 9-11. This selection of material is justified partly through our study of word frequency which showed that θεός occurs more frequently in these chapters than in the rest of the letter. Furthermore, this common feature corresponds to a thematic unity between chapters 1-4 and 9-11. The main theme of Romans from 1:16-17 is often understood as a message of salvation by faith. This interpretation stands in need of qualification in the light of what Paul actually says in the subsequent chapters. Why does Paul introduce this salvation as "for Jews first . . . ", and what bearing do his repeated discussions of Israel, in chapters 1-4 and 9-11, have upon this theme? Furthermore, why does he choose Abraham as his example of God's universal salvation by faith when he returns to his main theme in 3:21-4:25?

It is striking that when Paul speaks of salvation by faith he develops one particular aspect of this theme—its meaning for Israel and its implications for the Jews.[5] To the Jews, Paul's gospel meant a threat to Israel's right to salvation. Moreover, it was a serious problem to Christian Jews that most of their fellow-Jews rejected their message. Robin Scroggs describes the situation in this way:

> Paul has turned the traditional picture of Jewish piety and its interpretation of its history to the wall. ... He must answer the questions put by that piety, questions stemming out of the awareness that its very existence has been called into question. In the face of Israel's rejection of God's righteousness, both the value of the actual Israel and the trustworthiness of God are at stake.[6]

---

[4] This is one of the major functions of the prescript and thanksgiving sections of a letter, see W. Wuellner, "Paul's Rhetoric of Argumentation in Romans", *CBQ* 38 (1976) 335-37.
[5] Cf. N. A. Dahl, "Notes", 40.
[6] "Rhetorician", 277.

Paul wrote Romans in a situation in which Israel's "very existence
[had] been called into question". Not only that, but this crisis over
the identity of the Jewish community, acutely felt by the Christian
Jews, was linked with a crisis in their belief in God's trustworthiness.
The Christian Jews were here caught in the middle of a conflict
over loyalties in different directions. This conflict is most directly
brought to the fore in those instances in Romans 1-4 and 9-11
where Paul employs the literary style of a dialogue (or diatribe).[7]
Whether each one of these texts goes back to a real encounter or
not is of little consequence. Taken together, they convincingly
convey a picture of Paul engaged in discussions which he can draw
upon when he writes Romans.[8] He repeatedly introduces these
dialogues with questions that refer to the crisis in the understanding
of Israel's identity and in its trust in God (3:3, 27; 4:1; 9:6, 14;
11:1). It is on Paul's use of God-language in these and similar
discussion-texts in Romans 1-4 and 9-11 that we shall concentrate.
The passages are as follows: 2:1-6, 7-11; 3:1-8, (26) 27-31; 4:1-25;
9:6-13, 14-18; 11:1-6, 19-24, 25-32. At this initial stage we should
keep in mind that Paul's real or fictitious opponents in these texts
and the addressees of the letter are not necessarily identical groups.
Chapters 1-4 and 9-11 do not give much information about the
specific situation of the Christians in Rome. Rather, they describe
Paul's conflict with Jews and Jewish Christians over his mission
to non-Jews in general terms. However, the similarities between
Paul's arguments in the main parts of these chapters and his
arguments in the introductory and concluding sections of the letter
(which are explicitly directed towards to the Romans) suggest that
the topics from this general discussion were relevant in Rome also.[9]

---

[7] It is questionable whether one can speak of "diatribe" as a genre of its
own. There has been too heavy dependence upon R. Bultmann, *"Der Stil
der paulinische Predigt und die kynisch-stoische Diatribe"* (FRLANT 13,
Göttingen, 1910) in this matter. See the criticism by K. P. Donfried, "False
Presuppositions in the Study of Romans", *CBQ* 36 (1974) 342-49; and E. A.
Judge, "St. Paul and Classical Society", *Jahrbuch für Antike und Christentum*
15 (1972) 33; cf. further the recent discussion of the classical evidence in
Diatribe in Ancient Rhetorical Theory (The Center for hermeneutical studies
in Hellenistic and modern culture, Protocol series 22, Berkeley, Calif., 1976).
[8] N. Schneider, *Die rhetorische Eigenart der paulinischen Antithese* (Hermeneutische Untersuchungen zur Theologie 11, Tübingen, 1970) 68-69.
[9] See below, 217-19, and 219, n. 36. A useful collection of articles about
the *Sitz im Leben* of Romans is found in *The Romans Debate* (ed. K. P.
Donfried, Minneapolis, 1977).

(a) 2:1-6:   "For he will render to every man according to his
works"

2:7-11:   "For God shows no partiality"

These two axioms about God's impartiality stand within the
first section of Paul's long judgment speech against his fellow Jews.
This section contains the first group of accusations. As a whole
Rom 1:18-3:20 resembles the judgment speeches by the Old
Testament prophets, especially by Amos.[10] Every Jew would agree
with Paul's pronunciation of judgment on the godless Gentiles,
1:18-32, but then he turns around and directs his accusation
against Israel. It is on this note that he starts the dialogue in 2:1
where he addresses his audience in the second person singular:

2:1-2   Therefore you have no excuse, O man, whoever you are, when
you judge another, for in passing judgment upon him, you con-
demn yourself, because you, the judge, are doing the same things.
We know that the judgment of God rightly falls upon those who
do such things.

(οἴδαμεν ὅτι τὸ κρίμα τοῦ θεοῦ ἐστιν κατὰ ἀλήθειαν ἐπὶ τοὺς τὰ
τοιαῦτα πράσσοντας, 2:2).

Here v. 1 is the actual accusation.[11] Then v. 2 states the reason why
the one who passes judgment on others, but himself performs the
same acts, shall not escape condemnation. God's judgment will
fall upon those who do this. The introduction with οἴδαμεν shows
that Paul here refers to an accepted fact;[12] this concept of God's
judgment was a common basis for Paul and his audience. These
two verses introduce the theme for this section and give an outline
for Paul's argumentation in the following verses:[13] the accusation
against the Jews ("man") comes first, and is then justified by a
reference to God's judgment (in v. 4 his mercy).

---

[10] See Amos 1-2. His oracles are first directed against Israel's neighbours,
1:1-2:3, but then with a surprising turn he indicts also Judah, 2:4-5, and
Israel, 2:6-16.

[11] Against R. Bultmann ("Glossen im Römerbrief", TLZ 72 (1947) 200)
and Käsemann (An die Römer (HNT 8a, 3d revised edition, Tübingen, 1974)
50) who hold 2:1 to be a gloss. But see C. E. B. Cranfield, The Epistle to the
Romans (International Critical Commentary, Edinburgh, 1975) 141.

[12] See 3:19; 7:14; 8:22, 28 etc.; cf. Bauer, 1100; and W. D. Burdick,
"Οἶδα and γινώσκω in the Pauline Epistles", New Dimensions in New Testa-
ment Study (ed. R. Longenecker and M. Tenney; Grand Rapids, 1976) 347.
Cf. also Rom 14:10.

[13] See J. Weiss, "Beiträge zur paulinischen Rhetorik", Theologische
Studien für B. Weiss, (Göttingen, 1897) 216-20.

Accusation   Sentence

2:3a λογίζῃ δὲ τοῦτο, ὦ ἄν-
θρωπε ὁ κρίνων τοὺς τὰ τοιαῦτα
πράσσοντας καὶ ποιῶν αὐτά,   3b ὅτι σὺ ἐκφεύξῃ τὸ κρίμα τοῦ
                                              θεοῦ;

2:4a ἢ τοῦ πλούτου τῆς χρηστό-
τητος αὐτοῦ καὶ τῆς ἀνοχῆς καὶ
τῆς μακροθυμίας καταφρονεῖς,   4b ἀγνοῶν ὅτι τὸ χρηστὸν τοῦ
                                              θεοῦ εἰς μετάνοιάν σε ἄγει;

2:5a κατὰ δὲ τὴν σκληρότητά
σου καὶ ἀμετανόητον καρδίαν
θησαυρίζεις σεαυτῷ ὀργὴν   5b ἐν ἡμέρᾳ ὀργῆς καὶ ἀποκα-
                                              λύψεως δικαιοκρισίας τοῦ θεοῦ,
                                          6 ὃς ἀποδώσει ἑκάστῳ κατὰ τὰ
                                              ἔργα αὐτοῦ.

Paul is here arguing that man's wrongdoings, even that of the
Jews, will meet with God's judgment. The one follows from the
other; this is expressed through parallel statements. The relative
clause in v. 6: ὃς ἀποδώσει ἑκάστῳ κατὰ τὰ ἔργα αὐτοῦ, that is attached to v. 5, goes beyond this parallel structure. Thus it adds
weight to Paul's argument, and in fact becomes his final and
decisive argument.[14]

V. 6 serves both as a conclusion to the discussion in 2:1-5 and as
an introduction to the next paragraph, 2:7-11. This section has a
chiastic structure where vv. 7 and 10 form one pair of parallels and
vv. 8 and 9 another.[15] In vv. 7-8 Paul says that God gives eternal life
to those who do good, whereas his wrath comes upon those who do
wrong. When this statement is repeated in vv. 9-10, an explanation
is added: it is for "the Jew first and also the Greek", 9b and 10b.
This would in itself suffice as a conclusion to Paul's argument, but
it is warranted by another axiomatic statement in 2:11: οὐ γάρ ἐστιν
προσωπολημψία παρὰ τῷ θεῷ. Thus v. 11 is an exact parallel to v. 6;
here too Paul closes the discussion with a reference to a long-held
belief in God.

---

14 Käsemann, Römer, 53; Weiss, "Rhetorik", 217.
15 J. Jeremias, "Chiasmus in den Paulusbriefen", ZNW 49 (1958) 149.
Cf. further K. Grobel, "A Chiastic Retribution-Formula in Romans 2",
Zeit und Geschichte. Dankesgabe an R. Bultmann zum 80. Geburtstag (ed.
E. Dinkler, Tübingen, 1964) 255-61 and the survey in Schneider, Antithese, 41.

In each instance Paul uses an axiomatic expression of traditional beliefs in God as a concluding argument. He wants to prove that the Jews are subject to the judgment of God in the same manner as non-Jews. Paul voices his protest against the idea that the Jews had secured a special position and had special rights and privileges before God. Even the expressions of faith in God wherewith Paul backs up his position are taken from within the tradition of the covenant between God and Israel. Now Paul separates them from this tradition and employs them to proclaim a judgment as universal as God's salvation, both of which are for Jews and Gentiles alike.[16] In 2:16, he concludes the next section with a reference to the judgment of God, parallel to 2:5-6: "on that day when according to my Gospel, God judges the secrets of men by Christ Jesus".[17]

(b) 3:1-8: "Let God be true"

Rom 3:1-8 has become a veritable storm-centre in Pauline scholarship. This is primarily due to the discussion over whether 3:4-5 form the starting point for the understanding of δικαιοσύνη θεοῦ in Paul or not.[18] This term occurs here in a context where several other expressions help to give it a clearer meaning. Among these phrases are τὴν πίστιν τοῦ θεοῦ 3:3; ἐπιστεύθησαν τὰ λόγια τοῦ θεοῦ 3:2; ὁ θεὸς ἀληθής 3:4; and not least the quotation from Ps 51:6 in 3:4: "Ὅπως ἂν δικαιωθῇς ἐν τοῖς λόγοις σου. This evidence points to a concept of God's δικαιοσύνη that stresses God's trustworthiness in his words and in his relationship to his people.[19] Actually this is the central question in Paul's deliberations in 3:1-8. In this section, as in the preceding one, Paul draws upon experiences from real controversies. It is no transcript of a discussion. Several of the problems that are raised are brought forward as rhetorical questions. But in v. 8 he makes a direct reference to contradictions from a real opponent.

---

[16] This is Paul's main point here; he is not discussing the apparent conflict between justification by faith and judgment according to works, which has puzzled interpreters; cf. N. A. Dahl, *Studies in Paul* (Minneapolis, 1977) 80.

[17] Against the suggestion that 2:16 is a gloss, Käsemann, *Römer*, 62f.

[18] E. Käsemann, P. Stuhlmacher and Ch. Müller argue that δικαιοσύνη θεοῦ is here a subjective genitive and that it indicates God's faithfulness as creator towards the world. This is denied e.g. by G. Klein, E. Lohse and G. Bornkamm; see the summary of the various positions in Bornkamm, "Theologie als Teufelskunst. Römer 3, 1-9", *Geschichte und Glaube* 2 (Gesammelte Aufsätze 4, BEvT 53, Munich, 1971) 140. The arguments and the positions are repeated in the discussion of Rom 4:17, cf. below, 105.

[19] N. A. Dahl, *Studies in Paul*, 128-29.

The immediate background to this passage is 2:17-29. There, Paul argues that any privileges that the Jews formerly held were no longer valid—not even circumcision. Cranfield summarizes the problem that Paul's teaching raised for the Jews (i.e. primarily for the Christian Jews and consequently for Paul himself) in this way: "If there then really is no advantage of the Jew and no profit in circumcision, this must mean either that the OT is a false witness or else that God has not been faithful to his word. *The question raised is nothing less than the question of the credibility of God*".[20] Thus not just the identity of the Jewish people, but even the trustworthiness of God were at stake.

In 3:1-8 Paul takes up this problem in four exchanges of questions and answers, *vv.* 1-2; 3-4; 5-6 and 7-8.[21] The objections to Paul's teaching that are voiced here are concerned either with the situation of Israel, partly including mankind in general, or with the faithfulness of God. In every instance, it is with a statement about God, mostly drawn from Jewish tradition, that Paul answers these objections.

The first question in 3:1 is directly related to the conclusion of chapter 2: "Then what advantage has the Jew? Or what is the value of circumcision?" The answer that Paul gives, "Much in every way", sounds surprising after 2:17-29, but then it is qualified in 3:2b: "To begin with, the Jews are entrusted with the words of God". The Jews themselves have no advantage—it rests entirely with God. *He* has given them his words (cf. 9:4).[22]

With ἐπιστεύθησαν in *v.* 2 Paul introduces a chain of words from the same root. They follow in the questions in 3:3: τί γὰρ εἰ ἠπίστησάν τινες; μὴ ἡ ἀπιστία αὐτῶν τὴν πίστιν τοῦ θεοῦ καταργήσει; The objection is here similar to the one in 3:1, but it is expressed directly as a question that affects God:[23] can it be that the lack of trust and faithfulness on the side of the Jews should make the faithfulness of God ineffective? In 3:4 Paul rejects this idea by exclaiming: μὴ γένοιτο. γινέσθω δὲ ὁ θεὸς ἀληθής. God is true to his

---

[20] *Romans*, 176-77; my italics; see also Dahl, *Studies in Paul*, 128-29.

[21] Bornkamm, "Teufelskunst", 142-46.

[22] If 2:17-28 provoked the question in 3:1, Paul's answer in 3:2-5 is prepared by 2:29c; "His praise is not from men but from God". Cf. K. Dreiergaard, "Jödernes Fortrin. En undersögelse av Rom 3:1-9", *Dansk Teologisk Tidskrift* 35 (1973) 81-101.

[23] This objection is raised as a rhetorical question: Cranfield, *Romans*, 180; Paul actually shares the view of his opponents; Bornkamm, "Teufelskunst", 143.

promises; this is an axiom that cannot be doubted. Moreover, in 4b it is supported by a quotation from Ps 51:6. Paul draws here on the Old Testament image of a lawsuit between Yahweh and his people. God is accused by his people of being unjust, but he is vindicated and appears as righteous.[24] The axiom that God is true, backed by the citation from Ps 51:6, closes the discussion.[25] The accusation against God is turned around—"man" (i.e. the Jews and Greeks of 3:9) stands as a liar.

Some misunderstandings might possibly arise from Paul's insistence that lack of faith on the part of man (the Jews) did not impede the faithfulness of God. The next round of arguments concerns these objections. The nature of the accusations raised against God in 3:5-7 is best understood in the light of the final accusation in *v.* 8. Paul's opponents misrepresent his message when they claim that Paul says: "Why not do evil so that good may come?" In 3:5 and 7 this is raised as a question that concerns the understanding of God. In the first part of each verse, the arguments from Paul's opponents draw on the "dogma" stated in 3:1-4, that God is faithful to his promises. However, then they make the inference that therefore God should not inflict his wrath upon the Jews.[26] Paul rejects this notion completely with μὴ γένοιτο in *v.* 6 and reaffirms it with ἐπεὶ πῶς κρινεῖ ὁ θεὸς τὸν κόσμον; Paul upholds the traditional teaching: that God shall judge the world is a given fact that no sophisticated speculation can withstand. He gives the same answer in *v.* 8 with the abrupt ὧν τὸ κρίμα ἔνδικόν ἐστιν. Paul does not really enter into discussions with his opponents; rather his answer is an absolute refutation.[27] Those who try to misconstrue the teaching of Paul and thereby defend themselves against God's wrath are themselves confronted with his judgment! Paul does not introduce this as a question to be debated, but rather as an absolute reality—from which no man can escape. The result is that those who accuse Paul of misrepresenting the true Jewish tradition about God now themselves have this tradition turned against them!

---

[24] See A. A. Trites, *The New Testament Concept of Witness* (SNTSMS 31, Cambridge, 1976) 35-47, 201.

[25] That God is faithful is not a philosophical concept; rather, it is related to his acts and to his words, especially in his judgment; cf. Quell and Kittel, "ἀλήθεια", *TWNT* I (1933) 235-38.

[26] Even this section is part of Paul's discussion with the Jews; against Bornkamm, "Teufelskunst", 144.

[27] C. J. Bjerkelund, "Nach menschlicher Weise rede Ich", *ST* 26 (1972) 95.

(c) 3:27-31: "God is one"

In this section Paul makes his teaching of "justification by faith" from 3:21-26 more pointed in a clearly polemical situation. The inherent controversy in his doctrine is here brought out into the open and applied to the major problem that faced him—the divisions between Jews and non-Jews that continued also among the Christians. Paul makes 3:21-26 end on an explicitly God-centred note: εἰς τὸ εἶναι αὐτὸν δίκαιον καὶ δικαιοῦντα τὸν ἐκ πίστεως 'Ιησοῦ. Then he goes on to draw the implications of this in two short exchanges of questions and answers, 3:27-28 and 29-30(31). The question of the privilege of Israel comes up in a way that resembles 3:1. Paul asks in 3:27a: ποῦ οὖν ἡ καύχησις; In terse expressions, without any explanations, Paul in v. 27b gives the answer that boasting is excluded through faith. This answer is backed up, however, by a statement in 3:28, introduced by λογιζόμεθα, indicating that Paul wants this to be commonly accepted: "For we hold that a man is justified by faith apart from works of law".[28]

In v. 27 Paul raised the question whether the Jews had any privilege in their relation to God in terms of καύχησις. The exchange in 3:29-30 takes up the same question,[29] this time explicitly focusing upon God's relationship to Israel: "Or is God the God of Jews only? Is he not the God of Gentiles also?" Paul gives a short answer in v. 29c: "Yes, of Gentiles also", but then he expands this answer in the same manner as in 3:28 with an axiomatic statement: "God is one" (3:30a). It is this belief, central both to Jews and to Greeks, that Paul here uses as a definite argument for his teaching.[30] But now he draws inferences that radicalize this commonly-held belief by describing God with a relative clause in v. 30b: ὃς δικαιώσει περιτομὴν ἐκ πίστεως καὶ ἀκροβυστίαν διὰ τῆς πίστεως.

---

[28] Cranfield, Romans, 220; "λογιζόμεθα is here used to indicate a faith-judgment, a conviction reached in the light of the gospel (see also on 6.11; 8.18; 14.14)". Similar statements in 3:19 and Gal 2:16 are introduced by οἴδαμεν, εἰδότες see n. 12. H. Schlier (Der Brief an die Galater (MeyerK 7, 12th edition, Göttingen, 1962) 91) characterizes Gal 2:16; 3:11; Rom 3:20, 28 as "die entscheidende Erkenntnis der paulinischen Botschaft".

[29] Against Klein, "Römer IV und die Idee der Heilsgeschichte", EvT 23 (1963) 427. He finds a break in Paul's argument between a strictly anthropological and a theological perspective; similarly Käsemann, Römer, 97.

[30] See now the illuminating study by N. A. Dahl, "The One God of Jews and Gentiles (Romans 3:29-30)", Studies in Paul, 178-91. For Paul's use of "God is one" in Gal 3:20, cf. below, 213-15. For Jewish theology at this point, cf. the bibliography in Maier, Geschichte, 162.

Ironically, using a traditional belief that all Jews would agree upon, Paul has drawn a conclusion with which most Jews would disagree. He has actually interpreted this common faith that God is one in the light of his main theme in Romans: that the righteous through faith, the Jew first and then the Greek, shall live; 1:16-17.

(d) 4:1-8, (9-12), 13-22, 23-25: God—"who justifies the ungodly" and "who gives life to the dead"

Romans 4 is written in a less polemical form than the other texts we have discussed. However, the element of dialogue is present here as well in the questions addressed to Paul's readers, e.g. in 4:1-2 and 9. Moreover, the style is characterized by a use of antitheses which have a function similar to the dialogues.[31] And Paul raises the same basic question about the identity of the people of God as in the passages we have studied earlier, cf. v. 1: "What then shall we say about Abraham, our forefather according to the flesh?" The frequent use of predications for God combined with πιστεύω, which is found only in this chapter, shows that faith in God is intimately linked to the question of God's people. Romans 4 divides into three main parts, vv. 1-8; 9-12 and 13-22, followed by a conclusion in vv. 23-25.[32] The predications of God are evenly distributed throughout the chapter in vv. 5, 17, 21 and 24. The use of antitheses is another typical feature of this chapter. The questions leading up to chapter 4 in 3:27, 29 and 31 are antithetical and thus in their form reflect the polemics of the situation in which they are used. The same is true of expressions that without sharing the formal structure of the antithesis nevertheless refer to opposite or opposing views.[33] A typical example is the beginning of Paul's discussion of Abraham in 4:2: "For if Abraham was justified by works, he has something to boast about, but not before God". This statement is supported with the citation of Gen 15:6, and it has been argued that the rest of the chapter is a midrash on this verse.[34] Various aspects of the quotation are discussed in the different parts of the chapter. Each section is introduced by an antithetically formed question or assertion:

4:4   τῷ δὲ ἐργαζομένῳ / τῷ δὲ μὴ ἐργαζομένῳ, πιστεύοντι δέ

4:9   ἐπὶ τὴν περιτομήν / ἢ καὶ ἐπὶ τὴν ἀκροβυστίαν

4:13   οὐ γὰρ διὰ νόμου / ἀλλὰ διὰ δικαιοσύνης πίστεως

---

[31] Schneider, Antithese, 68-71.
[32] See below, 108-16.
[33] Cf. 4:9, 12, 16, 23-24.
[34] P. Borgen, Bread from Heaven (NovTSup 10, Leiden, 1965) 47-50.

This antithetical structure is a formative element in chapter 4. Consequently, we need to study the participial predications of God and their function within the various subsections of the chapter in the light of this structure.

The ascription "God who justified the ungodly" is part of the antithesis that Paul develops in *vv.* 4-5. It can be outlined as follows:

v. 4	*v.* 5
a. τῷ δὲ ἐργαζομένῳ	τῷ δὲ μὴ ἐργαζομένῳ, πιστεύοντι δὲ ἐπὶ τὸν δικαιοῦντα τὸν ἀσεβῆ
b. ὁ μισθὸς οὐ λογίζεται κατὰ χάριν ἀλλὰ κατὰ ὀφείλημα.	λογίζεται ἡ πίστις αὐτοῦ εἰς δικαιοσύνην.

As an antithesis is a form of parallelism, we expect to find a greater or lesser degree of symmetry between the two parts. When, as in 4:5, one part is considerably longer, we must assume that there is a reason for this expansion. Considering the point that Paul is making here, it becomes clear that the predication "God who justifies the ungodly" is not an incidental addition that spoils the symmetry. Rather, it represents the pivotal point of Paul's argument![35] Contrary to our previous examples where Paul had recourse to traditional formulae, it is most likely that he coined this most controversial expression himself. The effect when this predication is added unto the antithesis between "work" and "faith", is that Paul puts the emphasis not on "faith" *per se*, but rather on *God*, in whom one believes. A similar structure is found also in *vv.* 17, 21 and 24, and as a result, the understanding of God is more directly the focus of interest than in other texts where Paul speaks of "faith".

Although 4:9-12 shows the same structure as the preceding and the following sections, it does not contain any predications of God. We will therefore pass over these verses and go directly to 4:13-22. In this section Paul illustrates his teaching of justification with a new and important theme—God's promise of land and descendants to Abraham. He introduces the promise in an antithesis: "The promise . . . did not come through the law but through the righteousness of faith", *v.* 13. This juxtaposition of "law" and "righteousness of faith" determines the structure of the rest of this section, 4:14-22. In 4:14-15 Paul develops the negative side—why the

---

[35] Käsemann, *Römer*, 104-5; against Weiss, "Rhetorik", 175.

promise was not through the law. His own position, that the promise was "through faith", is given an extensive treatment in 4:16-22. It is here that we find the predications of God in 4:17b and 21. In 4:17 these ascriptions stand within a parallel structure of two relative clauses (4:16-17b and 4:18) attached to "Abraham" in v. 16c.

a 16d ὅς ἐστιν πατὴρ πάντων ἡμῶν

b 17a καθὼς γέγραπται ὅτι Πατέρα πολλῶν ἐθνῶν τέθεικά σε

c 17b κατέναντι οὗ ἐπίστευσεν θεοῦ τοῦ ζῳοποιοῦντος τοὺς νεκροὺς καὶ καλοῦντος τὰ μὴ ὄντα ὡς ὄντα

c 18a ὃς παρ' ἐλπίδα ἐπ' ἐλπίδι ἐπίστευσεν

a 18b εἰς τὸ γενέσθαι αὐτὸν πατέρα πολλῶν ἐθνῶν

b 18c κατὰ τὸ εἰρημένον, Οὕτως ἔσται τὸ σπέρμα σου.

These two relative clauses have an almost chiastic structure where vv. 16d-17a and v. 18b-c form the brackets. Here Abraham is described as the father of many nations. This claim is supported by quotations from Gen 17:5 and 15:5 about the promise to Abraham. The parallel between v. 17b and 18a in the centre of the chiasmus expands Gen 15:6: "Abraham believed God and it was reckoned to him as righteousness". Here v. 18a, "in hope he believed against hope", elaborates on the situation in which Abraham believed. This corresponds to the description of God in v. 17b—the God who gives life to the dead is stronger than this hopeless situation. Positioned between the two promises to Abraham that he should become father of many nations, the predications in 4:17b serve as a guarantee. The descriptions of God as the one who gives life are given in order to support his words. We find the same theme in v. 21— Abraham was convinced that "God was able to do what he has promised".[36] God stands behind his words! In both cases the predications used of God are traditional—but not the thesis they support. Paul here employs these predications in his argument that Abraham was the father both of Jews and of non-Jewish Christians. This was also his underlying argument in 4:4-5, and in fact, 4:16-22 form a parallel to v. 5:

---

[36] V. 21 supports the statement in v. 20: "No distrust made him waver concerning the promise of God"; and provides the basis for trust in the promise of God; Schneider, *Antithese*, 71.

4:5 τῷ δὲ μὴ ἐργαζομένῳ, πιστεύοντι δὲ

ἐπὶ τὸν δικαιοῦντα τὸν ἀσεβῆ

λογίζεται ἡ πίστις αὐτοῦ εἰς
δικαιοσύνην.

4:16 οὐ τῷ ἐκ τοῦ νόμου μόνον
ἀλλὰ καὶ τῷ ἐκ πίστεως 'Αβραάμ . . . .
4:17 κατέναντι οὗ ἐπίστευσεν
θεοῦ τοῦ ζῳοποιοῦντος τοὺς
νεκροὺς καὶ καλοῦντος τὰ μὴ
ὄντα ὡς ὄντα
4:21 πληροφορηθεὶς ὅτι ὃ ἐπήγγελται δυνατός ἐστιν καὶ ποιῆσαι.
4:22 διὸ καὶ ἐλογίσθη αὐτῷ εἰς
δικαιοσύνην.

In both arguments the statements about God hold central positions. Compared to the shorter exchange in 4:4-5, however, an
additional theme in 4:13-22 is the emphasis on God as a guarantor
that his words will come true. Paul's emphasis on the reliability of
God's promise was related to the fact that the acceptance of non-
Jews into Christian communities threatened the traditional understanding of this promise. With his interpretation Paul linked God's
promise with the *new* community of circumcised and uncircumcised.
This becomes even more obvious in the conclusion to the chapter
in 4:23-25. Here we find the first specifically *Christian* predication
of God in this chapter, with a christological formulaic expression
attached to it. In the previous sections Paul has argued that faith
in God who "justified the ungodly", "raised the dead", and "called
the non-existent into being" created a community that in its
existence reflected these acts by God. Thus Jews and non-Jews,
circumcised and uncircumcised, were the seed of Abraham, and, like
him, were justified through faith. In this last section of the chapter,
Paul spells this out even more clearly. The preceding arguments
over the actual meaning of "justification" are by implication present
in *v.* 24. Here he speaks of "us" for whom faith will be reckoned to
justification, i.e. his contemporaries, including all the different
groups he has earlier mentioned. In conclusion Paul points out in
whom they believe—God "who raised from the dead Jesus our
Lord, who was put to death for our trespasses and raised for our
justification".[37]

This double description—of God and of Christ Jesus—serves not
only to identify the God of Abraham with a well-known Christian

---

[37] See p. 272 nn. 139-40.

predication. It is also Paul's final argument in the discussion carried over from the preceding sections. Paul strikes a familiar note by using a traditional formula that was acceptable to all Christians, whether Jews or non-Jews. The point he is arguing, however, is just as controversial in this final section as in any of the earlier parts of the chapter.

(e) 9:6-13: "Not because of works but because of him who called"

This text shows many similarities to 3:1-8. First, 9:1-5 prepares the question in 9:6 in the same manner as 2:17-29 led up to the objection in 3:1. In 9:1-5 Paul has enumerated the advantages of Israel—or rather, God's gifts towards Israel. But Israel, i.e. most of the Jews have rejected these gifts, and vv. 1-5 is Paul's prayer to God for his people. This wish-prayer expresses his strong loyalty towards his fellow Jews in a way not unlike the prayers of the Old Testament prophets. In this situation Paul once more has to face the question concerning the trustworthiness of the word of God. The urgency of this question is stressed by Martin Rese in his study of Rom 9:1-5; "Durch den Unglauben der Mehrheit der Juden wird die Frage der Besonderheit der Juden verschärft zur Frage nach der Wahrheit Gottes, es geht um Gott selbst und seine Treue zu seinem Wort".[38] Faced with this theological problem, Paul responds with a strong assertion in 9:6: "But it is not as though the word of God has failed".[39] But how could he possibly reconcile the fact that many of the Jews had rejected Christ (in whom the Christians found the fulfilment of God's promises) with the assertion that God's promise to Abraham and to Israel was steadfast? This situation had introduced an ambiguity into the terms "Israel", "children of Abraham", "children of God", etc. Paul solves this problem through making a distinction—he argues that not all from Israel are Israel, not all Jews rightly bear the name of Jews (cf. 2:28f). There are two parallel arguments in 9:7-13, vv. 7-9 and 10-13, the first using Abraham, the second using Rebecca as an example.[40] In both instances Paul states the historical "facts" as

---

[38] "Die Vorzüge Israels im Röm 9:4f und Eph 2:12", TZ 31 (1975) 215. Similarly Dahl (Studies in Paul, 143): "Paul has in mind God's promise to Israel; it is still valid. This is the sum and substance of what Paul wants to say in Romans 9-11".

[39] See p. 57 n. 4.

[40] Cf. A. T. Hanson, Studies in Paul's Technique and Theology (London, 1974) 87-90.

they were known through contemporary exegesis of the relevant
Biblical passages: only Abraham's descendants through Isaac were
recognized as his legitimate children, 9:7. Similarly, Rebecca
conceived two children at the same time but the elder, Esau,
became subservient to the younger, Jacob, 9:10-11a and 12b.
Clearly, the Jews descended from Jacob, not from Esau! The
traditions that Paul elaborates upon here were used by the Jews
when arguing against other groups that also claimed descent from
Abraham for themselves.[41] With this commonly accepted view as
his starting point, Paul goes on to sharpen it by antithetical definitions in 9:8 and 11b-12a.[42] In both instances they are supported
by scriptural quotations in 9:9 and 13. In v. 8 Paul defines the
ambiguous term "children of God" through the following antithesis:
"This means that it is not the children of the flesh (τὰ τέκνα τῆς
σαρκὸς) who are the children of God, but the children of the promise
(τὰ τέκνα τῆς ἐπαγγελίας) are reckoned as descendants". With this
distinction between σάρξ and ἐπαγγελία Paul's argument is brought
to an end.

In the section on Rebecca, Paul states his own position by way
of a final clause. The reason why the elder son should serve the
younger was ἵνα ἡ κατ' ἐκλογὴν πρόθεσις τοῦ θεοῦ μένῃ. Many of Paul's
arguments end with a ἵνα-clause. In these clauses Paul often speaks
of the ultimate goal for God's relationship with man, e.g. "that God
may be everything to everyone" (1 Cor 15:28). Normally, such a
statement, because of its eschatological nature, makes further
arguments superfluous.[43] However, in this particular case, Paul
deems it necessary to guard himself against misunderstandings.
Similar to v. 8 he does this by means of a definition of a vital part

---

[41] See 4 Ezra 3:13-16. Cf. also Jub. 15:30-31; 16:17, protesting against
the influence of Hellenism; S. Sandmel, "Philo's Place in Judaism", *HUCA*
26 (1955) 163-70. In later sources cf. *Tg. Neof.* Gen 16:5; *Tg. Ps.-J.* Gen
21:12; *Gen. Rab.* 53. But there were also attempts in apologetic and missionary literature to make Abraham the father of many of the surrounding
nations through Israel or through his sons by Ketura, e.g. 1 Macc 12:21;
Josephus, *Ant.* I 220-21, 239. See further G. Mayer, "Aspekte des Abrahambildes in der hellenistisch-jüdischen Literatur", *EvT* 32 (1972) 121-23; and
D. Georgi, *Die Gegner des Paulus im 2. Korintherbrief* (WMANT 11, Neukirchen, 1964) 63-65.

[42] Here the antithesis functions as a correction against a possible misunderstanding or to define an ambiguity, cf. Schneider, *Antithese*, 68-72.

[43] See E. Stauffer, "ἵνα und das Problem des teleologischen Denkens bei
Paulus", *Theologische Studien und Kritiken* 102 (1930) 232-57. Cf. also
G. Delling, "Zur paulinischen Teleologie", *TLZ* 75 (1950) 705-10.

of his argument, here, the phrase "God's purpose of election".[44]
Paul gives it a polemical turn and thereby contests the Jewish
usage of this term with the antithesis in 9:12a: οὐκ ἐξ ἔργων ἀλλ'
ἐκ τοῦ καλοῦντος.[45] As already noticed, the ascription ὁ καλῶν corresponds to the quotation from Gen 21:12 in Rom 9:7. Therefore
it is in itself not controversial. But when Paul sets it up antithetically to ἐξ ἔργων, it becomes highly polemical.[46] A large group
of Paul's antitheses deal with the differences between God and
man. "God" and "man" could only be spoken of together, but it
was necessary for Paul to do so in the form of an antithesis.[47] Thus
his argument in 9:6-12 ends with a statement about God within an
antithesis. After this, Paul allows for no more discussion, only one
additional citation from scripture follows in 9:13. His definition of
"God's purpose of election" has shown that "Bedingung der πρόθεσις
θεοῦ ist Gott selbst".[48]

(f) 9:14-18: "So it depends not upon man's will or exertion but
     upon God who shows mercy"

Since we have treated Paul's use of antitheses in his arguments in
some detail in the preceding section, we can pass over 9:14-18
rather briefly. By way of introduction Paul again considers an
objection that might be raised against his preaching: "What shall
we say then? Is there injustice on God's part?" His rejection of this
possibility is supported by a citation from Ex 33:15 to the effect
that God is free to show mercy to whomever he chooses. So far,
the matter of controversy in this exchange has not been sharply
defined. It is not until Paul draws the conclusion in an antithesis
in v. 16 that a clearer picture of the issues emerges. Here he says,
"So it depends not upon man's will or exertion, but upon God who
shows mercy (τοῦ ἐλεῶντος θεοῦ)". This is an exact parallel to the
antithesis in 9:12. The problem is the same—that of God's election
and rejection. This antithesis between "man" and "God" throws
light on the objection Paul referred to in v. 14: "Is there injustice

---

[44] Schneider, *Antithese*, 84. Apparently unknown to Schneider, this was
noticed in 1897 by E. Kühl, "Zur paulinischen Theodicee", *Theologische
Studien für B. Weiss*, 68.

[45] Michel, *Römer*, 233-34; Käsemann, *Römer*, 254-55.

[46] Similarly in Galatians with the contrast between ὁ καλῶν and "another
gospel", "man"; 1:6, 15.

[47] Typical examples are Rom 1:23; 2:29c; 9:12, 16; 1 Cor 3:7; 2 Cor 1:9;
cf. Schneider, *Antithese*, 87.

[48] Schneider, *Antithese*, 84.

on God's part?" [49] The underlying assumption was apparently that Israel had privileges that were violated through God's acceptance of Gentiles and his exclusion of the Jews. Earlier, e.g. in 3:2 and 9:8, 11-12, Paul has completely reinterpreted the meaning of these privileges by emphasizing that they are *gifts* of God and not rights.

Paul follows the same approach here. He draws upon tradition and quotations from Scripture when he describes God as ὁ ἐλεῶν.[50] However, the implications of this term become visible only when it is read in its antithetical position over against "man": ἄρα οὖν οὐ τοῦ θέλοντος οὐδὲ τοῦ τρέχοντος, ἀλλὰ τοῦ ἐλεῶντος θεοῦ. A quotation from Ex 9:16 follows the antithesis and must be read in light of it. Thus God's word to Pharaoh becomes an apt illustration of the position that Paul brought forth in *v.* 16. In 9:18 this position is summarized once more, this time without a negation.

Both in 9:6-13 and in 9:14-18 Paul's arguments are brought back to one last statement—a point beyond which there is no further discussion. When Paul here refers to God he does it in terms that came from tradition or arose from the context. However, these traditional statements are phrased as antitheses—they are expressions about God and man. Other passages that precede or follow immediately after the dialogues in 9:6-18 tell us more about the situation where this controversy took place. 9:1-5 point to the claim made by Jews (Christian Jews included) that they as a group stood in an unbroken continuity with God's promise to Israel in the past.[51] Contrary to this, Paul argued that another community now represented this continuity—i.e. the Christians, Jews and non-Jews.

When Paul speaks about the recipients of God's call, the children of Abraham, etc., he frequently does so in terms of "not only (Jews, circumcised etc.) but also (non-Jews, uncircumcised etc.)", cf. 4:12, 16. Here in chapter 9 Paul sees the new community as called out "not from the Jews only but also from the Gentiles" (9:24). This was a result of creation—not by man, but only by God.[52] Thus

---

[49] Schneider, *Antithese*, 71.

[50] See p. 24 n. 35.

[51] However, at the same time, Paul interprets these claims in 9:1-5 within his own theological concept; see Rese, "Vorzüge", 213-19. But there still remains a difference between the concept of Israel in these verses and that in 9:6-13. Against U. Luz (*Das Geschichtsverständnis des Paulus* (BEvT 49, Munich, 1968) 274) we agree with Käsemann (*Römer*, 249); "Offensichtlich versteht Pls das Phänomen Israel nicht weniger dialektisch als das des Gesetzes".

[52] See below, 252.

there is a close relationship between what Paul wants to convey through his expressions "not man, but God" (9:12, 16), and through this other figure of speech "not only Jews, but also Gentiles (9:24). Only an act of God could bring about this unity across old barriers. Consequently, also the scheme "οὐ μόνον ... ἀλλά" signals a polemical situation and is directed against Jews (Christian or non-Christian). With this Paul aims at breaking the Jewish mode of thinking about Jews and non-Jews as groups that were meant to keep separate also in the Christian community.

(g) 11:1-6: "God has not rejected his people whom he foreknew"

Although this passage does not contain a direct predication of God, a comparison with 9:6-18 justifies its inclusion in our survey. In this text Paul's introductory question presupposes a certain understanding of the relationship between God and his people: "I ask then, has God rejected his people?" 11:1.[53] After rejecting this possibility with μὴ γένοιτο, his immediate answer in 11:1b is to point to *himself* as a sign that the Jews were not rejected. In *v.* 2 he repeats the question, this time in the form of an emphatic negation with a significant addition: οὐκ ἀπώσατο ὁ θεὸς τὸν λαὸν αὐτοῦ ὃν προέγνω. This addition of ὃν προέγνω provides the key to Paul's proofs in the following verses. In his first example, from 1 Kings 19 (Rom 11:2b-4), Elijah is cast in a role similar to Paul's, complaining over his people, that there were no faithful left in Israel. The answer to Elijah is given in the words of God, that he has kept for himself 7,000 men who had not worshipped Baal. In 11:5 Paul draws the line to the present, when he speaks of "the remnant", i.e. the Christian Jews. This remnant was chosen by grace (κατ' ἐκλογὴν χάριτος), an expression that further characterizes ὃν προέγνω from *v.* 2.

Χάρις was commonly used in Jewish texts to characterize acts of God.[54] As Paul is arguing precisely against a theology that also spoke of God's χάρις, he has to define it, and he does so with the

---

[53] Ps 94:14 and 1 Sam 12:22 provide the most direct OT background; for its interpretation in Jewish tradition, cf. Billerbeck 3, 286. When Israel lament that God actually *has* rejected his people, e.g., Ps LXX 59:3, 12; Lam 3:31, it is with the firm conviction that he will restore them again.

[54] ןֵח and דֶסֶח are extensively used in the OT. The former is usually translated by the LXX with χάρις, the latter with ἔλεος, although there is no strict distinction between them. Philo often speaks of God's χάρις; cf. Conzelmann and Zimmerli, "χάρις", *TWNT* 9 (1973) 366-405. For Paul's theology of χάρις, see below, 256-61.

4

antithesis in v. 6: εἰ δὲ χάριτι, οὐκέτι ἐξ ἔργων, ἐπεὶ ἡ χάρις οὐκέτι γίνεται χάρις. Here χάρις and ἔργα are opposites, like ὁ καλῶν and ἔργα in 9:12. Consequently, χάρις characterizes *God*, not only as opposed to *man* in general (this Paul's opponents would agree with) but more specifically to man as the one *who does* works (cf. 4:4).

(h)   11:16-24: "God has the power to graft them in again"

Paul's argument in this section is similar to that in 2:1-16. It addresses the same question, but the roles are reversed. Romans 11:16-24 is not directed against Jews who sit in judgment over non-Jews, but against non-Jewish Christians who disregard the Jews and slight their fellow Christians among the Jews. In 2:1-11 Paul brought in two axioms about God as final statements to prove that everybody, the Jews included, were alike for God when it came to his judgment. Here the argument is reversed. In 11:16-24 Paul turns the privileges of Israel (interpreted as gifts of God's grace, cf. 3:2; 9:1-5) against non-Jewish Christians who boast of *their* status before God. The parable of the olive tree and the branches raises a number of intricate exegetical problems that cannot be discussed here.[55] Paul first states his presuppositions in v. 16:

If the dough offered as first fruits is holy, so is the whole lump; and if the root is holy, so are the branches.

The most natural interpretation of this picture is that it concerns Israel's ancestors and the present Israel.[56] Consequently in this text Paul takes Israel to represent the people of God—into which the non-Jewish Christians were accepted. In accord with this, his first argument in 11:17-18 closes with an admonition to remember that it is the root that supports the branches—not the opposite! The second round of arguments, 11:19-23, has a similar conclusion. As Paul switches back and forth from image to explanation it is at times difficult to follow his argument. However, in this passage he speaks of God in clear language. 11:19-21 are almost a direct parallel to 11:17-18.[57] The warning against boasting has a similar

---

[55] See the discussion in J. Munck, *"Christus und Israel, Eine Auslegung von Röm 9-11"* (Acta Jutlandica 28/3, Theology Series 7, Aarhus, 1956) 95-98.

[56] Käsemann, *Römer*, 298; Dahl, *Studies in Paul*, 151.

[57] Weiss ("Rhetorik", 241-42) over-elaborates when he attempts to divide *vv.* 17-24 into four parallel strophes. However, he is right in pointing out the parallel between the description of God in 22a: "note then the kindness and severity of God", and *v.* 23b: "God has the power to graft them in again".

conclusion, the difference being that God is brought directly into the picture: "For if God did not spare the natural branches, neither will he spare you" (v. 21). As in several other passages (e.g. 2:1-16; 3:6-8; 14:10-12), the haughty is confronted with the judgment of God. This is further developed in 11:22 where Paul points to God's kindness *and* his severity (ἴδε οὖν χρηστότητα καὶ ἀποτομίαν θεοῦ) to characterize his acts towards Israel and non-Jewish Christians, respectively. He expresses this antithetically: "severity towards those who have fallen, but God's kindness to you". But this is not a *static* situation that the non-Jews can make a ground for boasting, any more than the Jews could make claims upon God. The non-Jewish believers can be cut off from the mercy of God, if they do not remain within its scope (v. 22c). Likewise, the rejection of Israel is not final—it lasts only so long as Israel persists in its unbelief. Here Paul slides into the picture of the olive tree again when he points to God's power to receive back the people he rejected: δυνατὸς γάρ ἐστιν ὁ θεὸς πάλιν ἐγκεντρίσαι αὐτούς. This statement about the power of God is supported by an *a maiori ad minus* argument in v. 24.[58]

(i) 11:25-32: "For the gifts and the call of God are irrevocable"

Throughout this chapter, Paul has stressed that the fate of the (non-Jewish) Christians and that of Israel are inextricably bound together.[59] Therefore the non-Jewish Christians could not sever this link at will. This bond between the two groups becomes even more visible in Paul's concluding arguments in 11:25-32.[60] He does not here discuss the future of Israel *per se*, but as intertwined with the fate of the non-Jewish Christians. Therefore Israel's identity is described antithetically:

v. 28a   κατὰ μὲν τὸ εὐαγγέλιον ἐχθροὶ δι' ὑμᾶς,

v. 28b   κατὰ δὲ τὴν ἐκλογὴν ἀγαπητοὶ διὰ τοὺς πατέρας.

v. 29   ἀμεταμέλητα γὰρ τὰ χαρίσματα καὶ ἡ κλῆσις τοῦ θεοῦ.

---

[58] *V.* 24a states the more difficult deed, which God has already done; in consequence also the less difficult is possible, *v.* 24b. Paul uses similar arguments in 5:6-9, 10; 8:32; 1 Cor 6:2-3; cf. J. Jeremias, "Paulus als Hillelit", *Neotestamentica et semitica, Studies in Honour of M. Black* (ed. R. E. Ellis and M. Wilcox, Edinburgh, 1968) 92.

[59] See G. Eichholz, *Die Theologie des Paulus im Umriss* (Neukirchen, 1972) 284-301.

[60] See the discussion of recent interpretation by P. Stuhlmacher, "Zur Interpretation von Römer 11:25-32", *Probleme biblischer Theologie. G. von Rad zum 70. Geburtstag* (ed. H. W. Wolff, Munich, 1971) 555-70.

It is 11:28b in particular, concerning Israel's election, that is supported by the axiom in v. 29.[61] The combination of these two clauses, vv. 28 and 29, clearly shows that in Paul's mind the identity of Israel was linked to his understanding of God. But he can only speak of this link antithetically. Since Israel is also seen together with the non-Jewish Christians, its position in the present was ambiguous.[62] In consequence, v. 29 is not to be considered here as a "general statement", to Paul, this traditional Jewish confession holds true only in this antithetical position. 11:30-31 parallel and repeat v. 28, in that they elaborate further on the intertwinement between (the non-Christian) Israel and the (non-Jewish) Christians. Finally, in v. 32 Paul brings it all together in a theological conclusion before the great doxology (11:33-36): συνέκλεισεν γὰρ ὁ θεὸς τοὺς πάντας εἰς ἀπείθειαν ἵνα τοὺς πάντας ἐλεήσῃ. Here the opposite groups are brought together in τοὺς πάντας.[63] The differences in God's way of dealing with Jews and non-Jews in various periods are here summed up as parts of God's plan of salvation. Thus it becomes apparent that Paul's antitheses are an historical mode of speaking. Salvation and rejection, faith and disbelief are not given unchangeable positions; rather, they are part of an historical development towards a final goal: God's mercy to all men.

This does not solve the problem that is involved in talking antithetically of God. The difficulty that statements about God cannot be harmoniously reconciled into a unity remains. Also, by expressing it in this way Paul leaves the problem as a mystery (cf. 11:25) that cannot be proved by further arguments. Once more this is the end to the discussion—as well as the introduction to the doxology that forms the conclusion to all that Paul has said so far in Romans 9-11.

Our initial question concerned the function of statements about God in discussion texts in Romans 1-4 and 9-11. We claimed that Paul's understanding of God could only be grasped through such a

---

[61] Käsemann, Römer, 305, against P. Richardson (Israel in the Apostolic Church (SNTSMS 10, Cambridge, 1969) 127) who suggests that v. 29 is part of the antithetical structure in v. 28. He divides it accordingly, and takes God's χαρίσματα to correspond to v. 28a and his κλῆσις to 28b. Cf. further above, 27 n. 46.

[62] See the comment by Käsemann in n. 51.

[63] He does the same at other important points, see e.g. 1:16, 18; 3:19-20, 22-23; 10:11-13.

contextual study. The texts were selected to allow concentration upon Paul's use of God-language in a specific situation—his discussions with Christian and non-Christian Jews. Thus, these texts represent only one sector of Paul's application of God-language in Romans. However, this area is the one most important for a study of his concept of God. Here he stands within (as well as over against) Jewish belief in God. This raises above all the question of the relation between Paul's understanding of God and a Jewish understanding of God.

We have already pointed out that by using traditional expressions of God Paul chose a common starting point, a basis for mutual communication. However, Paul did not employ these common statements to emphasize the consent between himself and his opponents—on the contrary, he used them to support his own position in a situation of disagreement. Thus there was a discrepancy between a common basis in a set of ideas and values, and a strong disagreement at the same time. This situation is typical of conflicts within a group or between related groups where all lines of communication have not yet been broken off.[64] In Romans, Paul makes strong efforts to continue this communication, but it frequently takes on a polemical form. That is also the case when he not only knows, but even partly shares, the views that he is protesting against.

Paul most drastically turns a common basis against his opponents when he closes a discussion with a reference to the judgment of God, as, e.g., in 2:6, 11; 3:6, 8; 11:21. In these texts this quite literally is the final word. That God is judge, that he shall judge all men, etc., was common knowledge—but Paul brings it in here not as theoretical knowledge, but as a *reality* from which his opponents cannot escape. Thus a general statement about God was applied to a *situation* where it took on a new reality. Paul blamed the Jews for wanting to pass God's judgment onto others, 1:32; 2:2, and he put it back where it belonged—among themselves. The Jews had turned a "correct" belief in God as the judge of the world into a false statement about God when they (or the Gentile Christians in chapter 11) regarded themselves as exempt from his judgment.

When he uses traditional phrases about God as a final word, sometimes as an additional clause, Paul is concerned that God can

---

[64] J. Gager, *Kingdom*, 80-88.

be spoken of only in his relationship to man. This is more clearly
spelled out in contexts where statements about God are not added
at the end, but are integrated in the structure of the argument. It
still has the function of a *final* word in support of Paul's cause,
and it is directly related to this argument. Thus "traditional
statements" about God are brought into contemporary discussion.
There are two main ways in which Paul does this. One is through
final clauses when an expression about God is used to guarantee a
result, to bring about a change, or for some other purpose. One
example of this is the predication "God who raises the dead etc."
in 4:17. It provides support for Paul's claim that Jews and non-
Jewish Christians alike are the children of Abraham—and thus this
ascription was drawn into the polemics of the day. A predication
of God can also be combined with a clause in the future tense. Like
the final clause, this indicates a result or an aim in the future, cf.,
e.g., 3:30; 4:21, 24; 11:32. When Paul employs a final clause or
the future tense in this way, it conveys his vision for the Christian
community (and for the Jews). God is the God of the future and
of a community that is in the process of change, that is built up
through conflicts.

No sharp distinctions can be made between passages where a
concept of God concludes an argument and texts where it sums up
the whole point that Paul is making. The latter is especially true in
instances where the predication of God in its form draws upon the
vocabulary in that particular passage. Frequently a text starts
with a question about the relationship between God and Israel (the
believers). In the following Paul often speaks of God in *antitheses*,
e.g. in 3:4; 4:5; 9:12, 16; 11:6, 28. Such antitheses are used to
clarify Paul's own view of this relationship over against competing
views. In most cases, the antithesis is one between God and man.
However, this was not unique for Paul, his opponents among the
Jews would agree that "God" stands over against "man" and see
this as a fundamental distinction in their theology.[65] But when Paul
put "works", "privileges" etc. on the side of "man", as something
that is opposed to God, the antithesis became controversial to
Jews. In consequence, traditional expressions of belief in God took
on a new meaning when they were no longer alone or when they
were found within a controversial antithesis. The formulae them-

---

[65] See below, 144, 167-68.

selves had not changed, but they stood in a different context. Thus they expressed another relationship between God and man than in their former use.

It is impossible to extract a "doctrine" from the statements that Paul makes about God, isolated from their context—that would give a distorted picture of his teaching. But a presentation of Paul's understanding of God has to take into consideration the fact that he uses traditional forms.[66] However, it is an *interpreted* tradition that we find in Paul, and characteristically for Paul this interpretation takes the form of an antithesis. When Paul introduced statements about God into the discussion this represented a continuing interpretation of traditional belief in God. In our next chapter, we will suggest that this was a conscious effort on the part of Paul, that he was aware that "God" was under discussion.[67]

---

[66] Wire, "Pauline Theology", 10-11. However, she finds that the implicit theology, provided by the context, most of the time contradicts and negates the explicit theology of the traditional statements about God; cf. 260-77; see further our criticism, below, 286-87.

[67] Against Wire, "Pauline Theology", 11.

CHAPTER THREE

"THE NAME OF GOD IS BLASPHEMED AMONG THE GENTILES BECAUSE OF YOU"

Blasphemy-charges and the function of theology in conflicts [1]

Within the larger group of texts that we have discussed we will select some to focus more directly upon Paul's understanding of God versus his non-Christian Jewish opponents. In several passages Paul met with an objection or himself spoke of a possible misunderstanding that could arise. This was the case particularly in 3:3-8; 9:6, 14 and 11:1. The questions (in 9:6 the negation) in these texts have one common theme: whether the acts and words of God towards Israel are still valid.

The following list reveals a similar structure in these questions:

	A	B	C
3:3	τί γὰρ εἰ ἠπίστησάν τινες;	μὴ ἡ ἀπιστία αὐτῶν	τὴν πίστιν τοῦ θεοῦ καταργήσει;
9:6		οὐχ οἷον δὲ ὅτι ἐκπέπτωκεν	ὁ λόγος τοῦ θεοῦ.
9:14		μὴ ἀδικία	παρὰ τῷ θεῷ;
11:1		μὴ ἀπώσατο ὁ θεὸς	τὸν λαὸν αὐτοῦ;

God is characterized (either explicitly or implicitly) by a "quality" that is ascribed to him, or rather through a relationship between him and Israel (C). In every instance the question is the same, i.e., whether God has broken and nullified this relationship (B). Only 3:3 explicitly gives the reason why this question must arise (A). However, in 9:6, 14 and 11:1 the immediate context supplies the

---

[1] "Blasphemy" is here not used in the strict technical sense which developed in Rabbinic law. Under this law disciplinary actions were inflicted only in rare cases when somebody, despite warnings, had deliberately pronounced the name of God. This narrow interpretation of blasphemy did not exist at the time of Jesus and it is not presupposed in the NT use of the term. Under "blasphemy" we shall therefore include instances in which "the word", "the name", or "the law" etc. of God was slandered; this was regarded a violation of God himself, and of his power and glory. Cf. H. W. Beyer, "βλασφημία", *TWNT* 1 (1933) 620-24; and E. Lövestam, *Spiritus Blasphemia, Eine Studie zu Mk 3, 28f par Mt 12, 31f Lk 12, 10* (Scripta minora. K. humanistiska vetenskapssamfundet i Lund, 1966-67/1, Lund 1968) espec. 7-57.

answer. In 3:3 Paul gives the reason in very general terms as the unfaithfulness of the Jews towards God. From the other texts it becomes clear that this "unfaithfulness" was specifically related to their rejection of Jesus as the Messiah of the Christians, 9:1; 10:16, 21.

Paul's intentions in the different passages vary; 3:1-8 stand within a section dealing with God's judgment upon Jews and non-Jews, whereas the questions in chapters 9-11 introduce Paul's defence of a continued salvation for the Jews. In these chapters in particular, the questions voice a concern from within the Jewish community. The problem here is that according to the preaching of Paul, God acted outside the law. To a Jew this was unheard of and this led to the questions in 9:6 and 11:1: "But it is not as though the words of God have failed", and, "I ask, then, has God rejected his people?" Paul's rhetorical questions here are probably based on real objections. Luke is another witness to this when he deems it necessary to defend Paul against similar accusations. In Acts 21:28 he refers to the charges that the Hellenistic Jews brought against Paul: "This is the man who is teaching men everywhere against the people and the law and this place . . ." [2]

The objections in Romans 9 and 11 refer to traditional views on God, in most cases with a strong scriptural basis. To a Jew, the negation in 9:6: οὐχ οἷον δὲ ὅτι ἐκπέπτωκεν ὁ λόγος τοῦ θεοῦ, would bring to mind texts from scripture.[3] A close parallel is the latter part of Num 23:19: λαλήσει, καὶ οὐχὶ ἐμμενεῖ (cf. Rom 9:11, ἵνα ἡ κατ᾽ ἐκλογὴν πρόθεσις τοῦ θεοῦ μένῃ). μένω is the opposite of πίπτω and the words could be used antithetically.[4] The negation in 9:6 also resembles the first part of Num 23:19: οὐχ ὡς ἄνθρωπος ὁ θεὸς διαρτηθῆναι. Thus the objection in 9:6 would be closely associated with the discussion of anthropomorphisms in Judaism.[5] Within all

---

[2] J. Jervell, Luke and the People of God (Minneapolis, 1972) 163-74.
[3] E.g. Isa LXX 31:2 ὁ λόγος αὐτοῦ οὐ μὴ ἀθετηθῇ.
[4] Cf. Isa LXX 40:7 ἐξηράνθη ὁ χόρτος, καὶ τὸ ἄνθος ἐξέπεσεν, τὸ δὲ ῥῆμα τοῦ θεοῦ ἡμῶν μένει εἰς τὸν αἰῶνα. Similarly Ps LXX 101:12-13; cf. Jos 21:45; 23:14. See K. Berger, "Abraham in den paulinischen Hauptbriefen", Münchener Theologische Zeitschrift 17 (1966) 79-80; and D. Zeller, Juden und Heiden in der Mission des Paulus (Forschung zur Bibel 8, Stuttgart, 1973) 114 n. 131.
[5] Marmorstein, Rabbinic Doctrine 2, Essays in Anthropomorphism; C. T. Fritsch, The Anti-Anthropomorphisms of the Greek Pentateuch (Philadelphia, 1943); U. W. Mauser, Gottesbild und Menschwerdung (BHT 43, Tübingen, 1971) 23-28.

groups of Judaism it was discussed whether one could properly ascribe anthropomorphisms to God. This question is singularly absent from the New Testament. In line with Old Testament usage, the authors without hesitation employ images, parables, etc., from everyday human life to describe God and his acts. However, in the texts here under discussion Paul faces the same problem that lies at the heart of the controversy over anthropomorphisms—viz., that God must be described in such a way that it becomes clear that he is *God and not man*. Within this discussion, Num 23:19 is frequently referred to in Rabbinical sources as well as in Philo.[6] In Philo's treatises the thesis that "God is not man" takes on the character of a *hermeneutical principle*.[7] He uses it to distinguish between true and false teaching on a wide variety of questions. His terminology is that of Greek philosophy, speaking of the essence of God. The theme that he continuously emphasizes, however, is central to the Old Testament and to all branches of Judaism—God is trustworthy, he does not draw back, not even when man (i.e. Israel) is unfaithful and fails. In the light of this discussion the nature of the accusations against Paul from Jewish quarters becomes clear. If God, whom Paul proclaimed, was no longer true to his law and to his words to Israel, then God was no better than man—how could he be trusted any more? In other words—Paul's teaching was blasphemous!

In 3:3-8 Paul is met with the objection that his preaching and missionary practice have rendered God unpredictable. Paul's opponents argue that when God's law of justice and retribution is no longer accepted (8) the result is that God becomes an unpredictable and unjust judge. *V.* 5: ". . . what shall we say? That God is unjust to inflict wrath upon us?", and again *v.* 7: "But if through my falsehood God's truthfulness abounds to his glory, why am I still being condemned as a sinner?" This was the consequence some, here presumably Jews, would draw from Paul's gospel of justification by faith: the law was abolished. Also, libertinist groups could use this inference as an argument for their own practice.[8] However, in Romans 3 it is more likely that Paul's

---

[6] For the Rabbinic discussion, see below, 167-69.

[7] See below, 144.

[8] Paul's message could be distorted by only a small change in his vocabulary, cf. the objection in 3:7 with the distinctively Pauline phrase in 5:20. Paul's statement in 5:20-21 is followed in 6:1 by an objection similar to that in 3:5-8. However, his opponents in 6:1 and 15 are probably libertinists;

opponents argue from a legalistic point of view. This is obvious in 3:31, here the accusation is directly made against Paul that his Gospel overturns the law.

These four questions in 3:3; 9:6, 14 and 11:1 indicate a problem that lies under Paul's discussion in large parts of Romans, viz., that the Jewish faith in God was threatened. This was not a question of "doctrine"; rather, the objections focused on God in his specific relationship to Israel, his people. It was in this context that the Jews expressed their faith in God and in the trustworthiness of his words and promises—and it was this trust in a special relationship that was threatened through Paul's preaching.

Faced with the accusation that his teaching endangered the Jewish belief in God, Paul denied the charges against him. His answers are introduced by an emphatic μὴ γένοιτο, signalling that he stoutly defends the traditional belief in God.[9] In each case μὴ γένοιτο is followed by a more thorough explanation, in support of Paul's claim to be in accord with traditional faith.[10] This explanation frequently takes the form of a scriptural quotation or example from the Bible. Regularly, a predication of God concludes Paul's defence—most often, a reference to a traditional belief (as in 3:4; 9:12, 16 and 11:5). On the surface, Paul answers accusations from traditional quarters by recourse to more orthodoxy! However, as we have already pointed out and as Wire has most convincingly shown, his use of antitheses in these answers completely changes the implications of these traditional statements about God.[11] Nevertheless, when Paul argues the way he does, he claims his right to these expressions of Israel's faith in God. This is the God whom he preaches, and it was Paul's use of scripture that conveyed the right interpretation of God's acts towards Israel. As a result, he does not leave it to the non-Christian Jews to express their belief in traditional formulae—he appropriates them for himself and for the Christian kerygma.

Logically enough, Paul then turns the accusations around and contests the traditional interpretation of faith in God. His opponents

---

Käsemann, *Römer*, 157; while in 3:5-8 they were Jews, possibly Christian Jews.

[9] Cf. Wire's analysis of the μὴ γένοιτο-argument in "Pauline Theology", 151-77.

[10] 3:4 (Pss 116:11 and 51:6); 9:7 (Gen 21:12); 9:15 (Exod 33:19); 11:2-4 (1 Kings 19:10-18). See further the discussion of 3:31 below, 224-26.

[11] "Pauline Theology", esp. 194-222.

regarded his preaching of God as *blasphemous*. In return Paul characterizes their distorted rendering of his preaching as blasphemous. This he brings out in 3:8: καὶ μὴ καθὼς βλασφημούμεθα. When Paul is slandered, this slander is directed against his preaching at its central point: the significance of justification by faith. Consequently, their slander is actually directed against God! [12] By misrepresenting Paul's message, his opponents give a false idea of God's salvation. Therefore they are given the sentence of blasphemers: ὧν τὸ κρίμα ἔνδικόν ἐστιν 3:8.

If Paul in 3:8 delivered a veiled charge that his opponents among the Jews blasphemed against God, this is directly and unmistakenly expressed in 2:23-24:

> You who boast in the law, do you dishonour God by breaking the law? For, as it is written, "The name of God is blasphemed among the Gentiles because of you" (Isa 52:5).

In this passage, Paul interprets Isa 52:5 and turns it against the Jews, contrary to the intention of the original text.[13] Originally the prophetic text was directed against Israel's enemies. Their transgressions towards Israel and its subsequent suffering had the result that God was slandered among the "Gentiles", since he was unable to defend his people. Now Paul drastically turns this around and charges the Jews that *they* are the ones who dishonour God and blaspheme him by not doing his will.[14]

This motif recurs frequently in early Christian literature.[15] Mostly it is directed against *Christians* as a warning. If their lives

---

[12] See Michel, *Römer* 97. So also in Matt 5:11, although the word βλασφημέω is not used; Beyer, "βλασφημία", 622 n. 13.

[13] The text in Isa 52:5b: "Their rulers wail, says the Lord, and continually all the day my name is despised", is corrupt. C. Westermann (*Das Buch Jesaja. Kapitel* 40-66 (Das Alte Testament Deutsch 19, Göttingen, 1966) 201) suggests that "their rulers" refers to Israel's *oppressors* and not to their legitimate rulers. The LXX attempts to solve the problem by means of additions to the TM: (δι' ὑμᾶς διὰ παντὸς τὸ ὄνομά μου βλασφημεῖται (ἐν τοῖς ἔθνεσιν). Perhaps the δι' ὑμᾶς (although it in the LXX undoubtedly meant "because of your misfortunes") made it easier for Paul to turn the accusation against the Jews instead of their oppressors; Cranfield, *Romans*, 171. Käsemann (*Römer*, 67) suggests that Isa 52:5 was used in this way in Christian polemics even before Paul.

[14] B. Lindars, *New Testament Apologetic* (2nd impression, London, 1973) 22.

[15] To the following see W. C. van Unnik, "Die Rücksicht auf die Reaktion der Nicht-Christen als Motiv in der altchristlichen Paränese", *Judentum, Urchristentum, Kirche. Festschrift für J. Jeremias* (ed. W. Eltester, BZNW 26, Berlin, 1960) 221-34.

do not reflect the will of God, they will become a stumbling-block to non-Christians and cause them to blaspheme God.[16] Likewise, this admonition is found within the Jewish community. In Rabbinic literature it is often backed by a quotation from Ez 36:20: "But when they came to the nations, wherever they came, they profaned my holy name".[17] In the second century, the Christian apologists turned Isa 52:5 against the Jews and applied it as a prophecy referring to the conflict between Jews and Christians.[18] This second-century usage reflects the split between Jews and Christians. Paul still stands within the Jewish community and balances his judgment with the prophecy of salvation for Israel.[19] In Rom 2:23-4 he polemicizes a common theme and with a surprise effect uses it in an unexpected setting. The passage is extremely polemical against Paul's fellow Jews. He charges that they do not honour God, just as the non-Jews of chapter 1 (1:23), and that the Jews are worse off, since they ought to know better! They boast of their knowledge of the law, 2:23a, but at the same time they break the law, 23b! Thereby they contradict the very basis of their life and have come in an untenable position vis-a-vis God.[20] Although they may outwardly observe the law, they have transgressed its deeper intention. Paul therefore confronts them with God himself and his demands. The charge of blasphemy amounts to an accusation that they with their lives have brought false testimony against God. In the following verses, 2:25-29, Paul confronts the Jews with the results of their lives in various areas, particularly in relation to circumcision. The polemical, but at the same time positive, intention behind

---

[16] The best example is 2 Clem 13:3; see van Unnik, "Rücksicht", 221-24; and K. P. Donfried, *The Setting of Second Clement in Early Christianity* (NovTSup 38, Leiden, 1974) 53. Further examples include Ign. *Trall.* 8:2; Pol. *Phil.* 10:3-4; *Const. App.* III 5, 6; 1 *Clem.* 47:6. The motif, if not the actual warning against blasphemy, goes back to the first century; cf. 1 Thess 4:10-12; Col 4:5; also 1 Cor 10:32-33. In 2 Pet 2:1-2, Isa 52:5 is referred to in a denunciation of false teachers in the congregation. False teachers are actually called "blasphemers" in 2 Tim 3:2; Herm. *Sim.* IX 18:3; 19:1, 3.

[17] *Mek.* to Ex 15:2; b. *Yoma* 86a; cf. also CD 12:6-7; T. *Naph.* 8:6; van Unnik, "Rücksicht", 233. See further b. *Taʿan.* 23a; see G. Forkman, *The Limits of the Religious Community* (ConBNT 5, Lund, 1972) 106-8.

[18] Justin Martyr, *Dial.* 17; Tertullian, *Marc.* 2:23; 4:14; Cyprian, *Ep.* 13:3; cf. van Unnik, "Rücksicht", 224-25.

[19] P. Schmidt, "Die 'Ungläubigen' in der Bibel. Überlegungen und Beobachtungen zur soziologischen Funktion religiöser Begriffe", *Klio* 43-45 (1965) 424.

[20] See O. Michel, "Polemik und Scheidung", *Basileia, W. Freytag zum 60. Geburtstag* (ed. J. Hermelink und H. J. Margull, Stuttgart, 1959) 193.

Paul's argument is brought out by his introduction of the true Jew, *v.* 28f.[21] It is all summed up in *v.* 29 where this true Jew is described as circumcised in his heart ἐν πνεύματι οὐ γράμματι. Finally, a further definition is added in *v.* 29c: "His praise is not from man but from God".[22] In this passage, 2:17-29, Paul stresses the immediate connection between *God* and *the law* as God's command. This was common to Paul and his Jewish antagonists—but they would vary in the understanding of the law. Thus, Paul's complaint that the Jews did not keep the law implied that their total relationship to God and their understanding of him was endangered.

Not only in misrepresenting Paul's teaching of God's righteousness, 3:8, but even long before that, Israel was guilty of blasphemy against God. This is seen clearly in Paul's interpretation of the history of Israel when he launches the same accusation against them in 10:21, a passage that leads up to the question in 11:1. Here he cites another text from Isaiah, this time 65:2: "But of Israel he says, 'All day long have I held out my hands to a disobedient and contrary people' ".

What caused these mutual accusations of slander and of blasphemy against God? From the Christian side, it can in part be explained as a reaction to harassment and even persecution by the Jews.[23] Paul himself gives an example of this in 1 Thess 2:14-16:

> For you, brethren, became imitators of the churches of God in Christ Jesus which are in Judea; for you suffered the same things from your own countrymen as they did from the Jews, who killed both the Lord Jesus and the prophets, and drove us out, and displease God and oppose all men by hindering us from speaking to the Gentiles that they may be saved—so as always to fill up the measure of their sins. But God's wrath has come upon them at last!

---

[21] See the careful discussion by Richardson (*Israel*, 137-38) showing the fluctuation between traditional and new language in Paul's argument. This observation makes it possible for him to move beyond the stalled discussion of what group(s) Paul had in mind here.

[22] This antithesis sums up Paul's argument in 2:17-29; see Schneider, *Antithesis*, 79-83.

[23] See D. R. A. Hare, *The Theme of Jewish Persecution of Christians in the Gospel according to St. Matthew* (SNTSMS 6, Cambridge, 1967) 19-79; further J. D. M. Derrett, "Cursing Jesus (1 Cor XII:3): The Jews as Religious 'Persecutors' ", *NTS* 21 (1974-75) 544-54.

This statement is polemical in the extreme.[24] Paul blames the death of Jesus and the suffering of the Christians upon the Jews. The main charge against them, however, that brings judgment upon them, is that they attempt to stop the Christian mission to the non-Jews. Thereby they prevent the promise of God from being fulfilled! [25] Compared to this. Paul's polemics in Romans are quite subdued. However, the fear of persecution from the Jews is present here as well, this time with regard to Paul's own life, 15:31. Moreover, Paul is primarily concerned that the opposition from "the unbelievers" may make his journey to Rome and subsequent mission to Spain impossible to undertake. Again, it is their opposition to Paul's eschatological mission that is the ultimate sin of the Jews.

It is this *mission*, which started with *Jesus*, that is at the centre of the controversy between Paul and his opponents in Romans. This becomes apparent from Paul's own account. In 3:1-8 he defends God's faithfulness to his words even if he now—in Christ—acts outside of Israel and of the law. It is this "apart from the law" that causes the charge that Paul slanders God through his preaching. From Paul's proclamation of God's justice now revealed in Christ through faith (1:16f) his opponents drew the inference that this destroyed the law! Thus Paul presents the charges against him and his gospel as a direct result of his preaching of God's righteousness in Christ. The other side of God's salvation in Christ, Paul describes as the revelation of God's wrath over the world, Jews and non-Jews alike (1:18ff).[26] It is within this context that Paul alleges that the Jews blaspheme God through their lives. Although the context itself is not defined through Christological language, the *event* that brought about these charges is the same "Christ-event" to which the Jews reacted with their blasphemy charges. Like the Jews, Paul, in his accusations, focuses upon *the law*, claiming that the Jews distort their relationship with God by failing to keep the law. The

---

[24] See O. Michel, "Fragen zu 1 Thessalonicher 2, 14-16; Antijüdische Polemik bei Paulus", *Antijudaismus im Neuen Testament?* (ed. W. Eckert, N. P. Levinson and M. Stöhr, Abhandlungen zum christlich-jüdischen Dialog 2, Munich, 1967) 50-59.

[25] See the connection between persecution and charges of blasphemy in the description of Paul in 1 Tim 1:13; τὸ πρότερον ὄντα βλάσφημον καὶ διώκτην καὶ ὑβριστήν. 1 Tim 1:13 elaborates on Paul's own statements in 1 Cor 15:9; Gal 1:13; Phil 3:6 as well as on the description in Acts 9:4-5; 22:4-5; 26:9-11.

[26] G. Bornkamm, "Die Offenbarung des Zornes Gottes", *Das Ende des Gesetzes* (Gesammelte Aufsätze, BEvT 16, 5th edition, Munich, 1966) 1-33.

short exchanges in 2:23f and 3:5-8 confirm the impressions we get from the other texts under discussion. The controversy between Paul and his opponents arose on the commonly-accepted basis for Jews and non-Jewish Christians: the faith in one God, his election of Israel and his giving of the law. However, *both groups* claimed the right to this faith—to the exclusion of the other group: theirs was the law, they were the true Israel, they had the right understanding of God.

This is not to say that the generally-held view that Jews and Christians believed in the same God is wrong. It correctly represents the understanding both of Jews and of Christians in the first century. The common faith in God was taken for granted; only in the second century did Christian apologists find it necessary to state this explicitly.[27] But this faith in God did not remain unchanged. The controversy between non-Christian Jews and the Christians was not merely a conflict over faith in Jesus or over different attitudes to religious laws and rituals, Scripture, etc. These questions cannot be isolated and treated separately. The New Testament authors always discuss them *in their relation to God*—as the law of God or the word of God. But if the Jewish belief in God actually underwent a change—how can this change be measured? Was it a deviation from specific norms? This leads us to the question of "orthodoxy" and "heresy" in Judaism and early Christianity.[28] The inherent methodological problems in the discussion of this issue have become manifest in the recent exchanges between

---

[27] E.g. Justin Martyr, *Dial.* 11:1. In the second century the Christians had to defend their faith in God against attacks from the Gnostics and from Marcion, who contested that the Christian God was identical with the God of Israel, the Creator; cf. R. A. Morris, *God and World in Early Christian Theology*; and A. von Harnack, *Marcion. Das Evangelium von fremden Gott* (Leipzig, 1921) 147-60.

[28] The discussion on this issue was revived with the new edition of W. Bauer, *Rechtgläubigkeit und Ketzerei* (ed. with suppl. by G. Strecker, BHT 1, 2nd edition, Tübingen, 1964) and its English translation, *Orthodoxy and Heresy in Earliest Christianity* (ed. R. A. Kraft and G. Krodel, Philadelphia, 1971). Among recent contributions to this discussion of interest for the NT period are H. Köster, "Häretiker im Urchristentum als theologisches Problem", *Zeit und Geschichte*, 65-83; H. D. Betz, "Orthodoxy and Heresy in Primitive Christianity", *Interpretation* 19 (1965) 299-311; R. Kraft, "The development of the Concept of 'Orthodoxy' in Early Christianity", *Current Issues in Biblical and Patristic Interpretation, Studies in Honor of M. C. Tenney* (ed. G. F. Hawthorne, Grand Rapids, Mich., 1975) 47-59; I. Howard Marshall, "Orthodoxy and Heresy in Earlier Christianity", *Themelios* 2 (1976) 5-14. See also n. 29.

N. J. McEleney and D. Aune.[29] McEleney contested the commonly held view that Judaism represented an "orthopraxy" and *not* an "orthodoxy". However, his arguments are linked to a defence of the authority of the "orthodox" teaching of the Church in the New Testament.[30] Thus the role of theology in a religious community is overemphasized. McEleney presupposes the primary importance and influence of doctrine, without questioning this conception on the basis of historical evidence.[31]

In his criticism, D. Aune argues that the "belief system was definitely subordinate both in a functional and structural way to Jewish traditions of ritual practice and ethical behaviour".[32] However, this approach, too, is one-sided—as it tends to disregard the dialetic of ideology and practice. There are two issues involved here. First, there is the historical question: What were the reasons for conflicts within or between related groups, and for the subsequent split between Judaism and the Christian church? The reasons, to a large degree, can be described historically in social and political terms. In *Kingdom and community*, John Gager has successfully applied sociological patterns to the question of "orthodoxy" and "heresy".[33] He raises the question of the function of social conflicts and points out that conflicts have a group-binding function, in that the self-definition of a group is developed in the process of opposing another group. This is especially true of conflicts between groups with close ties (e.g. the early Christian communities as an off-shoot of Judaism). This closeness, combined with a strong desire to establish a separate identity intensifies the conflict.

---

[29] N. J. McEleney, "Orthodoxy and Heterodoxy in the New Testament", *Proceedings of the Catholic Theological Society of America* 25 (1971) 54-77; "Orthodoxy in Judaism of the First Century Christian Century", *JSJ* 4 (1973) 18-42; D. E. Aune, "Orthodoxy in First Century Judaism? A Response to N. J. McEleney", *JSJ* 7 (1976) 1-10.

[30] "Orthodoxy and Heterodoxy", 42.

[31] Cf. "Orthodoxy and Heterodoxy", 20: "The present separation of Judaism and Christianity is explicable historically *only* if one recognizes that there existed a firmly accepted Jewish orthodoxy in the first century and that this was even then a *definable* belief (actually expressed in part in the šemaʿ) which was accepted by all who called themselves Israelites" (McEleney's italics). McEleney does not here distinguish between actual historical reasons for the separation and their subsequent explanation in theological terms. It is the latter that we find in the NT.

[32] Aune, "Orthodoxy in First Century Judaism?", 10.

[33] 76-88.

Polemics and controversy do not give a correct description of the "real" situation but tend to distort it. This is true both of Paul's denunciation of the Jewish attitude to the law and of the hostility of the Jewish leaders towards Jesus as it is described in the Gospels.[34] Gager comments upon this:

> This is not to say that such enemies are created ex nihilo, but that the exaggeration of hostility, whether conscious or not, serves both to sharpen the group's identity and to strengthen its internal cohesion. At the very least, we may be certain that ideological struggles between kindred communities ought never to be taken at face value and that such struggles play a role in the formation of ideological and institutional structures of which the participants themselves are but faintly aware.[35]

This leads us to the second question, that of the interpretation of these socio-religious conflicts. As a result of their just protest against a dogmatic approach to an historical question, Aune and Gager almost dismiss this second question. But it should not be disregarded; rather, it must be understood as an historical question in its own right! New Testament polemics are an interpretation of historical events—in most cases, a theological interpretation. Different practices and traditions were considered to be prescribed by God, and he was the ultimate authority behind them. It was God who revealed himself in the various ordinances of the law and in the interpretation. According to the Gospels, both sides in the controversies between Jesus and the Pharisees claimed God as the authority behind their position.[36] From here there was only one step to the next stage, where this conflict over individual aspects of the law was actually expressed as a conflict over the understanding of God.[37]

Admittedly, this theological interpretation was a subsequent development, frequently serving as an explanation or justification of an already-established practice. However, in its turn this

---

[34] Michel, "Polemik", 193-94 n. 5.

[35] *Kingdom*, 88.

[36] See below, 69-71.

[37] See M. W. Shaw, *Studies in Revelation and the Bible* (Indianapolis, Ind. 1971) 77; "Once the first step toward differentiation has been taken in any movement, there usually follows a period of open conflict with the un-differentiated parent body which leads to mutual accusation, mutual excommunication, and finally to theological justification".

interpretation became an influential factor in shaping the social behaviour of early Christian communities. Thus there was a dialectic between practice and theology. The remarks by Wayne A. Meeks on the Johannine community are especially illuminating in this regard:

> I do not mean to say that the symbolic universe suggested by the Johannine literature is *only* the reflex or projection of the group's social situation. On the contrary, the Johannine dialogues suggest quite clearly that the order of development must have been dialectical: the christological claims of the Johannine Christians resulted in their becoming alienated, and finally expelled, from the synagogue; that alienation in turn is "explained" by a further development of the christological motifs (i.e. the fate of the community projected onto the story of Jesus); these developed christological motifs in turn drive the group into further isolation. It is a case of continual, harmonic reinforcement between social experience and ideology.[38]

It is particularly in the interpretation of scripture that this interdependence between theology and praxis becomes visible.[39] The sacred texts were regarded as speaking with authority to situations. At the same time, however, it was, to a large degree, the needs of the situation or an already established practice that governed the choice of a particular text as well as its interpretation. The various groups of Jews and Christians in the first century all accepted the scriptures as a means of revelation of God. Moreover, they expressed their own identity in their relation to God through this interpretation. It was not a static situation; rather, it was a continuous process whereby different groups adapted the texts to meet their specific needs. Moreover, as the claim to possess the true interpretation was exclusive and held against other groups, there was an extensive use of polemics.

This process of interpretation combined with controversy is aptly described by Dieter Georgi in his article "Der Kampf um die reine Lehre im Urchristentum als Auseinandersetzung um das rechte

---

[38] "The Man from Heaven in Johannine Sectarianism", *JBL* 91 (1972) 71.
[39] E.g. in the Qumran community. See N. A. Dahl, "Eschatologie und Geschichte im Lichte der Qumrantexte", *Zeit und Geschichte*, 3-18. Dahl is here concerned with "die Korrelation der soziologischen Struktur und Geschichte der Gemeinden mit ihrer eschatologischen Schriftauslegung und Messiaslehre", 12.

Verständnis der an Israel ergangenen Offenbarung Gottes".[40] He points out how the discussion between various Jewish groups in the pre-Christian period had formed hermeneutical models for interpretation which were later taken over by the Christians. The Qumran community is a typical example. They claimed to represent the true Jewish tradition. Their great interest in the interpretation of Scripture played an important part in this. They asserted that the scriptures were fulfilled in the sect, that *they* were the generation about whom scripture spoke.[41] As a logical consequence, they turned the words of judgment contained in the scriptures against their adversaries, particularly the priests in Jerusalem.[42]

It is within this tradition that we find the documents of the New Testament, and among them the letters of Paul. The New Testament is therefore in parts a highly polemical book. Otto Michel comments upon this in an interesting article, "Polemik und Scheidung": "Das Neue Testament ist weithin ein judenchristliches Buch, und doch trifft die neutestamentliche Polemik das Judentum zuallererst". The controversy was so bitter mainly because Jews and Christians shared the same belief in God, that he had chosen Israel his people and given them the Torah and also the eschatological wisdom. Michel points out that this conflict was not over partial issues only. Rather it concerned faith and existence in their totality:

> Der Kampf zwischen Christentum und Judentum geht lediglich um die Sendung Jesu und die Auslegung des Alten Testamentes, um den Anspruch der Gemeinde, das wahre Israel zu sein und um den neuen Weg zu den Heiden. Das ist aber kein Teilgebiet, sondern ein neues Wahrheitsverständis in Bezug auf das Ganze.[43]

These various elements were all linked together. They expressed the self-identity and the ethos of the community, that which gave it its distinctiveness and its norms. All Christian groups—though to a varying degree—found themselves in conflict with their surrounding Jewish milieu. By necessity they expressed this conflict in *theological terms*. They interpreted threats to the identity and existence of the community theologically. To break the law meant to dishonour God, to slander his people was an offence against him.

---

[40] *Antijudaismus im Neuen Testament?* 82-94.
[41] H. Braun, *Qumran und das Neue Testament* 2 (Tübingen, 1966) 308-9.
[42] IQHab 2:1-10 is a typical example, see Braun, *Qumran*, 320-21.
[43] 185 and 186.

Charges of blasphemy and similar accusations were ways of distancing oneself from a rival group—and at the same time of claiming the right to the issues at stake. This polemic was not only turned outwards, against clearly separate groups. In Romans we found it difficult at times to decide whether Paul spoke to Christian or non-Christian Jews. But we may safely say that Paul's polemics reveal conflicts within religious and social communities that are in the process of breaking apart.

Thus it is too simple to regard polemics as directed against a rival-group only. A consideration of the nature and function of the New Testament literature makes this obvious. It was primarily written for the use of Christian groups—it was not addressed to an hostile environment. Therefore polemics against "the others" had as its primary function to strengthen the group in its struggle for expansion and survival. The recording of successful discussions with rivals was a means of asserting the validity of one's own faith.

EXCURSUS

Polemics in the Gospels and Acts

In this excursus we will briefly point to some similarities between the polemical situation in Romans and that of the Gospels and Acts. In Romans, Paul employs the style of a dialogue and we argued that this was more than a literary device. Rather, it was based on real discussions. A decisive argument in favour of this thesis is the record of controversies between Jesus and his opponents in the Gospels.[44] They reflect the conditions of the Christian communities at the time of their redaction. There were discussions between Christians and (other) members of the synagogue—as well as between different groups within the Christian community. The most important issue was the role of the law (the Torah) in the community. In the synoptic Gospels it is raised as a question of keeping the law—Paul is more drastic in questioning the validity of the law.[45]

---

[44] C. H. Dodd, "The Dialogue Form in the Gospels", *Bulletin of the John Rylands University Library of Manchester* 37/1 (1954) 54-67; E. Lohse, "Jesu Worte über den Sabbat", *Judentum, Urchristentum, Kirche*, 78-89; P. von der Osten-Sacken, "Streitgespräch und Parabel als Formen markanischer Christologie", *Jesus Christus in Historie und Theologie*, 375-94.

[45] R. Bultmann, "Die Bedeutung des geschichtlichen Jesus für die Theologie des Paulus", *Glauben und Verstehen* 1 (2nd edition, Tübingen, 1954) 197: "Es ist klar, dass bei Jesus diese expliziten theologischen Gedankengänge

The closest parallel to Rom 2:17ff and the charges of blasphemy in *v*. 23-24 is found in Mark 7:1-23 par (Matt 15:1-20; Luke 11:37-41) in the discussion about ritual cleanness.[46] As usual, the starting-point is an episode in the life of Jesus and his disciples— this time it is the Pharisees watching the disciples eat without having performed the ritual handwashing. The terminology of the subsequent discussion is very similar to that in Rom 2:23-24. Although the content of the controversy is the same in all three synoptic Gospels, there is considerable variety in the terminology that is used. In Matthew it is a question of "transgressing the law". This is the same terminology as in Rom 2:23. The Pharisees and the scribes ask Jesus why his disciples transgress the traditions of the elders: Διὰ τί οἱ μαθηταί σου παραβαίνουσιν τὴν παράδοσιν τῶν πρεσβυτέρων; 15:2. Jesus counters their objection by asking why they use their traditions to transgress the commandments of God: Διὰ τί καὶ ὑμεῖς παραβαίνετε τὴν ἐντολὴν τοῦ θεοῦ διὰ τὴν παράδοσιν ὑμῶν; 15:3; cf. Rom 2:23: διὰ τῆς παραβάσεως τοῦ νόμου τὸν θεὸν ἀτιμάζεις; This text in Matthew gives a clearer picture of the dialogue than Romans 2:23-24, in that it also presents the objections made by the Jews. Each side charges the other with transgressing the law. The accusation from Jesus is made especially polemical in that "your tradition" is put pointedly over against "the commandment of God".[47] When the Jews claim that the minutiae of the law should be kept, they are acting against the commandment of God. The main thrust of the quotation from Isa 23:19 LXX in 15:7-9 corresponds to Paul's accusation in Romans 2—through their transgressions they contradict the alleged basis of their life:

> This people honours me with their lips, but their heart is far from me: in vain do they worship me, teaching as doctrines the precepts of men.

---

nicht vorliegen. Es erscheint mir aber als ebenso klar, dass sie nur den Gedanken Jesu in bestimmten historischen Antithesen explizieren. *Sie beruhen ja auf dem gleichen Grundmotiv*, das der Polemik Jesus zugrunde liegt; auf der Gegenüberstellung von Recht und eigentlichen Gotteswillen" (Bultmann's italics).

[46] See the discussion of this text by N. J. McEleney, "Authenticating Criteria and Mark 7:1-23", *CBQ* 34 (1972) 431-60.

[47] J. Schneider, "παραβαίνω", *TWNT* 5 (1954) 735. R. Bultmann (*Die Geschichte der synoptischen Tradition* (5th edition, Göttingen, 1961) 15-16) suggests that this passage reflects the situation of early Christian groups in Palestine.

Thus, in the various conflicts over the law, the Jews are eventually confronted with Jesus' preaching of God. This represents not so much a new concept of God, as a proclamation of his immediate presence, breaking all barriers that men had put up against him.[48]

This pattern of discussion, reflecting the controversy between Jews and Christians in the latter half of the first century, is found also in the second century. A text in case is Justin's Dialogue with Trypho. Here, too, there are mutual accusations that the other does not follow the commandments of God. In Dial 10:2-3 and 16:4 Justin makes the accusation that the Jews, after having killed Jesus, continued their disobedience against God.[49] By banning Christians from their synagogues they dishonoured not only them but even God himself! Justin uses words that are typically used for controversies in the New Testament, e.g. ἀτιμάζω and ἀθετέω.[50]

In Mark's version of the discussion over ritual cleanness, 7:1-13, ἀθετέω is one of the terms he uses to accuse the Pharisees and the scribes of setting aside the commandment of God, 7:9. Luke launches the same attack against them in another context as well, when he describes their reaction to the message of John the Baptist: "But the Pharisees and the lawyers rejected (ἠθέτησαν) the purpose of God for themselves, not having been baptized by him", 7:30.

Against this background, we realize that the accusation in Rom 2:23-24 that the Jews cause the name of God to be blasphemed, is a typically Pauline sharpening of an argument from the Christian side in a well-known polemical situation. The term "blasphemy" itself is not used in the synoptic "parallels" to Romans 2. However, strong accusations of not fulfilling the commandments of God and of misusing his words in effect amount to a charge of slander against God.[51] This discussion was not confined to the controversy between Christian groups and the synagogues—on the contrary,

---

[48] Becker, "Gottesbild", 105-26; Kümmel ("Gottesverkündigung", 40-68) argues that there was a conflict "im Gottesverständnis".

[49] καὶ νῦν τοὺς ἐλπίζοντας ἐπ' αὐτὸν καὶ τὸν πέμψαντα αὐτὸν παντοκράτορα καὶ ποιητὴν τῶν ὅλων θεὸν ἀθετεῖτε καί, ὅσον ἐφ' ὑμῖν, ἀτιμάζετε. Dial. 16.4.

[50] ἀτιμάζω: Mark 12:4 par. Luke 20:11; John 8:49; Acts 5:41; Rom2:23; ἀθετέω: Mark 7:9; Luke 7:30; 10:16; John 12:48; Gal 2:21 etc. ἀθετέω in Mark 7:9 is a parallel expression to παραβαίνω in Matt 15:2-3 and ἀφίημι in Mark 7:8; see C. Mauere, "ἀθετέω", TWNT 8 (1969) 159. Cf. also the use of ἀπιστέω etc., mostly directed against the Jews, e.g. Matt 13:58; Mark 6:6, but also as a warning to the disciples, e.g. Mark 9:24; Luke 24:11; see Schmidt, "Die 'Ungläubigen' in der Bibel", 410-34.

[51] Cf. Becker, "Gottesbild", 113-17.

the polemics can be almost as sharp in conflicts between Christians.[52] A case in point is Gal 2:18-21 where Paul concludes the report of his controversy with Peter. The terminology in these verses is similar to that of Romans 2 and Matt 15:1-9 par. In Gal 2:18 Paul says that if he should endeavour to build up again that which he tore down, i.e. the observance of the law, then he would appear as a transgressor (παραβάτης). That is—if he followed the law of Moses, he would transgress the commandments of God! [53] But instead, his life is now "in Christ" and he makes the confession that "I do not nullify the grace of God (οὐκ ἀθετῶ τὴν χάριν τοῦ θεοῦ), for if justification were through the law, then Christ died to no purpose", 2:21. The antithesis between χάρις and νόμος identifies this as a polemical statement against those who would not accept Paul's proclamation of salvation through the grace of God.[54] To Paul, this grace found its full expression in the life, death and resurrection of Christ. Consequently, for Paul, to reject the grace of God, was a theological term for the rejection of his own mission and preaching.

This connection between controversy and mission is also found in Luke's use of ἀθετέω. He makes it explicit in 10:16 in Jesus' speech when sending the seventy disciples. To reject Christian missionaries is to reject Jesus, and that again implies a rejection of God, who sent him: ὁ ἀθετῶν ὑμᾶς ἐμὲ ἀθετεῖ. ὁ δὲ ἐμὲ ἀθετῶν ἀθετεῖ τὸν ἀποστείλαντά με.[55] In Acts the rejection of the Christian mission is combined with charges of blasphemy. The terms βλασφημέω, βλασφημία are not always used, but the acts described by Luke serve to identify the situation: the missionaries shake the dust off their feet, tear their garments, etc., (13:51; 14:14; 16:22; 18:6; 22:22f).[56] These acts express strong reactions of displeasure, and judgment. And the reason is that God has been dishonoured and held in contempt—and thus such strong reactions were necessary. As in the controversy in Mark 7:1-23, the charges of blasphemy in

---

[52] Georgi, "Kampf", 93.

[53] Notice the connection between νόμος and παράβασις in Rom 4:15; 5:14 and Gal 3:19; cf. below, 263-66.

[54] Similarly Maurer, "ἀθετέω", 159. This is more plausible than the suggestion by Schlier, (Galater, 104) that Paul had to defend himself against accusations that he rejected the grace of God.

[55] Luke here comes close to the Johannine terminology of "sending", e.g. John 12:48; 17:18; see Miranda, Der Vater, 20.

[56] For the following, see H. J. Cadbury, "Dust and Garments", The Beginnings of Christianity 1/5 (ed. Kirsopp Lake and H. J. Cadbury, Edinburgh, 1933) 269-77.

Acts are mutual. In some instances it is the reaction of the Jews that is described in this way, at other times that of Christian missionaries.[57] In these confrontations the controversial issue is the mission to the non-Jews, in most cases Paul's preaching to the "God-fearers". In 22:21 the Jews interrupt Paul's speech just as he has said: "And he (i.e. God) said to me, 'Depart; for I will send you far away to the Gentiles'." Their reaction was to tear their garments, throw dust into the air and to demand that he was punished by death: "Away with such a fellow from the earth! For he ought not to live," 22:22. According to Luke, the Jews regarded the proclamation of God to the non-Jews as a rejection of Israel and of the law. It is the same accusation that the Jews bring forth against Stephen in 6:11-13. Stephen allegedly rejected the temple and the law. This accusation is directly linked to the charges that he spoke blasphemy against God and against Moses: 'Ακηκόαμεν αὐτοῦ λαλοῦντος ῥήματα βλάσφημα εἰς Μωϋσῆν καὶ τὸν θεόν.

It is Luke's main purpose in Acts to explain how God made the mission to the uncircumcised possible, without abolishing his special relationship with Israel.[58] It is therefore imperative for Luke to depict Paul and his co-missionaries as law-abiding Jews, and the Christians in general as true Jews. As a result, Luke had to face the problem of how to distance the Christians from the non-believing Jews. It is at this point that he introduces the apostolic and missionary preaching of Jesus as the Messiah. In his speech in Acts 13:16-41 Paul proclaimed that through the resurrection of Jesus the promise to the forefathers was fulfilled. The Jews answered by blaspheming Paul: ἀντέλεγον τοῖς ὑπὸ Παύλου λαλουμένοις βλασφημοῦντες, 13:45. This time it is Paul and Barnabas who react by shaking off the dust of their feet against them. Paul proclaims that he will now instead go to the Gentiles, leaving the Jews to the coming judgment (13:46, 51). Luke describes a similar controversy in 18:5-6, this time in the form of a short summary. The content of Paul's sermon is summarized as "the Christ was Jesus" (18:5). When the Jews opposed and slandered him (18:6a), Paul answers by shaking his garments and proclaiming judgment upon them: "Your blood be upon your heads. I am innocent. From now on I

---

[57] The Jews are described in Acts 22:22-24; Christian missionaries in 13:51; 14:14; 18:6.

[58] Jervell, Luke, 41-75, esp. 68-69. But cf. S. G. Wilson, The Gentiles and the Gentile Mission in Luke-Acts (SNTSMS 23, Cambridge, 1973) 219-33.

will go to the Gentiles" (18:6b). If Mark 7:1-23 par (Matt 15:1-20) shows similarities with Rom 2:23-24, this text in Acts 18 brings to mind Rom 3:6ff. Both in Acts 18 and in Romans 3 Paul's preaching is met by slander and blasphemy, and in a similar manner he proclaims God's judgment upon them. In Rom 3:8 this exchange is a literary form. In Acts 18 (and 13) we are close to the situation out of which it a-rose—the conflict between Christian missionaries and the synagogues.

It has been argued that Luke's description of the acts accompanying charges of blasphemy is only a formal literary device which has no actuality for his readers.[59] However, this is unlikely in view of other descriptions of missionaries and their behaviour (e.g. Mark 6:6b-13 par.; Luke 9:1-6; Matt 10:9-11).[60] Upon arriving in a town, the missionaries should stay with whomever was willing to take them into their house. If nobody would receive them, they were to shake the dust off their feet in judgment against that town and leave it to its fate. It is most probable that these instructions reflect the situation of early Jewish-Christian missions in Palestine.[61]

Time and again, the conflict between Christian missionaries and the non-believing Jews reaches its climax over the claim that the crucified Jesus was the Messiah, the fulfillment of God's promise. This is where the charges of blasphemy arose. In all likelihood there is here a continuity of provocations and accusations stretching back to the historical Jesus. It is not without reason that in the synoptic gospels the charges of blasphemy are the main cause for his being sentenced to death by the Sanhedrin, Mark 14:61-64 par. The Sanhedrin reacted either to Jesus' acceptance of the title "Son of God" or to his statement about the "Son of man" at God's right hand coming with angelic powers. The high priest performed the appropriate act—he tore his garments and charged that: "You have heard this blasphemy. What is your decision?", Mark 14:64a. And the Sanhedrin rendered the verdict that he deserved to die (14:64b).

It is not only in the passion narrative that the gospels depict Jesus as being accused of blasphemy. It had started already at the very beginning of his ministry. The most striking example is the story of Jesus' healing the paralytic and declaring that his sins are

---

[59] Cadbury, "Dust and Garments", 276; and E. Haenchen, *Die Apostelgeschichte*, (MeyerK 3, 15th edition, Göttingen, 1968) 471 n. 4.

[60] See H. Schürmann, *Das Lukasevangelium* I (HTKNT 3, Freiburg, 1969) 498-505, esp. 504-5.

[61] See G. Theissen, "Legitimation und Lebensunterhalt; Ein Beitrag zur Soziologie urchristlicher Missionäre", *NTS* 21 (1974-75) 192-200.

forgiven, Mark 2:1-12 par. (Matt 9:1-8; Luke 5:17-26). The Pharisees reacted with an accusation of blasphemy: "Why does this man speak thus? It is blasphemy! Who can forgive sins but God alone?", Mark 2:7. Thus in the Marcan version the life of Jesus is seen in light of this accusation of blasphemy that finally (cf. 14:64) led to his crucifixion and death.[62] This combination of healing story, controversy and passion in Mark (also in John 5:1-18) most likely reflects a situation where Christian healers had caused controversy and suffered persecution from the Jews.[63]

However, there can be no doubt that the conflicts with the Pharisees belong to the securely-established facts about the life of Jesus.[64] He healed, and included among his followers people who, socially and religiously, belonged to the periphery of Jewish society. These were provocative acts, and so his opponents among the Jews accused him of breaking God's commandments. His followers, however, interpreted these same acts as done by the power of God. Once more we can see how charges and counter-charges met in controversies between Christian and non-Christian Jews. The latter regarded the claim that sins could be forgiven "in the name of Jesus" as blasphemous (Mk 2:7). On the other hand, as they would not accept the Christian message that Jesus acted on behalf of God, they were met with charges of blasphemy against the Holy Spirit (Mk 3:28f). This accusation is similar to that in Stephen's speech in Acts 7:51: "You always resist the Holy Spirit. As your fathers did, so do you." Here the conflict between groups of early Christian enthusiasts and the Jewish establishment becomes visible.[65] And the purpose of the accusations was not only to denounce their opponents—they also served to strengthen the group-identity among the Christians themselves.

At least within some groups the controversy between Jews and Christians became embittered towards the end of the first century. The sharpened attitude from the synagogues probably was one reason;[66] open conflicts with the Roman state were another. This

---

[62] Von der Osten-Sacken, "Streitgespräch", 379.

[63] A. B. Kolenkow, "Healing Controversy as a Tie between Miracle and Passion Material for a Proto-Gospel", *JBL* 95 (1976) 623-38.

[64] For the following, see Von der Osten-Sacken, "Streitgespräch", 391-94.

[65] M. Hengel, "Zwischen Jesus und Paulus", *ZTK* 72 (1975) 193-95; see also Gager, *Kingdom*, 26-27.

[66] See n. 23. However, we should not over-estimate the measures which the synagogues took against Christians; and it is not proved that the intro-

attitude is evident in the Gospel of John.[67] Here the charges of
blasphemy which the Jews brought against Jesus become a recur-
rent theme, 5:18; 10:32-39; 19:7. Moreover, John's own accusations against the Jews are just as hard-hitting, even if he uses a
different terminology from the synoptic gospels. Whereas they
spoke of transgressing particular commandments, John is much
less specific in his charges. This does not mean that he is more
cautious. He uses drastic and categorical expressions. Frequently
they include such words as οἶδα and γινώσκω.[68] The Jews do not
know the one who sent Jesus, for only Jesus does, 7:28; 15:21.
They know neither Jesus nor his father, 8:19; 14:7. As a matter
of fact, they have *never* known God, even if they claim him to be
their father, 8:54. Their claim is false—the devil is their father,
8:44.[69] Thus John in several instances brings the conflict between
Jesus and the Jews back to a conflict over the relationship to *God*.
The rejection of Jesus amounted to nothing less than a rejection of
God! This is polemics in the extreme—John actually denies that
there is a common basis for Christians and non-believing Jews in
faith in God (as Paul presupposes in Romans). Behind this, we can
conjecture a group that has almost cut itself off from the synagogue
—although the imagery and exegesis in this gospel betray a close
relationship with Judaism.[70]

The trend towards isolation from other religious groups and from
the social and political society at large becomes even more apparent
in the Book of Revelation. This book mirrors the situation of
Christian communities in Asia Minor *c.* AD. 90-95.[71] The faithful
community is depicted almost as if in a cosmic battle, with all
religious and political powers of the time lined up against it. It

---

duction of the 'birkat hammīnīm' in the 18 Benedictions was primarily
directed against Christians. See P. Schäfer, "Die sogenannte Synode von
Jabne. Zur Trennung von Juden und Christen in ersten/zweiten Jh. n. Chr.",
Judaica 31 (1975) 54-64, 116-24.

[67] Cf. E. Grässer, "Die antijüdische Polemik im Johannesevangelium",
NTS 11 (1964-65) 74-90.

[68] Cf. J. Gaffney, "Believing and Knowing in the Fourth Gospel", *Theological Studies* 26 (1965) 215-41; and B. E. Gärtner, "The Pauline and
Johannine Idea of 'to know God' against the Hellenistic Background", *NTS*
14 (1967-8) 209-31.

[69] See N. A. Dahl, "Der Erstgeborene Satans und der Vater des Teufels
(Polyk 7 : 1 und Joh 8 : 44)", *Apophoreta*, 70-84; and E. Grässer, "Die Juden
als Teufelssöhne in Joh 8 : 37-47", *Antijudaismus im Neuen Testament*? 157-70.

[70] Meeks, "The Man from Heaven in Johannine Sectarianism".

[71] Kümmel, *Einleitung*, 341-44.

suffers the blasphemy of the false Jews, 2:9. Apart from this text, references to blasphemy are gathered in two passages, 13:1-6 and 16:9-21. Chapter 16 portrays the seven plagues that are brought over the world. However, this judgment of God does not bring men to repent (μετανοέω) or to glorify him (δίδωμι δόξαν); on the contrary, they blaspheme him, 16:9, 11! The most extraordinary use of "blasphemy" is found in 13:1-6.[72] The "beast" that is described here, with a head bearing a blasphemous name and with a mouth uttering blasphemous words, is the Roman state, i.e. its emperor! The beast is described in images from Daniel 7 and 4 Ezra 12. In addition, there are also similarities with the criticism of Antiochus Epiphanes in 1 Macc 1:20-28.[73] Thus the Roman empire is described as a satanic world-power. The blasphemy of the first beast against God in 13:1-10 is followed by the activity of the second beast, leading people astray to worship the first beast. Here the overwhelming reality of persecution and oppression is apparent.[74] In Revelation these events are mythologized. To characterize them as blasphemy against God is a last-ditch defence—as well as a confession of God in the midst of this crisis. The Christians here are in grave danger: their very existence is threatened to the utmost. Only an apocalyptic vision of the world can avert a complete breakdown of faith and identity.[75] Thus this is another example that the primary function of accusations against enemies of a group is to strengthen and to keep the community together. In consequence, polemics and propaganda are closely related—also, in that they respond to the inner needs of a community. It is worth noticing that some of the most harsh polemical statements are found in the context of missionary propaganda, where the ultimate goal is to bring the listeners to repentence and conversion. It is in discussion of the Christian mission to the non-Jewish world that the issue of the identity of the Christian community is most frequently raised. When converts to Christianity were not required to become Jews—i.e. to be circumcised—when they joined a community consisting mainly of Christian Jews, this question of identity became crucial.

---

[72] See J. Massyngberde Ford, *Revelation* (AB 38, New York, 1975) 210-30.
[73] Cf. also the similarities between Rev 13:6 and IQS 4:11 and CD 5:11-12.
[74] Kümmel, *Einleitung*, 334-38.
[75] Gager, *Kingdom*, 49-57. For a similar situation reflected in Jewish apocalyptic groups, see M. Hengel, *Judentum und Hellenismus* (WUNT 10, Tübingen, 1969) 354-57.

CHAPTER FOUR

GOD-LANGUAGE AND THE CHURCH OF JEWS AND NON-JEWS

In our preceding chapter we have seen that Paul used God-language to intensify conflicts with rival groups. In this chapter, we will study how he simultaneously turned this God-language inwards. He applies it to Christian communities in order to interpret their identity. Christian Jews caused the most pressing problem. Being Christians, but Jews as well, they stood in a double position where they represented a collective crisis of identity. More than non-Christian Jews, they were affected by Paul's proclamation that salvation was for "Jews and Greeks". We will argue that when Paul uses this phrase in conjunction with God-language, he intends to reinterpret the identity of Christian Jews and create a common basis for self-understanding among all Christians.[1]

This becomes apparent in Rom 3:29-30. The issue under debate is Paul's practice of including non-Jews into his churches without circumcision. Paul raises this as a theological question—i.e., it is immediately related to the understanding of God. His main point is that God can no longer be described primarily in terms of his relationship with Israel:

Or is God the God of Jews only?
Is he not the God of Gentiles also?
Yes, of Gentiles also, since God is one;
and he will justify the circumcised on the ground
of their faith and the uncircumcised through their faith.

In using the terms 'Ιουδαῖοι and ἔθνη in v. 29, Paul describes the world from a Jewish perspective.[2] The world consisted of the Jews,

---

[1] Cf. Dahl, *Volk Gottes*, 264-78; and R. Bultmann, "The Transformation of the Idea of the Church in the History of Early Christianity", *Canadian Journal of Theology* 1 (1955) 73-81.

[2] Also 9:24. Similarly, the terms 'Ιουδαῖος and "Ελλην, 1:16; 2:9-10;3:9; 10:12; περιτομή and ἀκροβυστία 2:25-27; 3:30; 4:11-12; περιτομή and ἔθνη 15:8. 'Ισραήλ and ἔθνη are used in chapters 9-11 to express *contrast*, not totality, 9:30-31, but see 11:25-26. These various expressions have a similar meaning in Paul, see H. Windisch, ""Ελλην", *TWNT* 2 (1935) 512-13. Cf. further N. A. Dahl, "Nations in the New Testament", *New Testament*

the people of God, on the one hand, and of "the nations" (the Greeks) on the other. Paul accepts this division, but from the common faith in God he draws the conclusion that there is no distinction between circumcised and uncircumcised. The underlying conflict here is sometimes described in terms of "particularism" versus "universalism". Paul is considered to have brought the trend toward universalism within Judaism to its logical conclusion.[3] However, this interpretation misses the point. From the prophets onwards, there was in Judaism an emphasis upon the proclamation of God as the God of the "nations" also.[4] And, especially in apocalyptic literature, this was described not only in historical but also in cosmic terms.[5] However, this "universalism" was tempered by the conviction that God had a special relationship with Israel, expressed through the giving of the Torah. The Torah, therefore, was the dividing line that God, the creator of the world, had set between Israel and other nations. It is this function of the Torah as dividing-line that is made obsolete when Paul says that God will justify the circumcised and uncircumcised "through faith". This "universal" statement in 3:30 is bracketed by two antithetical expressions in 3:28 and 31, contrasting "faith" and "law". Through these two verses we are able to define the issue at stake more clearly. Paul's mission broke down national barriers that were upheld by Jewish Torah-piety. On the other hand, his preaching created another division—between those who accepted the Christian kerygma and those who rejected it. Instead of the Torah as the dividing-line between Jews and non-Jews came faith in Christ, distinguishing believers from non-believers.[6] Paul's conclusion that

Christianity for Africa and the World: Essays in Honour of Harry Sawyerr (ed. M. E. Glasswell and E. W. Fashole-Luke, London, 1974) 54-68.

[3] C. H. Dodd, *The Epistle of Paul to the Romans* (London, 1934) 63. Käsemann (*Römer*, 97-98) makes a distinction similar to that between "particularism" and "universalism" when he describes Paul's argument too much in terms of a contrast between God the creator and the Rabbinic God of the covenant. However, Paul sees the contrast not so much between creation and covenant as between law and faith; cf. N. A. Dahl, *Studies in Paul*, 178-91, esp. 191; see further the criticism of Ch. Müller, below, 286.

[4] For the following section, see Dahl, *op. cit.*, Maier, *Geschichte*, 20-23, and W. D. Davies, *Paul and Rabbinic Judaism* (revised edition, London, 1955) 58-85.

[5] See Hengel, *Judentum*, 330-57.

[6] H. Ridderbos, *Paul: An Outline of his Theology* (Grand Rapids, Mich., 1975) 340; "in this new concept of the people of God given in the revelation of Christ a new restriction and in a certain sense a new particularism is

the salvation of the one God is "universal" is therefore not a "general" statement: it is directly applied to the creation of Christian communities. It is against this background of controversy over missionary practice in the early church that we should study other texts where Paul speaks of "Jews and Greeks".[7]

Another passage that shows how Paul can use an "universal" statement about "the Jew first and also the Greek" to make an attack upon the traditional barriers around the synagogue is Rom 2:9-10. This passage that proclaims the same judgment upon Jews and non-Jews is bracketed by statements that describe God as the impartial judge (2:6 and 11).

> There will be tribulation and distress for every human being who
>   does evil,
> the Jew first and also the Greek,
> but glory and honour and peace for every one who does good,
> the Jew first and also the Greek.

The universality of God's judgment is here brought to bear upon another aspect of the controversy between the synagogue and Christian missionaries. Following the example of the prophets and John the Baptist, Jesus and Christian missionaries after him proclaimed judgment upon the unrepentant Jews. The latter protested by pointing to their privileged status as the people of God, Matt 3:7-10; John 8:30-44.

The embittered discussion over the trustworthiness of the word of God to Israel in 3:1-8 belongs to the same context of controversy.[8] It finds its conclusion in a statement about "Jews and Greeks" in v. 9:

> What then? Are we Jews any better off? No, not at all; for I
> have already charged that all men, both Jews and Greeks, are
> under the power of sin . . .

Since we have already commented upon 3:29-30, let us here point out only that this passage in fact parallels 3:26. There Paul said that God wanted "to prove at the present time that he himself is

---

implied". On the similar function of the Torah and of Christ within Judaism and early Christianity respectively, cf. W. D. Davies, *Paul*, 147-76; and ''Torah and Dogma; A Comment'', *HTR* 61 (1968) 87-105. However, for his suggestion that Christ represents a "new" Torah, see the critical remarks by E. P. Sanders, *Paul and Palestinian Judaism* (London, 1977) 511-15.

[7] Cf. N. A. Dahl, *Volk Gottes*, 239-40.

[8] Notice the similarity between Rom 3:8 and Acts 18:5-6, see above, 74.

righteous and that he justifies him who has faith in Jesus". It is not absolutely clear what Paul is aiming at with this "general" remark. However, in the polemics of 3:29-30 the issue under discussion is directly identified. Here God's salvation "at the present time" of "him who has faith in Jesus" becomes visible! It takes the form of the acceptance by Jews and non-Jews of the preaching of Christian missionaries and of a fellowship where both groups are included! This is made even more specific in Chapter 4 where the predications of God are followed by descriptions of the children of Abraham.

In 4:11-12 and 16, Paul describes the believers in the same terms as in 3:30, i.e. as "circumcised" and "uncircumcised". There is no direct statement about God in 4:9-12. However, 4:10 has a function similar to the predications in 4:5 and 17, when Paul says that Abraham's faith was reckoned to him as righteousness. From this act of God Paul draws conclusions for the relationship between Jews and non-Jews in his congregations when he says in 4:11-12:

> The purpose was to make him father of all who believe without being circumcised and who thus have righteousness reckoned to them, and likewise the father of the circumcised who are not merely circumcised but also follow the example of the faith which our father Abraham had before he was circumcised.

The description in 4:16 precedes the predication of God in *v.* 17:

> That is why it depends on faith, in order that the promise may rest on grace and be guaranteed to all his descendants—not only to the adherents of the law but also to those who share the faith of Abraham, for he is the father of us all.

In these texts the various groups are not so clearly identified as we might have wished.[9] We would like to be able to distinguish between non-believing Jews, Christian Jews and finally non-Jewish Christians. That the picture here is so vague as to make clear-cut divisions difficult probably reflects the real situation at the time. Many Christian Jews would still regard themselves as so much a part of the synagogue that they did not become identifiable as a separate group.

However, when we try to point out the various groups in these texts we must keep in mind the purpose of Paul in this chapter. He does not discuss the question of the seed of Abraham in general

---

[9] See below, 112 n. 18, 250-51.

terms, but in a context where he speaks of the identity of the Christians, those "who have faith" (3:26, 30). Consequently, when he speaks of "those of the law" and of "the circumcised", Paul first of all thinks of Christians Jews. He argues that they, too, belong to the people of God on the basis of faith. However, the text as it stands does not exclude the interpretation that the Jews as such—believers in Christ or not—are also the children of Abraham. In fact, this is implied when Paul discusses the salvation of *all* of Israel in chapter 9-11. There it is Israel and *not* the Christian groups that is the focus of Paul's interest.

In chapter 9:6-13 and 14-18 Paul discusses the faithfulness of God towards Israel, as well as his freedom to act as he wants. Through his use of predications of God in *vv.* 12 and 16 Paul defines the special relationship between God and Israel. In contrast to this, however, in 9:24 he draws conclusions that specifically concern the *Christian* churches.

9:22-24   What if God, desiring to show his wrath and to make known his power, has endured with much patience the vessels of wrath made for destruction,
in order to make known the riches of his glory for the vessels of mercy, which he has prepared beforehand for glory,
even us whom he has called, not from the Jews only but also from the Gentiles?

This passage bears many similarities to 3:25-30. First, there is a more "general" description in 9:22-23: God will show his wrath over the "vessels of wrath" that he has so long been patient with (cf. 3:25). The positive element is introduced by ἵνα: "in order to make known the riches of his glory for the vessels of glory" (cf. 3:26). In the light of the preceding discussion Paul's readers should be able to identify the two different "vessels" of which he speaks. However, in what follows Paul makes the identification absolutely clear by applying the metaphor directly to the Christians: "even us whom he has called, not from the Jews only but also from the Gentiles" (cf. 3:30). The terms are 'Ιουδαῖοι and ἔθνη as in 3:29. This turn from the discussion of Israel to a description of "the new community" is prepared through a common vocabulary.[10] Like the "true Israel" in 9:6-13, this "vessel of mercy" is also brought into

---

[10] Compare a) τοῦ ἐλεῶντος θεοῦ *v.* 16, ὃν θέλει ἐλεεῖ *v.* 18 with ἐπὶ σκεύη ἐλέους *v.* 23, and b) ἐκ τοῦ καλοῦντος *v.* 12 with οὓς καὶ ἐκάλεσεν *v.* 24.

existence through the call of God. In *v.* 24 we can almost see how Paul points to his integrated congregations of Jews and non-Jews as an illustration of his thesis.[11] They were visible manifestations of the assertion that the people of God were brought into existence through his mercy.

In these texts where God was discussed, Paul spoke to both Jewish and non-Jewish Christians. From some of them, especially among the first Christian community in Jerusalem, Paul met with objections that had to be answered. They argued that when Paul included God-fearers into his churches without circumcision he made God appear unfaithful to his people. In doing this, Paul transgressed the traditional borders of Israel. In consequence, when Paul defended his proclamation of God and claimed to uphold the traditional faith of Israel, this also amounted to a defence of his missionary practice. He argued that the new "separatist" groups at the periphery of the synagogues—or even in some cases already separated from them—were *not* a threat to faith in God as the God of Israel. On the contrary, these groups were visible expressions of God's faithfulness and mercy! It was in small, scattered communities in Asia Minor, Greece, Italy, etc., where Jews had ventured an experiment of unprecedented fellowship with non-Jews, that the God of Israel was now visible! Only when this was accepted was a true understanding of God possible.

So far, we have only discussed passages containing statements about God. To fill out the picture, we will also include other texts where "Jews and Greeks", "circumcised and uncircumcised", or similar terms are found, to see if there is the same connection here between a "universal" statement and a real situation. These texts include 1:16-17; 10:11-13; 11:25-26 and 15:8-9.

1:16 For I am not ashamed of the gospel: it is the power of God for salvation to every one who has faith, to the Jew first and also to the Greek.

This thematic statement at the beginning of Romans combines two inter-related and unseparable themes. First, Paul gives his own interpretation of εὐαγγέλιον θεοῦ from 1:2-4 through the introduc-

---

[11] This verse has caused commentators many difficulties, cf. Michel, *Römer*, 248 and Käsemann, *Römer*, 264. Here Dodd (*Romans*, 160) is more suggestive: "Until now the argument has moved on abstract and academic lines, now it suddenly touches concrete reality".

tion of δικαιοσύνη θεοῦ in *v.* 17. Second, he describes the addressees of God's gospel. Paul defines "every one who has faith" by an appositional description: "to the Jews first and also to the Greek".[12] Similarly in 1:5, after the summary of the gospel Paul introduces his call to preach it "among all the nations". These two expressions (ἐν πᾶσιν τοῖς ἔθνεσιν and 'Ιουδαίῳ τε πρῶτον καὶ "Ελληνι) emphasize the different aspects of the universal impact of the gospel. In *v.* 5 Paul stresses primarily the non-Jewish world whereas he strikes another note in *v.* 16 by saying "the Jew first". This inherent tension corresponds to Paul's argument in the rest of the letter, and also confirms the thesis that his "universalism" is always applied to a specific situation. In *v.* 5, the mention of his calling as an apostle to the nations serves to legitimate his letter to the Romans. Similarly, "to the Jews first and also to the Greek" in *v.* 16 is a statement that defines the universal claims of the gospel in a specific context. Even when Paul makes "general" theological statements about God and the world, they are related to the more immediate questions of his letters. Therefore, Paul already at the outset places the issue of unity between Jews and non-Jews in the perspective of the revelation of the righteousness of God.[13]

10:11-13 The scripture says, "No one who believes in him will be put to shame".
For there is no distinction between Jew and Greek;
the same Lord is Lord of all and bestows his riches upon all who call upon him.
For, "every one who calls upon the name of the Lord will be saved".

As in 1:16, the definition, in this case οὐ γάρ ἐστιν διαστολὴ 'Ιουδαίου τε καὶ "Ελληνος is added to "every one who believes". In 1:1-17 the context was God-centred: it was "the gospel of God" that opened up salvation for Jews and Greeks alike. In contrast to

---

[12] "Jews and Greeks" or similar expressions are added as an explanation to "the one who has faith" in 10:11 also; cf. 3:30; 4:11-12, 16.

[13] M. Barth, "Jews and Gentiles: The Social Character of Justification in Paul", *Journal of Ecumenical Studies* 5 (1968) 241-67. We agree with Barth's thesis: "For the two themes, justification by faith and unity of Jew and Gentile in Christ, are for him obviously not only inseparable but in the last analysis identical", 258. Unfortunately, however, his study is marred by a highly polemical (and unecumenical!) attitude towards contemporary (German) Lutheran interpretation of Paul. See further N. A. Dahl, "The Doctrine of Justification: Its Social Function and Implications", *Studies in Paul*, 95-120.

this, the same assertion in 10:11-13 is given a distinctively christological motivation: "The same Lord is Lord of all, and bestows
his riches upon all who call upon him". Again there is a direct
connection between the central message of Paul's kerygma (cf. *v.* 9
"Jesus is Lord") and his description of the Christian community.[14]
Probably "vision" or "prophecy" would be more adequate terms
than "description". Paul's inferences about the structures of the
new communities were descriptive in that he could point to some
examples among his own congregations. In fact, Paul has here
again theologized his own experience and practice. However, the
examples that Paul could point to were not representative for all,
probably not even for most Christian groups in his time. When
turned against his adversaries, his "universalism" became a
criticism of the social structure within many Christian groups,[15]
especially predominantly Jewish-Christian groups. There are
similar passages to 10:11-13 in Gal 3:28, and also in Peter's speeches
in Acts 10:34-36 and 15:9-11.[16] They point to the controversy
whether God-fearers and other non-Jews should be circumcised, as
the original Sitz-im-Leben for Paul's statement in 10:11-13.

It was the mission to the non-Jewish world that spurred this
controversy. To Paul, however, it was this very mission that was
the source of unity between "Jews and Greeks". In his role as
apostle to the nations Paul saw himself as working towards the
unification of all mankind through the gospel.[17] His mission to the
nations did not set them apart from Israel, or imply God's rejection
of Israel. Rather, Paul regarded his missionary work as an eschatological event whereby Jews and non-Jews were inseparably linked.
This theme becomes increasingly important in the latter part of
Romans. It is this unity—now hidden, but to be revealed at the
parousia—that Paul sets forth as "a mystery" in 11:25-26:

---

[14] τοὺς ἐπικαλουμένους αὐτόν (i.e. ὁ κύριος) is not a description of individual
believers but a title for *Israel* taken over by the Christians; cf. 1 Cor 1:2;
Acts 9:14, 21; 22:16; 2 Tim 2:22; Dahl, *Volk Gottes*, 206.
[15] L. E. Keck, "On the Ethos of Early Christianity", (1974) 450.
[16] Jervell, *Luke* 65-67. Notice also how Luke contrasts Ἰουδαῖοι and
Ἕλληνες, ἔθνη in Acts, esp. when he describes how Christian missionaries
left the Jews to go to the Greeks. Ἕλληνες and ἔθνη do not refer to non-Jews
in general, but most often to "God-fearers", e.g. 13:46; 14:1; 17:4; 18:6;
see Windisch, "Ἕλλην", 510; and Hengel, "Zwischen Jesus und Paulus",
164-65.
[17] Hengel, "Die Ursprünge der christlichen Mission", *NTS* 18 (1971-72)
17-24.

Lest you be wise in your own conceits, I want you to understand this mystery, brethen; a hardening has come upon part of Israel, until the full number of the Gentiles come in, and so all Israel will be saved . . .

Recent studies have established that the use of μυστήριον in Paul and in "the Pauline school" (i.e., Ephesians and Colossians) is directly linked to the theme of *mission*.[18] In several texts, especially Eph 3:2-12, Col 1:24-29 and Rom 16:25, this is primarily understood as the inclusion of the non-Jewish world. In contrast to this, Paul in 11:25-26 is not only concerned with the non-Jews, but also stresses the salvation of the Jews.[19] He does this in a vision of eschatological dimensions that eventually leads up to the concluding doxology in 11:33-36. When Paul unfolds this salvation-history, he relates it to the controversy from 11:11 onwards.[20] The mystery of God's salvation of the Jews is Paul's final refutation of Christians who held the Jews in contempt.

Likewise in Rom 15:7-13 it becomes apparent that "eschatological unity" is related to the social structure of Christian groups.

15:8-9a   For I tell you that Christ became a servant to the circumcised to show God's truthfulness, in order to confirm the promises given to the patriarchs, in order that the Gentiles might glorify God for his mercy.

In 15:7 Paul repeats the main theme from his admonition to "the weak" and "the strong" in chapter 14 by saying: "Welcome one another, therefore, as Christ has welcomed you, for the glory of God". He supports this exhortation by referring to Christ as an example of obedience. Attempts have been made to identify "the strong" and "the weak" in chapters 14-15 with the non-Jewish and Jewish Christians respectively.[21] Although this explanation is not

---

[18] See R. E. Brown, "The Semitic Background of the New Testament *Mysterion*", *Bib* 39 (1958) 426-48; 40 (1959) 70-87; cf. further L. Cerfaux, *La théologie de l'Eglise suivant Saint Paul* (Unam Sanctam 10, 2nd revised edition, Paris, 1948) 229-67.

[19] Brown, "Mysterion", 446. For the salvation of Israel in Romans 11, see W. D. Davies, "Paul and the People of Israel", *NTS* 24 (1978) 4-39.

[20] J. La Grand Jr. ("τὸ μυστήριον: The New Testament Development of the Semitic Usage", unpubl. Th. M. diss., Calvin Theological School (Grand Rapids, Mich., 1976, 74-83) goes beyond Brown's study in his focus on the situation of controversy that is reflected in Paul's use of τὸ μυστήριον.

[21] In recent years especially P. Minear, *The Obedience of Faith* (SBT 2/19, London, 1971); and K. P. Donfried, "False presuppositions in the study of

quite convincing, the example of Jesus uniting Jews and non-Jews must in some way be related to the situation in Rome. The imagery that Paul introduces was well enough known to the Romans to bear upon their own situation. On the other hand, it has wider implications in that it reflects Paul's missionary discussions— and, being included in his letter to the Romans, it continues his discussions with Christian Jews.

The relationship between the various parts of vv. 8 and 9 has been much discussed. It is best to take Christ in the role of servant both to περιτομῆς ("in order to confirm the promises") and to τὰ δὲ ἔθνη ("in order that the Gentiles might glorify God").[22] Paul's ultimate goal is to unite both groups in praising God. He emphasizes this with his quotations from the Bible in vv. 9-12. This exhortation to praise God constitutes a central theme in Romans.[23] Paul does not conceive of this praise as a liturgical act only—it is to be rendered through all activities of life.[24] Consequently, in his discourse on the sinfulness of the world in 1:18ff it is Paul's main accusation that man has occupied the place of God, and has not given God the praise and glory that are his due! Paul sums up the goal of history, as he sees it, in the doxology in 11:33-36. When history is brought to its fulfilment, God—and not man—stands at its centre. In 15:5-12, when "the weak" and "the strong" as well as the Jews and the Greeks unite in glorifying God, they partake in the fulfilment of history. Their unity in praise is an eschatological sign! Rom 15:7-12 is, in a way, a summary of Paul's gospel in this letter. It parallels the introduction in 1:3-7,[25] and develops the major questions from

Romans"; against R. J. Karris ("Romans 14:1-15:13 and the Occasion of Romans", CBQ 35 (1973) 155-78) who finds in Rom 14-15 a general paraenesis. For a survey of different solutions see W. Schmithals, Der Römerbrief als historisches Problem (Studien zum Neuen Testament 9, Gütersloh, 1975) 95-107. We agree with Schmithals in finding Paul's concern for unity the most important theme of the letter. However, his limiting this to the Roman scene only and his reconstruction of the actual situation in Rome are not convincing.

[22] Käsemann, Römer, 372. Cf. the discussion of 15:8-9 in J. Thuren, Hedningarnas offerliturgi (Skrifter utgivna av Samfundet för missiologi och ekumenik 18, Helsinki, 1970) 24ff.

[23] G. H. Boobyer, "Thanksgiving" and the "Glory of God" in Paul (Leipzig, 1929) 79ff. R. D. Webber, "The Concept of Rejoicing in Paul" (Ph.D. diss., Yale university, 1970) was not available to me.

[24] See e.g. Rom 12:1-2, cf. E. Käsemann, "Gottesdienst im Alltag der Welt", Exegetische Versuche und Besinnungen 2 (3rd edition, Göttingen, 1970) 198-204.

[25] B. Olsson, "Rom 1:3f enligt Paulus", SEÅ 37-38 (1973) 261-67.

chapters 1-4 and 9-11. At the same time it also concludes the parenaetical section in chapters 12-15! These features combine to form a striking illustration of the centrality and importance of "unity" in Paul's argument in Romans.

His picture of an eschatological unity is brought to bear upon a situation at the "local" level that was characterized by a lack of unity. It was a question of unity between groups within a community, between a community and the apostle, or at times between groups of Christian communities. Both with regard to the organizational structure and with regard to the self-identity of Christian groups, the situation at this time was very confused.[26] At least in some communities, different religious or even social and economic groups were not integrated, but remained as separate parties. The churches also faced the problem of establishing clear lines of authority. Various groups of apostles, missionaries or representatives from the church in Jerusalem all claimed charismatic authority over the congregations.[27] The issue of mission to non-Jews and of fellowship between circumcised and uncircumcised Christians was an obstacle to social unity both within the Christian community at large and within individual groups. These various examples point to a situation where the Christians were in the process of emerging as a new social entity, but not yet clearly defined or with a structured organization.

Paul addresses himself to all of these questions in Romans. Since he has not himself preached in Rome, he first of all has to establish his own authority. He gives advice to "the weak" and "the strong" on questions from social life, i.e., he tries to work out a basis for unity despite varying practice concerning their relations to the society that surrounded them.[28] Above all, Paul's main concern is the integration of Jews and non-Jews into one body through his worldwide mission. This was the motivating force when Paul insisted upon the collection from non-Jewish or mixed congregations outside Palestine to the church in Jerusalem. In 15:14-33, Paul shares his concern over this collection with the Romans. The

---

[26] See Gager, *Kingdom*, 66-92.
[27] See J. H. Schütz, *Paul and the Anatomy of Apostolic Authority* (SNTSMS 26, Cambridge, 1975) esp. 1-34, 249-80; and G. Theissen, "Legitimation und Lebensunterhalt", 192-221.
[28] One of the issues at stake was the eating of unclean food, i.e. meat from "pagan" offerings, Rom 14:14; Käsemann, *Römer*, 362.

motif of eschatological unity is used as an inducement to co-opera-
tion and sharing between groups that were geographically and
partly also ideologically separated.[29]

It is with striking regularity that phrases like "for the Jew first
but also for the Greek", etc., are used to characterize God or his
way of acting. The number of such phrases in Romans is too high
to be overlooked—1:16-17; 2:9-10; 3:9, 29-30; 4:11-12, 16; 9:24;
10:11-13; 11:25-26; 15:8-9. However, the significant point is not
that these expressions are numerous, but that they are concentrated
at central points in the letter where Paul formulates his message in
thematic statements. In Romans, this frequently means a statement about the righteousness of God. Thus the final reason for
unity lies in the revelation of God's righteousness. The unity that
Paul urges his communities to adopt is based on nothing less than
an act of God.

The phrase, "for Jews and Greeks", is not the only way in which
Paul speaks of unity. Although it is closely connected with the
central message in 1 Corinthians and Galatians also, in these letters
other images for unity are more common, e.g. "the body (of Christ)"
or "a building".[30] In Romans these images are found especially in
chapters 5-6 and 12-14. The idea of the unity of mankind is not
original to the New Testament—it is found in the Old Testament, in
Hellenistic philosophy, and in Oriental mythology.[31] Contemporary
religious cults and philosophical schools emphasized the unity of
mankind and the equal value of all men (if not women). However,
Paul does not simply rehearse a common stock of philosophical
ideas. Nor is his conception of unity between Jews and non-Jews
inherent in traditional Jewish faith in God, although he invokes
God (especially the oneness of God, Rom 3:30; Gal 3:20) as the
decisive argument for his thesis. Just as the Hellenistic idea of unity
and equality did not break down social barriers, so the Jewish faith
in one God did not produce "integrated" congregations. In consequence, even if Paul could draw upon both sources, this does not
fully explain the vigour of his argument.

---

[29] D. Georgi, *Die Geschichte der Kollekte des Paulus für Jerusalem* (Theologische Forschung 8, Hamburg, 1965) 79-87; K. F. Nickle, *The Collection.
A study in Paul's strategy* (SBT 48, London, 1966) 111-43.

[30] For a complete list see P. Minear, *Images of the Church in the New
Testament* (Philadelphia, 1960).

[31] See H. Baldry, *The Unity of Mankind in Greek Thought* (Cambridge,
1965).

What then is the centre of Paul's concern when he argues for unity between "Jews and Greeks"? Since in Romans he draws upon and generalizes experience from his mission, similar expressions in earlier letters may point more directly to a situation or an experience. This is the case in 1 Cor 12:13 and Gal 3:27-28. In both instances the phrase, "Jews and Greeks", is used together with other terms ("male and female", "slave and free"), illustrating distinctions that were broken down within Christian communities. Other passages as well give evidence that Paul in Gal 3:27-28 actually points to the Christians as a group with a new social structure.[32] This is also reflected in Col 3:10-11 and Eph 2:11-22.[33] Col 3:10-11 combines a similar formula with the idea of the "new creation" in the image of Christ. Similarly in Ephesians, the terminology is that of "nations and Israel" and "uncircumcised and circumcised".

In these texts the use of "Jews and Greeks" etc., is related to the inclusion of believers into the "new" community in a more direct way than in Romans, in that these passages reflect a liturgical practice in Pauline congregations. In 1 Cor 12:13 Paul refers to baptism accompanied by ecstatic experiences:

For by one Spirit we were all baptized into one body—Jews or Greeks, slaves or free—and all were made to drink of one Spirit.

Furthermore, this unity, confirmed by baptism, is described with the image of the body of Christ. At the outset of the letter, in 1:13-17, it is this baptismal experience to which Paul refers in his exhortation to unity among the Corinthians. Gal 3:27-28 shows similar traits:

For as many of you as were baptized into Christ have put on Christ. There is neither Jew nor Greek, there is neither slave nor free, there is neither male nor female, for you are all one in Christ Jesus.

---

[32] Esp. 4:8-10; cf. H. D. Betz, "Spirit, Freedom and Law", *SEÅ* 39 (1974) 145-60.
[33] See J. Jervell, *Imago Dei. Gen 1, 26f im Spätjudentum, in der Gnosis und in den paulinischen Briefen* (FRLANT 76, Göttingen, 1959) 245-46. For Colossians see also M. D. Hooker, "Were there False Teachers in Colossae?", *Christ and Spirit in the New Testament. In Honour of C. F. D. Moule* (ed. B. Lindars and S. M. Smalley, Cambridge, 1973) 328; similarly Minear, *Images of the Church*, 211: "The image of the body of Christ thus served as a way of describing a social revolution".

Here there is no direct reference to "the body of Christ". However, the same idea is expressed in a phrase that is characteristic of Paul—"to be in Christ".[34] There can be no doubt that these texts mirror early Christian experience. It was through baptism and the manifestations of the Spirit that new members—including non-Jews—were brought into the Christian community. It was in this act that the old religious and social barriers were most visibly broken down. Luke in his interpretation of the break-through of the mission to the non-Jewish world likewise traces this event to baptism and the outpouring of the Spirit, Acts 10:44-48; 11:15-18.[35] Apparently, Paul can draw not only on a common experience but also on an earlier interpretation of this experience. In his formulae, Paul makes theological inferences from experiences in the life of Christians—and he brings this interpretation to bear upon Jewish tradition. Gal 3:27-28 is especially illuminating in this respect. Here he combines the idea that "you are all one in Christ" as an expression of Christian identity, with the concept that they are also "Abraham's offspring".[36] Paul retains this Old Testament and Jewish expression for the identity of the believers and uses it of the Christians—but he interprets in light of Christian experience. This passage prepares Paul's way of speaking of "Jews and Greeks" in Romans. Here too, the Christ-event at the end of time is the basis for Paul's arguments, but in most cases it is not made explicit. We noticed how Paul in Romans speaks of God instead of Christ. This corresponds to the way he expresses the group-identity of the Christians in terms of "seed of Abraham", "Israel" and "people (of God)". This implies not only that Paul interprets Christian experience as *theology*, but that he can also express it as *history*.

When Paul speaks of "Jew and Greek", he is concerned with the unity between all Christians, be they Jews or non-Jews. Therefore, it is equally important to Paul that the non-Jews shall be included and that the Jews shall remain in the community of Christians.

---

[34] See F. Neugebauer, *In Christus, Eine Untersuchung zum paulinischen Glaubenverständnis* (Göttingen, 1961); further M. Bouttier, *La condition chrétienne selon Saint Paul* (Nouvelle série théologique 16, Genève, 1964), and Dahl, *Volk Gottes*, 224-25; Cerfaux, *L'Eglise*, 201-18.

[35] See G. W. R. Lampe, "The Holy Spirit in the Writings of St. Luke", *Studies in the Gospels. Essays in memory of R. H. Lightfoot* (ed. D. E. Nineham, Oxford, 1955) 196-200.

[36] Dahl, *Volk Gottes*, 225: "Sachlich ist der Kirchenbegriff des Paulus aber derselbe, ob er nun vom "Volke Gottes" oder vom "Leibe Christi" spricht". See also Cerfaux, *L'Eglise*, 215-18, and Ridderbos, *Paul*, 393-95.

This latter point has not always been sufficiently recognized.[37] When Paul proclaimed that the distinction between "Jews and Greeks" was made obsolete, this was a direct attack not only upon non-Christian Jews, but upon Christian Jews as well. It was their identity that was most directly affected by Paul's preaching and missionary activity. Paul does not make sharp distinctions: when he characterizes his opponents as "Jews" he might very well be speaking of Christian Jews. However, it is sometimes possible in his argument to distinguish between Christian and non-Christian Jews. This is the case in texts where Paul struggles with the major problem that confronted Christian Jews—why did the Jews, by and large, reject the gospel, whereas many non-Jews accepted it? [38] As we have already noticed, it is in Rom 9-11 that Paul most frequently raises this question. Paul's way of speaking about "Jews and Greeks" in these texts differs from what we have found earlier. Here Jews and Greeks are not equal; rather, the advantage is on the side of the latter group. Not only have the Jews lost their privileges, but the non-Jews are even in a better position than the Jews. We find the first example in 9:30-31:

> What shall we say then? That the *Gentiles who did not pursue righteousness* have attained it, that is, righteousness through faith, but that *Israel* who pursued the righteousness which is based on law did not succeed in fulfilling that law.

The same idea is expressed through a quotation from Isa 65:1-2 in 10:20-21:

> Then Isaiah is so bold as to say, "I have been found by those who *did not seek me*; I have shown myself to those *who did not ask for me*". But of *Israel* he says, "All day long I have held out my hands to a disobedient and contrary people".

In 11:25-26, Paul contrasts a part of Israel that has been hardened and the full number of the non-Jews:

> . . . a hardening has come upon part of Israel, until the full number of the Gentiles come in, and so all Israel will be saved . . .

---

[37] But see e.g. Dahl, *Volk Gottes*, esp. 237-46; and Munck, *Christus und Israel*; further n. 43.

[38] In this debate, proof-texts from Scripture played an important part, see E. E. Ellis, *Paul's use of the Old Testament* (Edinburgh, 1957), 121-24 and B. Lindars, *Apologetic* 158-159, 241-44.

Compared with the first two passages, there is a new element here. Not only has Paul revealed "the mystery" of the salvation of Israel as an eschatological event; he has emphasized also that it is "all Israel" that will be saved—whereas a part of it is now hardened. Who then make up the part that is *not* hardened? The answer to that question is found in 11:1ff. Here Paul counters the objection that God has rejected his people by pointing to himself—as an Israelite and descendent of Abraham—and in *v.* 5 "a remnant, chosen by grace", (λεῖμμα κατ' ἐκλογὴν χάριτος). Paul repeats his argument in 11:7 in a verse that is strikingly similar to 9:30-31:

What then? *Israel* failed to obtain what is sought. The *elect* (ἡ δὲ ἐκλογή) obtained it, but the rest were hardened.

"*Israel* failed to obtain what it sought"—but another group did! In 9:30 it was the non-Jewish Christians—here it is the remnant, i.e., the Christians among the Jews.[39] In this text Paul compares Christian and non-Christian Jews. Paul sees a split between "all Israel" that had received the promises, and that part of it where the promises were now fulfilled—and this split would remain until the end of the world (11:25-27 and 11:15). Paul has the remnant in mind also in 9:11 when he speaks of ἡ κατ' ἐκλογὴν πρόθεσις τοῦ θεοῦ.[40] Here he gives a definition of the true Israel and the seed of Abraham as those who have their being ἐκ τοῦ καλοῦντος. This corresponds to the description of the believers of his own time— God had "called them out" from Jews and non-Jews. When using the metaphor of the remnant Paul possibly adopts a term that Christian Jews used about themselves.[41] However, in 11:6 he defines

---

[39] Dahl, *Volk Gottes*, 242-44; Käsemann, *Römer*, 289-91; G. Schrenk, "λεῖμμα", *TWNT* 4 (1942) 215-21.

[40] Notice the use of ἐκλογή also in 11:5, 7, 28; cf. Michel, *Der Brief an die Römer* (MeyerK 4, 13th edition, Göttingen, 1966) 233-34 n. 6.

[41] There is no similar use of ἐκλογή and λεῖμμα in the NT to support this suggestion. Paul introduces them as well-known terms (cf. "children of Abraham" in Galatians 3 and Romans 4) and then defines them by typically Pauline antitheses. But cf. J. Jeremias, "Der Gedanke des 'Heiligen Restes' im Spätjudentum und in der Verkündigung Jesu", *ZNW* 42 (1949) 184-94. Jeremias stresses that Jesus envisaged himself as gathering the *people of God*, not the remnant. This view is argued in the Gospels also, e.g. Matt 13:24-30. Against Jeremias, there is evidence that the Christians (Christian Jews) when under pressure from their surroundings described themselves as "the few", Matt 7:14; "the chosen", Matt 22:14; "the little ones", Matt 10:42; "the poor ones", Matt 11:5;—i.e. terms which distinguished them from "the others", Matt 22:14; see G. F. Hasel, "Remnant", *IDBSup* (1976) 736. There is a striking similarity between the description in Luke 8:9-10 par.

it by means of an antithesis—"By grace . . . no longer on the basis of works". In this way Paul completely removes the notion of the law that was central to a Jewish use of "remnant".[42] Nevertheless, even with this polemical interpretation, Paul's intentions towards the Christian Jews in *vv.* 5-7 are positive. They are accepted and included as Jews—but Paul gives his own definition of the basis for their acceptance. Their identity as remnant can now only be understood in terms of "by God's grace". What Paul asks of them is nothing less than to accept *his* definition of their identity!

Paul goes to great lengths in his efforts to include the Jews—even if his polemics against their theology would seem to exclude them. What is the reason for this apparent dichotomy? His intentions at this point have frequently been misunderstood. Scholars have argued that Paul intended to take away from the Jews their position as the people of God. The (primarily German) discussion over "Heilsgeschichte" is a pertinent illustration.[43] To a large degree this discussion centred on Paul's view on the *history* of Israel— without enough awareness of the factors that made Paul take up this question. To Paul it was above all a question that concerned not the past but his contemporary fellow-Jews! He was himself a Jew and lived among Jews, and he desired to live in fellowship with them—especially the Christians amongst them. There were certain limits, however, to this fellowship. His controversy with the judaizers in Galatia makes this clear. Their attempts to bring the Torah into force among non-Jewish Christians are met with absolute rejection. Admittedly, many of Paul's arguments from Galatians are also found in his letter to the Romans. Even so, his intentions in this letter are different—his arguments are here directed towards the *inclusion*, not the rejection, of Christian Jews.[44]

Mark 4:10-12, Matt 13:10-17 and that of Rom 11:7-8. We find "you" (i.e. the disciples) or "the remnant" on the one side and "the others" on the opposite side. In both instances, "the others" are characterized by similar quotations from Isa 6:9 and 29:10, about the hardening of the people.

[42] Käsemann, *Römer*, 290-291.

[43] See below, 104-05. The debate on the American scene is oriented more towards the contemporary situation; and most scholarly studies are influenced by the ongoing ecumenical discussions between Jews and Christians. See e.g. W. D. Davies, "Paul and the people of Israel"; and the more popular study by K. Stendahl, *Paul among Jews and Gentiles* (Philadelphia, 1976).

[44] The differences between Galatians and Romans are succinctly stated by Jervell, "Brief", 68-69.

Thus Paul's attitude towards the Jews has two sides. It is positive as long as there is a hope that they might be included in the new community—but negative towards those who rejected outright his preaching and mission. This double attitude is mirrored in Rom 15:30-31:

> I appeal to you, brethren, by our Lord Jesus Christ and by the love of the Spirit, to strive together with me in your prayers to God on my behalf, that I may be delivered from the unbelievers in Judea, and that my service for Jerusalem may be acceptable to the saints . . .

Paul here turns to the Romans with a direct request.[45] He asks them to unite in prayer to God with him. First that when he arrives in Jerusalem, he shall be saved from οἱ ἀπειθοῦντες, i.e., the non-believing Jews. Second, that the collection he is bringing with him must be accepted by οἱ ἅγιοι i.e., the Christian Jews. We have already mentioned how important this collection was to Paul as a visible expression of his conception of his own mission to the non-Jewish world. When in 15:30 he speaks of going to Jerusalem to deliver it, he obviously envisages this as a means of securing the unity between the Christians in the missionary areas and the church in Jerusalem. As a bond of unity it implied obligations for both parts—in that it expressed mutual recognition between the two groups of Christians. Even this caused a problem to the Christian Jews in Jerusalem. When Paul prays that his service may be acceptable to them, this implies nothing less than their acceptance of uncircumcised Christians into their Jewish fellowship. In Paul's view the prophecy of the pilgrimage of all nations to Jerusalem at the end of time was fulfilled when the uncircumcised entered into the church.[46] But this was offensive to many Christian Jews—because it meant that the "nations" had arrived at Zion *before* the Jews! In consequence, when Paul presented the leaders of the church in Jerusalem with his collection, he simultaneously presented them with the problem of their loyalties and their identity. For them to accept the collection meant to choose—socially and theologically—the followship with "mixed" Christian groups in the Diaspora

---

[45] Paul's use of παρακαλῶ shows how important this request was to him, see Bjerkelund, *Parakalo*, 156-59.

[46] Paul here interprets an early Christian application of a theme from the OT (Isa 2:2ff); cf. Hengel, "Mission", 19-21, further Georgi, *Geschichte der Kollekte*, 84-86.

over against the fellowship of law-abiding Jews.[47] This was not only a problem for the church in Jerusalem. A similar conflict developed outside Palestine where small Christian groups came into existence at the periphery of the synagogues. The controversy over table-fellowship in Antioch reflects this (Gal 2). Here extreme Jewish-Christians convinced Peter and other missionaries that their identity as Jews was more important to them than the bond between the Christians themselves.

Against this, Paul put the emphasis upon this bond between Christians, especially through the image of "being in Christ". However, in Romans he speaks much more frequently of "Israel" as well as of "the seed (children) of Abraham". Both terms were much closer to *Jewish* identity than to a specifically Christian one. And it was not Paul's intention to destroy this Jewish identity—any more than he wanted to destroy a traditional understanding of God. Much more, he *interprets* them—both the concept of God and the identity of his people. Paul retains traditional statements about God and about Israel, but he defines them, especially through his use of antitheses. When he says that God's election is steadfast he immediately goes on to characterize it—it is "by grace" only (cf. 9:6-13, 14-18; 11:1-7; 4:16). It is this election "by grace" that represents the *new* identity for Israel and for Christian Jews. The Jews were the people of God only "by grace"—however, this did not negate the fact that God had given his words and his promise to the Jews in the first place.

With his use of "Jews and Greeks" in Romans, Paul wants to include both groups. In Acts, Luke has a similar approach to the question of the mission to the non-Jews. However, he develops a scheme where the Jews constitute the "true" people of God whereas the non-Jews form an "associate" people.[48] Differently from Luke, Paul establishes the unity between the two groups by setting forth a new identity for the Christian Jews—an identity that is based not on the law but on grace. As a result, in Romans Paul does not preach a "Jewish-Christian" gospel—but it is a gospel also for the

---

[47] From Acts 21-26, we know that Paul met with criticism both from Christian and from non-Christian Jews, and that his mission was not accepted by all, see Jervell, "Brief", 67 and *Luke*, 153-83. Faced with the question of conflicting loyalties, Christian Jews did *not* choose the fellowship with non-Jewish Christians; cf. O. Cullmann, "Dissensions within the Early Church", *New Testament Issues* (ed. R. Batey, London, 1970) 119-29.

[48] Jervell, *Luke*, 41-74.

Jews! Paul's extensive use of scripture to support his arguments is related to this main purpose.[49] He brings in quotations from scripture to support his thesis that God had *always* acted "by grace". In consequence, non-Jews had always been included in the promises that God gave to Israel. Although Paul used commonly accepted exegetical methods, his conclusions were unacceptable to most Jews. However, it was not Paul's intention that Christian Jews should reject his reading of their history. Rather, it was his hope that they would be persuaded by it—e.g., so that they would accept as their father Abraham who believed *before* he was circumcised, 4:10-12. Thus, the Jew Abraham could become the father both of Christian Jews and non-Jews; it was possible for both groups to identify with him. With modifications we can probably say the same of Paul's description of the "true" Jew in 2:28-29 as a contrast figure to the "historical" Jew that Paul condemns in 2:17-27.

Conclusions

In this chapter we have combined two groups of texts that turned out to share many similarities. The first group consisted of the passages we discussed in chapter two—discussions or dialogues over the role of Israel and the faithfulness of God in the new situation that was brought about by the Christian mission to the non-Jewish world. Paul based the defence of his position on statements about God. From these statements he drew the inference that Jews and Greeks were in the same position—be it under the wrath of God or under his mercy. Paul was here addressing Christian communities consisting of Jews and non-Jews. Although Paul almost exclusively employed God-language, it was in response to criticism of his missionary preaching about Christ. Hence these texts took us to the centre of Paul's proclamation of his gospel, as it is found in Romans. As a second group of texts we brought in other passages where Paul spoke of "Jews and Greeks", etc. These texts confirmed our hypothesis—they turned out to be among the central expressions of Paul's kerygma in Romans, 1:16-17; 10:11-13; 15:7-9. In most cases "Jews and Greeks" or similar terms occurred as appositions or were added as explanations to "the one(s) who believe(s)".

---

[49] A typical example is the quotation from Hosea in Rom 9:25-27; see below chapter 8 n. 82; see further the discussion of Paul's use of Hab 2:4 (Rom 1:17); Isa 28:16 (10:11); and 59:20; 27:9 (11:26-27) in Ellis, *Paul's Use of the Old Testament*, 119-21; and Lindars, *Apologetic*, 201-3, 244-45.

From this we gathered that Paul saw a direct link between the Christian message and the visible expression it found in a community of believers that encompassed both Jews and non-Jews.

There is a striking but often overlooked similarity between this relationship of theory and practice in Romans and in 1 Corinthians. Paul's main argument in the first chapters of 1 Corinthians is that there is a close connection between the *content* of his preaching and the *forms* through which it is expressed.

These forms are the preaching and the life of the apostle as well as the social composition of the church in Corinth. A gospel that is "the foolishness of God" cannot be proclaimed in wisdom-language, 1 Cor 1:21ff; 2:1ff. Nor can a church that is called into existence through this gospel be a church of the wise and the rich—its members are weak and low and poor. We cannot read 1 Cor 1:26-29 as an accurate description of the social structure of the Christian community in Corinth in the first century.[50] It is rather an idealized description of the founding period that is used as a criticism of the contemporary social structure of the church. In doing this Paul employs a traditional method of criticism.[51] His argument is that if the community received its life from the gospel, this gospel should also influence the organization and structure of that community.

Theology plays a similar part in Paul's letter to the Romans, although in a different historical and religious situation. In 1 Corinthians Paul characterized his gospel as "foolishness" among the weak and the poor, thus using a terminology that reflected the philosophical debate and the social structures in Corinth. In

---

[50] G. Theissen ("Soziale Schichtung in der Korinthischen Gemeinde", *ZNW* 65 (1974) 232-72) emphasizes that although Paul speaks about the social situation from a theological perspective, terms such as τὰ μὴ ὄντα etc. retain their sociological value. According to Theissen the church in Corinth had many members from the middle class. Similarly H. Kreissig, "Zur sozialen Zusammensetzung der früchristlichen Gemeinden im ersten Jahrhundert U. Z.", *Eirene* 6 (1967) 91-100. Against this, W. Wuellner rejects the possibility of drawing sociological conclusions from 1 Cor 1:26-28 in "The Sociological Implications of 1 Corinthians 1:26-28 Reconsidered", *Studia Evangelica* IV (TU 122, 1973) 666-72.

[51] Cf. how the OT prophets held up an idealized picture of the forty years in the wilderness as the founding period of the people. They measured the contemporary Israel against this ideal; e.g. Jer 2:1-3; Hos 2:14-20; Amos 5:25-27. Cf. also the comments by Gager (*Kingdom*, 28) on the description of poverty within early Christian groups in the Gospels: "Thus we are forced to conclude that the ideology of poverty does more than simply mirror social reality. It exaggerates and idealizes this reality".

Romans, the gospel as a proclamation of God's faithfulness finds its form in a church that includes both "Jew and Greek", "circumcised and uncircumcised". If groups among the Christians refuse to admit both Jews and non-Jews on an equal basis, then their very preaching of God is in danger of becoming false witness of him. Then God is rendered unfaithful!

In the introduction we suggested that Bultmann's thesis was inadequate, when he said that "if a man will speak of God, he must evidently speak of himself". From the texts that we have discussed it is more to the point to say that, for Paul, to speak about God is to speak about his people! Paul's use of statements about God is directly related to his defence for a religiously and socially integrated community of Christians. In Paul's interpretation, traditional statements about God were employed to legitimate his missionary practice as well as the Christian churches that resulted from that practice. When these same expressions were turned against Paul's Jewish-Christian opponents, however, they took on a *critical* function. Again, his criticism concerned not only their theories but even more their practice, the way their self-understanding was expressed in religious and social structures. Thus when Paul applies theological statements to a particular situation or structure, it represents in part a sociological description—culled from his own experience with his churches. But in his theological reflection these experiences are generalized and applied to other structures as well. Paul referred to God as the absolute authority behind them and he could therefore claim universal acceptance of them.

As we notice, there are different theories about the historical forces behind the controversy and subsequent schism between church and synagogue. However, there can be no doubt that Paul followed Jewish and early Christian tradition when he interpreted this social and religious conflict as a theological disagreement. More than any other New Testament author (except perhaps for John) he sharpened the polemics by saying that this was a controversy where the understanding of God was at stake. Through his own calling Paul became convinced that God was free to act as he chose and that his acts were expressions of grace. This conviction was the basis for his polemics against the Jews—be they Christian or non-Christian. At the same time his proclamation of God who acted in this way had a *positive* function—to express the identity of the Christian church, for Jewish and non-Jewish Christians alike.

PART TWO

IN DEFENCE OF THE PROMISE OF GOD

Tradition and polemics in Rom 4:13-22

In the first part of this study we looked at Paul's use of general statements about God in Romans. We found that Paul expressed the conflict between Jews and Christians about their identity as a conflict about the understanding of God. Thus the two problems— the identity of the people of God, and faith in God himself—were inextricably linked. Consequently, when the identity of the people was in question, faith in God was inevitably brought into the controversy. In this second part we shall study in more detail Rom 4:13-22, a passage which illustrates this in a special way. We noticed earlier that there is in Romans 4 an unusually large number of statements about God. Moreover, in 4:5, 17, (21), 24-25 they occur in a unique combination with πιστεύω or πίστις. Thus, when Paul speaks of faith in this chapter it is characterized by a God-centred description. As we shall see, this theological character of Romans 4 is most easily recognized in 4:13-22. In this section statements about God are directly associated with the promise to Abraham. In his interpretation of this promise, Paul emphasizes that Abraham was the *father* of many nations. Paul is apparently here facing a situation where the right to the title "children of Abraham" was contested, and in this controversy he refers directly to faith in God.

This particular aspect, which is the key to the function of Romans 4 within the letter as a whole, has been neglected in most studies. The variety of questions addressed to this chapter bears witness to the importance attributed to Romans 4 both within Paul's teaching and for present-day theology.[1] Some of the questions are prompted

---

[1] See some recent studies where the titles indicate the particular interests of the author: U. Luz, *Das Geschichtsverständnis des Paulus*, 168-86; E. Käsemann, "Der Glaube Abrahams in Römer 4", *Paulinische Perspektiven*, (Tübingen, 1969) 140-77; H. Boers, *Theology out of the Ghetto. A New Testament Exegetical Study Concerning Exclusiveness* (Leiden, 1971) 82-104; F. Hahn, "Genesis 15:6 im Neuen Testament", *Probleme biblischer Theologie* 90-107; H.-J. van der Minde, *Schrift und Tradition bei Paulus* (Paderborner theologische Studien 3, Munich, 1976) 68-106; see also n. 2.

by contemporary discussions in systematic theology more than by problems in the text itself. The discussion between G. Klein and U. Wilckens in the 1960s about "salvation history" ("Heilsge-schichte") was a typical example.[2] They discussed whether or not Paul in Romans 4 and Galatians 3 developed a history of salvation. Another approach is more common, focusing upon Paul's description of faith in Romans 4. From this perspective the chapter, in particular 4:17-22, reads as a description of "das Wesen des Glaubens Abrahams".[3] By implication this is often simply identified with "das Wesen des christlichen Glaubens", since Abraham is understood as the prototype for our present day situation. In recent years the implicit dangers in this approach have been exposed most clearly by J. Jeremias in his study "Die Gedankenführung in Röm 4. Zum paulinischen Glaubensverständnis".[4] Jeremias understands this chapter in a psychological and individualistic sense which is far removed from the historical position of Paul's argument.[5] Paul's emphasis on theology, i.e. upon God, in Romans 4

---

[2] U. Wilckens, "Die Rechtfertigung Abrahams nach Römer 4", *Studien zur Theologie der alttestamentlichen Überlieferungen. Festschrift für G. von Rad* (ed. R. Rendtorff and K. Koch, Neukirchen, 1961) 11-27; idem, "Zu Römer 3:21-4:25", *EvT* 24 (1964) 586-610; G. Klein, "Römer IV und die Idee der Heilsgeschichte, *EvT* 23 (1963) 424-47; idem, "Exegetische Probleme in Römer III. 21-IV. 25", *EvT* 24 (1964) 676-83. Cf. also the summary to the debate by E. Goppelt, "Paulus und die Heilsgeschichte: Schlussfolgerungen aus Römer IV und 1 Kor X. 1-13", *NTS* 13 (1966-67) 31-42.

[3] Cf. Hahn, "Genesis 15:6", 103.

[4] *Foi et salut selon S. Paul* (AnBib 42, Rome, 1970) 51-58. Cf. the opening line: "Nirgendwo hat Paulus so präzise gesagt, was er unter "glauben" verstand, wie in Röm 4". Similarly P. Althaus, *Der Brief an die Römer* (NTD 6, 10th revised edition, Göttingen, 1966) 49. But see the criticism of Jeremias by R. Pesch, W. C. van Unnik and others in the discussion following his lecture, *Foi et salut selon S. Paul*, 59-65. It is Rom 4:17-22 in particular which is characterized as a description of faith, cf. e.g. Michel, *Römer* 114; Wilckens, "Rechtfertigung", 125.

[5] See the criticism of this approach by K. Stendahl, "The Apostle Paul and the Introspective Conscience of the West", *HTR* 56 (1963) 198-215; further the rejoinder by E. Käsemann, "Rechtfertigung und Heilsgeschichte im Römerbrief", *Paulinische Perspektiven*, 108-39; see finally, K. Stendahl, *Paul among Jews and Gentiles*. Bultmann (Theologie, 281-82), too, uses Romans 4 (but not 4:17-21, see below, 202) for an existentialist interpretation of faith; see the criticism of his position by E. P. Sanders, *Paul and Palestinian Judaism* (London, 1977) 490-91. This very important study appeared too late to be taken into account for the major parts of this study. However, since I find that some of what I have vaguely seen, Sanders has developed clearly and at great length, I have tried to indicate this in the footnotes, in chapter 8 in particular.

has often gone unnoticed, especially in studies which focus upon the psychological character of faith. However, this neglect has not been total. E. Käsemann, followed by Ch. Müller and P. Stuhlmacher, singled out the designation of God in 4:17 for special attention.[6] This verse is their main proof when they insist that for Paul, justification by faith is an expression of God's activity as creator and as the reviver of the dead. K. Berger and E. Lohse, among others, have protested strongly against this attempt to link justification by faith with creation theology.[7] However, even if we find this aspect of Käsemann's interpretation justified, he and his followers have put too much emphasis upon 4:17, in isolation from its context.[8]

Our own approach is different. We shall draw upon the conclusions from our short study of the designations of God used in Romans 4 and their function in the literary context. Paul's style in Romans is characterized above all by his use of antitheses. They constitute the main mode of argumentation and reveal by their form a pattern of conflict or opposing views which lies under the discourse in chapter 4. Frequently Paul's argument stops here, with the antithesis, but at times he takes the discussion one step further and introduces a statement about God as a warrant for his claim. This is the case in Rom 4:5, 17, 21 and 24 where appellations of God are Paul's last word in the discussion. From these observations of the structure of Romans 4 we now want to proceed to a study of the historical and theological aspects of the argument which Paul carries out in 4:13-22. In consequence, it is within this argumentative situation that the appellation of God in 4:17 must be studied. Studies of Romans 4 have frequently emphasized the questions of "works" and circumcision in the first part of the chapter (vv. 1-12). Paul's arguments and their background in Jewish exegetical rules

---

[6] Käsemann, most recently in *Römer*, 116-17; P. Stuhlmacher, *Gerechtigkeit Gottes bei Paulus* (FRLANT 87, 2nd revised edition, Göttingen, 1966) 227; Ch. Müller, *Gottes Gerechtigkeit und Gottes Volk* (FRLANT 86, Göttingen, 1964) 53, 97-100.

[7] K. Berger, "Abraham in den paulinischen Hauptbriefen", 72 n. 50; E. Lohse, "Die Gerechtigkeit Gottes in der paulinischen Theologie", *Die Einheit des Neuen Testaments* (Göttingen, 1973) 210-27; G. Klein, "Gottes Gerechtigkeit als Thema der neuesten Paulus-Forschung", *VF* 12/2 (1967) 1-11.

[8] See H. H. Schmid, "Schöpfung, Gerechtigkeit und Heil. Schöpfungstheologie als Gesamthorizont biblischer Theologie", *ZTK* 70 (1973) 12-13; cf. further, "Rechtfertigung als Schöpfungsgeschenk", *Rechtfertigung*, 403-14.

in this passage have also been scrutinized.[9] Not surprisingly, most interpreters have focused on Abraham's obedience to the law in their study of Jewish traditions about Abraham. Apart from the interest shown in 4:17, the passage which follows this verse has received less attention. There has been no thorough study undertaken of the background to 4:13-22 and the promise to Abraham. Most commentators only venture general suggestions on the matter.[10] F. Hahn has pointed out that Paul employs traditional material in 4:17b-22.[11] He draws this inference from a comparison with Heb 11:8-19, a passage which shows many similarities with Romans 4, although there is no literary dependence upon Paul. Starting from another presupposition, H.-J. van der Minde comes to a rather different conclusion.[12] He takes up a suggestion by O. Michel that Romans 4 was originally an independent midrash.[13] Purely on internal grounds he establishes a pre-Pauline Christian tradition comprising Rom 4:3, 11a, 12, 13, 16, 17a and 18c. Thus, for 4:17-22, van der Minde agrees with most exegetes, who find in this paragraph Paul's own formulation of the nature of faith.

Whatever traditional material Paul was using, he integrated it into his own argument. Therefore, before studying Paul's adaptation of traditions about Abraham, we shall give an outline of the structure of Romans 4. In order to avoid unnecessary duplication of other studies we shall concentrate upon issues that are of particular concern to us: Paul's emphasis upon God in this chapter; the question of unity in 4:13-22 and of the function of 4:17 within this paragraph. Since the traditions behind Romans 4:13-22 have not been adequately studied, we shall devote a rather long chapter to this question. Was the heavy emphasis upon God in this chapter prefigured already in the traditions which Paul used? Furthermore, we shall ask if the traditions contained in Jewish and early Christian writings support our suggestion concerning the unity of 4:13-22. In chapter 7 of our study we shall raise the question of Paul's

---

[9] J. Jeremias, "Zur Gedankenführung in den Paulinischen Briefen", *Studia Paulina. In honorem J. de Zwaan* (Haarlem, 1953) 149-51; idem, "Paulus als Hillelit", 88-94.

[10] Their interest is primarily focused on Paul's interpretation of the promise of the land as "world" and how this interpretation is prepared in Judaism; cf. e.g. Michel, *Römer*, 121; Cranfield, *Romans*, 239-40; and, with special emphasis on the apocalyptic background, Käsemann, *Römer*, 112-13.

[11] Hahn, "Genesis 15:6", 105 n. 61.

[12] *Schrift*, 78-83.

[13] Michel, *Römer*, 114.

use of the promise motif in Galatians and in other passages in Romans apart from chapter 4. Thereby we hope to establish the function of this motif within Paul's preaching and within the controversies over his missionary practice. In the following chapter we are directly concerned with Paul's interpretation of traditional material in Rom 4:13-22. His interpretation hinges on the traditional statement in 4:17, and it is therefore upon this designation that we shall focus our attention.

CHAPTER FIVE

THE STRUCTURE OF PAUL'S ARGUMENT IN ROMANS 4

In Romans 4, Paul uses a midrashic pattern.[1] When he brings in the Abraham-story to answer questions about the identity of the Christian community, he introduces his answer by means of a quotation from Gen 15:6: 'Επίστευσεν δὲ 'Αβραὰμ τῷ θεῷ, καὶ ἐλογίσθη αὐτῷ εἰς δικαιοσύνην. Throughout the chapter, Paul frequently cites or refers to this verse. He uses it to divide his exposition into smaller units (3-8; 9-12; 13-22; 23-25). In some instances a reference to Gen 15:6 occurs both in the introduction and in the conclusion to a unit, e.g., in the sub-unit 3-5, as well as in 9-11(12) and 23-24(25). In the sub-unit 6-8 the reference to Gen 15:6 in v. 6 represents Paul's interpretation of the quotation from Ps 32:1-2 in vv. 7-8. In 4:13-22 on the other hand, Paul's interpretation by means of Gen 15:6 comes at the end of the passage in v. 22. Paul in part uses direct quotations, in part reformulations or allusions to Gen 15:6. In 4:5, 9, 22 and 23 we find almost direct quotations from parts of the text whereas 4:6, 11 and 24 are examples of a more free use of the verse.

However, the most characteristic feature in Paul's use of Gen 15:6 is his strong concentration upon the second half of the verse ἐλογίσθη αὐτῷ εἰς δικαιοσύνην.[2] Undoubtedly, Paul is always conscious of the first half of the verse also; the two parts belong inseparably together. But it is not accidental that when in 4:6, 11, 22 and 23 Paul sums up the content of each passage, it is by quoting or paraphrasing the second half of Gen 15:6. This cannot be fully explained by the common practice of quoting only a part of the verse, whereby the full context was implied. Rather, Paul's usage must be compared with the contemporary Jewish use of Gen 15:6. Here

---

[1] Cf. P. Borgen, *Bread from Heaven* (NovTSup 10, Leiden, 1965) 47-50. "Midrashic" is here used in a wide meaning, see M. P. Miller, "Midrash", *IDBSup*, 596-97. For the following, cf. H.-W. Heidland, *Die Anrechnung des Glaubens zur Gerechtigkeit* (BWANT 4/18, Stuttgart, 1936) 118-28; K. Kertelge, *"Rechtfertigung" bei Paulus* (NTAbh NT 3, Münster, 1967) 185-95; Hahn, "Genesis 15:6"; J. A. Ziesler, *The Meaning of Righteousness in Paul*. (SNTSMS 20, Cambridge, 1972) 180-85, 195-96.

[2] Kertelge, (*Rechtfertigung*, 189 n. 153) too, notices the frequent use of λογίζομαι in vv. 3, 4, 5, 6, 8, 9, 10, 11, 12, 23, 24.

the emphasis was put upon the first part of the verse: "Abraham believed God", and it was understood as Abraham's faithfulness towards God.[3] In contrast to this Paul's stress on "it was reckoned to him as righteousness" represented a conscious break with Jewish understanding of faith.[4] By repeating Gen 15:6b he underlines that justification is an act of God which is not due to any merit of Abraham's. This is apparent even in those instances where Paul uses only the first part of Gen 15:6. Sometimes he makes additions to the quotation or allusion, most notably in 4:5, 17 and 24. Here the additions contain a description of God in whom Abraham (or the Christians of Paul's time) believed.[5]

4:5 πιστεύοντι δὲ ἐπὶ τὸν δικαιοῦντα τὸν ἀσεβῆ

4:17 ἐπίστευσεν θεοῦ τοῦ ζωοποιοῦντος τοὺς νεκροὺς κτλ.

4:24 τοῖς πιστεύουσιν ἐπὶ τὸν ἐγείραντα Ἰησοῦν τὸν κύριον ἡμῶν ἐκ νεκρῶν

Such definitions of πιστεύω or πίστις are rare when Paul speaks of faith in God.[6] Here they are found three times within one chapter, in the exposition of one single text, Gen 15:6. This is quite exceptional and requires consideration. Moreover, if we also take into account two other examples of predications of God from the immediate context, in 3:26 and 30, it makes the concentration of God-language even more remarkable.

Rom 4:1-8

When Paul introduced Gen 15:6 as his interpretation of the Abraham example in Rom 4:3, he employed the very text which his opponents used to describe Abraham. Paul therefore had to give Gen 15:6 a new interpretation which supported his own argument.[7] It follows that 4:4-5 with its example about labour and wages represents Paul's own exegesis of Gen 15:6. The interpretation in

---

[3] See below, 129.

[4] D. Lührmann, "Pistis im Judentum", ZNW 64 (1973) 37.

[5] In some instances the believers are described, 4:11, 18, 19, in terms which correspond antithetically with those used of God, e.g. in 4:17.

[6] None of the other predications we studied in part I was linked to πίστις/πιστεύω. The absolute use of πιστεύω is more characteristic of Paul: it occurs 12 times in Romans (e.g. 1:16; 3:22; 10:4). πιστεύω with a noun in dative or with a prepositional phrase is found more frequently in other NT writings than in Paul. See Bultmann, "πιστεύω", TWNT 6 (1959) 203.

[7] Cf. Kertelge, Rechtfertigung, 192-93.

these verses hinges upon the meaning of λογίζομαι.[8] Paul's sole
argument against "rewards for work" in 4:4 is simply that they
would not be reckoned as gifts. He presupposes here that it is
inherent in λογίζομαι that it is κατὰ χάριν, describing an act by God.[9]
Similarly, he introduces the antithesis between τῷ ἐργαζομένῳ and
πιστεύοντι without any further explanation; it is regarded as a given
fact.[10] The explanation of λογίζομαι by means of κατὰ χάριν in v. 4
corresponds to the description of the man who believes in v. 5. τῷ
πιστεύοντι is here qualified not through a description of the believer,
but of God: [11] "And to one who does not work but trusts him who
justifies the ungodly (τὸν δικαιοῦντα τὸν ἀσεβῆ), his faith is reckoned
as righteousness". In each case Paul refers to a typical act of God
as his main argument for the interpretation of Gen 15:6. The most
polemical and provocative argument in his controversy with Jews was
this description of God in Rom 4:5, that he justifies the ungodly.[12]

In v. 6 it becomes even more apparent that it was God and his
way of dealing with people that were at the centre of Paul's argument. His introduction to the quotation from Ps 32:1-2 at the same
time serves to interpret it. This verse, too, is based on Gen 15:6b
when Paul says: "So also David pronounces a blessing upon the
man to whom God reckons righteousness apart from works (ὁ θεὸς
λογίζεται δικαιοσύνην χωρὶς ἔργων)". There are two noteworthy
elements here. First, God appears *expressis verbis* as the subject for
λογίζεται. Even if the passive forms in 4:4, 5 implied that God was
the agent, here there can be no doubt that Paul speaks of an act
by God himself. Secondly, this verse sheds more light on Paul's
concept of λογίζομαι when he adds that it is χωρὶς ἔργων. This is an
addition similar to "by grace" in v. 4. Once more the emphasis is
put upon an act of God.[13] This time Paul even speaks in general

---

[8] Heidland, *Anrechnung*, 119-20; Kertelge, *Rechtfertigung*, 189-92, esp.
190 n. 154; Hahn, "Genesis 15:6", 101; but see Cranfield (*Romans*, 230-32),
who emphasizes *faith*.

[9] D. J. Doughty, "The Priority of χάρις. An Investigation of the Theological Language of Paul", *NTS* 19 (1972-73) 165-67.

[10] Käsemann, *Römer*, 104.

[11] Cf. Käsemann, *Römer*, 106; "Paulus muss sagen, wer Gott ist, um den
Glauben zu bestimmen".

[12] Stuhlmacher, *Gerechtigkeit Gottes*, 227; "Röm, 4, 5 ist, gerade weil die
Stelle theologisch spricht, die polemische Mitte der paulinischen Recht-
fertigungslehre". See above, 22, n. 29.

[13] Michel, *Römer*, 118; "In Römer 4:6-8 tritt das schenkende Handeln
Gottes in diesem Zuspruch noch stärker heraus als in Röm 4:3-5".

terms of "man" as the benefactor from God's act—faith or the
believer from the previous verses are not even mentioned. The
citation from Ps 32:1-2, focusing upon forgiveness of sins, also
contains the word λογίζομαι. This was probably the reason why
Paul quotes this particular passage here.[14] It is possible that he
considered Psalm 32 as a whole to be a fitting illustration of the life
of Abraham.[15] However, it is more likely that he took the psalm to
refer to the contemporary situation. In that case we can here see
a link with Rom 3:24-26. In his "dogmatic" passage in 3:21-26
Paul employed an early Christian tradition about the death of
Jesus as expiation for sins to describe how God founded a new
community.[16] In 4:25 Paul repeats this early tradition, this time
using a christological formula. It is the same motif which Paul uses
in 4:7-8.[17] His interpretation in 4:6 stresses that God now gives
forgiveness for sins (regarded as a sign of the people of God) even
to those who are outside the Jewish covenant.

Rom 4:9-12

The central problem in this passage concerns the identity of the
children of Abraham. The section starts with a question which was
prompted by the quotation from Psalm 32: "Is this blessing
pronounced only upon the circumcised, or also upon the uncircumcised?" (4:9). This question is similar to that in 4:1-2; the only
new element is the antithesis between περιτομή and ἀκροβυστία.
Here, too, it is Gen 15:6 (this time in an adapted form) which
provides the answer: "We say that faith was reckoned to Abraham
as righteousness" (4:9b). Again λογίζομαι is the important term.
V. 10 repeats the question from v. 9 and combines it with Gen 15:6b
πῶς οὖν ἐλογίσθη; ἐν περιτομῇ ὄντι ἢ ἐν ἀκροβυστίᾳ. In his answer, Paul
builds on the witness of the biblical texts themselves: the justification of Abraham is recorded in Genesis 15, before his circumcision
in chapter 17. Consequently, Paul can say that Abraham was given

---

[14] This is according to the *gezera sava* rule, the second of the exegetical rules
of the school of Hillel; see J. Jeremias, "Zur Gedankenführung in den
paulinischen Briefen", 149-50.
[15] See the suggestion by A. T. Hanson, *Studies*, 55-58.
[16] P. Stuhlmacher, "Zur neueren Exegese von Röm 3:24-26", *Jesus und
Paulus*, 330-32.
[17] In the light of Rom 3:25; 4:7-8 and 25, notice how frequently Paul
refers to contemporary praxis among Christians (baptism, eucharist) and a
traditional interpretation which stressed the forgiveness of sins through
these acts.

circumcision only as a sign of his righteousness by faith, 4:11a. Now Paul has made his point in a theological interpretation of the life of Abraham. Even if there is no direct predication of God in this passage there is a close parallel between *v.* 10: God reckons the faith of *the uncircumcised* to righteousness, and *v.* 5: God justifies *the ungodly*. However, the goal of Paul's argument is not reached until 4:11b-12 when he draws inferences from his theological interpretation of the life of Abraham to his own time. The connection between the two is established by εἰς τὸ which expresses the divine purpose. The two stages in Abraham's life: that he was reckoned righteousness as uncircumcised (4:10) and afterwards given circumcision as a sign of his righteousness while uncircumcised (4:11a), correspond to the two groups of descendants. This happened in his life in order that (εἰς τό) he should become father of the uncircumcised believers (4:11b), as well as of the circumcised ones, who followed the example of the uncircumcised Abraham (4:12). Between the description of the two groups of descendants Paul inserts another final clause: εἰς τὸ λογισθῆναι αὐτοῖς τὴν δικαιοσύνην. Just as Paul in 4:6 used forgiveness of sins as an example of justification, in 4:11-12, to be children of Abraham is understood in the same way. Thereby the theological importance of the inclusion of Jews and non-Jews into the same community is brought to the centre of attention. In *v.* 12 Paul probably refers to *Christian* Jews—but neither here nor in 4:16 does Paul give an explicit Christian definition of "children of Abraham". In fact, both passages are rather ambiguous. It seems that Paul does not make strict distinctions between Christian and non-Christian Jews.[18]

---

[18] Paul seems to refer to two groups of circumcised in *v.* 12, and only the second group are qualified as believers:

καὶ πατέρα περιτομῆς τοῖς οὐκ ἐκ περιτομῆς μόνον
ἀλλὰ καὶ τοῖς στοιχοῦσιν τοῖς ἴχνεσιν τῆς ἐν ἀκροβυστίᾳ πίστεως
τοῦ πατρὸς ἡμῶν Ἀβραάμ.

The problem is frequently solved by correcting the second τοῖς to αὐτοῖς, so that the antithesis would refer to Christian Jews only. However there is no Mss. evidence for this. Even an interpretation in the light of similar passages, e.g. 2:28-29 and 9:6-13 (Luz, *Geschichtsverständnis*, 175-76; Käsemann, *Römer*, 109-10), does not completely explain away the ambiguity (cf. Minde, *Schrift*, 71-72 n. 15), especially since 4:16 is also ambiguous. It seems best not to exclude the possibility that Paul includes (non-Christian) Jews as well. If he does, it is because he speaks from the perspective of the final eschatological salvation, cf. the final clauses in 4:11-12 and 16; similarly, to 4:16, Klein, "Römer IV", 439.

Rom 4:13-22

In 4:9-12, Paul raised the question of the identity of the children of Abraham and gave his answer by drawing implications from Gen 15:6. Although this passage was linked to the preceding verses by *v.* 9, it was set apart by the discussion of circumcision. The same is true of 4:13-22, which addresses the same question about the children of Abraham, as did 4:9-12, but has as its particular motif *God's promise* to Abraham and to his descendants. Many commentators have failed to recognize the unity of this passage, and have frequently divided it into 4:13-16(17) and 4:17(18)-22.[19] The main reason for this division is the predication of God in 4:17b, which seems to represent a drastic break in Paul's argument. However, 4:17b is not so much a dividing line between two passages as the focusing point of a unit with one coherent theme. In the first place, the suggestion of a division in *v.* 17 breaks up the unity between the two relative clauses in 4:16d-17a and 18.[20] These clauses run parallel; in each of them Paul quotes the promise from Gen 17:5 that Abraham should become the father of many nations. Secondly, ἐπαγγελία or ἐπαγγέλλομαι occur throughout this section (4:13, 14, 16, 20, 21), and are found in this part of chapter 4 only. Thirdly, Pauls' argument comes to an end first with his quotation from Gen 15:6 in 4:22: "That is why his faith 'was reckoned to him as righteousness' ". We noticed earlier as a typical feature of Paul's style in Romans 4 that he brings sections or sub-sections to completion by quoting or alluding to Gen 15:6b (4:6, 11, 24).

The antithesis was an integral part of Paul's discussion in 4:4-6 and 9-12.[21] It is found in 4:13-22 as well; in 4:13 it is introduced as one between νόμος and δικαιοσύνη πίστεως. The argument which follows is similar to that of the preceding passages. The only difference is that the negative argument (why the adherents of the

---

[19] The unity of the passage is emphasized by C. K. Barrett, *A Commentary on the Epistle to the Romans* (London, 1957) 85, 92; P. Althaus, *Römer*, 43-45; Käsemann, *Römer*, 112. The latter part, 4:13-22, cannot easily be subdivided into smaller sections. There is no natural division between 4:16 and 17 (against e.g. A. Nygren, *Commentary on Romans*, (London, 1952) 178-9; Schlatter, *Gottes Gerechtigkeit*, 168; Jeremias, "Röm 4", 55), nor between 4:17 and 18 (Against e.g. Michel, *Römer*, 114; H. W. Schmidt, *Der Brief des Paulus an die Römer* (Theologischer Handkommentar zum Neuen Testament 6, Berlin, 1962) 85; Cranfield (*Romans*, 224-25) who puts the division between 17a and 17b).

[20] Cf. above, 43.

[21] Cf. above, 41-42.

8

law shall not inherit the promise) is worked out in more detail
(4:14-15). The argument for Paul's own thesis (that the believers
are the heirs to the promise) in 4:16 is similar to that in 4:4: in
both instances it is κατὰ χάριν. That the promise should be by grace
and also be secure for all descendants of Abraham (εἰς τὸ εἶναι
βεβαίαν τὴν ἐπαγγελίαν παντὶ τῷ σπέρματι) is the ultimate goal for
Paul's argument. Thus, there is again a correspondence between an
act of God ("by grace" and "guaranteed promise") and the conclusion that it is "for all".[22] This is Paul's theological basis when he
claims that the believing non-Jews should be included with the
Jews (4:16c), and the same is true in 4:17-18. It follows that the
predication of God in 4:17b is not abruptly introducing resurrection
of the dead as a new theme into the discourse. Rather, in its context
it functions as a guarantee for the promise that Abraham should
become the father of many nations. It was "in the presence of
(κατέναντι)" this God that Abraham received his promise, that is,
it was through faith and not through the law.[23] Similarly, in 4:2,
Paul says that if Abraham was justified by works, he had something
to boast about, but then he concludes: "but not before God". In
4:19-21, Paul describes Abraham's reaction to God's promise of
Isaac (Gen 17:17). According to Paul, Abraham believed, but, as
in 4:16, Paul describes this faith by speaking about God: "he gave
glory to God, fully convinced that God was able (δυνατός ἐστιν) to
do what he had promised" (4:20-21).

This verse concludes a passage which as a whole is centred
around the promise of God. The promise is first introduced in *v.* 13,
and in *v.* 16 it is given its fullest description, that it is by grace and
steadfast to all the descendants of Abraham. In 4:17 Paul uses a
predication of God to support his argument that the promise is
both for Jews and for non-Jews. Finally, in *v.* 21 he describes God
as "able to do what he had promised". This credal statement reads
as a conclusion to the story of God's promise to Abraham. It could
be, therefore, that Paul has used here a tradition about the promise
to Abraham, which he has then incorporated into his own structure
with the quotation from Gen 15:6 in *v.* 22. Unlike the previous
passages, in this section Paul does not quote Gen 15:6 until the end.

---

[22] Doughty, "Priority", 167-88.
[23] For the grammatical construction, see Bauer, 833. The New English
Bible translates: "This promise, then, *was valid before God*, the God in whom
he put his faith, the God who makes the dead live etc.".

The citation serves both as Paul's conclusion and as his interpretation of the story. With this citation, Paul interprets God's trustworthiness to his promise to Abraham and to his descendants as an expression of the righteousness of God, similar to the foregiveness of sins in 4:6-8.

Rom 4:23-25

In this concluding section, Paul's application of the Abraham-story reaches its goal. He has argued that it was through an act of God that Abraham was reckoned righteous and that Jews and non-Jews became the children of Abraham. Now he turns directly to his contemporaries. That scripture is written for the present readers (v. 23) is a hermeneutical notion common to Judaism.[24] It is Paul's résumé of what scripture actually said which is significant: ὅτι ἐλογίσθη αὐτῷ. By quoting this part of Gen 15:6, it is the Abraham-story as an *act of God*, so to speak, which Paul brings before his readers. Thus this quotation is an accurate summary of his exposition of Gen 15:6 throughout the chapter. In addition, Paul expounds Gen 15:6a, this time with a Christian predication of God, with a christological formula added to it. They are both known from early Christian tradition. With these formulae Paul refers back to 3:21-26 and also points towards the description of Christian life in chapter 5.[25] Thus the exposition of the life of Abraham is bracketed by references to Paul's own time. Moreover, it was the contemporary situation and the Christian faith that formed the actual starting point for Paul's interpretation.

This sketch of Paul's argument in Romans 4 has shown that it was consistently based on the same theological grounds in the various sections (3-8; 9-12; 13-22; 23-25). Paul referred to Gen 15:6b in the conclusion to every paragraph. Moreover, the use of λογίζομαι from Gen 15:6 implied that this was an act of God himself. Paul's conclusion in each section was warranted by various considerations. First of all, it was bolstered by faith in God expressed in the designations in 4:5, 17, 21 and 24. It was also implied in the term κατὰ χάριν (4:5, 16), describing an act of God. Thirdly, final clauses could also be used as an argument, in so far as they expressed an

---

[24] In Paul see also Rom 15:4; 1 Cor 10:11 (and 2 Cor 3:14), cf. Philo, *Abr* 4 (quoted below, 272, n. 141).

[25] The direct reference to the death and resurrection of Christ links this passage to 3:21-26 and 5:1-11 (cf. 4:25a with 3:21-26, and 4:25b with 5:1).

eschatological goal. Thus, our outline has decisively shown that explicit references to God play an important part in Romans 4. Moreover, there is a high concentration of such motifs in 4:13-22. On internal grounds, we have found that these verses constitute a unit. The main theme of this section is the promise made to Abraham and his faith in it. This is in itself a motif which stresses God's initiative in acting and in this respect it differs somewhat from the former examples Paul referred to, *viz.* the works of Abraham and of his circumcision. In Rom 4:13-22, justification is identical with God's trustworthiness towards his promises and towards his words, as in 3:5. Therefore, Paul's teaching about justification must be seen in the context of his interpretation of scripture, understood as God's promises to Israel and his history with his people.[26]

Consequently, we shall ask to what extent Paul stands within a Jewish exegetical tradition when he speaks of the promise and the acts of God in 4:13-22. It is well known that the expression in 4:17 is part of traditional belief. However, the different answers given by van der Minde and Hahn leave unanswered the question of traditions in Rom 4:13-22 at large. In our next chapter, we shall try to answer these questions by a study of the interpretation of the Old Testament tradition about the promise to Abraham among Paul's contemporaries.

---

[26] Cf. N. A. Dahl, *Studies in Paul*, 105-8.

CHAPTER SIX

GOD AND HIS PROMISE TO ABRAHAM

First century appropriations

In the processes of redaction of the various strata of the Pentateuch, the writers used the material speaking of the promise to Abraham to illuminate the contemporary situation of Israel. As a result, the Pentateuch in its final stage contained material reflecting various political and religious situations. This process of re-interpretation continued in inter-testamental Judaism, with the difference that the biblical tradition about Abraham was now fixed. This meant that there was in scripture a common stock of material to which interpreters in different periods and circumstances could go back.

We shall not try to establish a history of tradition by forcing Jewish material into Paul's "background". Instead we will point out various expressions of this process of re-interpretation in the first century A.D. as various groups and authors grappled with the question of what God's promise meant to them. In Alexandria in the first decades of the century, Philo used the Abraham-figure as a means of strengthening the identity of his fellow Jews. A few years later Paul made the promise a centre for his polemics against other Jews (Christian and non-Christian) when defending the legitimacy of his missionary communities. In the latter part of the century ἐπαγγελία was a central term to Luke and to the author of Hebrews, but now apparently without Paul's strong polemics against other Jews. Finally, the fall of Jerusalem caused many Jews to turn to God's promise again—and to question his faithfulness to them. These questions were reflected in apocalyptic and early Rabbinic writings in the last decades of the first century or at the turn of the second century A.D.

In different ways, these various groups attempted to appropriate the Old Testament narratives of the promise to Abraham. And they were roughly contemporary and almost certainly independent applications of the same material. Nevertheless there is a striking similarity in motifs and in composition between many of these various interpretations. These similarities cannot be fully explained

by the fact that they could all draw upon the same passages from
the Bible. There must have been a broad tradition of interpretation
that could be appropriated in addition. By comparing the Abraham
narrative in its various interpretations we hope to establish a firm
ground to distinguish between traditional material and Paul's
adaptation of it in Rom 4:13-22. Since we are concerned with this
common tradition, it would be arbitrary to divide Jewish interpretations from Christian interpretations, and we shall therefore
discuss them in one chapter. They are more or less contemporary
enterprises; however, except for Philo, they are all later than Paul.
They are included, therefore, because they contain traditions that
are older than the writings themselves. It is only the picture of
Abraham in 1 Clement which shows any influence from a Pauline
theology.

A. *Preparing the way:*
The Old Testament and the earliest interpretations

In the Old Testament there is no Hebrew term equivalent to
ἐπαγγελία.[1] Thus, it is the context and the description of a situation
more than a particular vocabulary that indicate that one particular
text is what we would think of as a "promise". The Old Testament
texts themselves frequently refer to God's *word*, דבר, he *speaks*,
אמר.[2] Another much used expression is *the oath of God*, שבועה, he
has *sworn* to do something, נשבע.[3] When we speak of "promise" it
has only *positive* connotations, whereas דבר and שבע are much more
ambiguous: God's word and his oath could bring both salvation and
punishment, e.g., Num 14:20-35. Consequently, when we use the
term "promise" when speaking of the Old Testament, we must be
aware that we to some extent impose upon this material a category,
and thereby an interpretation, from a later period.

There can be no doubt that God's promise to the fore-fathers
constituted one of the major themes of the Old Testament. It is
not easy, however, to assess its relative importance compared to

---

[1] Schniewind and Friedrich, "ἐπαγγελία", *TWNT* 2 (1935) 575.
[2] In passages ascribed to J, the promises are frequently introduced by
ויאמר יהוה or with the formula וירה (אליו) יהוה, e.g. Gen 28:13; 12:1; 13:14;
H. H. Schmidt, *Der sogenannte Jahwist. Beobachtungen und Fragen zur
Pentateuchforschung* (Zürich, 1976) 146-47.
[3] Niphʿal of שבע, e.g. Gen 22:16; 50:24; Exod 33:1; Num 11:12; Deut
7:8 etc., see H.-G. Link, "Schwören", *Theologisches Begriffslexicon zum NT*
2/2 (1971) 1107.

other motifs.[4] Outside of the Pentateuch, references to the divine promises to the fathers are few and far between. The exodus from Egypt and the giving of the Torah at Mount Sinai were regarded as being of greater consequence than the promise to Abraham. In addition, creation came to play an increasingly important role, especially in post-exilic literature.[5] Even within the Pentateuch itself the function of the promise is not easily defined.[6] This should warn us not to overestimate the importance of "the promise to the fathers". The attempts to the see the promise motif as the link between the Old and the New Testaments are to some extent forced upon the material. Still, it is significant that it is to the idea of the promise that Paul turns when he speaks of the identity of the Christians in discussions with Jews and Jewish Christians.[7] It is not within the scope of this study to outline the historical development of the promise motif throughout the Old Testament. Therefore, we content ourselves to pointing out some aspects of this motif which became influential in inter-testamental Jewish literature.

In the Pentateuch, the promise to Abraham is interpreted in such a way as to relate acts of God in history to the contemporary situation. The tradition of God's promise to Abraham belongs to

---

[4] See W. D. Davies, *The Gospel and the Land* (Berkeley, Calif., 1974) chapter 5, 75-158: "Cautionary considerations".

[5] E.g. Deutero-Isaiah, where the exodus from Egypt is combined with the creation motif in the concept of a new creation, e.g. 41:17-20; 42:14-16; 43:16-21; cf. W. H. Schmidt, *Alttestamentlicher Glaube und seine Umwelt*, 157-64; see further below, 239, n. 34.

[6] Recently a number of studies have called into question the traditional solution to the problem of the Pentateuch. The patriarchal narratives are at the centre of a debate which has focused upon the theology of the Yahwist and the dating of the first redaction of the Pentateuch. This new Pentateuch criticism tends to date the Yahwist to the Deuteronomic period, i.e. in the 7th century B.C. Cf. J. van Seters, *Abraham in History and Tradition* (New Haven, Conn., 1975); and "Confessional Reformulation in the Exilic Period", *Vetus Testamentum* 22 (1972) 448-59; R. Rendtorff, *Das überlieferungs-geschichtliche Problem des Pentateuchs* (BZAW 147, Berlin, 1976); H. H. Schmid, *Jahwist*. Similar viewpoints are found in J. Hoftijzer, *Die Verheissungen an die drei Erzväter* (Leiden, 1956). *Journal for the Study of the OT* 3 (1977) provides a good introduction to this new approach to Pentateuchal criticism, with contributions from i. a. Rendttorff, van Seters and Schmid. However, as the debate is still unresolved, in this short survey we shall follow the more traditional approach represented by C. Westermann and others, see n. 8.

[7] Romans 4; 9:4-13; Galatians 3; 4:21-31.

old strata of material.[8] In fact, some of it may well go back to a
pre-Israelite situation. In a recent study Claus Westermann argues
that it is necessary to distinguish between various promises—of the
land, of a son, of numerous descendants, etc.[9] Among these he
considers the promise of *a son* to be the oldest. Frequently two or
more promises were combined and as time went on, the distinction
between them was blurred. As the promise of *the land* was directly
related to the political position of Israel, this promise took on a
special importance. In *Die Landesverheissung als Eid*, Norbert
Lohfink studies the promise of the land in Gen 15:18. He argues that
Genesis 15 contains the oldest tradition about the promise to
Abraham that has been preserved. As distinct from its later interpretation,[10] this early tradition holds that the promise of God was
unconditionally given. There were no requirements attached to it.
Lohfink underlines this when he argues that כרת יהוה את אברם ברית
in Gen 15:18 does not mean "to make a covenant", as an act
between two parties. Rather, it implies that God swore an oath to
secure his promise to Abraham.[11] The main thrust of Lohfink's
interpretation is indirectly supported by H. E. White in his article
"The Divine Oath in Genesis".[12] White points out that in a number
of passages in Genesis the promise is introduced by the divine self-
presentation, e.g. in 26:24:

> I am the God of Abraham your father; fear not, for I am with
> you and will bless you and multiply your descendants for my
> servant Abraham's sake.

Other examples are Gen 12:6, 7; 28:13-15; 35:9-15. The self-
introduction ("I am the Lord of Abraham, etc.") functions as an
introduction to an oath: "Yahweh seems to give his promissory
oath to man and to name himself as the guarantor of the oath".[13]
These studies point in the same direction—in the earliest tradition

---

[8] C. Westermann, *Verheissungen*; R. E. Clements, *Abraham and David*
(SBT 2/5, London, 1967); N. Lohfink, *Landesverheissung als Eid. Eine
Studie zu Gen 15* (SBS 28, Stuttgart, 1967); see also Davies, *Gospel*, 3-158.

[9] *Verheissungen*, 123-49. The promise of a son in Gen 15:2, 3; 16:11;
18:10, 14 belongs to the oldest stratum of this tradition.

[10] Cf. how the promise is made dependent upon Abraham's obedience,
e.g. Gen 18:19; 22:15; 26:5; see Westermann, *Verheissungen*, 121-22.

[11] *Landesverheissung*, 101-8.

[12] *JBL* 92 (1973) 165-79. But cf. the criticism in Schmid, *Jahwist*, 121-27.

[13] 173. Deut 32:39-40 gives an example of this close affinity between
self-presentation and the divine oath; cf. also Ezek 20:5.

about the divine promise there was a strong emphasis on the promise as an *act of God*. That God guaranteed his promises through an oath meant that they could be trusted. The descendants of Abraham could have recourse to them in periods of distress.

And that was exactly what they did! The various promises concerned Israel's existence as a people and their right to the land of Canaan. Therefore, in periods of religious, social and political conflicts with neighbouring countries the question of the validity of the promises was bound to be raised. The often precarious position of Israel among her neighbours was defended through a theological interpretation of God's promise. Thus, the use of the Abraham-tradition in the Old Testament reflects a need to legitimize Israel's position, to give guarantees and hope when the identity, sometimes even the very existence, of the nation was threatened. Further-more, the promises to Abraham could even be used as support for an expansionist politics—e.g., when Gen 12:1-3 puts great stress on the promise that the nations of the earth would receive blessing for themselves in Abraham.[14] This reflects the political situation under David and Solomon when Israel's borders were stretched out "from the river of Egypt to the great river—the river Euphrates" (Gen 15:18).[15] Similarly, as God's promise to Abraham was regarded as an oath, so was that to David and his descendants, e.g. in Ps 132:11:

> The Lord swore to David a sure oath
> from which he will not turn back:
> "One of the sons of your body
> I will set on your throne . . . "[16]

Here, the notion that it was the oath of Yahweh that was the basis for the relationship between him and Israel came to the fore again. In the exodus-tradition, on the other hand, the main thrust was upon the responsibility of Israel to keep its oath to Yahweh.[17]

---

[14] The same is said of the Davidic king in Ps 72:17, see Clements, *Abraham and David*, 58-59, and J. Schreiner, "Segen für die Völker in der Verheissung an die Väter", *BZ* NF 6 (1962) 1-31.

[15] This description of Israel was probably added in the reigns of David and Solomon; Lohfink, *Landesverheissung*, 115; but see Schmid, *Jahwist*, 125-26. Cf. the use of this motif in Sir 44:21 and IQapGen 21:12-14.

[16] The promise of the land in Gen 15:7 was later referred to as God's *oath*, e.g. Gen 24:7; 26:3: Exod 13:5, 11; 32:13; Num 14:16; Deut 1:8, 34-35, see n. 3. The oath to David in Ps 132:11 is paralleled in 2 Sam 3:9 and Ps 89:3-4, 34-35; see Lohfink, *Landesverheissung*, 108, 113.

[17] Cf. Exod 34:10-16; Josh 24; Judg 2:1-5; Lohfink, *Landesverheissung*, 109-13.

The pre-exilic prophets did not mention the promise to Abraham. This possibly reflects a criticism of the way in which the promise had been linked with the Davidic dynasty and its cult. However, in other circles of the same period the tradition of the promise was preserved—most significantly in Deuteronomy. Again as a reflection of the political situation, Deuteronomy is primarily interested in the promise of *the land*. It is often referred to simply as God's *oath*, that which he had sworn to Abraham, Isaac and Jacob. Since the Sinai covenant was central in the theology of Deuteronomy, the oath to the patriarchs served as a kind of prophetic anticipation of this covenant. On the other hand, the possibility of a *tension* between the oath to the patriarchs and the Sinai covenant is raised: what happens when Israel is unfaithful to the covenant and the people rightly deserve to be punished and expelled from the land? This problem is extensively dealt with by J. Hoftijzer in *Die Verheissungen an die drei Erzväter*. He has a tendency to over-schematize and to create a rigid system where the tension between promise and law ("Verheissung" and "Gesetz") becomes the driving force in the development of Old Testament tradition.[18] However, other scholars have also noticed this tension. When Israel with their sins had broken the covenant, they were no longer entitled to inherit the promised land. This was not only a question that concerned Israel's inheritance. Ultimately, even the trustworthiness of Yahweh became problematic, as Clements points out: "... the probability is raised that the original fulfilment of Yahweh's oath might be brought to nothing. Does this then cancel the divine promise to the patriarch?"[19] This problem is raised succinctly in Deut 4:30-31 and 9:25-29. Both texts are concerned with the sufferings inflicted upon Israel by her enemies—thereby threatening the fulfilment of God's promises to his people. These sufferings, defeats, etc., were interpreted theologically, as a result of Israel's sin. Moreover, unfulfilled promises were also turned against God who was accused of being without power to fulfil them. Thus in Deut 9:28 the author alludes to the polemics from the enemies of Israel:

> lest the land from which thou didst bring us say "Because the Lord was not able to bring them into the land which he promised them, and because he hated them, he has brought them out to slay them in the wilderness."

[18] Less dogmatic, speaking of two covenants instead of promise versus law, is W. Zimmerli, "Sinaibund und Abrahambund", *TZ* 16 (1960) 268-80.
[19] *Abraham and David*, 67.

Against these accusations, Moses, in his intercessary prayers, appeals to God's promise to the patriarchs, which he had fulfilled in the exodus:

Remember thy servants, Abraham, Isaac, and Jacob, do not regard the stubbornness of this people . . . (9:27)

In a parallel text in Exod 32:13, the reference to the patriarchs is explicitly a reference to God's promise to them:

Remember Abraham, Isaac, and Israel, thy servants, to whom thou didst swear by thine own self, and didst say to them, "I will multiply your descendants as the stars of heaven, and all this land that I have promised I will give to your descendants, and they shall inherit it for ever."

Similarly, Deut 4:31 stresses that God is faithful to his oath:

for the Lord your God is a merciful God; he will not fail you or destroy you or forget the covenant with your fathers which he swore to them.

The witness of Deuteronomy is that God's faithfulness is stronger than Israel's sins—and even stronger than the mockery from the nations!

The exile and the post-exilic restoration of Israel represented another challenge to the continuing process of interpreting the promise. Again, it was the very faith in God that was brought into question, as van Seters points out:

"Who is the God of the fathers?" . . . precisely this question was the burning issue of those in exile after 587 B.C. For what hope could the Jews of the exile have in Yahweh as the God of the fathers of the exodus and in the covenant promises made with them, which covenant was now broken (so Jeremiah, Ezekiel, and Deuteronomy)? The answer for them in this situation is that Yahweh is the God of the patriarchs, and all the covenant promises made with them and spelled out so fully by this Pentateuchal source are still valid. Thus to confess Yahweh as the God of the patriarchs is to exercise faith in these promises of restoration.[20]

In the prophets of this period, however, there are not many references to Abraham or the other patriarchs. Also, there is not always

---

[20] "Reformulation", 457.

a clear distinction between the promise to the patriarchs and to the fathers of the exodus. But when the promise is mentioned, it is with an emphasis upon God's oath and the trustworthiness of his promise.[21]

The most extensive re-interpretation of the promise in the early post-exilic period is found in P's account of God's covenant with Abraham in Genesis 17. In pre-exilic times the exodus from Egypt and the covenant at Sinai had been regarded as the most important event in the life of Israel. Now, in a critical period for the people, the group behind P made God's covenant with Abraham the basis for their interpretation of the history of Israel.[22] P describes the covenant as "an everlasting covenant", ברית עולם thereby asserting its permanent validity as well as its unconditional character:

I will establish my covenant with him as an everlasting covenant for his descendants after him (Gen 17:19).[23]

Within this covenant, as P sees it, God's commitment towards Israel is stronger than Israel's disobedience and sin. As was the case in Deuteronomy, God remembers his covenant and his promise and therefore saves his people from complete extinction.

This interpretation in the P-document was indicative of a widespread process of adaptation that apparently had its centre in priestly circles. Similar ideas are found in liturgical texts from post-exilic times, e.g. Ps 105:6-11; Neh 9:7-8; 1 Chr 16:14-18. Here confession of sins is combined with the praise of God, who remembers his covenant, and his words, i.e. his promises, to the patriarchs:

He is mindful of his covenant for ever,
of the word that he commanded,
for a thousand generations,
the covenant which he made with Abraham,
his sworn promise to Isaac,
which he confirmed to Jacob as a statute,
to Israel as an everlasting covenant,
saying, "To you I will give the land of Canaan
as your portion for an inheritance" (Ps 105:8-11).

---

[21] Abraham is mentioned in Isa 41:8; 51:1-2; Ezek 33:24; the promise as an oath occurs in Ezek 20:5-6, 15, 28, 42.

[22] See Clements, *Abraham and David*, 70-78; Zimmerli, "Sinaibund".

[23] This expression is frequently found also in the prophets of the exilic period, cf. Isa 55:3; 61:8; Jer 32:40; Ezek 16:60 etc.

God's faithfulness was regarded as a reason for Israel to be confident; in fact, it was the only reason for confidence. Thus, God's faithfulness to his promise became a guarantee for Israel's election, which was based not upon any merit of Israel but upon God's oath. A late example of this tradition is found in the Benedictus, Luke 1:72-73:

> to perform the mercy promised to our fathers,
> and to remember his holy covenant,
> the oath which he swore to our father Abraham [24]

Through the different strata of the Old Testament tradition, with varying emphasis on the role of Abraham, there were common elements concerning the promise from God. His words were based on *an oath*, and therefore they remained absolutely trustworthy (e.g., Gen 15:18; 22:16; Exod 32:13; Deut 4:31). Other texts characterized his words as an "eternal covenant" (Gen 17:19; Ps 105:11). And God was also said to remember the patriarchs (Deut 9:27), his oath to them (Exod 32:13) or his covenant (Lev 26:42, 45). Thus the emphasis upon *God as the guarantor of his promise* ran through the various texts, as a sub-structure, so to speak.

The collection of scriptures consisting of the Law, the Prophets and the Writings had been more or less established at the very latest by *c.* 200 B.C. This meant that the basis had been laid for future development of the Abraham-tradition. When new material about the life of the patriarch was later added, it took the form of interpretation and application of the biblical material to the contemporary situation. It was in this inter-testamental period that the literary genres *midrash* and *targum* were developed.[25] The promise to Abraham does not figure prominently in the Jewish literature of this period.[26] Abraham is depicted primarily as an example of obedience towards God and to his commandments in the Torah. This emphasis is easily understandable on the background of the political and religious situation in Palestine during the Hellenistic and Roman periods. Different reactions towards increasing foreign

---

[24] Cf. Ps 105:42 (1 Chr 16:15-16); see also Luke 1:54-55. Luke 1:68-75 is probably pre-Lukan, of Jewish origin, see Schürmann, *Lukas* 1, 84-90.

[25] See R. Bloch, "Midrash", *DBSup* 5 (1957) 1263-71.

[26] W. D. Davies, *Gospel*, 107-8; but see further Mayer, "Aspekte der Abrahambildes", and D. J. Harrington, "Abraham Traditions in the Testament of Abraham and in the 'Rewritten Bible' of the Intertestamental Period", *Studies in the Testament of Abraham* (ed. G. W. E. Nickelsburg, SBL Septuagint and Cognate Studies 6, Missoula, Mont., 1976) 165-71.

influence in political and cultural spheres are reflected in Jewish literature. The *Book of Jubilees* is in several ways a forerunner for the kind of piety that was later found in Qumran, and it has a largely negative attitude to non-Jewish influence.[27] Since it follows faithfully the outline of Genesis, as a matter of course it narrates the various promises to Abraham. However, through a number of additions the author's main intention becomes clear—it is to assert the exclusiveness of the Jews and the blessings of the Torah (e.g., 12:2-5; 13:20, 26; 15:26, 31-34; 16:26-27).

In other circles—including religious and political leaders as well— there was a more open attitude towards Greek commerce and culture. This openness was often combined with a desire to retain Jewish identity. The Wisdom of Jesus the Son of Sirach probably represented such views.[28] In the long list of heroes in chapter 44, the description of Abraham draws upon material from Genesis 17 and 22. Thus, the promise appears to be a result of his obedience. But above all we should notice Sirach's openness towards the non-Jewish world here [29]—the quotations from Gen 17:5 and 22:17-18 speak of Abraham as a father for many nations and of the blessings that should come upon the nations (τὰ ἔθνη) through the promise to Abraham:

> Abraham was the great father of a multitude of nations,
> and no one has been found like him in glory;
> he kept the law of the Most High,
> and was taken into covenant with him;
> he established the covenant in his flesh,
> and when he was tested he was found faithful.
> Therefore the Lord assured him by an oath
> that the nations would be blessed through his posterity,
> that he would multiply him like the dust of the earth,
> and exalt his posterity like the stars,
> and cause them to inherit from sea to sea
> and from the River to the ends of the earth (Sir 44:19-21).

In still other groups, partly consisting of people who were economically and politically oppressed, there was a strong resent-

---

[27] Sandmel, "Philo's Place", 159-70.

[28] Th. Middendorp, *Die Stellung Jesu ben Siras zwischen Judentum und Hellenismus* (Leiden, 1973) 162-64.

[29] Middendorp, *Die Stellung Jesu ben Siras*, 164-66; similarly the promise to Isaac in Sir LXX 44:23 see Middendorf, 55-56.

ment towards foreign dominance as well as towards the Jewish
political and religious establishment. The Maccabean uprising was
characterized by its insistence upon a strict observance of the
Torah.[30] It was required since the identity of Israel was made
visible in the observance of the Torah. The description of Abraham
in 1 Macc 2:52:

Ἀβραὰμ οὐχὶ ἐν πειρασμῷ εὑρέθη πιστός,
καὶ ἐλογίσθη αὐτῷ εἰς δικαιοσύνην;

fits very well this radical pattern for Jewish life that was set by
Mattathias in his exhortation to his sons in 2:50:

Now, my children, show zeal for the law, and give your lives for
the covenant of our fathers.

In 1 Macc 2:52, Abraham becomes an ideal for a national and
religious resistance movement. In other circumstances he was
associated with the fate of Jewish martyrs, most notably in 4
Maccabees, a homily probably from Egypt in the first century A.D.[31]
The seven brothers and their mother are described as "sons of
Abraham" and "a daughter of Abraham", and they are brought to
suffer because of their obedience to the Torah.[32] They hope to
share the eternal life of Abraham, Isaac and Jacob, who already
live to God. In the idea of the resurrection of the righteous it is
implicit that they shall be together with the patriarchs, without
whom Israel would be incomplete.[33]

Abraham is mentioned in two documents that are frequently
identified with the Qumran community. The first is the Damascus
document where Abraham is described as obedient to the law:

Through it, the children of Noah went astray, together with their
kin, and were cut off.
Abraham did not walk in it, and he was accounted friend of God
because he kept the commandments of God and did not choose
his own will (CD 3:1-3).[34]

---

[30] Cf. E. Bickermann, *Der Gott der Makkabäer* (Berlin, 1937).

[31] See J. C. H. Lebram, "Die literarische Form des Vierten Makkabäer-
buches", *Vigiliae Christianae* 28 (1974) 81-96.

[32] E.g., 6:17, 23; 7:20; 13:17; 18:23.

[33] For this concept in 4 Macc and in other Jewish literature, see G. W. E.
Nickelsburg, *Resurrection, Immortality and Eternal Life in Intertestamental
Judaism* (Harvard Theological Studies 26, Cambridge, Mass., 1972) 34-35,
109-11, 141-42.

[34] Abraham is mentioned in passing in CD 12:11 (his covenant) and in
16:6 (his circumcision).

The children of Noah and Abraham are here used by the author as examples in the conflict between the Essenes and the Jewish religious establishment of his own time, as it is expressed in CD 3:10-21. It was "with the remnant which held fast to the commandments of God, He made His Covenant with Israel for ever, revealing to them the hidden things in which all Israel had gone astray." (3:12-13)

The *Genesis Apocryphon* from Qumran Cave I is based on Genesis, but with haggadic additions.[35] Although it is often referred to as a Qumran document, J. Fitzmyer finds but scant traces of specific Qumran teachings in it. In fact, he considers it impossible to distinguish any particular exegetical or theological interest in the composition of the work.[36] However, there is one text that reveals a strong interest in the promise of the *land*, I *QapGen* 21:8-14;

8. God appeared to me in a vision of the night and *said to me,* "Go up to Ramath-Hazor, which is to the north of

9. Bethel, *the place where you are* dwelling; *lift up your eyes and look to the east, west, south and north* (Gen 13:14) and see *all*

10. this *land which I am giving to you and to your descendants forever"* (Gen 13:15). The next day I climbed up to Ramath-Hazor and I looked at the land from

11. this height, from the River of Egypt to Lebanon and Senir, and from the Great Sea to Hauran, and all the land of Gebal as far as Kadesh, and at all the Great Desert

12. which is (to the) east of Hauran and Senir as far as the Euphrates. And he said to me, "To your descendants I shall give all this land; they will inherit it forever.

13. *I shall make your descendants* as numerous *as the dust of the earth which no man can number; so too your descendants will be without number.* (Gen 13:16) *Rise, walk about,* and go (around)

14. to see how great is *its length* and how great is *its width. For I shall give it to you* (Gen 13:17) and to your descendants after you for all ages."

Through the repetition of "to you and *your descendants after you*" the author takes care to relate this promise to his own times. The

   [35] See G. Vermes, *Scripture and Tradition in Judaism* (SPB 4, Leiden, 1961) 96-126.

   [36] *The Genesis Apocryphon of Qumran Cave* I (Biblica et Orientalia 18, Rome, 1966) 11-12.

description of the land may well have eschatological overtones pointing to the tradition about Eden with the four rivers of Paradise.[37]

The description of Abraham in I Macc 2:52 (similarly Sir 44:20); ἐν πειρασμῷ εὑρέθη πιστός, represents an interpretation of Gen 15:6: ἐπίστευσεν 'Αβραὰμ τῷ θεῷ. Here Gen 15:6 is combined, not with the promise in Gen 15:5, but with his faithfulness when God tested his obedience, in particular in Genesis 22.[38] This was also a very common conception in the first century A.D. It is found in James 2 and it is mirrored in Paul's polemics in Galatians 3 and 4 as well as in Romans 4. However, a reconstruction from polemics in the New Testament may easily result in a one-sided and largely negative description. In the first place, the *promise* to Abraham had not completely been forgotten—although it did not occupy a place of prime importance.[39] Furthermore, Abraham as an example of obedience needs to be seen within the larger picture of the function of the Torah in Judaism.[40] The casuistry of the Pharisees was more "down to earth", whereas apocalyptic groups tended to push the demands towards the impossible. However, both groups were concerned with the salvation not only of the individual but of Israel as a whole. In apocalyptic circles, rigorous demands to keep the commandments of the Torah represented a revolutionary projection of a new world order, expressing strong criticism of the laxity of the time. The Pharisaic criticism was less severe, but it shared the basic assumption that Israel's observance of the Torah would bring about the Messianic age—and thereby the ultimate fulfilment of all promises. In evaluating the Jewish picture of Abraham we should always bear in mind the needs which arose from the practical situation. A reconstruction of the history of Abraham was always brought to bear upon the contemporary situation of a community, be it Jewish or Christian.

---

[37] R. de Langhe, "La terre promise et le paradis d'après l'Apocryphe de la Genèse", *Scrinium Lovaniense. Mélanges historiques, Etienne van Cauwenbergh* (Univ. de Louvain, Receuil de travaux d'histoire et de philologie, 4/24, Louvain, 1961) 126-35.

[38] F. Hahn, "Genesis 15:6", 94-98. For the Akedah tradition see G. Vermes, *Scripture and Tradition in Judaism*, 193-227; R. Le Déaut, *La nuit pascale* (AnBib 22, Rome, 1963); and most recently, R. J. Daly, "The Soteriological Significance of the Sacrifice of Isaac", *CBQ* 39 (1977) 45-75.

[39] In addition to the texts already mentioned, see also I Macc 4:10; 2 Macc 1:2; *Pss. Sol.* 9:9; *As. Mos.* 3:9; *T. Levi* 15:4.

[40] For a short but useful summary, see Maier, *Geschichte*, 20-23.

B. *Philo and the promise to Abraham—encountering Greek Alexandria*

1. *Philo in Alexandrian Judaism*

As the first proselyte and one who even became the ancestor of the Jews, Abraham was a popular figure in Jewish preaching as well as in missionary propaganda to Non-Jews (in the Diaspora) in the first century.[41] It is only to be expected that he should play an important role in the works of Philo also, particularly since most of his writings are commentaries on various chapters of Genesis.[42] Abraham was both the ancestor and an example for all Jews. A description of him therefore expressed the author's ideas about Jewish identity and ethos. All interpreters made the Genesis narrative their starting point, but they expressed their own views partly by adding new material and partly by their selection of material from the Biblical text. Whereas, for example, the Palestinian Targums paid great attention to texts dealing with covenant and circumcision, Philo hardly mentioned these topics. Thus, Philo did not stress the distinction between Jews and non-Jews so much as the Palestinian Targums. However, this difference is partly due to varying attitudes towards mission to non-Jews: to Jews in Palestine this was not such an urgent issue as in the Diaspora.[43]

In Philo's exposition, two events in Abraham's life were more important that others. The first was his departure from Mesopotamia to go to Canaan (Genesis 11-12), the other occurred when God changed his name from Abram to Abraham (Genesis 17). Philo frequently comes back to these events both in his commentaries on

---

[41] See D. Georgi, *Gegner*, 63-82; W. L. Knox, "Abraham and the Quest for God", *HTR* 28 (1935) 55-60; L. H. Feldman, "Abraham the Greek Philosopher in Josephus", *Transactions and Proceedings of the American Philological Association* 99 (1968) 143-56.

[42] Philo deals with the Abraham narrative in *Migr.*, *Heres.*, *Mut.*, *Abr.*, *Quaes. Gen.*, and to some extent also in *Congr.* and *Fuga.* The major study of Philo's use of the Abraham tradition is S. Sandmel, "Philo's Place in Judaism: a Study of Conceptions of Abraham in Jewish Literature", *HUCA* 25 (1954) 209-37, and 26 (1955) 151-332, reprinted, N.Y. 1971 (this edition referred to in parenthesis); cf. further his "Abraham's knowledge of the Existence of God", *HTR* 44 (1951) 137-39.

[43] Cf. Knox, "Abraham and the Quest for God", 59-60. The covenant may have been more important to Philo than is generally recognized, cf. A. Jaubert, *La notion d'alliance dans le judaïsme aux abords de l'ère chrétienne* (Patristica Sorbonensia 6, Paris, 1963) 414-37; however, he interpreted it within his own theological system; see E. P. Sanders, "The Covenant as a Soteriological Category and the Nature of Salvation in Palestinian and Hellenistic Judaism", *Jews, Greeks and Christians*, 25-38.

Genesis 12 and 17, and in other books where they occur as independent motifs.[44] Moreover, Philo's narrative at this point follows the same structure both in the more literal interpretation in the Expositions, intended perhaps for non-Jews, and the allegorical treatises that were written more specifically for Jews.[45] To Philo, Abraham's departure from Mesopotamia and his change of name were, in a deeper sense, expressions of a corresponding change in his life. Allegorically, Abraham's migration symbolized the journey of the soul towards God.[46] Similarly, the change of name was a confirmation of what had happened in the migration. The allegorical meaning of the change was a transition from trust in the created world to trust in God, the creator himself.

Compared with the Old Testament, Philo's allegories spiritualized the texts and almost neglected their historical value. However, this allegorical interpretation addressed the contemporary scene much more directly than any historical exposition could have done. Philo's admonition to distrust the created world and trust in God alone amounted to a rejection of Hellenistic and Egyptian mythology. This rejection had not only a polemical function, but also a paraenetic function. Philo told the Abraham story in order that his readers should follow the example of Abraham.[47] If his migration and change of name symbolized the journey of the soul and a change in character, these were events that were not bound to history, but could happen at any time. With his exhortations Philo addressed his fellow Jews as well as Alexandrian Hellenes who showed interest in Jewish religion. Therefore his use of the Abraham story gives us information about Philo's understanding of the relationship between the Jews and their non-Jewish neighbours in Alexandria.

In *Virt.* 175-86, a treatise on conversion, Philo describes the spiritual journey of proselytes in terms similar to those used of Abraham. This chapter is characterized by a reconciliatory attitude towards proselytes and God-fearers.[48] A little later in the same book

---

[44] On Abraham's migration, see *Migr.* 1-35; *Abr.* 60-88; *Leg. All.* III 83-84; *Heres.* 98-99. On his change of name, see in particular *Mut.* 60-76 (129); *Cher.* 4-8; *Gig.* 62-65; *Quaes. Gen.* III 43.

[45] Sandmel, "Philo's Place", 228 (107), but see Georgi, *Gegner*, 79-80 n. 1.

[46] A typical example is *Abr.* 68.

[47] See *Abr.* 4, cf. Sandmel, "Philo's Place", 318 (197).

[48] Similarly chapters 187-227; also *Spec. Leg.* I 51-52. The missionary intention behind these passages is emphasized by Jaubert, *Alliance*, 388-90.

Philo once more stresses the close contact between the proselytes and Abraham when he says that the patriarch was a "canon of the proselytes" (οὗτος ἅπασιν ἐπηλύταις εὐγενείας ἐστι κανών (*Virt.* 219)). But Philo has spiritualized even the term ἐπηλύτης so that he could in fact use it also of Jews.[49]

Despite this positive attitude towards proselytes, Philo rarely speaks of a mission to the nations outside of Israel. He seldom elaborates on passages from Genesis where the blessings on the nations were part of the promise to Abraham.[50] Moreover, he pays scant attention to the promise of a great posterity. When he does comment upon this promise, it is with an allegorical interpretation. In *Heres.* 277-79 Philo discusses the promise in Gen 12:2, that God would make Abraham the father of a great nation. Philo follows traditional exegesis in ascribing this promise to Israel, but then he goes on to allegorize it. Israel is the new race "which observes and contemplates all the things of nature", i.e. the nation that sees God.[51] However, Philo's allegorization is based on the existence of a Jewish community that considered itself to be the promised nation. When Philo spiritualized this promise it represented an interpretation of the empirical Israel, a religious ideal which he set for his fellow Jews.[52] We find an example of this in the exposition of the promise in Gen 15:5: "Look toward heaven, and number the stars, if you are able to number them. Then he said to him, 'So shall your descendants be' ". Philo does not here identify the large number of Jews spread out over the world of his time as the proof that the promise had been fulfilled. Instead he starts with the observation that the promise did not say τοσοῦτον, i.e. "so many", but οὕτως, i.e. "so, such as". Consequently the promise was not concerned with the numbers of believers, rather, it intended "to picture the soul of the Sage as the counterpart of heaven", (*Heres.* 88).[53] Another example may be found in the *De Mutatione Nominum*, a

---

[49] K. G. Kuhn, "προσήλυτος", *TWNT* 6 (1959) 732.

[50] But see *Migr.* 118-24 on Gen 12:3.

[51] This is based upon Hebrew etymology, see the discussion in Jaubert, *Alliance*, 411-12. This is another favourite theme in Philo's writings, see e.g. *Leg. All.* II 34; *Plant.* 58-60; *Abr.* 57; *Quod Deus* 144.

[52] Cf. M. Harl, *Philon d'Alexandrie, Quis rerum divinarum heres sit* (Oeuvres 15, Paris, 1966) 16-17. Hereafter referred to as Harl, *Oeuvres* 15. Other vols. of this edition are referred to in the same way.

[53] This is a stoic ideal, see Harl, *Oeuvres* 15, 95-97; cf. Philo's interpretation of Gen 15:5 in *Leg. All.* III 39-41, where he omits "so shall your descendants be".

verse-by-verse commentary on Genesis 17. We shall concentrate on Philo's exposition of Gen 17:4-5, God's promise to Abraham:

4a. Behold, my covenant is with you,
  b. and you shall be the father of a multitude of nations.
5a. No longer shall your name be Abram, but your name shall be Abraham,
  b. for I have made you the father of a multitude of nations.

In his comments upon this passage, Philo omits both *vv.* 4b and 5b, concerning the promise that Abraham should be the father of many nations.[54] Instead he links *v.* 4a: "my covenant is with you" directly to *v.* 5a: "Your name shall be Abraham", and in his exposition focuses upon the importance of the change of name.

This almost existentialist understanding of the promise, directly relating it to Philo's own time, is apparent also in Philo's exposition of Genesis 15, *Quis Rerum Divinarum Heres.* Already the first paragraph illustrates this when Philo asks: τίς ὁ τῶν θείων πραγμάτων κληρονόμος ἐστίν; (*Heres.* 1). The promise of *descendants* and of *land* in Gen 15:5 and 7 have in Philo's allegory become τὰ θεία πράγματα, i.e. wisdom and knowledge of God (*Heres.* 98, 101).[55] The fulfilment of the promise of land and descendants is described in terms similar to those used of Abraham's migration. Philo urges his readers to turn from the created world to the creator, to ascend from the material sphere to the immaterial. Thus in Philo's interpretation of the two narratives there is, so to speak, a common sub-structure. Philo found the exegetical basis for this identification of the two in Gen 15:7, where the migration from Mesopotamia and the promise of the land are mentioned in the same passage (*Heres.* 96-99).

Not only the promise of the land but also the promise of a son, Isaac, was explained within the same outline. In the case of this last promise Philo takes as his point of departure the meaning of Isaac in Hebrew, where יִצְחָק comes from the same root as "joy, laughter". Consequently Isaac symbolizes the joyful, ecstatic experience of God where man enjoys the *unio mystica.* Whenever "laughter" is mentioned with reference to the birth of Isaac, Philo ascribes this

---

[54] *Mut.* 57-60. However, Philo includes Gen 17:4b in *Quaes. Gen.* III 42.
[55] Similarly in the short comment upon the promise of the land in Gen 15:8 in *Heres.* 313-16. On Philo's interpretation of "the land", see Davies, *Gospel,* 120-23.

allegorical meaning to it.[56] In fact, Philo interprets *every* incident in the life of Abraham according to this same pattern. Be it Abraham's migration, his change of name, or the promise and subsequent birth of Isaac—Philo's message is the same: Abraham, i.e. the true believer, turns away from this material world towards God, in order to share his "joy" and "good things".

From these samples we get the impression that Philo used the authority of the Abraham figure to legitimate his own theology and preaching. At times his interpretation was controversial, and he had to face objections that were raised against his picture of Abraham: was there really any reason to praise Abraham for his faith more than anyone else (*Heres.* 90)? Further, what was the significance of adding only one letter to the name of the patriarch? (*Mut.* 60-62; *Quaes Gen.* III 43). Finally, if Abraham was an exemplary believer, why did scripture record that he doubted? (*Mut.* 181). Philo employs the same method in countering these various objections. He measures them against his theology in its narrower sense, i.e., his understanding of God. Those who said that there was nothing special about Abraham's faith revealed that they had never grasped how difficult it was to trust in God alone and in nothing else, (*Heres.* 90-93).[57] In the same manner also those who ridiculed the one-letter change from Ἀβράμ to Ἀβραάμ were actually mocking God. They had failed to see the allegorical meaning of that change (*Mut.* 61-65). Philo's argument in *Mut.* 181 runs along similar lines: it amounts to blasphemy to suggest that Abraham, who was after all only a man, could be completely without doubt. That would be to make him like God himself! [58] In every instance Philo countered his opponents on the grounds that their objections represented a distorted theology in which they did not properly distinguish between God and man, between faith in God and faith in the created world.[59] In other words, their theology blurred the distinc-

---

[56] The source for this interpretation was Gen 21:6: "And Sarah said, 'God has made laughter for me' ". Philo also applies it to Gen 17:17; 18:13 (the three texts are combined in *Leg. All.* III 217-19), etc. As a result, this is one of the most frequently recurring themes in his treatises, see Sandmel, "Philo's Place", 294-97 (173-76); further H. Lewy, *Sobria ebrietas. Untersuchungen zur Geschichte der antiken Mystik*, (BZNW 9, Giessen, 1929) 34-41.

[57] Philo employs the term μόνος θεός, see Harl, *Oeuvres* 15, 30-31; and Delling, "Μόνος θεός", *TLZ* 77 (1952) 469-76.

[58] See below, 162-63.

[59] Similar discussions are found in *Abr.* 177-99; *Somn.* I 92-94; *Quod Deus* 20-32; see H. A. Wolfson, *Philo* I (Cambridge, Mass., 1948) 59.

tion between Jewish faith on the one hand and Hellenistic and Egyptian religion on the other.

Does this use of the Abraham tradition help us to answer the question of Philo's place within Judaism of his time? On this issue there is still no consensus.[60] On the one hand, his interpretation is couched in terms taken from Hellenistic philosophy. The general tendency of his works has even been described as gnostic. On the other hand, Philo shows close knowledge of Jewish traditions of interpretation and frequently expounds Biblical passages verse-by-verse in true Rabbinic fashion. From the point of view of a history of ideas, this makes it difficult to classify Philo. Even if one should reach a definite conclusion along these lines, the scope of such a study may be too narrowly defined, if it does not also include the *historical* setting. This is to some extent true, for instance, of Samuel Sandmel's thorough study, "Philo's Place in Judaism", in which he investigates the interpretation of the Abraham narrative in Philo. Sandmel is able to show in detail how Philo is influenced by Greek language and philosophy. He finds only the most superficial similarity with Rabbinic Judaism—and that can easily be explained on the basis of their common source in Scripture. It is Sandmel's final verdict that Philo represents such a complete Hellenization of Jewish faith as to be "a marginal, aberrative version of Judaism".[61] Since Sandmel's work was published in 1955 several studies have shown conclusively that there was no clear division between "Palestinian" or "Rabbinic Judaism" on the one hand and

---

[60] For this discussion see H. Thyen, "Die Probleme der neueren Philo-Forschung", *TRu* 23 (1955) 230-46; more recently the excellent survey by R. Arnaldez, "Introduction générale", *Oeuvres* 1 (1961) 17-112; as well as R. Arnaldez et al., "Philon d'Alexandrie", *DBSup* 7 (1966) 1288-1351; cf. also the conference by the French Philo project. *Philon d'Alexandrie. Lyon 11-15 Septembre 1966* (Paris, 1967).

R. G. Hamerton-Kelly ("Sources and Traditions in Philo Judaeus", *SP* 1 (1972) 3-26, summarizes the results from earlier efforts by W. Bousset, I. Heinemann, E. R. Goodenough, et al. to identify traditions, especially philosophical ones, in Philo, and proposes methods for such a study of traditional material. The arguments for a connection between Philo and a (Hellenistic) Jewish Gnosticism, advanced particularly by Goodenough and H. Jonas, have become more widely accepted in recent years; see B. A. Pearson, "Friedländer revisited. Alexandrian Judaism and Gnostic Origins", *SP* 2 (1973) 23-39. Philo's knowledge of Rabbinic tradition is still discussed, but the earlier absolute positions on one side or the other can now be said to belong to the past, cf. the balanced discussions by R. Cadiou and J. E. Menard in "Philon d'Alexandrie", *DBSup* 7, 1290-1304.

[61] This is Sandmel's conclusion in "Philo's Place", 332 (211).

"Hellenistic Judaism" on the other.[62] Moreover, Sandmel judges Philo from the point of view of a "normative" Jewish theology and history of religious ideas. To a large extent he disregards the relationship between Philo's works and a specific historical situation. This last point deserves more attention than the bare outline we can indicate here.[63] The historical setting for Philo's works was Alexandria in the first century A.D., and Philo was above all a preacher and interpreter of sacred history for his own community.[64] Even his apologetic and missionary treatises must be understood from this perspective.[65] What Philo said about Abraham in these writings was intended for Greeks who had had at least some contact with the synagogue and some sympathy for Jewish religion. Philo's polemics against Hellenistic and Egyptian religion and philosophy could have only a negligible or even an adverse effect upon critics and adversaries of the Jews. It is unlikely that his treatises would be widely spread outside Jewish circles. His exhortations could have had a positive influence only upon someone who was already sympathetic to Jewish religion. Philo's presentation of Abraham might induce them to sever the remaining links with their old religion and turn decisively to the Jewish faith. This is similar to the effect it would have had upon *Jewish* readers as well! Philo's polemic against Hellenistic philosophy was, more than anything, a warning to his fellow Jews in Alexandria not to follow Greek and

---

[62] Especially Hengel, *Judentum*; see the conclusion, 453-63.

[63] See the important article by A. V. Tcherikover, "Jewish Apologetic Literature Reconsidered", *Symbolae Raphaeli Taubenschlag dedicatae* 3 (EOS. Commentarii Societatis Philol. Polonorum 48/3 1956, Warsaw, 1957) 169-93. Here he criticizes traditional scholarship for almost exclusive concentration on theological ideas. However, the interaction between ideology and social and political history has not been completely neglected; see especially E. R. Goodenough, *The Jurisprudence of the courts in Egypt* (New Haven, Conn., 1929), and *The Politics of Philo Judaeus* (New Haven, Conn., 1938). Further M. Pohlenz, *Philo von Alexandreia* (Nachrichten der Akademie der Wissenschaften zu Göttingen, Hist.-Phil. Kl. 1942) 409-88; more recently, P. Borgen, *Bread from Heaven*. Arnaldez (*Oeuvres* 1, 22-43) gives a balanced discussion of this interest in the relationship between philosophy and practice in Philo. On the historical situation of the Jews in Alexandria at the time of Philo, see V. A. Tcherikover, "Prolegomena" in his edition of *Corpus Papyrorum Judaicarum* 1 (Cambridge, Mass., 1957) 1-111; cf. further the article by him cited in n. 67.

[64] This is stressed especially within French Philonic studies, see Arnaldez, *Oeuvres* 1, 22-43; cf. further H. Thyen, *Der Stil der jüdisch-hellenistischen Homilie* (FRLANT 65, Göttingen, 1955) 7-11.

[65] For the following, see in particular Tcherikover, "Literature".

Egyptian mythology. This was not a matter of religion only—the identity of the Jewish community as a social and political entity was at stake. When Greek religion was made to look inferior to the Jewish, the Jews' confidence in their own religion and in their commitment to their own social group was strengthened. Thus Philo's polemics served an important political purpose.

Philo himself belonged to a small group of rich, well-educated Jews with contacts in the Greek establishment. Therefore he knew the temptations that the Greek city held for the Jews on the upward move well. Even so, the Jews had to resist these temptations, as Philo said in his comment upon Gen 21:12:

> And if he (Abraham), filled with gratitude towards the education by means of which he was brought into union with virtue, thinks it harsh to reject it, he shall be brought to compliance by an oracle of God: "In all that Sarah saith to thee, listen to her voice" (*Leg. All.* III 245).

In this passage Philo contrasts the teaching of the encyclica (represented by Hagar), with true wisdom and virtue (Sarah). He recognizes the value of the encyclical education, but only as one step towards that full wisdom and insight which are found only in Jewish religion. Peder Borgen points out that this discussion was directly related to the relationship between Jews and Greeks in Alexandria at the time of Philo.[66] One of the burning issues was the question of education. If Jewish youths were allowed into Greek schools, it ensured that they would be accepted into the Greek society of Alexandria at large. Thus this discussion of "encyclical education" versus "virtue" in *Leg. All.* III 245 concerned vital social and political questions. For the individual Jew who managed to slip into Greek society, many opportunities were open. However, the relationship between the large Jewish community as a whole and the Greek (and Egyptian) city became increasingly uneasy during Philo's lifetime, with mounting tensions between them.[67] The main issue was that of civil rights for the Jews. They were organized as a separate group with substantial rights, but desired to become citizens of the Greek city—a move which the Alexandrians strongly resented.

---

[66] *Bread from Heaven*, 108-11, 124-27.

[67] See V. A. Tcherikover, "The Decline of the Jewish Diaspora in Egypt in the Roman Period", *Journal of Jewish Studies*, 14 (1963) 1-32.

Philo gives a telling description of this in his *Ad Flaccum* and *Legatio ad Gaium*.[68] In *Gaium*, we find Philo cast in a political role as a respected leader in the Jewish community in Alexandria. Together with other Jewish leaders, he went on an embassy to the Emperor Caligula in Rome to argue the Jewish case against the Greeks after the riots against the Jews in Alexandria in A.D. 38. The *Legatio ad Gaium* is the most political of Philo's books, but even so, it has as its introduction a theological treatise (1-7). In this introduction Philo describes Israel as the nation "who sees God". A little later he calls them "the race of suppliants"—who therefore are under God's πρόνοια, his providential care. What is the function of this theological passage within the treatise as a whole? W. A. Meeks suggests that *Gaium* 1-7 actually prepares the ground for the criticism of Caligula later in the book.[69] In *Gaium* 75 and 114-19, we hear that Caligula claimed to be God and that he usurped all justice, making himself the fount of law. According to Philo the Jews were the only ones to protest against this, and therefore they were persecuted. The description of the Jews in *Gaium* 1-7 justified their stand—a people "who sees God", who had the true knowledge of the creator, could not bow to the claim of a mere man to be divine. Thus Philo's theology had clear political implications here as well.

This was likewise the case when he used Moses as an example or commented on other texts from Exodus relating to the Israelites in Egypt. These texts were easily applicable to the situation of the Alexandrian Jews of his time. Again the apologetic and paraenetic go together. If the narratives from Exodus were a veiled chastisement of the opponents of the Jews in Alexandria, the description of Moses directed the Jews to the Torah as the norm for their life.[70] Together with other Jews, Philo shared the conviction that the Torah formed the basis for Jewish life. Sometimes Philo's stand on this issue appears to be hidden in his mysticism. In his allegorical interpretation the historical Israel all but disappears, and Philo seems to speak only of the individual soul, on its spiritual journey

---

[68] Edited, with comments, by E. M. Smallwood, *Philonis Alexandrini Legatio ad Gaium* (Hereafter referred to as Smallwood, *Gaium*, Leiden, 1961).

[69] "The Divine Agent and his counterfeit in Philo and the Fourth Gospel", *Aspects of Religious Propaganda in Judaism and Early Christianity* (ed. E. S. Fiorenza, Univ. of Notre Dame Center for the Study of Judaism and Christianity in Antiquity 2, Notre Dame, Ind., 1976) 51-53.

[70] Meeks, "Agent", 48, 51-52.

towards God. But this mysticism was not without relation to the historical situation. As a preacher, Philo gave illustrations of how this union with God was to be achieved. His exhortation to follow the example of Moses, who desired "to live to the soul alone and not to the body", was followed by a very concrete illustration of those who did *not* live "to the soul alone":

> they nevertheless look down on their relations and friends and set at naught the laws under which they were born and bred, and subvert the ancestral customs to which no blame can justly attach, by adopting different modes of life, and, in their contentment with the present, lose all memory of the past (*Vita Mos.* I 31).

From this we gather that to live "to the soul" above all implied to show loyalty to the Jewish community and its traditions in its struggle for identity and survival.

From Philo's polemics we learn about various groups among the Jews in Alexandria. As far as we can gather, the situation was not unlike that of Palestine. Religious attitudes (especially concerning the Torah) often corresponded with certain political positions, and both were influenced and shaped by social and economic factors.[71] Jews from the lower classes had, for the most part, little contact with Hellenistic, upper-class culture. Their religious and social identity found expression in a literal interpretation of the Torah, as well as in a rejection of Hellenistic influence. A diametrically opposite attitude was found among some upper class Jews who had left their Jewish faith altogether in order to become assimilated into the economic and social life of Greek Alexandria. From Philo's treatises we get the impression that some of these renegade Jews even employed arguments taken from the literalists in order to ridicule Jewish religion.[72] In between these two groups there was a third one, probably consisting of Jews from the middle and upper classes, if Philo is a typical example. Their economic and cultural interests demanded an open attitude towards the Greek city; at the same time their controversies with the Greeks made them retain a specific Jewish identity. It is within this last group that we find a man like Philo, whose position and influence W. A. Meeks describes thus:

---

[71] Tcherikover, "Literature", 190-93.
[72] E. g. *Conf.* 2-3; *Agr.* 157; see M. J. Shroyer, "Alexandrian Jewish Literalists", *JBL* 55 (1936) 277-279.

All Philo's writings are intended to facilitate his fellow Jews' maintaining a delicate balancing act. On the one hand, by his allegorical interpretation of the Torah, made possible by his sophisticated philosophical eclecticism, he showed that one could accept as the Jews' own the highest values of the "Greek" civilization which were aspired to by the urbane classes of Alexandria (in contrast to the native Egyptians, whom he treats with disdain, or the city "rabble"). On the other hand, he insists upon absolute loyalty to the Jewish *ethnos* and to its scriptures, laws and traditions.[73]

In his polemics against other groups, Philo's attitude varied from outright condemnation of defectors from Judaism to a considerably milder attack on the literalists, who probably were Jews of a Pharisaic type.[74] Quite frequently, Philo accepts their literal interpretation as a first step, but he argues that it does not grasp the deeper meaning of a Biblical passage. The true sense was revealed only by an allegorical interpretation. In practicising this allegorical exegesis Philo could draw upon earlier traditions from an Alexandrian "school" of interpretation.[75] However, the allegorists themselves were not a coherent group. Some of them apparently went so far as to reject altogether the literal meaning of the Torah, with its commandments.[76] Against these Philo showed no leniency, since their attitude opened the way for the complete assimilation of Judaism by Hellenistic culture and philosophy.

It is difficult to judge what effect Philo's preaching and writing had upon the groups he intended to reach. By their very nature his philosophically-worded allegories would appeal only to educated Jews and to their sympathizers among the Greeks in Alexandria. There are no signs that his openness towards non-Jews produced

---

[73] "Agent", 32.

[74] See the discussion of Philo's polemics in Wolfson, *Philo* 1, 55-86; E. Brehier, *Les idées philosophiques et religieuses de Philon d'Alexandrie* (3rd edition, Paris, 1950) 61-66; also Shroyer, "Literalists", 261-84.

[75] This thesis, set forth by Bousset, *Jüdisch-christlicher Schulbetrieb in Alexandria und Rom* (FRLANT NF6, Göttingen, 1915), has been confirmed by later studies; cf. H. Hegermann, *Die Vorstellung von Schöpfungsmittler im hellenistischen Judentum und Urchristentum* (TU 82, Berlin, 1961) 6-87; despite the recent criticism by A. Nissen in his learned, but too dogmatic study *Gott und der Nächste im antiken Judentum* (WUNT 15, Tübingen, 1974) 419-23.

[76] *Migr.* 16, 89-90.

immediate results in the form of active Jewish proselytizing.[77] Somewhat ironically, Philo's influence became much greater after his lifetime, and above all upon the interpretation of the Old Testament in the Early Church.[78]

In our study of Philo's use of the promise to Abraham, we shall take a closer look at the similarities between his exegesis and that of other Jewish groups. Although we shall focus on Philo's interpretation, we shall compare it at every point with traditions from other Jewish groups, especially those in Palestine, but including those in Babylonia. The starting point for our comparison will be the *Targum Neofiti*, which represents an early form of the Palestinian Targumic tradition.[79]

2. *The promise is steadfast*

That God swore an oath (e.g. in his promise to Abraham in Gen 22:16-17) was a popular motif in Jewish tradition. In Philo it occurs in several passages, of which *Leg. All.* III 203-8, *Sacr.* 91-96 and *Abr.* 273 are especially noteworthy. H. Köster has compared these passages with Hebr 6:13-20, which also quotes Gen 22:16-17, and he has identified an underlying common tradition.[80] Between Hebrews 6 and the passages in Philo there are similarities in terminology as well as in the sequence of particular motifs and their function in the context. In every passage it is of particular importance that the word of God secured by an oath is firm and steadfast, (βέβαιος).[81] This word of God is his promise to Abraham, a promise which both Philo and the author of Hebrews regarded as valid for their own generation also. According to Köster, the author of

---

[77] Dahl, *Volk Gottes*, 276.

[78] See the material collected in the classic study by C. Siegried, *Philo von Alexandria als Ausleger des Alten Testament* (Jena, 1875) esp. 303-97.

[79] The Palestinian Targums are useful for the study of Jewish traditions in the first century; cf. the recent survey of Targumic studies by M. McNamara, "Targums", *IDBSup* (1976) 859-61. Although the Targums in their present form are too late to be relied upon in a reconstruction of first century Judaism (see Sanders, *Paul*, 25-29), when compared with sources of a known date, e.g. Philo or the NT, they can be used to trace the development of (exegetical) traditions; see R. Le Déaut, "Targumic Literature and New Testament Interpretation", *Biblical Theology Bulletin* 4 (1974) 243-89, esp. 243-45.

[80] "Die Auslegung der Abraham-Verheissung in Hebräer 6", *Studien zur Theologie der alttestamentlichen Überlieferungen*, 95-109.

[81] Hebr. 6:16, 19; *Leg. All.* III 203-204, 207; *Sacr.* 93; *Abr.* 273; cf. *Somn.* I 12.

Hebrews was in many ways more conservative than Philo, in that
he kept closer to a literal interpretation. The most prominent
example of this is found in their exegesis of the promise of *the land*.
In his allegory, Philo understands this in anthropological terms, as
referring to the soul of the believer. Hebrews, on the other hand,
has preserved a more historical concept, interpreting it in cosmological terms as a reference to the celestial city.[82]

However, even in Philo there are more traditional elements than
those which Köster has noticed. The influence of an earlier or contemporary interpretation is visible in the structure of his argument
as well as in particular passages where he explicitly refers to views
other than his own. The outline of Philo's argument is strongly
influenced by the Biblical text(s) that he is quoting. At first sight
both *Leg. All.* III 203-8 and *Sacr.* 91-96 appear to be isolated
treatises, completely separate from the context. The reference to
God's oath seems only to be an excuse for Philo's real concern,
which is to discuss whether anthropomorphisms can be legitimately
used to describe God. However, a closer look at the introduction to
each text reveals that both passages are linked to the tradition of
the promise made to the ancestors. Philo sees this promise fulfilled
in the life of the perfect (τέλειος) and wise (σοφός) man, i.e., the
true believer (*Sacr.* 90, *Leg. All.* III 203, cf. 217). The gift of the
promise distinguishes him from the "self-lover" (φίλαυτος, *Sacr.* 52).
Allegorically this is "sense" (αἴσθησις, *Leg. All.* III 200, 216), whose
life is filled with sorrow and pain.[83] Philo regards fulfilment in terms
of spiritual existence to be the true interpretation of the promise.
We have already pointed out that this represented his ideal for the
historical Israel. In *Leg. All.* III 203 it is the quotation from Gen
22:16-17 which actually introduces Paul's discussion of the oath of
God. This is not true in *Sacr.* 91-96. However, this treatise on the
oath of God follows immediately after a section dealing with the
promise to the fathers. The introduction to *Sacr.* 91: "But, when he
tells us that God sware an oath", refers to the account of Abel's
sacrifice in 89: "And thus he fulfilled the sacred ordinance, 'It shall

---

[82] H. Braun, "Das himmlische Vaterland bei Philo und im Hebräerbrief",
Verborum Veritas. Festschrift für C. Stälin zum 70. Geburtstag (ed. O. Böcher
and K. Haacker, Wuppertal, 1970) 319-27.

[83] *Leg. All.* III 203-10 is inserted as a contrast in an interpretation of
Gen 3:16a ("I will greatly multiply your pain in childbearing") starting in
200 and continuing in 211. Similarly *Leg. All.* III 217-19 (with Gen 17:15-17;
18:11-13 and 21:6) is a contrast to 216 (Gen 3:16b).

be when the Lord thy God has brought thee into the land of the Canaanites, as *He sware to thy fathers—'* " (Exod 13:11). This promise is now fulfilled in the believers, according to Philo's spiritual exegesis of the promise of the land in *Sacr.* 90: "The fittest time indeed is when God has brought thee where reason is tossed to and fro, that is to the land of the Canaanites. *He brought thee there in no random manner, but according to His own oath*". Thus the discussion of God's oath, although in itself dealing with the question of anthropomorphisms, functions in the larger literary context as a support for Philo's interpretation of the promise. This is the same combination of motifs which we find in Rabbinic literature when Num 23:19, speaking about the steadfastness of the word of God, is said to refer to the promise to the patriarchs.

In *Leg. All.* III 203-8 and *Sacr.* 91-96 Philo frequently refers to the views of others. From the remarks he makes, we can assume that his opponents were probably Jews who, like Philo himself, were offended by the use of anthropomorphic language about God. Already before Philo's time there were "allegorists" in Alexandria who objected to a literary interpretation of anthropomorphisms in the Scriptures.[84] As a result, they protested against the idea that God was said to swear an oath. In *Sacr.* 91-96 Philo takes the same position. He introduces this section by asking if one can justifiably say that God swore, and supports the view (which he ascribes to a large number of people) that one cannot say this (μυρίοις ἔδοξεν ἀνοίκειον εἶναι, *Sacr.* 91). Philo continues this line of thought when he explains why anthropomorphisms are unacceptable. In doing this he points to God himself: God does not need anybody else as his witness, for nobody is his equal. His words are in themselves trustworthy, and are no different from an oath. Among men an oath is deemed necessary to prove one's trustworthiness. With God the opposite is true: he himself is trustworthy and lends credibility to his oath (οὐ γὰρ δι' ὅρκον πιστὸς ὁ θεός, ἀλλὰ δι' αὐτὸν καὶ ὁ ὅρκος βέβαιος, *Sacr.* 93).

Philo's main argument against anthropomorphisms (which he also used in this discussion), was based on Num 23:19:

---

[84] See esp. the fragment of Aristobulus in Eusebius, *Praep. Ev.* XIII 12, 9-16, cf. Arnaldes, *Oeuvres* 1, 51-54, and N. Walter, *Der Thoraausleger Aristobulos* (TU 86, Berlin, 1964) 141-48.

God is not man, that he should lie,
or a son of man, that he should repent,
Has he said, and will he not do it?
Or has he spoken, and will he not fulfil it?

Most frequently, Philo quoted only the first part of the verse "God is not man", to stress the difference between God and man. This was one of the main ideas in Philo's religious world, so important that it functioned almost as an hermeneutical principle in his treatises.[85] But since Moses had used human terms to describe God, there must have been a reason for this also. The only explanation Philo could find was that Moses had written out of a concern for man. The human mind was not able to grasp the true nature of God, and therefore it was a concession to human weakness when Moses said that God had sworn an oath.[86] In this interpretation Philo agreed with the view of another group among his contemporaries. Many Jews were apparently content with a literal interpretation of the narrative where God was said to swear an oath, and they did not feel the need to discuss this topic in depth. We find this view reflected in the *De Abrahamo*, where Philo gives an almost literal interpretation of the Biblical text. When he mentions God's oath to Abraham in *Abr.* 273 there is no criticism of the notion that God was said to swear. Instead he explains *why* God was said to have done this. It was in order to confirm his promise, so that Abraham's faith would be more secure and firm than before.

After his rejection of the idea that God can be said to swear in *Sacr.* 91-96 and his acceptance of it without discussion in *Abr.* 273, it is surprising to find that Philo actively defends the notion in *Leg. All.* III 203-8. The description he gives of God in this text is similar to that in the former passages: "let God be his own most sure guarantee and evidence (ὁ δὲ θεὸς αὐτοῦ πίστις ἔστω καὶ μαρτυρία βεβαιοτάτη, 208). Similarly to *Sacr.* 91, Philo quotes the objections from the "allegorists": "Some have said that it was inappropriate for Him to swear" (204). But in this case he rejects their objections and argues that that it was proper to say that God swore to confirm his promise: "Good is it both that he confirmed (βεβαιῶσαι) his

---

[85] See *Quod Deus* 51-73; *Sacr.* 101; *Quaes. Gen.* II 54; cf. now N. A. Dahl and A. Segal, "Philo and the Rabbis on the Names of God", *JSJ* 9 (1978) 6-10.

[86] See *Quod Deus* 60-69; cf. N. A. Dahl, "Widersprüche in der Bibel. Ein altes hermeneutisches Problem", *ST* 25 (1971) 9.

promise by an oath, and that He did so by an oath befitting God" (203). Why did Philo here take a different position from that in *Sacr.* 91-96 and disagree with the allegorists, whose views he generally shared? In both instances he applied the same theological criterion, that God is without equal.[87] But when it came to the application of this principle, Philo's interpretation was influenced in each particular passage by the quotation from the Bible. This quotation left such a strong influence on his exposition that it made his answer in *Leg. All.* 203-8 contradict that of *Sacr.* 91-96. When quoting Gen 22:16 in *Leg. All.* III 203 Philo emphasizes the first part of the quote: *"By myself I have sworn,* saith the Lord".[88] Apparently Philo understands this passage as a statement of God's uniqueness vis-a-vis man. In consequence, he draws the conclusion that nobody else, i.e. no man, must swear by God—that is blasphemous! (*Leg. All.* III 207) Once more Philo has employed his main theological principle, which in this instance resulted in an outright rejection of the common legal practice among Jews of swearing oaths.[89] In *Sacr.* 91-96 he modifies this position, another indication that the interpretation there comes closer to the traditional teaching of an Alexandrian "school".

These various positions which Philo took on the question of God's oath give us a telling illustration both of Philo's dependence upon tradition, and of his freedom with respect to it. In Alexandria he stood in a tradition of teaching which employed allegorical exegesis. But he could also draw upon a more literal interpretation of the Bible, *viz.* that offered by Pharisaic groups.[90] Common to all groups in their interpretation of Gen 22:16-17 was the conviction that the promise of God was trustworthy, and that it was confirmed by God's word or his oath. It was over the question of whether one could say that God was actually swearing that the discussion arose. Philo's criterion here was his theology as it was expressed by Num

---

[87] Cf. *Leg. All.* III 203 and *Sacr.* 91.

[88] Cf. a similar exegesis based on a seemingly unimportant pronoun in Gen LXX 15:4 in *Heres.* 68-69.

[89] See I. Heinemann, "Philo's Lehre vom Eid", *Judaica, Festschrift für H. Cohen* (Berlin, 1912) 109-18.

Philo's opposition was based on his concept of the wise man (*Sacr.* 91-96 and *Leg. All.* III 204) as an image of God—whose word is an oath, without swearing, cf. S. Daniel, *Oeuvres* 24 (1975) 236 n. 3.

[90] See H.-F. Weiss, "Zur Frage der historischen Voraussetzungen der Begegnung von Antike und Christentum", 318-19; further A. Nissen, *Gott und der Nächste im antiken Judentum,* 20-31.

23:19: "God is not man". As the situation changed, so did Philo's interpretation of God's oath, but his theological principle remained the same.

3. "All things are possible with God"

Philo's interpretation of Gen 22:16-17 was a telling example of how he could draw upon contemporary exegesis, preaching and discussions. Above all, he continued and developed an allegorical exposition of the Biblical material. The same is true in a group of texts where he deals with the promise of Isaac in Genesis 17 and 18, either discussing the promise itself or the recording of his birth in chapter 21. In Philo's allegorical interpretation the two situations symbolized the same event: God creating his life in the soul of the believer. But here, too, Philo builds on traditions of a more literal interpretation. We find a typical example of this is his narration of Gen 18:1-15 in Abr. 107-32. This treatise, De Abrahamo, was probably written as an introduction to Jewish faith for non-Jewish readers, and here Philo follows the simple style of the Biblical narrative.[91] First of all he gives a straightforward report of the story of the three men and their visit to Abraham (107-13). Then follows a literal interpretation (114-18), and finally an allegorical one (119-32).[92] Similarities between the different parts tell us that Philo in his allegorical exposition continues and develops tendencies that were found in the literal interpretation—some of them even in the narrative itself.

The episode from Genesis 18 is told as an example of Abraham's hospitality, in contrast to the inhospitableness of the Egyptians which Philo has described in detail in the preceding chapters (89-106). In his interpretation of the story Philo explains Abraham's hospitality as an expression of the highest virtue, i.e. fear of God (θεοσέβεια, 114). By setting these two examples up against one another, Philo has created a striking contrast: Abraham, the ancestor of the Jews, was treated ungenerously by the Egyptians, while he himself was a model of the highest virtue for which he was rewarded by God. The allusions to the situation in Alexandria

---

[91] J. Gorez, Oeuvres 20 (1966) 14; but see, on the influence from Hellenistic biography, A. Priessnig, "Die literarische Form der Patriarchenbiographien des Philon von Alexandrien", MGWJ 37 (1929) 145-48.

[92] The introductions in 114 and 119 indicate the transitions. Similarly Sandmel, "Philo's Place", 240-42 (119-21); against Gorez (Oeuvres 20, 18) who divides into two parts only: narrative (107-18) and allegory (119-32).

at the time of Philo are unmistakable and could hardly have passed unnoticed by his readers. Thus Philo has prepared the way for a polemical use of the Abraham tradition.

When first narrating the story itself in *Abr.* 107-13, Philo uses little of the extra-Biblical material that was available in the contemporary tradition. There Abraham's hospitality towards strangers was a popular motif, and it was frequently interpreted as a means of proselytizing.[93] The idea that God's promise to Abraham was a reward for his hospitality was common to most elaborations on this story. However, the connection that we find in Philo between hospitality (φιλοξενία) and fear of God (θεοσέβεια) was a product of Hellenistic religiosity. We meet with the same combination in Christian Jewish sources towards the end of the century, notably in 1 *Clem* 9ff.[94]

There is in Philo's version of the story in Abr. 107-32 (as in the treatise in general) a mixture of traditional rhetorical elements and allegorical interpretation. This makes it difficult to distinguish between traditional material and Philo's own contributions.[95] However, an observation by G. Delling helps us to identify Philo's intentions behind the story as it now stands.[96] Delling points out that Philo here employs the same terminology as when describing the miracles during the forty years of Israel in the desert. Examples of such terminology are found especially in the conclusion to the literal interpretation of the story in *Abr.* 118:

It is a marvel (τεράστιον) indeed that though they neither ate nor drank they gave the appearance of both eating and drinking. But this is a secondary matter; the first and greatest wonder (τερατωδέστατον) is that, though incorporeal, they assumed human form to do kindness to the man of worth. For why was this miracle worked (ἐθαυματουργεῖτο) save to cause the Sage to perceive with clearer vision that the Father did not fail to recognize his wisdom?

---

[93] See L. Ginzberg, *The Legends of the Jews* I (Philadelphia, 1913) 240-45; and D. Beer, *Leben Abrahams nach Auffassung der jüdischen Sage* (Leipzig, 1859) 37-40; further, R. B. Ward, "The Works of Abraham, James 2 : 14-26", *HTR* 61 (1968) 286-88.

[94] Cf. O. Knock, *Eigenart und Bedeutung der Eschatologie im theologischen Aufriss des ersten Klemensbriefes*, (Bonn, 1964) 228-30, and G. Brunner, *Die theologische Mitte des ersten Klemensbriefes* (Frankfurter theologische Studien 11, Frankfurt, 1972) 77-80.

[95] The dilemma is apparent in Hamerton-Kelly, "Sources and Traditions", 12.

[96] "Wunder-Allegorie-Mythus bei Philon von Alexandreia", *Studien zum Neuen Testament und zum hellenistischen Judentum*, 109.

Philo's purpose in telling this story about Abraham, his hospitality and his fear of God now becomes clear. By depicting the reward as the result of a divine miracle, he wanted to emphasize that the God of Abraham—and of the Jews—was the God who worked miracles.[97] This insistence upon the miraculous in the literal interpretation which Delling noted, even finds its parallel in the narrative itself, especially in *Abr.* 110-13:

> After feasting not so much on the viands prepared for them as on the good will of their host, and on this example of great and unbounded generosity, they presented him with a reward sur-passing his hopes by promising him the birth of a son born in wedlock. And this promise, which was to be made good in the next year, was given through one and that the highest of the three (110).

In contrast to the Septuagint which, like the Hebrew, had no specific word for the promise, Philo uses the term ὑπισχνέομαι. In the allegorical interpretation in Abr. 131-32 the giver of the promise is identified as God himself. Moreover, Philo affirms that the out-come of the promise is guaranteed, in that it will be fulfilled (βε-βαιωθησομένην) in the following year. We find a typical expression taken from miracle narratives in the statement that the reward was greater than Abraham could have hoped (ἆθλον ἐλπίδος μεῖζον *Abr.* 110) [98] Philo elaborates on this theme in the following descrip-tion of the patriarch and his wife:

> But to Abraham and Sarah the thing seemed incredible, and therefore they did not pay serious regard even to the promises of the three. For as they had passed the years of parenthood, their great age had made them despair of the birth of a son (διὰ μακρὸν γῆρας ἀπεγνώκεσαν παιδὸς σποράν, *Abr.* 111).

That they had actually given up every hope underlines the motif of hopelessness. Then Philo goes on to contrast this situation with the power of God. Once more he expands elements that were already present in the text of Genesis 18 itself. In this case it is the admonition of Sarah in 18:14 LXX that he singles out for special attention:

---

[97] Cf. Priessnig, "Literarische Form", 146.
[98] See the parallels in nn. 111 and 112.

So the scripture says that the wife first laughed at the words and afterwards, when they said, "Is anything impossible with God" (μὴ ἀδυνατεῖ παρὰ τῷ θεῷ πᾶν ῥῆμα)? was ashamed and denied her laughter, for she knew that all things were possible with God (πάντα γὰρ ἤδει θεῷ δυνατά) a truth (δόγμα) which she had learnt long ago and even from the cradle (*Abr*. 112).

The original reproach, "Is anything impossible with God" is here repeated as a positive affirmation, "all things are possible with God". This second time it is attributed to *Sarah*—against the intention of the narrative in Genesis itself. The importance of this statement is stressed even more when Philo characterizes it as a δόγμα. Finally, the conclusion of the narrative corresponds to that of the literal interpretation in 118, in that it focuses upon the theme of knowing God:

It was then, I think, that she first saw in the strangers before her a different and grander aspect, that of prophets or angels, transformed from their spiritual and soul-like nature into human shape (*Abr*. 113).

Sarah's confession that "all things are possible with God" signifies growth in knowledge of God. Throughout his interpretation Philo has made this "dogma" the centre of the narrative: in fact, it serves as the guarantee for the promise. At the same time, this confession was at the centre also of Philo's polemics. The contrast between the inhospitable Egyptians on the one hand and Abraham and Sarah on the other was accentuated by this description of the God of Abraham. Thus the expression that "all things are possible with God" served as a theological criterion that divided believers from non-believers, i.e., Jews from Egyptians—and Greeks!

Although it was Genesis 18 that was the original context of this confession Philo applied it to several other similar narratives. In *Quaes. Gen.* III 56, he attributes it to Abraham when he received the promise of Isaac in Gen 17:17. Inserted between two allegorical expositions of this verse, we can distinguish a third, more literal one: [99]

---

[99] *Quaes. Gen.* III 56 is a shorter parallel to the discussion of Gen 17:17b in *Mut.* 177-201, both give three different expositions. *Quaes. Gen.* III 56a and c parallel *Mut.* 177-80 and 188-201, respectively, but the central section, *Quaes. Gen.* III 56b is both in content and in its simple literal form quite unlike the allegorical interpretation in *Mut.* 181-87.

Behold, our body has passed (its prime) and has gone beyond the age for begetting. But to God all things are possible, even to change old age into youth, and to bring one who has no seed or fruit into begetting and fruitfulness. And so, if a centenarian and (a woman) of ninety years produce children, the element of ordinary events is removed, and only the divine power and grace clearly appear.

This passage represents a literal interpretation of the popular theme of the miraculous childbirth.[100] The story of Sarah bearing Isaac in old age was only one of many similar stories in which God was said to have opened the closed womb of a woman.[101] In Philo's allegorical interpretation this motif played a role similar to that of Abraham's migration or his change of name—it was a symbol of God's creation of new spiritual life.[102] However, in this passage in *Quaes. Gen.* III 56 there is no trace of allegory. God shows his power by rejuvenating Abraham's body in order that he should become the father of Isaac. What we have found in this literal exegesis hidden between the two allegories, bears similarities to the rendering of Gen 18:10 in the Palestinian Targums as well as to Rabbinic explanations of that text.[103] This is another example that the literal expositions in Philo correspond closely to contemporary and later interpretations by Jews in Palestine and Babylonia.

In *Quaes. Gen.* IV 17, however, the motif of child birth is allegorized in Philo's comments upon Gen 18:13-14. He explains away

---

[100] For the history of interpretation of the biblical tradition see O. Michel and O. Betz, "Von Gott gezeugt", *Judentum, Urchristentum, Kirche*, 3-23; and also M. Dibelius, "Jungfrauensohn und Krippenkind", *Botschaft und Geschichte* 1 (ed. G. Bornkamm, Tübingen, 1953) 22-37 (but see criticism below, 240, n. 39).

[101] The Rabbis spoke of the three keys of God, which he used to give life; he opened the closed womb (birth), the closed heaven (rain) and the closed grave (resurrection), see b. *Sanh.* 113a, 92a; b. *Ta'an.* 2a, 8a. According to another tradition Sarah did not have a womb, and therefore God gave her one, so that she could bear a child; cf. *Gen. Rab.* 47 and 53, to Gen 17:16 and 21:1; *LAB* 23:8.

[102] R. A. Baer, *Philo's Use of the Categories Male and Female* (ALGHJ 3, Leiden, 1970) 51-64.

[103] *Tg. Ps.-J.* Gen 18:10 reads: "And one of them said, 'I will certainly return to thee in the coming year *when you are well* (ואתן קיימין), and, lo, Sarah thy wife shall have a son' ". Cf. the translation by Etheridge: *"You shall be revived"*. This interpretation of Gen 18:10 understands the renewal of the year in the MT to refer to the new life given to Abraham and Sarah; so also in the Peshitta, and in Rashi to Gen 18:10; cf. J. Bowker, *The Targums and Rabbinic Literature* (Cambridge, 1969) 211.

the idea that Gen 18:14 was originally a reproach (this notion was preserved in *Abr.* 112), and immediately ascribes to Sarah the question: "Can it be that anything is impossible for God?" Moreover, Sarah is no longer the historical person who bears Isaac; rather, she symbolizes the soul in which God sows his joy: "For she wonders that when all the necessary and plausible conditions have been removed by which birth can be successfully accomplished, a new act shall be shown by God in the whole soul for the birth of joy and great gladness, which in Armenian is called 'laughter' and in Chaldean 'Isaac' ". The "mystical" language that Philo employs here is probably a way of describing in transcendental language experiences of ecstacy and of prophetic inspiration.[104]

There are two other episodes where Philo ascribes to Abraham the confession that "everything is possible with God". In *Quaes. Gen.* III 2, it is added to Abraham's answer to the promise from God in Gen 15:8. Finally, in *Abr.* 175, Philo inserts it in the story from Genesis 22. Faced with Isaac's question of how to find a sacrificial lamb in the wilderness, Abraham answers with this confession to the power of God. This story is in Philo's rendering so to speak a heightened parallel to that of Gen 18. It is interpreted along similar lines by Josephus in *Ant.* I 222-36.[105]

When we look back upon this last group of texts, we find that Philo has used this statement about the power of God to interpret the promise to Abraham within the framework of a miracle story. This is particularly characteristic of his *literal* exposition where he follows a tradition of interpretation that was similar to that found in the Palestinian Targums and in Rabbinic literature. However, the formula itself, "all things are possible with God", is not found in these other sources. It probably originated among Greek-speaking Jews in Egypt.[106] It is first found in the Septuagint, in texts where the idea (but not the actual formula) was present in the Hebrew text. The best-known example of this is Gen 18:14, others are Job

---

[104] Baer, *Male and Female*, 55-57.

[105] See the direct parallel to *Abr.* 175 in *Ant.* I 227; cf. further Abraham's speech in I 228-38, whereby Josephus interprets this narrative in the same way as the story of the crossing of the Red Sea; cf. H. W. Attridge, *The Interpretation of Biblical History in the Antiquitates Judaicae of Flavius Josephus* (Harvard Dissertations in Religion 7, Missoula, Mont., 1976) 88-90, 93 no. 1.

[106] W. C. van Unnik, " 'Alles ist dir möglich' (Mark 14:36)", *Verborum Veritas*, 31-32.

10:13; 42:2 and Zech 8:6.[107] The concept that God was all-powerful is found in Jewish writings later than the Septuagint,[108] but this special expression occurs only in Philo and in Christian literature of the first century.[109] However, Philo uses it so frequently, especially in his literal expositions, that we can assume that this confession was well-known among Jews in Egypt at his time. Its use in the Gospels probably indicates that it was also part of the religious language of first-century Palestine.

Apart from the patriarchal narratives, Philo refers to the belief that "all things are possible with God" especially when commenting upon miracles from Exodus. In Philo's rendering, these narratives have many motifs in common. Philo's interpretation frequently takes the form of speeches or prayers, whereby he expresses his theological concern. One characteristic example (which has a close parallel in Josephus *Ant.* II 330-33) [110] is Moses' speech at the Red Sea (*Vita Mos.* I 173-75). As a general rule, the Israelites found themselves in a hopeless position, e.g. described as παρ' ἐλπίδα.[111] As a result, they lost hope and surrendered to despair.[112] Any hope of deliverance was outside the power of man; when Israel was rescued by a miracle, it was only because "all things are possible with God".[113] The ultimate goal of Philo's expositions, here as well as in the Abraham story, was to bring his readers to accept this faith in God.

In their form the narratives of Abraham, Moses and the Israelites in the desert are similar to Josephus' rendering of them in the *Antiquitates Judaicae*.[114] Both Philo and Josephus are influenced by Hellenistic hero-biographies,[115] but they share a *theological* concern

---

[107] Job 10:13 and 42:2 combine a negative statement (found in Gen 18:14) and a positive one, in a similar manner as does Philo in *Abr.* 112, see Job 42:2: οἶδα ὅτι πάντα δύνασαι, ἀδυνατεῖ δέ σοι οὐθέν.

[108] See van Unnik, "Alles ist dir möglich" 32; and Marmorstein, *Rabbinic Doctrine*, 160-76.

[109] Mark 10:27 par. (Matt 19:26; Luke 18:27); 14:36; Luke 1:37(Gen 18:14).

[110] See Attridge, *Interpretation*, 76-81.

[111] *Jos.* 12, 208, 238; *Vita Mos.* I 58, 182, 187, 250; cf. also II 259; *Spec. Leg.* II 217. For the following, see Delling, "Wunder", 77-89.

[112] Cf. *Spec. Leg.* II 219: οὐκ ἐλπίσασιν; *Abr.* 175; ἀπογινώσκεις, (cf. *Abr.* 112); further *Vita Mos.* I 170-72.

[113] *Vita Mos.* 173; *Abr.* 175; *Jos.* 244.

[114] This is true in particular of the speeches in the *Antiquitates* whereby Josephus gives the narrative a theological interpretation. Here he frequently speaks of God's providence (πρόνοια), e.g. II 222-23, 330-33; IV 185; Attridge, *Interpretation*, 71-107.

[115] For Philo, see Priessnig, "Form", 145-55.

that goes beyond a mere praise of the Old Testament heroes. The praise given to them only points towards God, cf. e.g. Delling's comment upon the Moses narrative: "Offenbar will er nicht in erster Linie Moses als Thaumaturgen herausstellen . . . in erster Linie erscheint auch bei Philon (wie bei Josephus) Gott als der Wundertäter. Philon betont (und dass im Unterschied zu Josephus) kaum, dass Wunder die Frömmigkeit des Gottesmannes kundtun . . . " [116] Delling has also pointed out that when Philo describes God's miraculous assistance to his people, he has not allegorized or explained away motifs that might seem offensive to Greeks.[117] The miracle narratives give us an example of Philo's preaching faith in the God of Israel, over against all other beliefs. The mixture of polemical and missionary intentions behind his treatises becomes obvious when he describes how the Egyptians reacted to the miracle of the ten plagues inflicted upon them. They realized that this was not the result of human labour but had been "brought about by some divine power to which every feat is easy" (*Vita. Mos.* I 94). But even if they were forced to admit this, they did not repent and therefore they were even more severely punished.[118]

The miracles are in some respects parallel to creation, which Philo regards as another proof of God's power to do the impossible. Philo polemicizes against the Egyptians and their belief in the divinity of heavenly beings. In this context the confession that "everything is possible with God" is used by Philo to express faith in the true God of the Bible, in contrast to all mythology and pantheistic cosmology.[119] Philo here continues the Old Testament polemics against gods other than Yahweh when he describes them as being without power. Compared with the Old Testament passages which form the basis for Philo's narratives, he employs terms that are more explicitly *theological* (in a narrow sense) when describing the divine assistance. That "all things are possible with God" and that his help is "against all hope" are themes central to his interpretation. The miracle that God works does more than relieve the actual need, it also serves as a guarantee for future assistance. In *Sacr.* 91-

---

[116] Delling, "Wunder", 76-77.
[117] See Delling, "Wunder", 80.
[118] A more direct missionary motif would seem to be present in *Spec. Leg.* I 282. Here, "everything is possible with God" is used of his power to bring erring souls back to him, a task which is impossible to others; cf. Mark 10 : 27; further, *Somn.* I 87-91.
[119] *Op.* 46; see Delling, "Wunder", 114-23.

96 and *Leg. All.* 203-8, the divine promise was confirmed by God's oath. In *Abr.* 110-18, a similar promise was warranted by the miracle of God's appearance. Philo's literal exposition of the Abraham story, *Abr.* 107-18, is distinguished by certain elements which characterize it as a miracle story. It contains motifs and descriptions that were part of a reformulation of the biblical text which was probably already traditional before Philo's time.

When Philo spoke of a God for whom everything was possible, his statements had a double function. He proclaimed the superiority of the Jewish faith to non-Jews who were attracted to Judaism by its monotheism. At the same time, the extremes of his polemic against Egyptian religion served to strengthen the Jews in their faith. This last intention Philo explicitly brings to the fore in several texts where he adds this confession of the nature of God.[120] One of them is the episode of the Israelites crossing the Red Sea. When the Israelites are being pursued by the Egyptians, Moses encourages them: " 'Do not lose heart', he said, 'God's way of defence is not as that of man . . . what is impossible to all created being is possible to Him only, ready to His hand' " (*Vita. Mos.* I 173-4). Similarly in the desert, Moses pointed to former blessings from God as a reason to trust in him: "We must trust God (πιστεύειν δεῖ τῷ θεῷ) as we have experienced His kindness in deeds greater than we could have hoped for" (*Vita. Mos.* II 259).

With the formula, "all things are possible with God", Philo emphasized God's power to rescue his people when they were in danger. As a result, the expression took on a distinctively Jewish character which is even more striking when we consider the contexts in which it was used. In *Abr.* 113, it occurred in a section where Abraham's hospitality and piety were contrasted with the inhospitableness and false pretentions of the Egyptians. The same is true of its use in several of the miracle stories from Exodus, in which the Israelites were rescued from Egyptian oppression. The biblical setting of several of the narratives about Abraham and Moses in Egypt gave them a direct relevance to the situation of the Jews in Alexandria at the time of Philo. Abraham and Moses were exemplary men who upheld the principles of Jewish religion in inhospitable surroundings. By focusing on these texts Philo grasped the opportunity they gave him to strengthen the identity of the

---

[120] Moses' speech in Josephus, *Ant.* II 330-33 has a similar function, see Attridge, *Interpretation*, 104-6.

Jewish community vis-à-vis an hostile environment. In this way, he theologized a conflict that had to a large extent arisen over political and economic questions.

4. *Gen* 15:6 *and the promise to Abraham*

We shall now turn to Philo's use of Gen 15:6 within the wider context of his interpretation of the Abraham story. It has often been assumed that Jewish interpreters invariably read this verse in light of Genesis 22, as the prime example of Abraham's obedience towards God. However, a closer look at Philo's writings shows us that this assumption is not quite correct. It is true that Philo, too, regarded Abraham's sacrifice of Isaac as the highest example of his faith in God. But when it comes to actual quotations of Gen 15:6 (most often the first part of the verse only), they are found in passages where Philo has focused on the *promise* made to Abraham in Genesis 12, 15, 17 and 18.[121] Furthermore, on several occasions the quotation from Gen 15:6 serves as an hermeneutical principle which determines the interpretation of the text in question. It is in the interpretation of Gen 12:1-5 that Philo first turns to Gen 15:6. In *Migr.* 43-44 he comments upon God's command in Gen 12:1: "Go from your country and your kindred and your father's house to the land that I will show you". Philo starts with the observation that the promise is spoken in the *future* tense and not in the present: εἰπὼν οὐχ ἣν δείχνυμι ἀλλ᾽ "ἣν σοὶ δείξω". His explanation runs as follows:

> Thus he testifies to the trust which the soul reposed in God, exhibiting its thankfulness not as called out by accomplished facts, but by expectations of what was to be. For the soul clinging in utter dependence on a good hope, and deeming that things not present are beyond question already present (ἤδη παρεῖναι τὰ μὴ παρόντα) by reason of the sure steadfastness of Him that promised them (διὰ τὴν τοῦ ὑποσχομένου βεβαιότητα) has won as its meed (ἆθλον) faith, a perfect good, for we read a little later "Abraham believed God" (*Migr.* 44).

Philo here describes Abraham's faith recorded in Gen 15:6 as a *reward* from God for his trust in the promise. The soul that trusts

---

[121] Gen 15:6 is quoted or alluded to together with other biblical passages in *Migr.* 44 (Gen 12:1); *Heres.* 90, 94, 101 (Gen 15:6-8); *Mut.* 177 (Gen 15:4; 17:17), 186 (Gen 17:17): *Quod Deus* 4 (Gen 22:9): *Leg. All.* III 228 (Num 12:7). In some passages Gen 15:6 is not combined with any other text: *Abr.* 262; *Virt.* 216; *Praem.* 27.

God's promise of the future already anticipates its fulfilment.[122] Philo here speaks of the promise of the new creation, i.e., the unity of the believer with God. This is in a real sense a *creatio ex nihilo*.[123] This creation can happen now, Philo says, in the soul of the wise man who experiences union with God. Philo can use his own experiences of ecstatic inspiration as an illustration (*Migr.* 34-35). But these moments are rare for most men, and therefore Philo exhorts his readers to believe even before it happens, while they are still on their way towards the fulfilment of the promise. But it is only because God, who gave the promise, is steadfast that man can have this firm faith (*Migr.* 44). We found the same motif in Philo's interpretation of Gen 22:16-17, and in that of Genesis 18: God, who gives the promise, is himself its guarantor. Therefore man can trust in the promise, even before it is fulfilled, because God is steadfast.

The description of Abraham as one who trusted in God without doubting met in some instances with difficulties from an unexpected quarter—*viz.* the biblical narratives themselves! The passages concerned were above all Gen 15:2, 8 and 17:17, which describe Abraham's reactions to the promise from God. In these texts Abraham raised questions that could easily be understood as objections to what he had heard:

Gen 15:2 But Abraham said, "O Lord God, what wilt thou give me, for I continue childless, and the heir of my house is Eliezer of Damascus".

15:8 But he said, "O Lord God, how am I to know that I shall possess it?"

17:17 Then Abraham fell on his face and laughed, and said to himself, "Shall a child be born to a man who is a hundred years old? Shall Sarah, who is ninety years old, bear a child?"

The last passage, which tells us both that Abraham laughed and that he questioned the promise, has a parallel in the description of Sarah in 18:12 LXX: "And Sarah laughed in herself saying, 'The

---

[122] Cf. *Mut.* 157-65.

[123] Philo has no doctrine of "creatio ex nihilo" in the sense of creation of the world from a non-existent material. Instead he speaks of God who brings the non-existent into life, i.e. it is more a soteriological than a cosmological term; see H.-F. Weiss, *Untersuchungen zur Kosmologie des hellenistischen und palästinischen Judentums* (TU 97, Berlin, 1966) 59-72; against Wolfson, *Philo* I, 300ff.

thing has not as yet happened to me, even until now, and my Lord is old' ".[124]

A literal interpretation of these texts would find that Abraham doubted God's promise. This was the most common Rabbinic interpretation.[125] Moreover, even Philo testifies to this in *Abr.* 110-12, as we have already seen, and also in *Leg. All.* III 85, where he states that Abraham doubted. This is an example of how Philo sometimes incorporated traditional material into his treatises without making it conform to his own views. In this case the literal interpretation contradicts his allegorical exegesis.[126] In several of his treatises Philo discusses the possibility that Abraham could have doubted, but only to reject it. A typical example of his interpretation of Gen 15:8 is found in *Heres.* 100; of Gen 17:17 in *Mut.* 177-80 and *Quaes. Gen.* III 56.[127] In *Mut.* 177 Philo introduces the problem in this way:

> Because in saying "Shall this happen to one of a hundred years", he seems to doubt the birth of Isaac in which in an earlier place he was said to believe, as was shown by the oracular words delivered a little time before. Those ran "He shall not be thine heir, but one who shall come from thee", and then immediately followed the words, "And Abraham believed God and it was accounted to him for righteousness".

Philo is here faced with the problem of contradictions in the Scriptures.[128] How can two contradictory statements, in this case Gen 17:17 and 15:6, be reconciled? In this passage it is Gen 15:6 which carries most weight. Since Abraham responded with faith to the promise given in Gen 15:5, his response to the promise in 17:16 must be similar. Gen 15:6 therefore functions as Philo's proof-text and determines the interpretation of 17:17. He solves the problem

---

[124] The LXX differs from the MT; עֶדְנָה, "pleasure", remains untranslated, or possibly it was understood as an adverb of time, "hitherto, still", and therefore translated in ἕως τοῦ νῦν. Philo follows the LXX in *Mut.* 166, but is closer to the MT in *Leg. All.* III 218; see H. E. Ryle, *Philo and Holy Scripture. The Quotations of Philo from the Books of the Old Testament* (London, 1895) 72.

[125] The list given by Ginzberg, *The Legends of the Jews* 5, 227; needs to be corrected; see *Tg. Ps.-J.* Gen 15:13; *b. Ned.* 32a; *Pesiq. R.* 47:3; *Exod. Rab.* on Exod. 31:2; 5:22; *Rab. Eccl.* 4:3, 1; *Rab. Cant.* 1:4, 1.

[126] See C. Mondésert, *Oeuvres* 2 (1962) 218-19 n. 3.

[127] Cf. the interpretation of Gen 15:2 in *Heres.* 1-33.

[128] Dahl, "Widersprüche", 8-10.

of apparent contradictions between the two passages by minimizing
the notion of doubt in Gen 17:17. Philo achieves this by stressing
the fact that Abraham spoke only in his mind and not with his
mouth, i.e. he did not express his doubt aloud. Thus he comes to
the conclusion that "since doubt was not consistent with his past
belief, Moses has represented the doubt not as long-lived, or prolonged to reach the mouth, but staying where it was with the swiftly
moving mind" (*Mut.* 178).[129] The exposition of Gen 15:8 in *Heres.*
100-2 follows similar lines. Philo does not quote Gen 15:6, but he
does refer to it when introducing his discussion of Abraham's doubt
by saying: "Now perhaps it may be said that this question is
inconsistent with the belief ascribed to him" (μάχεσθαι τοῦτο τῷ
πεπιστευκέναι) (*Heres.* 101). Once more the witness of Gen 15:6 is
decisive: there can be no doubt that Abraham believed. In this
case Philo solves the problem of contradictions by making a fine
distinction: Abraham believed that he would inherit wisdom,
according to God's promise, and he was merely asking *how* this
would happen. Thus Abraham's doubt is again made to look
insignificant, and his reaction to the promise is brought into line
with his reaction in Gen 15:6.

Philo is the first interpreter explicitly to make Gen 15:6 his rule
for the interpretation of Abraham's questions in 15:8 and 17:17.
However, even if most Rabbinic commentators accepted that
Abraham doubted, Philo's interpretation was not totally unfore-
shadowed in earlier tradition. Already in the *Book of Jubilees* there
is a tendency to clear Abraham from any suspicion of doubt. The
rendering of Gen 17:17 in *Jub.* 15:17 is a telling example: "And
Abraham fell on his face and *rejoiced*, and said in his heart: 'Shall
a son be born to him that is a hundred years old, and shall Sarah,
who is ninety years old, bring forth?'" The idea that Abraham
rejoiced over the promise is repeated in other passages in *Jubilees*,
an indication that this change in the text of Gen 17:17 was the
result of a conscious interpretation.[130] Philo continues this line of
interpretation when he describes the laughter of Abraham and
Sarah in Gen 17:17 and 18:12 as χαρά.[131] In the Palestinian Targums
we can detect a tendency to diminish the notion of doubt in Abra-

---

[129] See also *Quaes. Gen.* III 56.
[130] *Jub.* 14:19-21; 17:2-4; 16:27.
[131] See n. 56.

ham's laughter.[132] However, Gen 15:6 is not used as an argument
for this interpretation. And the passages in which Gen 15:6 is
used to characterize Abraham, e.g., Sir 44:20 and 1 Macc 2:52, are
of a different type. There we find other texts, in particular Gen 22,
introduced to define Gen 15:6, so that as a result Abraham's faith
is understood as faithfulness. In contrast to this, in the passages
we have discussed here, Philo has brought in Gen 15:6 to qualify
other texts. Moreover, Philo was first of all concerned with Abraham's attitude towards God's promise. Thus, in addition to the
familiar interpretation of Gen 15:6 which he shares, Philo has
developed the use of Gen 15:6 as a proof-text to solve difficult
questions of interpretation.

A comparison with the Palestinian Targums will put Philo's
interpretation of Abraham's question into a wider context. There
are many features common to Philo and the Targums in their
treatment of this problem, but there are also significant dis-
similarities. Both in the Targums and in Philo's treatises, the
attitude of Abraham was interpreted in light of contemporary
issues. Since Abraham was the ancestor of the Jews his attitudes
set an example for his descendants. In fact, the interpretation of
his reaction tells us how the Jews in every generation responded
to the promise from God. Thus the interpretation of the texts in
question (Gen 15:8; 17:17; 18:12)gives an indication of the writer's
conception of Israel's relationship to God at a central point. The
Palestinian Targums as well as later Rabbinic writings explained
Abraham's reactions in the light of the introduction of circumcision,
to them the single most important factor in Israel's identity. This
determines the explanation of Gen 17:3 and 17 in *Tg. Neofiti*.
When Abraham responded to the promise from God by falling to
the ground, it was because he was not yet circumcised.[133] Circumcision was a requirement for a true relationship with God, and *Tg.
Neofiti* stresses the importance of it with its description of Abraham
after he was circumcised. In Gen 18:1 it is told that Abraham was
sitting in the door to the tent when the three wayfarers, i.e. God

[132] *Tg. Neof.*; *Tg. Ps.-J.*; *Frg. Tg.* Gen 17:17 render ויצחק in the MT with
ותמה "he was astonished, he wondered"; cf. M. Jastrow, *A Dictionary of the
Targumim etc.* 2 (N.Y. 1950) 1675. *Tg. Onq.* Gen 17:17 goes even further and
reads וחדי "he rejoiced"; Jastrow, *Dictionary* 1, 426. Cf. further John 8:56;
see n. 251.
[133] *Tg. Neof.* Gen 18:1; cf. *Tg. Ps.-J.* Gen 17:3; Ber. Rab. 46:6 and47:3
(to Gen 17:3 and 17).

himself, visited him. This symbolized the change that had taken place; when circumcised one could stand and even sit in the presence of God.[134] In a similar manner *Tg. Ps. Jon.* explains Abraham's disbelief in Gen 15:8 by relating it to a central event in the history of Israel, in this case the exile in Egypt. In Gen 15:13 it is told that God warned Abraham of this trial. *Tg. Ps. Jon.* and other Rabbinic interpreters combined these two passages from Gen 15 and suggested that it was because of Abraham's disbelief that God inflicted this severe punishment upon his descendants.[135] Thus, even when they were understood as expressions of disbelief, Abraham's questions were made to serve a purpose in the divine history with Israel.

Philo, for his part, also considered Abraham's questions in the light of what he regarded as constitutive factors in the life of Israel. He constantly urged his readers to believe in God, not in a created thing, and it was an example of this faith he found in Gen 15:6: "Abraham believed God". This was a motif common in Greek philosophy and the emphasis on the distance from anything created gave it gnostic overtones.[136] But it also had direct social and political implications, since to Philo this faith was the distinct mark of Israel's identity vis-a-vis Hellenistic influence.[137]

We discovered earlier that the centre of Philo's exposition of a text or discussion of a problem is to be found in his teaching about God. When he argued so strongly that Abraham *did* believe in God, Philo's position was warranted by his theology in its narrow sense: Abraham's faith in God was founded in God himself! When Abraham trusted in unfulfilled promises it was because God, who gave them, was steadfast (*Migr.* 44). It was only at a superficial level that his hope was directed towards promises of visible rewards: their ultimate goal as well as their foundation was God himself.[138] Philo takes the same general approach to this issue, but it is expressed in

---

[134] See further e.g. *Pirqe R. El.* 29; *Num. Rab.* 12:8.

[135] *b. Ned.* 32a; *Gen. Rab.* 44. Some Church Fathers who continued Philo's line of interpretation referred to this opposite view, cf. Ephraem Syrus (4th c.) *Fragments on Genesis*: in R. Devreese, *Les anciens commentateurs grecs de l'Octateuque et des rois* (Studi e testi 201, Rome, 1959) 68; cf. further references in Ginzberg, *Legends* I 235, 244; with nn. in vol. 5, 227-28, 237.

[136] H. Jonas, *Gnosis und spätantiker Geist* 2 (FRLANT 63, Göttingen, 1954) 117.

[137] See the exposition of Gen 15:6 in *Abr.* 262-65 and his criticism of economic and political opportunism.

[138] Cf. H. Braun, *Wie man über Gott nicht denken soll. Dargelegt an Gedankengängen Philo's von Alexandria* (Tübingen, 1970) 82-83.

various ways in the different texts. In *Heres*. 101 Philo sees Abraham's firm conviction that he will inherit the promised goods, as based on the divine promise itself: πάντως κατὰ τὰς θείας ὑποσχέσεις βεβαίως κατείληφεν. In the exposition of that same text, Gen 15:8, in *Quaes. Gen.* III 2 this motif is even more explicitly stated: "I know that Thou art Lord and ruler of all things and that Thou canst do all things and that there is nothing impossible with thee". Abraham's faith is based on God's power to fulfil his promise. Since Philo understands Abraham's questions in Gen 15:8 and 17:17 as expressions of faith, the response by God in the following verses cannot be regarded as a reproach. Instead, Philo reads them as confirmation from God who both renews his promise and guarantees it.[139]

Not surprisingly, Philo's exegesis of Sarah's laughter and her question in Gen 18:12-13 follows the same pattern. He starts from the notion that "everything is possible with God", and makes Sarah's reaction conform to this belief (*Abr.* 113: *Quaes. Gen.* IV 17). Similarly when he says that Sarah's question expressed not disbelief, but belief, it was because God is faithful. The text in question is Gen 18:12 LXX:

> And Sarah laughed in herself, saying "The thing has not yet happened to me, even until now, and my lord is old".

Philo gives a Targum-like rendering of this verse, following the Septuagint version closely and inserting his own exposition into the text:

> For again we find Sarah laughed, saying in herself, "Not yet has this befallen me till now", this unstudied, self-sprung good. Yet He that promised (ὁ δ' ὑποσχόμενος) she says, is "my Lord" and "older" than all creation, and I must believe him (ᾧ πιστεύειν ἀναγκαῖον, *Mut.* 166).[140]

Against the original meaning of the text Philo takes "my lord is old" to refer to *God*. God is further described as the giver of the promise, who deserves Sarah's trust. Here, too, Philo finds the foundation for faith in God himself and in his promise. This exegesis seems forced, and most Rabbis understood "my lord is old" as a reference to Abraham. However, we also find in the Targums and

---

[139] *Leg. All.* III 85; *Heres.* 96, 102; *Mut.* 253; *Quaes. Gen.* III 58.
[140] A parallel in *Leg. All.* III 218.

in later Rabbinic exegesis an interpretation similar to that of Philo.[141]

That it was God's promise and his steadfastness that made it possible for men to believe in him, emerges as a prominent theme in Philo's writings. As a last example of the importance of theology in his explanations of Abraham's questions, we may mention *Mut.* 181-87. Here Philo turns against those who reject the notion that Abraham showed any doubt at all. We noticed earlier that in the preceding passage, *Mut.* 177-80, Philo argued that Abraham's doubt was only passing and almost negligible. This interpretation of Gen 17:17 he based on a comparison with Gen 15:6, the latter serving as a proof-text. However, in 181-87, Philo takes the position that Gen 15:6 did *not* eliminate the possibility that Abraham doubted. Unlike the preceding passage, in *Mut.* 181-87 Gen 15:6 is not Philo's proof-text, but is itself the text in need of explanation. Philo refers to both Gen 15:6 and 17:17 in the introduction in *Mut.* 181: "But perhaps it may be said, why did he, when once he had believed (ὅτι πεπιστευκώς) admit any trace or shadow of doubt altogether", but then he focuses upon Gen 15:6. He turns against his opponents to prove that, when drawing the conclusion that doubt was impossible on the part of Abraham, they have mis-understood the real meaning of the proof-text. Consequently, Philo proceeds to provide his own interpretation of Gen 15:6. He does this by introducing a second quotation, this time from Deut 32:8, and he concludes by returning to the original text, Gen 15:6. Finally, this last quotation is followed by another supplementary text, Gen 32:25, 31. This is a typical example of the homily pattern that Borgen found in several passages in Philo.[142] The formal structure is especially interesting for a comparison with Paul's interpretation of Gen 15:6 in Romans 4, but for the moment it is the content of the passage that concerns us. Philo's exegesis of Gen 15:6 in *Mut.* 181-87 is determined by the quote from Deut 32, acting as a proof-text: θεὸς πιστός, καὶ οὐκ ἔστιν ἀδικία ἐν αὐτῷ. Philo's argument is based on the comparison of ἐπίστευσε in Gen 15:6 and πιστός in Deut 32:8. That God was πιστός, was a statement

---

[141] Beer (*Leben Abrahams* 159-60 n. 413) suggests that Philo here follows a midrashic interpretation. Can we see a reaction against such an interpretation in the amendation in *Tg. Neof.* I and *Tg. Ps.-J.*, saying, "my Lord *Abraham*?" From a much later period, see *Ber. R.* 48:7, attributed to R. Judah b. R. Simon (early 4th c.).

[142] *Bread from Heaven*, 28-58, esp. 46-51.

that could be used only of him. When Philo's opponents claimed that Abraham had a perfectly firm faith, they made him like God! Here, too, we find that Philo refuted his attackers by using this statement about God as his argument. The quotation from Deut 32:8 gives Philo the opportunity to rehearse the main theme of his theology: God is One and of a single nature, whereas man consists of a mixture of opposing forces, good and evil.[143] When Philo finally draws his conclusion by returning to Gen 15:6, he adds a significant qualification to the quotation: πεπίστευκεν οὖν Ἀβραὰμ τῷ θεῷ, ἀλλ' ὡς ἄνθρωπος πεπίστευκεν. Abraham believed— but only as a man! Even Gen 15:6 must be brought in line so that this assertion of Abraham's faith should not be understood as a threat to God's absolute majesty.

5. *Conclusions*

Philo's expositions of the Abraham story, which remained basically the same throughout his writings, were addressed to the various groups he was preaching to: Jews, proselytes and God-fearers. His admonition against Hellenistic religion and philosophy served a function not only in missionary propaganda, but also in Philo's teaching to the Jews themselves. To them it represented a warning not to be lured away by popular beliefs, but to retain their religious identity. Like other Jews, Philo found this identity expressed in the life of Abraham. Unlike the Rabbis and the Targums, he did not stress that Abraham was the ancestor of the Jews, the first to receive circumcision and a covenant. To Philo, Abraham's *faith* was more important, and in his allegorical interpretation Abraham signified every true believer.

The literal interpretation of the Abraham narrative shared many features with the interpretation of the Palestinian Targums and Rabbinic literature. More than these, however, Philo made his theological viewpoints explicitly known. The promise made to Abraham and Sarah was described in terms similar to those used of the miracles at the Red Sea and in the desert. The typical conclusion to these miracle stories was that "all things are possible with God". Thus there were two characteristic aspects in Philo's teaching. One was his specifically theo-logical concern, the other his emphasis on faith. These two met in his exposition of Gen 15:6:

---

[143] Cf. R. Bultmann, "πιστεύω", *TWNT* 6 (1959) 202-3; and Braun, *Gott*, 18-23.

"Abraham believed God". This verse occupies a central position in his discussion of several other texts, and it is directly related also to the promise of Abraham. Philo's exegesis proves that in Judaism, Abraham's faith was not understood as a "work" only. Although this notion was never absent in Philo's exposition, it was always subordinate to the idea that faith was a gift from God and that it found its basis in him alone. Even Philo's discussion of whether Abraham and Sarah actually showed disbelief, must be seen against the background of Rabbinic and Targumic exegesis, to which it stands in partial opposition. Thus Philo and his exegesis were not an isolated phenomenon in first century Judaism. In particular in his literal interpretation of the Abraham story we found him to be in close contact with contemporary exegetical discussions in Alexandria. The most significant new feature of his work, was his use of Gen 15:6 as a proof-text in these discussions.

C. A first-century crisis in Palestine reflected in Apocalyptic and Rabbinic writings

The fall of Jerusalem and the destruction of the Temple in A.D. 70 caused serious problems for the political, social and religious life of all Jews in Palestine.[144] It was in this period that the Pharisees came to power as a moderate political group that could negotiate with the Romans. Equally importantly, they were able to re-organize Jewish religion so that it could adapt to a post-Temple situation This transition was not so easy for groups with more fervent apocalyptic expectations. Not only were their hopes crushed, but the very trustworthiness of the word of God, which they had claimed to be preaching, was thrown into doubt. This discrepancy between the promises and actual experience resulted in widespread doubt as to whether God was able to fulfil his promises.[145]

The apocalypses of 4 Ezra and 2 Apoc. Bar. addressed themselves to this situation in an attempt to counter such doubts.[146] Conse-

---

[144] Maier, Geschichte, 92-98; further, J. Neusner, "Judaism in a Time of Crisis. Four responses to the Destruction of the Second Temple", Judaism 21 (1972) 313-27.

[145] The same scepticism was voiced in the accusation that the God of Israel was "old" and no longer able to help his people. This accusation was caused by the destruction of the Temple, cf. Gen. Rab. 10:8; Esth. Rab. 7:13; A. Marmorstein, Rabbinic Doctrine, 170-175.

[146] For the following see W. Harnisch, Verhängnis und Verheissung der Geschichte: Untersuchungen zum Zeit- und Geschichtsverständnis im 4. Buch

quently they had to face objections brought forward by disillusioned believers, and to some extent they have included these objections in their writings.[147] 4 Ezra especially offers a good illustration of this. Each one of a series of arguments is introduced with a glorification of God who created the world and made Israel his chosen people (3:4-27; 5:23-27; 6:38-54). However, this praise is followed in every instance by a complaint about the present situation of Israel (3:28-36; 5:28-30; 6:55-59). By implication, this amounted to an accusation against God,[148] and it was directly voiced as a doubt about the trustworthiness of his promises to Israel. In 4:23 it is the reliability of the law—as a proof of Israel's election and as a guarantee for the covenant—that is in question:

Why is Israel to the heathen given over for reproach,
thy beloved people to godless tribes given up?
The Law of our fathers has been brought to destruction,
the written covenants exist no more.

Similarly in 6:59, which contains an allusion to the promise of the land:

If the world has indeed been created for our sakes, why do we not enter into possession of our world (saeculum).[149]

4 Ezra 3:13-15 speaks specifically of God's acts towards Abraham, and the author mentions acts that were of special importance to him and his contemporaries:

Him (Abraham) thou didst love, and unto him only didst thou reveal the end of the times secretly by night; and with him thou didst make an everlasting covenant, and didst promise him that thou wouldst never forsake his seed.

Esra und in der syr. Baruchapokalypse (FRLANT 97, Göttingen, 1969). The origins of 4 Ezra and 2 Apoc. Bar. are probably to be found in Palestine in the last decades of the first century A.D.; Verhängnis, 15.

[147] Harnisch, Verhängnis, 64-65 and 86-87. Cf. A. F. J. Klijn's suggestion ("The sources and the Redaction of the Syriac Apocalypse of Baruch", JSJ I (1970) 75-76) that the author is correcting expectations about the restoration of the country and the temple "held by the more militant groups among the Palestinian Jews who were still present after the fall of Jerusalem".

[148] Harnisch, Verhängnis, 20-23.

[149] Here saeculum broadens out the promise of the land to mean also the future world, e.g. 7:26; 8:52-53; cf. Davies, Gospel, 145-48. A similar use of saeculum in a non-temporal sense is often found in LAB, see G. Delling, "Die Weise, von der Zeit zu reden, im Liber Antiquitatum Biblicarum", NovT 13 (1971) 306-8; cf. also Paul's use of κόσμος in Rom 4:13.

Against a scepticism that doubted whether God would fulfil his promises, 4 Ezra and 2 *Apoc. Bar.* argued for a God-centred view of history: the delay of the fulfilment was according to God's mysterious plan.[150] Thus, they were able to retain their eschatological expectations, but they purified them of speculations about fixed times for their fulfilment. Although their solution did not have the same widespread political and organizational consequences as that of the Pharisees, it nevertheless represented a considerable *theological* achievement. W. Harnisch describes it in this way: "Man wird diesen durch die Negation der Skepsis erzwungenen Entwurf apokalyptischen Denkens als eine theologische Apologie der Verheissung kennzeichnen dürfen. Sie sucht die Wahrheit des göttlichen wortes zu rechtfertigen und der faktisch dominierenden Erfahrungen der Ferne Gottes standhalten".[151]

Also written between A.D. 70 and 132, probably in Palestine, was Pseudo-Philo's *Liber Antiquitatum Biblicarum.*[152] It is not an apocalyptic work, but an haggadic narration of Biblical history from Adam to King Saul. The author was concerned to emphasize the Torah as the absolute norm for Israel. However, the crisis of year 70 had shattered the basis for confidence in God's plans and promises in the Torah. As a result, it was first necessary to rebuild trust in God.[153] One way of doing that was to prove how God in the course of history actually *had* fulfilled his promises. Accordingly, when narrating Biblical history, the author sometimes inserts references to earlier promises that had now been fulfilled,[154] e.g. in 15:5, on Num 13-14:

Behold, this is the seed unto which I spake saying: "Your seed shall come into a land that is not theirs, and the nation whom they shall serve I will judge." And I fulfilled my words and made their enemies to melt away, . . .

---

[150] See 4 Ezra 4:34-37 and 2 *Apoc. Bar.* 20:1-6; 22:1-8; 23:1-7; cf. Harnisch, *Verhängnis*, 268-321.

[151] Harnisch, *Verhängnis*, 326; cf. also 318.

[152] Ch. Dietzfelbinger, Pseudo-Philo; *Antiquitates Biblicae* (Jüdische Schriften aus hell.-röm. Zeit 2/2, Gütersloh, 1975) 9-10.

[153] See G. Delling, "Von Morija zum Sinai. (Pseudo-Philo Liber Antiquitatum Biblicarum 32:1-10)", *JSJ* 2 (1971) 14-15.

[154] See O. Eissfeldt, "Zur Kompositionstechnik des Pseudo-Philonischen Liber Antiquitatum Biblicarum", *Interpretationes ad Vetus Testamentum pertinentes S. Mowinckel septuagenario missae* (also as *NorTT* 56, Oslo 1955) 53-71.

Another characteristic example is the hymn of Deborah in chapter 32, which is quite different from the original one in Judges 5.[155] It looks back upon God's salvific acts towards his people through history, with Abraham and Moses as central figures. In conclusion of this part of the hymn, Deborah sings:

> The Most Mighty hath not forgotten the least of all the promises which he made with us, saying: Many wonders will I perform for your sons. And now from this day forth it shall be known that whatsoever God hath said unto men that he will perform, he will perform it, even though men die (32:13).[156]

When the author has thus proved that God is faithful to his words and to the covenant, he can proceed to exhort Israel to trust in God without wavering.

So far, we have discussed texts from the last decades of the first century, the *Liber Antiquitatum Biblicarum* being possibly a little later. So early a date cannot be given with any certainty to other midrashic or Rabbinic sources. However, in many cases they contain material that is very old, hence we may legitimately include a few examples to show a continuity of Jewish traditions at this point. In a recent article,[157] O. Hofius has collected many Rabbinic texts relating to the interpretation of Num 23:19:

> God is not man, that he should lie,
> or a son of man, that he should repent.
> Has he said, and will he not do it?
> Or has he spoken, and will he not fulfil it?

When interpreted, this verse was in many instances combined with references to the promise made to Abraham. Thus this text also was regarded as directly relating to the contemporary situation and the quest for the fulfilment of God's promise. *Tg. Pseudo-Jonathan* to Num 23:19 shows how this text and passages from Genesis about the promise to Abraham were linked together:

---

[155] See Delling, "Von Morija zum Sinai", 1-18.
[156] See further 9:4; 13:10; 19:2; 23:1; 30:7; 32:12. The covenant, the promises, the Torah etc. are described as eternal (*sempiternus*), e.g. 9:8; 11:2, 5; 13:7; see Delling, "Zeit", 305-21.
[157] "Die Unabänderlichkeit des göttlichen Heilsratsschlusses", *ZNW* 64 (1973) 135-45.

The word of the living and eternal God, Master of the world, Lord, is not as those of men. For a man speaks, and then takes back his word. Nor do His works resemble those of the children of flesh, who take counsel among themselves and then renounce their decisions. *But the Master of all the universe declared that He would multiply this people as the stars of heaven, and that he would give to it the land of Canaan.* Can He speak and not act? Is He able not to accomplish that which he has declared? [158]

Similarly also in the late *Num. Rab.* 20:20 to Num 23:19:

God is not a man, that he should lie. He is not like a mortal. If a mortal acquires friends he gives them up on finding others who are better, but He is not so. *He cannot turn back on the oath to the first Patriarchs.*[159]

In the same midrash, 23:8, there is another exposition of Num 23:19, in which the promise to Abraham in Gen 15:5 and Deut 1:10 (which could be read as a description of its fulfilment) are added as proofs that "God is not a man that He should lie".[160]

Hofius does not discuss the function of this motif, but it clearly continues the Old Testament and Apocalyptic usage. When God's unchangeability and faithfulness were recognized to lie behind the promise made to Abraham, Israel's trust in God was correspondingly strengthened. The conviction that, in the end, God would keep his promise to Abraham was fundamental to the identity of the Jews, especially after they were spread over large parts of the world. We shall here mention an exposition by R. Eleazar b. Azariah in the *Mekilta* to Ex 14:15:

For the sake of their father Abraham I will divide the sea for them, as it is said: "For He remembered His holy word unto Abraham His servant" (Ps 105:42). And it is written: "And He brought forth His people with joy" (Ps 105:43).

---

[158] Translation from G. Vermes, *Scripture and Tradition in Judaism*, 151-52. The promise is mentioned but not spelled out in the rendering of Num 23:19 in *Tg. Neofiti, Tg. Onqelos, Frg. Targum* and *Peshitta*; Vermes, 151.

[159] A parallel in *Tanh. Num.* balak 13.

[160] A parallel in *Tanh. Num.* masse 7. We find an early example of the use of Num 23:19 as an axiomatic statement in the discussion between R. Eliezer and R. Joshua (ca. 90 A.D.) *Sebu.* 35b; Schniewind and Friedrich, "ἐπαγγελία", *TWNT* 2 (1935) 577. See further Dahl, "Widersprüche in der Bibel", 10-11.

It was in order that the promise made to Abraham should be fulfilled that God was obliged to rescue Israel. There are several other expositions of this verse, in some of which the deliverance at the Red Sea is ascribed to the merits of Abraham.[161] But it is significant that this example of an early interpretation follows the line of thought from Deut 9:27-29 and Ex 32:11, i.e. that it was because of his promise to the patriarchs that God had rescued his people.[162]

Within Christian tradition, Heb 6:13-20, which dates from the last decades of the first century, presents the same combination of God's promise to Abraham and the notion that his words are unchangeable.[163] Within Egyptian Judaism, Philo bears witness to the same tradition earlier in the century. Hofius makes a sharp distinction between Philo's interpretation on the one hand and that of Hebrews and Rabbinic writings on the other.[164] He finds that the latter share a way of thinking about God's faithfulness to his words in terms of his acts in history, through which the promises are fulfilled. In contrast to this, Hofius contends, Philo had a speculative and philosophical concept of the unchangeability of God. However, we concluded that Philo built on the same tradition of interpretation which formed the basis also of Rabbinic exegesis.[165] In Philo's treatises *Leg. All.* III 203-8 and *Sacr.* 89-96, there is the same combination of texts and motifs as in Rabbinic literature: the word of God is different from that of man, and his "word" is above all his oath to the ancestors to give them Canaan. One cannot therefore argue, as Hofius does, that Hebrews necessarily builds on a Rabbinic rather than on a Philonic tradition. Rather, they are all independent adaptations of a common tradition.

D. *A Jewish promise for Christian Jews: Acts 7:2-8 in Luke's interpretation*

Among early Christian authors no one has incorporated Jewish traditions into his own composition more directly than Luke. The most comprehensive description of the life of Abraham in his works is found in Acts 7:2-8. In our study of this passage we are

---

[161] One exposition attributed to R. Banaah, speaks of Abraham's merits in Gen 22:3; another, attributed to Shema'yah, ascribed Abraham's merits to his faith, quoting Gen 15:6.
[162] I am grateful to Professor Otto Betz, Tübingen, for this observation.
[163] See below, 184-85.
[164] "Unabänderlichkeit", 139-44.
[165] See above, 142-43.

greatly indebted to the essay by N. A. Dahl, "The Story of Abraham in Luke-Acts".[166] In a recent study J. Kilgallen has confirmed the main thesis of Dahl's argument concerning the importance of Acts 7:2-8, in particular vv. 6-7, for the speech as a whole.[167]

The Abraham narrative introduces Stephen's defence speech in Acts 7:1-53. This speech is a survey of the history of Israel, emphasizing the role of Moses and finally reaching a climax in a discussion of the true worship of God. Many commentators find that the speech does not fit its context, in that it does not answer the accusations against Stephen in 6:10, 13-14.[168] They have therefore argued that the speech is simply a Jewish summary of the history of Israel, mostly without any particular bias. It is clear, however, that this tradition comes from Greek-speaking Judaism. Moreover, it has been suggested that 7:1-34 is directly taken over from the synagogue, whereas the Moses narrative in 7:35-53 was part of a Jewish-Christian homily.[169] In another attempt to place the speech in its historical setting some have argued that it actually goes back to the group of Greek-speaking Christian Jews around Stephen himself.[170] Still another suggestion focuses upon traits that point towards a Samaritan origin.[171] This discussion needs not detain us here. Our study is based on the assumption that the Abraham story in Acts 7:2-8 is Jewish in character, from Greek-speaking Judaism, but that Luke himself has adapted it for use within the theology of history which he develops in Acts 7. Furthermore, at least in 7:2-8 there is no need to suppose the existence of an inter-

---

[166] *Studies in Luke-Acts, Essays presented in honor of P. Schubert* (ed. L. E. Keck and J. L. Martyn, Nashville, Tenn., 1966) 139-58.

[167] *The Stephen Speech. A Literary and Redactional Study of Acts 7:2-53* (AnBib 67, Rome, 1976). For differing view-points cf. E. Haenchen, *Die Apostelgeschichte*, 225-44; M. Dibelius, *Aufsätze zur Apostelgeschichte* (ed. H. Greeven, 3rd edition, Göttingen, 1957) 143-46.

[168] E.g. Dibelius, *Aufsätze*, 143.

[169] F. Hahn, *Christologische Hoheitstitel*, 382-85 (FRLANT 83, Göttingen, 1963); cf. also Hengel, "Zwischen Jesus und Paulus", 186; and Dibelius, *Aufsätze*, 143-46. Dibelius, however, regards 7:35-53 as a Lukan composition.

[170] Especially M. Simon, *St. Stephen and the Hellenists in the Primitive Church* (London, 1968) 59-77; and M. Scharlemann, *Stephen. A Singular Saint* (AnBib 34, Rome, 1968) 12-108. But see against this Hengel, "Zwischen Jesus and Paulus", 186-90.

[171] Cf. e.g. C. H. H. Scobie, "The Origins and Development of Samaritan Christianity", *NTS* 19 (1972/73) 390-414; see the textual evidence for this theory in M. Wilcox, *The Semitisms of Acts* (Oxford, 1965) 27-35; see however, the criticism of the Samaritan theory by E. Richard, "Acts 7: An Investigation of the Samaritan Evidence", *CBQ* 39 (1977) 190-208.

mediate Jewish Christian or more specifically Samaritan source between a non-Christian Jewish tradition and Luke, especially since we hold that Luke wrote his Gospel and Acts for Christian Jews.[172]

When Luke started his summary of Israel's history with Abraham he was not only following the traditional sequence of events. Rather, he emphasized the motif of *promise* by making it the beginning of a history characterized by a progression from *promise to fulfilment*.[173] In Acts 7:2-8 Luke focuses upon the major events in the life of Abraham:

1. God revealed himself to Abraham and commanded him to leave his country to go to the land that God would show him (Gen 12:1) (7:2-3).
2. Abraham migrated from Mesopotamia via Haran (Gen 11:31) to Canaan (7:4).
3. God gave him no share in the land (7:5a).
4. However, when Abraham was still without child, God promised the land to him and to his posterity (7:5b).
5. Abraham was warned of the exile in Egypt for his descendants (Gen 15:13-14), but God also promised to rescue them and bring them into their own land to worship him (Ex 3:12) (7:6-7).
6. Abraham received circumcision (7:8a).
7. He had descendants: Isaac, and after him Jacob and the twelve patriarchs (7:8b-c).

This narrative is rather similar to summaries of the Abraham story in the Old testament and in Jewish literature.[174] However, there are some significant changes whereby traditional motifs take on a new importance within Luke's composition as a whole. Compared with the account in Gen 11:31-12:9, Luke has altered

---

[172] In most studies on Luke-Acts, there has been a dichotomy between a recognition of the large amount of Jewish material on the one hand, and the insistence that Luke nevertheless wrote for non-Jewish Christians, with a "universal" outlook, on the other. For an alternative view, making the Jewish character of Luke-Acts to bear more directly upon our construction of the historical position of Luke, see above all Jervell, *Luke and the People of God*; further G. Lohfink, *Die Sammlung Israels*.

[173] This is questioned by J. Kilgallen, *Speech*, 43-44. This is the major point of disagreement between his interpretation and that offered by Dahl and others.

[174] Cf. Josh 24:2-4; Neh 9:7-8; Ps 105:8-11; Isa 51:1-2; Wis 10:5; Sir 44:19-21.

the sequence of events in Acts 7:2-3. The revelation of God to Abraham is brought forward to the very beginning of the story, *before* Abraham departed to Haran: "The God of Glory appeared to our father Abraham when he was in Mesopotamia, before he lived in Haran—". With this change, which is known from other Jewish sources also,[175] Stephen's speech is given a typically Lukan introduction. In Luke-Acts, a revelation of God or of his angel is frequently used to introduce an episode, and this revelation then determines the course of events that follows.[176] Further examples in chapter 7 include *vv.* 30, 35, 38 and 53. The description of Abraham as "our father" in 7:2, and the identification of the promised land in 7:4 as "this land in which you are now living", serve to relate the Abraham story to the contemporary situation. They effectively link the promise to Israel, and Abraham is identified as the father of the Jews. Luke speaks to Jews living in the promised land, which God had promised Abraham without giving him "even a foot's length". The fact that Luke introduces this motif, *viz.* that Abraham did not see the fulfilment of the promise, but does not elaborate upon it, indicates that it was an integral part of his tradition. It occurred in other outlines of the Abraham narrative as well and was probably a popular motif among Jews in the Diaspora. It is found both in Hebrews and in Philo's treatises, where in both cases it is interpreted allegorically.[177] However, Luke does not spiritualize this theme. Nor is it likely that he employs the portrait of Abraham living outside the promised land as an argument for Christian mission to Jews or even non-Jews in the Diaspora.[178] Rather, we must look for the function of this motif of the patriarch in exile in his own land within the context of Acts 7. In 7:17 Luke introduces the Moses story as the fulfilment of the promise to Abraham: "But as the time of the promise drew near, which God had granted to Abraham ..." Like Abraham, Moses is also described as an exile in 7:29. Consequently, when God expelled the nations before the Jews so that they could enter Canaan (7:45), the promise in 7:5 was fulfilled, and the exile of

---

[175] See Gen 15:7; Josh 24:3; Neh 9:7; Hebr 11:8; Philo, *Abr.* 62-67; Josephus, *Ant.* I:154.

[176] E.g. Luke 1:11, 26; 2:9; 9:30-31; Acts 9:3; 16:9; 26:13 etc.; see Schürmann, *Lukas* I, 23-24.

[177] Hebr. 11:8-9; Philo. *Conf.* 79; *Virt.* 216-18.

[178] S. G. Wilson, *The Gentiles and the Gentile Mission in Luke-Acts*, 135-36; but cf. Davies, *Gospel*, 269-71.

Abraham and Moses was brought to an end. In the episodes in Acts 7:5, 17, 29 and 45, Luke is thus unfolding his scheme "from promise to fulfilment". Since the promise to Abraham was fulfilled within the history of Israel, Luke has no need to project fulfilment into the Christian era. This was a promise to Israel, and it was related to the Jews among his contemporaries as a part of their history.

The traditions that are contained in 7:6-7 are even more central to Luke's argument, not only in Stephen's speech, but in his two-part work as a whole. Luke here combines the warning of the exile and the promise of deliverance in Gen 15:13-14a with a quotation from Exod 3:12: "and after that they shall come out and worship me in this place" (λατρεύσουσίν μοι ἐν τῷ τόπῳ τούτῳ). In Rabbinic exegesis Gen 15:13 was frequently used to give a negative picture of Abraham: it was because Abraham lacked faith in God that his descendants were punished with exile.[179] This notion is totally absent in Acts 7. It is not the idea of exile as a punishment, but rather of the fulfilment of God's promise to rescue his people which is central to Luke's interest. Consequently, 7:6-7 determine Luke's composition of traditional material in the rest of the speech.[180] Even more than v. 5, they provide the main theme for Luke's development of "proof from prophecy" from the Abraham story, via the fulfilment in the Moses' narrative and into Luke's own days. In the section dealing with Moses Luke describes how the warning of trials came true (7:17-19), and also how God fulfilled his promise to rescue Israel (7:25, 30-45, esp. 34, 36). Whatever Luke's sources for Acts were, he has made a substantial revision to make them fit into his theological programme.

Although the promise was fulfilled in the time of Moses and Joshua, the quotation from Exod 3:12 that "they shall come out and worship me in this place" was directly related to a controversy in Luke's own time. Probably as a result of this controversy the text of Exodus which said ἐν τῷ ὄρει τούτῳ was changed to ἐν τῷ τόπῳ τούτῳ. With this change the text effectively becomes part of Luke's defence for Stephen, in answer to the accusations against him in 6:13-14: "This man never ceases to speak words against this

---

[179] See n. 135.
[180] See Dahl, "Abraham", 143-47; and Kilgallen, *Speech*, 36-44. Dahl emphasizes the motif of fulfilment of the promise, Kilgallen more that of the true worship.

holy place (κατὰ τοῦ τόπου τοῦ ἁγίου τούτου) and the law; for we have
heard him say that this Jesus of Nazareth will destroy this place"
(τὸν τόπον τοῦτον).[181] Luke here introduces the question of *true
worship* which is the main issue in the last part of Stephen's speech,
which discusses the tabernacle in the desert and the Temple of
Solomon (7:44-53).[182] In this section of the speech, the quotation
from Isa 66:1 in 7:49-50 is not necessarily used to criticize the
Temple as such. Rather, it is a question of the legitimate use of the
Temple—Luke is disputing the Jewish claim upon it. Stephen's
accusations against his persecutors in 7:51-53 are similar to Jesus'
speech against the Pharisees in Luke 11:46-52. It is in this context
that the words about the Temple are part of the accusations against
the Jews. They are accused of not having followed the command of
Exod 3:12, to worship God "in this place". To Luke the question of
the legitimate Temple worship was inextricably bound up with the
question of recognizing Jesus as the lord of the Temple. To him,
Jesus was the presence of God in the Temple.[183] Luke sees the
connection between Jesus and the Temple established already
from before his birth, and the confrontations between Jesus and
the Jewish leaders are in a sense conflicts over the right to the
Temple.[184] We find the same picture in Acts, where Christians Jews
are portrayed as worshipping in the Temple: they, and not the
unbelieving Jews, are the true worshippers of God! [185] When Luke
focused on the command to worship God "in this place" (Acts 7:7),
he brought into the Abraham narrative the main issue in the conflict between Christian Jews and their non-Christian fellow Jews.

Acts 7:2-8 is unmistakably Jewish; only its context reveals that
it is here used in a controversy between Jews. We may say that
Luke's interpretation of the history of Israel, drawing on a common
tradition, is in defence of a partisan argument. To Luke there could
be no doubt that the promises to Abraham had been fulfilled in the

---

[181] Many commentators have overlooked this connection between 7:7 and
6:13-14, and instead they have seen in the use of τόπος a reference to Sichem,
another indication of a Samaritan source behind Acts 7; cf. Scobie, "Samaritan Christianity", 395.

[182] See Kilgallen, *Speech*, 37-39, 87-95; and Dahl, "Abraham", 145-47; but
cf. the criticism of Dahl's argument by Wilson, *Gentiles*, 134-135.

[183] K. Baltzer, "The Meaning of the Temple in the Lukan Writings",
HTR 58 (1965) 272-77.

[184] Cf. Luke 1:8-25; 2:31-39, 41-50; 4:9-13; 13:31-35; 19:28-48.

[185] E.g. 3:1-10; 4:1-2; 5:19-21; 21:29-30; 28:26-27 (the temple-vision
in Isa 6:9-10).

history of Israel. Abraham was the father of the Jews and the promised land was no other than Palestine. Moreover, Luke made no effort to weaken the reference to circumcision in Acts 7:8. It was not only the invidual motifs which were traditional, but also their sequence in Acts 7:2-8 followed a traditional pattern. Luke's most original contribution to the composition was his use of quotations from Gen 15:13-14 and Exod 3:12. With this quotation Luke made the Abraham story his starting point for a continuous chain of events, which ran all through the history of Israel and finally pointed towards Jesus.[186] It is noteworthy that in this summary in Acts 7:2-8 Luke does not even allude to Abraham's sacrifice of Isaac. It may be that this example of Abraham's obedience did not fit into Luke's plans in this introduction to Stephen's speech. In the passage as it now stands, Luke does not turn Abraham into a model for Christian or Jewish life. Abraham remains an historical person in his own time, and he is linked to Luke's contemporaries as the first in a long line of ancestors (cf. 7:2, 4, 51-53). It appears that Luke is primarily interested in describing Abraham as the man with whom God initiated his dealings with Israel. Moreover, in the largest part of 7:2-8 *God* is the grammatical subject (7:2, 3, 5a, 5b, 6, 7, 8a) whereas Abraham figures in this capacity only in 7:4, 5c and 8b. Luke has thus continued and emphasized a tradition of interpretation focusing upon *God and his activity*.[187] In this interpretation God and his trustworthiness with respect to his promise to the forefathers of Israel figured more prominently than the exemplary character of the patriarchs.

This impression is confirmed by an examination of other passages where Luke refers to the tradition about Abraham. The Jewish character of this tradition is apparent in the two hymns in Luke 1:46-55 and 68-75.[188] Luke has incorporated Jewish or early Jewish-Christian hymns almost directly into his own composition. Typical of their hymnic style, both hymns are very much God-centred, praising him for his assistance to his people, Israel. This assistance is described in terms of God's remembering his oath and

---

[186] Cf. Stephen's accusations that the Jews had rejected Jesus, Acts 7:51-53; see Kilgallen, *Speech*, 101-4.

[187] See Kilgallen, *Speech*, 42-43; and Scharlemann, *Stephen*, 63. Notice how Acts as a whole is God-centred in its christology and ecclesiology; Lohfink, *Die Sammlung Israels*, 85-92.

[188] See Schürmann, *Lukas* I, 77-79, 88-94. Luke 1:68-75 and 76-79 did probably not originally form one unit.

his words to Abraham, cf. Luke 1:54-55: "He has helped his
servant Israel, in remembrance of his mercy (μνησθῆναι ἐλέους) as
he spoke to our fathers, to Abraham and to his posterity forever".
Similarly in 1:72: "to perform the mercy promised to our fathers
and to remember his holy covenant (μνησθῆναι διαθήκης ἁγίας αὐτοῦ)
the oath which he swore (ὅρκον ὃν ὤμοσεν) to our father Abraham".
When God fulfils his promise to Abraham, it is a characteristic
motif that he does so by bringing about a complete reversal of the
relationship between Israel and her enemies. This change which is
a sign of God's final, eschatological act of salvation is described in
political and socio-economic terms,[189] as e.g. in 1:52-53: "he has
put down the mighty from their thrones, and exalted those of low
degree, he has filled the hungry with good things, and the rich he
has sent empty away". The same idea is present in 1:67-75 in the
promise that God will rescue his people from their enemies. In its
hymnic form this motif is similar to the promise of deliverance
from Egypt in Acts 7:6-7. On the whole Luke 1:73-75 provides a
remarkable parallel to central parts of the Abraham tradition in
Acts 7:2-8.[190] Thus it is another witness to Luke's use of traditional material as a starting-point when he developed his own
theological programme. As in Acts 7, the references to Abraham in
Luke 1:53-55 and 72-75 have not been Christianized, we are here
dealing with a completely Jewish picture of Abraham. Not the
passages themselves, but only the wider literary context indicates
that this Jewish tradition is here used in a controversy where Luke
claims to represent the true tradition. Luke's use of the "reversal"-
theme as well as his understanding of the true worship of God are
illustrative examples. We found that the question of the true
worship of God was a main issue in the polemic of Acts 7:40-53.
Luke was convinced that God could only be found and worshipped
in Jesus. It was a sign of the true Israel that it served God (Luke
1:74, 2:37; Acts 7:7; 26:6-7), and now Luke claimed that the
Christian Jews fulfilled this obligation. As followers of Christ
among the Jews they constituted a separate community, but they
were in full continuity with Jewish tradition, particularly with the

---

[189] Schürmann, Lukas 1, 76.
[190] God gave his promise or swore an oath (Luke 1:73, Acts 7:6) that he
would rescue the descendants of Abraham from their oppressors/enemies
(Luke 1:74; Acts 7:7), so that they could serve (λατρεύω) God (Luke 1:75;
Acts 7:7).

promise of the resurrection. This is the main issue that is raised in Paul's speeches in Acts 24:14-15 and 26:6-8.[191] Even if resurrection in these passages is spoken of in general terms only, it was implicitly the belief in the resurrection of Jesus that was at the centre of the discussion. Only once (in Acts 3:25-26) does Luke spell this out directly. Here he refers to the resurrection of Jesus as the fulfilment of God's promise to send a new prophet (Deut 18:15, also in Acts 7:37) and to bless all nations in the seed of Abraham (Gen 22:18).

Although Luke constantly stressed that the promise was given to the Jews (cf. Acts 3:17-26) he was aware that this message was received by one group of Jews only. This gave his exhortations their polemical twist. The "reversal" in the hymns in Luke 1 was used of Israel and her neighbours; now Luke applies it to a conflict *within Israel*. In the prophecy in 2:34, Jesus is described as the source of this conflict: "This child is set for the fall and rising of many in Israel, and for a sign that is spoken against (ἀντιλεγόμενον)". At the very end of his work Luke describes the Christian Jews as a sect that were spoken against (ἀντιλέγεται, Acts 28:22, cf. 28:19). In the narratives in the Gospel, Israel is divided over Jesus and his ministry. We sense from Luke's writings that this reflects a division in Luke's own time where the Christian Jews constituted a minority. Their claim to represent the true Israel met with little acceptance. In this conflict Luke again takes direct recourse to the Abraham tradition. He argues for the inclusion of outsiders into Christian groups on the ground that they were "sons" or "daughters of Abraham", 13:16; 19:9. Behind Luke's gospel we perceive groups of Jewish Christians who had to defend their legitimacy over against the larger part of Jewish society—as well as against non-Jewish Christians. They did this by recourse to God's promise to Abraham —as a promise to all Jews. From Luke's use of the Abraham tradition we can see that he did nothing to alter its Jewishness. There was only one new element which in most cases was only implicitly present, that the promise to Abraham had now found its fulfilment in Jesus. However, in a situation of conflict between Christian and non-Christian Jews, even this implicit proclamation became controversial.

---

[191] Jervell, *Luke*, 153-83, cf. below, 271.

E. *Trusting in God's promise. Abraham in Heb* 11:8-19

The list of heroes from the past in Hebrews 11 is in many respects similar to the outline of Israel's history in Acts.[192] However, the author of Hebrews has not combined this list of exemplary figures into a continuous history. Chapter 11 must be seen in the context of the letter as a whole, its purpose is not to argue for a successive development of promise and fulfilment.[193] Instead, the author's main concern is clearly paraenetic, and the traditions contained in chapter 11 are interpreted accordingly. The writer achieves this first of all by his use of πίστει, which has been added almost as a formulaic introduction to the various examples.[194] In consequence the patriarchs and other heroes become exemplary figures, since πίστει refers to the author's definition of faith in 11:1-3.[195] This definition is eschatological in its outlook, and similar views recur in sections where the author comments upon the traditions used, especially 11:13-16 and 39-40.

The question of sources behind Hebrews 11 has been much discussed. The material is commonly divided into three groups: 11:3-12 and 17-31, the examples of both groups having the introductory πίστει, and 11:32-38, which has a different style altogether.[196] The insertion of the author's own comments in 11:13-16 makes it more difficult to see the structure of the underlying source. We should have expected this comment to be added at the end of one group of examples, and this is the presupposition behind the division between 11:3-12 and 17-31. However, this means sepa-

---

[192] Cf. Dahl, "Abraham", 142; C. P. M. Jones, "The Epistle to the Hebrews and the Lucan writings", *Studies in the Gospels*, 122-24; W. Manson, *The Epistle to the Hebrews* (London, 1951) 25-46; O. Michel, *Der Brief an die Hebräer* (MeyerK 13, 12th edition, Göttingen, 1966) 422. Manson and, more critically, Michel suppose a common background for Acts 7 and Hebrew 11 in an early Hellenistic Christian tradition. Against this see Grässer, "Der Hebräerbrief 1938-1963", *TRu* 30 (1965) 191; but cf. Michel's reply in *Hebräer*, 554.

[193] Köster, "Abraham-Verheissung", 107.

[194] It is used 19 times in chapter 11, see G. Schille, "Katekese und Taufliturgie", *ZNW* 51 (1960) 114-15.

[195] E. Grässer, *Der Glaube im Hebräerbrief* (Marburger theologische Studien 2, Marburg, 1968) 45-57; also H. Dörries, "Zu Hebr. 11:1", *ZNW* 46 (1955) 196-202.

[196] Cf. Michel, *Hebräer*, 380-81, 390-91; and H. Windisch, *Der Hebräerbrief* (HNT 17, 2nd revised edition, Tübingen, 1931) 99, 103. Windisch finds seven examples introduced by πίστει in 11:3-12 and eleven in 11:17-31. See further the summary of the discussion in Grässer, "Hebräerbrief 1938-1963", 153-54.

rating the Abraham example in 11:8-12 from that in *vv.* 17-19 and attributing them to different groups of examples. This is unlikely, since the similarities between the various parts of the Abraham story clearly suggest that they originally formed a unit. O. Michel has pointed in the right direction with his observations on the material surrounding the episodes from the life of Abraham.[197] The actual list of Old Testament heroes of faith starts with Abel, Enoch and Noah in 11:4; furthermore, 11:23-31 comprise one unit, describing Moses and the exodus from Egypt. Basing ourselves on an analysis of the content, we shall suggest therefore that the traditional material underlying Heb 11:4-31 described three groups of Old Testament witnesses:

1. heroes from the very earliest time (4-7),
2. the patriarchs, with Abraham as the main figure (8-12, 17-22),
3. Moses and Israel in the desert (23-31).

Structured in this way, the similarities between Hebrews 11 and other Jewish summaries of the history of Israel become apparent. We notice in particular the parallel sections in Sir 44:16-18; 19-23 and 45:1-5. Moreover, when Heb 11:8-12 and 17-22 are seen as one unit,[198] we realize that the outline of the narrative corresponds to that of Acts 7:2-8.

We find the closest parallel between Acts 7 and Hebrews 11 in the first episode that is recorded, Abraham's departure for Canaan and his life as an exile in the promised land (Acts 7:2-5, Heb 11:8-10). Hebrews and Acts are the only New Testament writings to speak of this event,[199] and the similarities suggest that they have drawn on the same Jewish source. However, in its interpretation of this motif in 11:10, Hebrews goes beyond the tradition of Acts 7. The next paragraph in Heb 11:11-12, which is related to the promise of Isaac in Genesis 17 and 18, has no direct parallel in Acts 7. Instead the promises of land and of a son are combined in an abbreviated version in Acts 7:5b: "(God) promised to give it to

---

[197] *Hebräer*, 383, 406.

[198] Similarly A. Vanhoye, *La structure littéraire de l'épître aux Hébreux* (Studia Neotestamentica, Studia 1, Paris, 1963) 182-91. He finds five sub-units in 11:8-22: 8-10, 11-12, 13-16, 17-19, 20-22.

[199] Parts of Gen 12:3 and 7 are quoted in Gal 3:8, 16 but Paul is interested only in the promise and not in Abraham's departure from Mesoptamia. Cf., however n. 245, to Rom 4:13. In Jewish interpretation this was an extremely important theme, since it was so closely associated with Abraham's fight against idolatry; cf. Vermes, *Scripture*, 83-90.

him in possession and to his posterity after him, though he had no child". Compared with Acts 7:5 the longer version in Heb 11:11-12 shows more interest in the promise of many descendants, and also in the description of Abraham and Sarah and their faith in God. Each version has some material that is not duplicated in the other, e.g. circumcision in Acts 7:8a and more importantly, the sacrifice of Isaac in Heb 11:17-19. However, both Luke and the author of Hebrews conclude the story of Abraham in a similar way, by drawing the line from Abraham via Isaac and Jacob to the twelve patriarchs, Hebrews again expanding this motif.[200]

Both in content and in the actual outline, there is a great deal of correspondence between the Abraham narratives in Hebrews 11 and Acts 7. Hebrews 11 shares with Acts 7 the main themes of the Abraham story, which we described as coming from a Greek-speaking Jewish tradition, probably from the Diaspora.[201] The main difference is found in their interpretation of this material. Acts 7:2-8 is much closer to the simple style of the biblical narratives, whereas Hebrews has developed this tradition in a particular direction. It is to this interpretation of the tradition in Hebrews that we now turn.

1. 11:8-10: *"whose builder and maker is God"*

Abraham is introduced as one who was called by God. Thereby it is emphasized that it was a command from God that started this series of events in the life of Abraham. The notion that Abraham was obedient corresponds to the emphasis on obedience in paraenetic sections in Hebrews.[202] So far there is nothing new in the narrative of Hebrews compared with Acts 7. However, already in Heb 11:8 the author introduces a characteristic topic when the goal for Abraham's migration is described as εἰς τόπον ὃν ἤμελλεν λαμβάνειν εἰς κληρονομίαν. The use of τόπος instead of γῆ for the land of Canaan shows that the goal is not clearly defined.[203] This notion is picked up in v. 8b: "and he went out, not knowing where he was to

---

[200] Heb 11:20-22, esp. 11:20, shows similarities with Jewish testament literature, cf. for this literature, A. B. Kolenkow, "The Genre Testament and Forecasts of the Future in the Hellenistic Jewish Milieu", *JSJ* 6 (1975) 57-71.

[201] Dahl, "Abraham", 142.

[202] See 5:8-9; cf. R. Leivestad, "Jesus som forbilde ifølge Hebreerbrevet", *NorTT* 74 (1973) 195-206. The connection between πίστει and ὑπήκουσεν in 11:8 is based on Hebrew's conception of faith as a response to the spoken word, cf. below, 189-90.

[203] Michel, *Hebräer*, 392.

go". The idea of the promise figures prominently in 11:9, where it is mentioned twice. In the first instance it is used to describe the land, γῆν τῆς ἐπαγγελίας, in the next to portray Isaac and Jacob as τῶν συγκληρονόμων τῆς ἐπαγγελίας. This emphasis upon the promise is contrasted with the portrait of Abraham living as a stranger (παρῴκησεν) in the very land of the promise, cf. Gen 23:4. In Acts 7 this theme was part of an historical narrative, and Abraham's exile was ended, so to speak, when his descendants entered the promised land. His life as a stranger could thus be regarded as one of his trials. Hebrews' version of the same theme has been interpreted along similar lines, e.g. by O. Michel: "Der Einzug in das gelobte Land bringt keinen Abschluss, kein Ende der Probezeit, kein Aufhören der Versuchung. Im Gegenteil, die neue Situation verlangt neuen Glauben und neuen Gehorsam. Das Leben der Patriarchen steht also äusserlich im Widerspruch zur empfangenen Verheissung".[204] However, Michel offers here an exegesis not so much of Heb 11:9 as of Acts 7:5 or of the common tradition behind them. Hebrews' version of the story differs from that of Acts 7:2-5 above all in the addition in 11:10. This verse must be considered Hebrews' own interpretation of the traditional material in 11:8-9. In its symbolic interpretation Abraham's position as a stranger in the land has positive connotations. It was of vital importance that Abraham did *not* take possession of the land, for Canaan was not the promised land! Instead, Abraham expected the heavenly city, whose builder is God! As a commentary on the traditional story, *v.*10 is closely related to the eschatological outlook in 11:13-16 and 39-40.[205] Thus we perceive a difference between the traditional material shared with Acts 7 and Hebrews' own interpretation. However, even in this interpretation Hebrews stands within a continuing tradition.

A comparison with the allegorical exegesis of Philo illustrates this clearly. Since there was probably no direct literary influence from Philo upon Hebrews,[206] we are dealing with independent witnesses

---

[204] *Hebräer*, 393.

[205] A. Vanhoye, (*Structure*, 186-87) finds 11:8-10 and 13-16 to be parallel; both paragraphs describe faith which has not yet obtained the fulfilment of the promises; similarly E. Käsemann, *Das wandernde Gottesvolk* (FRLANT 55, 4th edition, Göttingen, 1961) 16-19; Grässer, "Hebräerbrief 1938-1963", 226.

[206] See the discussion of various viewpoints in Grässer, "Hebräerbrief 1938-1963", 155; and Michel, *Hebräer*, 552-53. Cf. also the detailed but hyper-critical study by R. Williamson (*Philo and the Epistle to the Hebrews*, ALGHJ 4 (Leiden, 1970) in which he refutes the views of C. Spicq, *L'épître aux Hébreux*, 2 vols. (Paris, 1952-53).

to the same tradition of interpretation. Commentators have pointed out the many individual parallels between Heb 11:8-10 and passages from Philo. However, more important than single phrases or motifs are examples of similarities in structure and argument. In this respect we find the closest parallel in *Virt.* 212-19. Here we are told that Abraham, guided by his insight into divine truth and by divine inspiration, left his country (212-14). He was regarded by the people of Canaan as a *king* (Gen 23:6; *Virt.* 216). Philo interprets this event spiritually: he describes Abraham as "this lone wanderer without relatives or friends" (Gen 23:4), who put his trust in nothing created, but only in God (218). Finally, in 219 Philo pictures the land to which Abraham went in allegorical terms similar to Heb 11:10. We find another parallel, this time to Heb 11:9-10 only, in *Conf.* 77-79. As an example of those who have their citizenship in heaven (77-78), Philo quotes the words of Abraham to the Canaanites: "I am a stranger and sojourner with you" (Gen 23:4; *Conf.* 79). As in Philo's writings, the Abraham of Hebrews 11 is a witness to true faith in God. The description of God in 11:10: ἧς τεχνίτης καὶ δημιουργὸς ὁ θεός in fact serves as a guarantee for the hope in an heavenly city. Similarly, the eschatological hope as it is expressed in 11:13-16 and 39-40 is warranted by an act of God himself (11:16b and 40a). It is well known that Hebrews represents a more literal interpretation of the Old Testament texts than Philo. Thus, the author of Hebrews understands the promise of the "land" in eschatological terms, as the "heavenly city", whereas Philo has spiritualized it and described it in what we may anachronistically call psychological terms.[207] However, this does not hide the fact that their elaborations upon the literal tradition which Acts 7 represents follow the same structure—and therefore must be ascribed to the same tradition.

2. 11:11-12: *"he considered him faithful who had promised"*

In Heb 11:11-12, we learn that Abraham was strengthened to beget Isaac, and through him the promise of a great posterity was fulfilled. Textual problems in v. 11 suggest that in this verse, and probably in others as well, the introductory πίστει was added afterwards on to a tradition that was already fixed.[208] The main problem of this verse concerns the grammatical subject; is it Abraham or

---

[207] See e.g. Braun, "Das himmlische Vaterland", 319-27.
[208] Schille, "Katekese", 114.

Sarah? The sexual imagery implied in the use of καταβολήν strongly suggests a masculine subject in v. 11,[209] all the more since the subject in v. 12 is masculine. In the text as it now stands, however, the subject appears to be καὶ αὐτὴ Σάρρα(στεῖρα).[210] The easiest solution would be to explain this as a gloss,[211] in which case this episode is a direct parallel to the other examples from the life of Abraham. However, this suggestion lacks manuscript support, and must be rejected. M. Black has pointed to the best solution to this riddle. He reads καὶ αὐτῇ Σάρρᾳ στεῖρᾳ as a "Biblical Greek circumstantial clause" and suggests the translation: "By faith, *even although Sarah was barren*, he (Abraham) received strength for procreation, even though he was past the age".[212] The ambiguities in the text at this point cannot be explained only as text-critical problems. It is likely that the distinction between Sarah and Abraham has become blurred just because they were often described in similar terms. That was not so much the case in the Genesis narrative itself, as in the later interpretations of the promise of Isaac. In Philo, not only Abraham but Sarah also was portrayed as an example of faith, and the same confessions of faith in God were ascribed to both of them. The confession in Heb 11:11, that God was faithful to his promise, is similar to that ascribed to Sarah in Philo's exposition of Gen 18:12.[213] Perhaps the present confusion in the text of Heb 11:11 is a result of the writer's efforts to reconcile two different versions of the same tradition.

In 11:11-12, we hear that the promise to Abraham and Sarah was fulfilled: δύναμιν . . . ἔλαβεν and ἀφ' ἑνὸς ἐγεννήθησαν. This notion was a part of the tradition which the author of Hebrews took over without modifying it. It contrasts strongly with his own view when he says in v. 13 that the patriarchs died *without* receiving fulfilment, μὴ κομισάμενοι τὰς ἐπαγγελίας. Not only in 11:11-12, but also in 6:13-15 the promise to Abraham was described as something which

---

[209] καταβολή refers to the sexual function of the male, F. Hauck "καταβολή", *TWNT* 3 (1938) 623; further M. Black, "Critical and Exegetical Notes on three New Testament Texts Hebrews XI, 11, Jude 5, James 1.27", *Apophoreta*, 39-41. But see the evidence for its use referring to a woman in Spicq, *Hébreux* 2, 348-49.

[210] We follow P 46 and include στεῖρα; see Black, "Hebrews XI.11", 41.

[211] Cf. G. Zuntz (*The Text of the Pauline Epistles*, London, 1953, 15-16, 34) who considers it a "primitive corruption" which has come in already in P 46.

[212] "Hebrews XI.11", 41-42.

[213] Cf. *Mut.* 166; *Leg. All.* III 218; *Abr.* 112, *Quaes. Gen.* IV 17; see above, 161-62.

was fulfilled in the lifetime of the patriarch. There are other similarities also between the two passages. In his study of the use of the
Abraham-tradition in Hebrews 6, H. Köster finds two major motifs
which were present already in the sources behind Hebrews: "1. Die
Betonung des göttlichen Schwures, und damit die bleibende und
natürlich über Abraham selbst hinausgehende Gültigkeit der Verheissung zu erweisen. 2. Das Paradigma Abrahams, der das bleibende Vorbild des Vertrauens (Glaubens) auf die göttliche Zusage
ist".[214] The first theme is elaborated upon in 6:13-14, with the
quotation from Gen 22:16-17a: "For when God made a promise to
Abraham, since he had no one greater by whom to swear, he swore
by himself, saying: 'Surely I will bless you and multiply you' ".
Then in 6:15 Abraham is depicted as an example of patience,
receiving the promise: ἐπέτυχεν τῆς ἐπαγγελίας. We have already
discussed similar texts in Philo where he referred to traditional
views about the oath of God. The main point both for Philo and
for more traditional interpreters was that the oath made God's
promise steadfast and trustworthy.[215] In Heb 11:11-12, we recognize
the same two motifs as in 6:13-15. Abraham (and/or Sarah) is an
example of faith. His trust in God is described in 11:11: πιστὸν
ἡγήσατο τὸν ἐπαγγειλάμενον. At the same time, however, this is a
statement about *God*, who is faithful to his promises. Thus it
parallels 6:13, where God is described as the giver of his promise to
Abraham.[216] The content of the promise is the same—a large
posterity. In 6:14, it is spelled out in a quotation from Gen 22:17.
In 11:12 we find: "descendants as many as the stars of heaven and
as the innumerable grains of sand by the seashore". This is not a
direct quotation, rather, it is a conflation of expressions from several
similar texts, especially Gen 13:13; 15:5; 22:17 and Exod 32:13.
It is these last two texts that are closest to the actual terminology
of Heb 11:12.[217] Common to both is the fact that in their original
context they are preceded by a reference to the oath of God.[218]

---

[214] "Abraham-Verheissung", 103.

[215] Cf. above, 141-46.

[216] See also 10:23.

[217] Cf. Heb 11:12b: καθὼς τὰ ἄστρα τοῦ οὐρανοῦ τῷ πλήθει, with Ex LXX
32:13: ὡσεὶ τὰ ἄστρα τοῦ οὐρανοῦ τῷ πλήθει. Exod 32:13 is the only one
among the Old Testament texts mentioned which has τῷ πλήθει. Cf. Heb
11:12c: καὶ ὡς ἡ ἄμμος ἡ παρὰ τὸ χεῖλος τῆς θαλάσσης ἡ ἀναρίθμητος with
Gen LXX 22:17: ὡς τὴν ἄμμον τὴν παρὰ τὸ χεῖλος τῆς θαλάσσης.

[218] Exod 32:13: "Remember Abraham, Isaac, and Israel, thy servants,
to whom thou didst swear by thine own self, and didst say to them . . .".
Gen 22:16 is the well-known text about God's oath, quoted in Heb 6:13.

Moreover, the citation in Heb 11:12 continues where 6:14 left off in its quotation from Gen 22:16-17. Caution is required lest we attribute too much importance to textual minutiae. Most probably, the conflated quotation in 11:12 was the result of quoting from memory and not of precise textcritical editing work. Even so, it is obvious that Heb 11:11-12 belongs thematically to the same tradition as 6:13-15. It is actually a more direct and concrete example of the main tenor of the earlier passage: God who swears an oath to confirm his promise, is faithful and will fulfil it. That Abraham is the ancestor of the Jews is not a prominent theme in this context. The reference to a great number of descendants signifies rather an openness towards non-Jews. If this is so, it supports the assumption that the tradition behind Hebrews 11 can be found in Jewish circles of a "Hellenistic" type, i.e. with their open attitude towards non-Jews, whether in Palestine or in the Diaspora. Perhaps we find an embryonic form of this tradition in Sir 44:21, where God's oath to Abraham is followed by the promise of descendants and of land, a conflation of Gen 15:5 and 18.[219]

The author of Hebrews has not attempted an explicitly Christian interpretation in 11:11-12. Michel's suggestion, that he saw the promise fulfilled in the Christian community,[220] is true only by implication, since the passage is used in a letter to Christian groups. There is nothing in the text itself to support this thesis. Rather, we must say that the author has been true to the intentions of his material. Instead of altering the tradition, he has argued for his own view in the following section, 11:13-16, which is inserted before the last episode from Abraham's life in 11:17-19. In a previous passage, Heb 2:16-18, however, the term "the seed of Abraham" is clearly appropriated for the Christians.[221]

3. 11:17-19: *"He considered that God was able to raise men even from the dead"*

This section on the sacrifice of Isaac has no direct parallels in Acts 7 or in Paul's use of the Abraham tradition. It is found, however, in Jas 2:21-24; but there it is used for a different purpose. In Hebrews 11, it is put within the same framework as the earlier

---

[219] See above, 126.

[220] *Hebräer*, 397.

[221] A thorough study of this passage is found in J. Swetnam, "Jesus and Isaac: A Study of Heb 2:5-18" (submitted as Ph.D. dissertation to Oxford University, 1978).

episodes. Once more, God's promise to Abraham is the main motif. The structure of this passage is similar to that of 6:13-15 and 11:11-12: [222]

1. Abraham is characterized as "he who had received the promises" (11:17b), and then the promise itself is quoted: "Through Isaac shall your descendants be named" (Gen 21:12, Heb 11:18a).
2. The promise is fulfilled when Abraham receives Isaac back, so to speak, from the dead: ὅθεν αὐτὸν καὶ ἐν παραβολῇ ἐκομίσατο (11:19b).

Here the promise is fulfilled in a situation in which there was even less hope than in that described in 11:11-12. It was through Isaac that Abraham had received the fulfilment of the promise in the first place, and now God commanded him to give him back! Throughout all ages Jewish tradition has regarded this as the ultimate trial which Abraham had to face, and it has extolled him for his obedience.[223] This was the proof *par excellence* of the trust which Abraham showed in God. Hebrews' introduction to the story in 11:17 follows this approach when it says that "by faith (πίστει) Abraham, when he was tested (πειραζόμενος) offered up Isaac". This is similar to the praise of the patriarch in Sir 44:20: ἐν πειρασμῷ εὑρέθη πιστός. The version in Jas 2:20-25 shows parallel features. Here, Abraham's willingness to sacrifice Isaac is quoted as evidence for his righteousness by faith (Gen 15:6).[224] However, the exposition in Heb 11:17-19 belongs to a different tradition of interpretation in which this example is used for another purpose. The conclusion to the story focuses on the fulfilment of the promise in spite of a hopeless situation. This fulfilment was grounded solely in the power of God to do what he had promised. It is spelled out in Abraham's confession in 11:19a: λογισάμενος ὅτι καὶ ἐκ νεκρῶν ἐγείρειν δυνατὸς ὁ θεός. This is an interpretation drawing theological conclusions from the event, similar to 11:10: "whose builder and maker is God",

---

[222] A. Vanhoye (*Structure*, 187-89) parallels 11:11-12 and 17-19. Both represent positive phases and (unlike 11:8-10 and 13-16) record the fulfilment of the promise. Furthermore, both sections are concerned with the promise of descendants, and speak of the power of God (11:11, 19) which conquers death (11:12, 19).

[223] For the extensive literature on this subject see the references in Le Déaut, *La Nuit pascale*, 132-33 n. 3; and R. J. Daly, "The Soteriological Significance of the Sacrifice of Isaac", 48-49 nn. 7-12.

[224] See Hahn, "Genesis 15:6", 96-97.

and 11:11b: "he considered him faithful who had promised". Considered in this context, we realize that 11:17-19 also belong to the same tradition as the earlier examples in chapter 11 and 6. The underlying motif is the unchangeability of the promise of God, which is frequently combined with the idea that God's words are like an oath. It is the faithfulness of God towards his words more than the obedience of Abraham which is the concern of Heb 11:17-19. Once more, it is examples from Philo more than anything which show this to be part of a broad Jewish tradition. Moreover, Heb 11:17-19 may be the earliest witness to a Rabbinic interpretation of the Akedah, otherwise found only in much later sources. In these sources, Benediction 2 from the Tefillah is added to this story: when Isaac was brought back to life, he exclaimed together with Abraham: "Blessed be God who revives the dead".[225]

There is no reason to think that the author of Hebrews made large alterations in the traditional material he had received. However, from the introduction in 11:17 we gather that he himself probably regarded this as an example of the trials of Abraham. Thus, this episode is important within the context of his exortations elsewhere in the letter. Here the Christians are frequently described as facing trials. This is also an important theme in the christology of the letter. Christ himself has been tempted and tried, therefore he can now help those who suffer temptations (2:18; 4:15). When it says that Abraham received Isaac back ἐν παραβολῇ, this addition possibly points to the general resurrection as the *real* fulfilment of the promise.[226] Hebrews' own interpretation in 11:1-3 (10), 13-16 and 39-40 provides a frame of reference for this assumption that the promise is not yet fulfilled in its reality. However, we find no explicitly christological interpretation here, the confession of God "who revived the dead" in *v.* 19 is not explicitly linked to faith in the resurrection of Jesus. However, in 13:20 a similar Old Testament designation of God is used to describe the resurrection of Jesus as an act of God.[227]

---

[225] *Pirqe R. El.* 31; cf. Le Déaut, *La Nuit pascale,* 206; and S. Spiegel, *The last trial* (N.Y. 1967) 28-37, for other medieval sources. For the use of this benediction in other contexts cf. below, 237, n. 24.

[226] Michel, *Hebräer,* 402-3; against Spicq (*Hébreux* 2, 354-55) who draws upon the exegesis of the early Church fathers for a christological interpretation.

[227] Cf. Isa LXX 63:11 and the Old Testament formula "I am the Lord who brought you up out of the land of Egypt", Lev 11:45 etc.; see Delling, "Gottesprädikationen", 16-17, 34-35; and Michel, *Hebräer,* 535-38.

4. Conclusions

There is at times in Heb 11:8-19 a discrepancy between material from tradition and the intentions of the author himself, which he voices in his inserted comments. In particular, the examples in 11:11-12, 17-19, and in 6:13-15 in their rendering of the tradition correspond to the "promise and fulfilment" theology of Acts 7: the promise too of God can be trusted, because the promise to Abraham was fulfilled in its time. In the actual text of these examples the author of Hebrews has retained this element of fulfilment. However, they were incorporated into a composition where the main theme was that the patriarchs did *not* see the fulfilment (11:13, 39). This tension between two different ways of speaking of the promise was noticed by E. Käsemann in *Das wandernde Gottesvolk*.[228] He makes this tension a major factor in the theology of Hebrews. According to Käseman, it was because of this tension that Christian life is described as a "Wanderschaft". The Christian community was always on the way to the final consummation of the promise. In this study, we have followed the suggestion of Köster which qualified the observations made by Käsemann. Köster ascribes this tension between fulfilled and not-yet-fulfilled promises to the tension between the sources of Hebrews and the theology of the author himself.[229] His attempts to locate Hebrews in a tradition of interpretation that was also represented by Philo proved to be fruitful. This does not imply that they had the same world-view or theology, but that they developed the material from a more traditional viewpoint (e.g., as represented by Acts 7) along the same lines. A typical example was Heb 11:8-10 where all the various features were found in Philo's *Virt.* 212-19. Moreover, unlike Acts 7, but again like Philo, the various episodes from the Abraham story in Hebrews 11 ended on an explicitly God-centred note. Each of them contained a confession of God (11:10, 11 and 19). The strategic position of the various statements about God within each story corresponded to that in Philo. It is apparent that the author of Hebrews was above all concerned to stress the power and the trust-worthiness of God. The different use of Genesis 22 in Hebrews 11 and in James 2 was an illuminating example. James 2 emphasized the trust and obedience of Abraham, whereas Hebrews

---

[228] 11-19.
[229] "Abraham-Verheissung", 104-5.

11 above all stressed that *God* was trustworthy. However, despite the differences, the version in Hebrews 11 was also part of a Jewish tradition, but a different situation required this emphasis upon God.

At the same time, the episodes from the life of Abraham were introduced by πίστει, characterizing him as an exemplary figure. This did not diminish the importance of the emphasis upon God, rather, it made theology a warrant for the paraenesis of Hebrews. Apparently, the author of Hebrews wrote to a group—or groups— of Christians who were about to lose faith in God.[230] In particular, they doubted that the promises—of resurrection, of a new world etc.—would come true. It was not enough, in this situation, to point to the ancestors, and the fact that God's promise to them had been fulfilled. The author of Hebrews faced the formidable task of constructing a solid theological basis for trust in the promise of God. This he achieved by bravely facing the situation—that the promises to the Christians were as yet unfulfilled—and by turning this situation into a theological virtue. Even the promises to the fore-fathers had not been fulfilled—or at best, only in a shadowy way and not in a real sense. God had not wanted them to see the fulfil-ment until the believers at the time of Hebrews were included as well. Hence the emphasis on God, that he was able to do what he had promised. In Heb 11:8-19, the author makes no explicit reference to Christ. However, in 6:13-20 the promise to Abraham is a prefiguration of that which God gave the believers in Jesus. In his study of that passage, Köster concluded that the author of Hebrews wished to do more than to depict Abraham as a paradigm for the believer.[231] Rather, he wanted to describe God's promise and oath to him as a type of the way God acted with believers in Jesus. Abraham was above all an example that God was faithful, that his words were steadfast and that he always fulfilled his promises. This is the principal importance of the confessions of God in chapter 11. They are concrete expressions of God's promises, and they warrant the fulfilment of them. Central to the exhorta-tions to retain faith is Hebrews' emphasis on the words of God, that God has spoken. [232] Most statements about God refer to him as one who speaks, promises, etc. God is the one who speaks—and

---

[230] Grässer, "Hebräerbrief 1938-1963", 223-27.
[231] "Abraham-Verheissung", 107-8.
[232] E.g. 1:1-3; 2:3; 3:7-11, 15; 6:4-5; see Käsemann, *Gottesvolk*, 12.

man is urged to listen to his words. The theological centre of Hebrews is found in this understanding of the word of God. This letter proclaims an *audible* gospel, so to speak,[233] and not a visible, "heilsgeschichtlich" gospel.

F. *Post-Pauline interpretation in* 1 *Clement* 10

Our last example of Christian use of the tradition of the promise to Abraham is taken from 1 *Clement* 10. Unlike Acts 7 and Hebrews 11, 1 *Clement* is probably influenced by Paul's interpretation of the Abraham tradition. However, it is also a witness to an older, typically Jewish tradition and therefore we may legitimately include it in our survey. The outline of the portrait of Abraham in 1 *Clement* 10 follows what we may call the Jewish exemplary tradition. The introduction in 10:1 represents a typical summary of this tradition: "Abraham, who was called 'the Friend', was found faithful in his obedience to the words of God" (πιστὸς εὑρέθη ἐν τῷ αὐτὸν ὑπήκοον γενέσθαι τοῖς ῥήμασιν τοῦ θεοῦ). Together with Enoch and Noah (9:3-4), and Lot and Rahab (11-12), Abraham is used as an example to support Clement's exhortation to obedience. The episodes from Abraham's life that follow in chapter 10 are introduced as examples of obedience. First comes Abraham's departure from his country (10:2). It was a result of his obedience, δι' ὑπακοῆς and was done in order that "he might inherit the promises of God" (κληρονομήσῃ τὰς ἐπαγγελίας τοῦ θεοῦ). This correspondence between obedience and reward is expressed even more directly in 10:7a: "Because of his faith and hospitality (διὰ πίστιν καὶ φιλοξενίαν) a son was given him in his old age". As a final proof of Abraham's obedience, in 10:7b Clement mentions his sacrifice of Isaac: "and in his obedience he offered him as a sacrifice to God on the mountain which he showed him".

It has been suggested that there was a direct literary influence of Hebrews 11 upon 1 *Clement* 10.[234] Both chapters mention the same

---

[233] Cf. K. Haacker, "Creatio ex audito. Zum Verständnis von Hbr 11:3", *ZNW* 60 (1969) 279-81.

[234] Most recently by D. A. Hagner, *The Use of the Old and New Testament in Clement of Rome* (NovTSup 34, Leiden, 1973) 184-86. But see P. Drews (*Untersuchungen über die sogen. Clementinische Liturgie im VIII Buch der apostolischen Konstitutionen* (Tübingen, 1906) 23-40) who suggests that Clement and Hebrews derived the material from a Jewish tradition independently of one another. Similarly open to this possibility is R. M. Grant, *First and Second Clement* (The Apostolic Fathers 2, by R. M. Grant and H. H. Graham, N.Y. 1965) 32.

episodes from the life of Abraham: his departure from Mesopotamia, the birth of a son, and finally the sacrifice of Isaac. But in the last two episodes in particular, the differences are even more noteworthy than the similarities. In I *Clem.* 10:1-2, 7, there is none of the emphasis upon God and his faithfulness to his promise which was so important in the parallel passages in Hebrews 11. Instead, I *Clement* follows a tradition similar to that of Jas 2:21-24: the sacrifice of Isaac is above all a sign of Abraham's obedience. Similarly, the birth of a son was a reward for Abraham's hospitality. This last motif was widespread in Jewish use of the Abraham tradition, and Clement here resembles Philo, *Abr.* 107-18. Thus I *Clem.* 10:1-2 and 7 is a typically Jewish collection of examples with its main interest on the *obedience* of Abraham. As such, it was well suited for Clement to incorporate in his exhortation to the rebels in the congregation in Corinth.[235]

However, it appears that Clement has incorporated into this framework material from a tradition which focused upon the *promise* made to Abraham. This tradition is represented by a catena of quotations in 10:3-6, and it is here that we find the closest parallels to the Abraham narrative in Acts 7 and Hebrews 11. This series of quotations include Gen 12:1-3; 13:14-16 and 15:5-6. It is introduced by the final words in 10:2: κληρονομήσῃ τὰς ἐπαγγελίας τοῦ θεοῦ, which are similar to expressions in Acts 7:5 and Heb 11:8-9. In his first quotation from Genesis 12, unlike Luke who quotes only 12:1 (Acts 7:3), Clement includes also vv. 2-3, thereby bringing God's *promise* more into focus. This tendency is emphasized when Clement, in the next paragraph, quotes Gen 13:14-16 in full. These verses also speak of a promise, both of the land, and of descendants as many as the dust of the earth. This was one of several similar texts that Luke drew upon in Acts 7:5. Finally, in I *Clem.* 10:6 the promise of a great posterity is repeated, this time with a citation from Gen 15:5 about descendants outnumbering

---

[235] See H. Chadwick, "Justification by Faith and Hospitality", *Studia Patristica* 4 (TU 79, Berlin, 1961) 281-85; Hagner (*Old and New Testament*, 250-51) suggests that Clement is directly dependent upon James 2 in his use of Abraham, Lot and Rahab as examples of hospitality. L. Sanders (*L'hellénisme de saint Clément de Rome et le paulinisme* (Studia Hellenistica 2, Louvain, 1943, 77) finds parallels to the hospitality motif in the stoic-cynic diatribe. However, the broad Jewish tradition behind this motif has not been sufficiently recognized by these writers; see R. B. Ward, "The Works of Abraham", 285-87. Similar to I *Clem.* 10, Abraham's hospitality and his sacrifice of Isaac are combined in in Philo, *Abr.* 167.

the stars. There is a parallel to this in Heb 11:12. This group of quotations from Genesis is centred on the same motif—the promise of land and of posterity. The passages that are quoted give an outline that is similar to that of the Abraham narrative in Acts 7:2-7 and Heb 11:8-12. In Acts and especially in Hebrews these events from the life of Abraham were given an interpretation, in I *Clement* 10 they are found merely as a series of texts.[236] The fact that I *Clem.* 10:6 concludes this collection with Gen 15:6 makes it probable that the collection itself had a Christian origin. With this quotation Abraham's faith is understood in light of the promise from God. Consequently, this group of texts belongs to a tradition of interpretation similar to that in Acts, Hebrews, and Romans 4. However, as we learned from Philo, this tradition also was of Jewish origin. In addition to the quotation from Gen 15:6, it is first of all Clement's use of the story of the patriarchs in chapters 30-32 which suggests that he is influenced by this tradition in its Christian, more specifically its Pauline, version.

However, when Clement incorporated this group of texts he made it conform to his own outline, depicting Abraham as an ideal of obedience. He does this through a skilful redaction of the chapter. His remarks in 10:2 serve both to introduce the quotation from Genesis 12, and to interpret it. In the quotation itself, the promise of God is the main theme, but in Clement's introduction the main theme is Abraham's obedience.[237] The same is true of his introductory remarks to Gen 13:14-16: here, he makes a small but significant alteration in the text.[238] Gen 13:14 says that Lot parted from Abraham, whereas Clement makes Abraham leave Lot, and receive the promise thereafter. According to Jewish interpretations of Genesis 13, Lot is to blame too for his selfishness in claiming the best land for himself.[239] In consequence, to part from him becomes

---

[236] J. A. Fischer (*Die Apostolischen Väter* (Munich, 1957) 7) thinks that groups of combined quotations in I *Clement* in several cases go back to collections taken over by the Christians from Hellenistic synagogues. Similarly R. M. Grant, *First and Second Clement*, 10-13. Grant does not in his list include the citations from Genesis in 10:3-6; however, they do seem to fit some of his criteria for discerning anthologies of Old Testament quotations (adopted from P. Prigent); "(4) a series of citations independently attested by several authors; and (5) the use of a series of citations for a purpose different from that for which they were collected", 10.

[237] Cf. A. W. Ziegler, *Neue Studien zum ersten Klemensbrief* (Munich, 1958) 95-97.

[238] Ziegler, *Neue Studien*, 96.

[239] Cf. Philo, *Migr.* 148-50.

an example of virtue, similar to Abraham's departure from his father's house. With these changes, Clement has interpreted the catena of quotations in 10:3-6 according to his own intentions. Thus, Gen 15:6 in 1 *Clem.* 10:6 is now understood in the light of Clement's introduction in 10:1: *viz.* that Abraham was found faithful (πιστός) because of his obedience. This is O. Andrén's conclusion also in his study of the concept of righteousness in 1 Clement.[240] However, Andrén fails to see that there is a tension in Clement (similar to the one we found in Hebrews) between one group of traditional material focusing upon the obedience of Abraham, and another where the promise was the main theme. This observation, *viz.* that Clement has incorporated various strands of the Abraham tradition into his discourse, helps us also to understand 1 *Clement* 30-32 better. The relationship between these chapters and Paul's teaching of justification by faith has been much discussed.[241] The expressions in 32:4, for example, have a genuinely Pauline ring:

And therefore we who by his will have been called in Christ Jesus are not made righteous by ourselves, or by our wisdom or understanding or piety or the deeds which we have wrought in holiness of heart, but through faith by which Almighty God has justified all men from the beginning of the world . . .

In chapters 30-31 Clement seems to contradict this; the content of these chapters can be conveniently summed up in the statement in 30:3: "Let us . . . be justified by deeds not by words". In both instances, Clement employs examples from the Old Testament. In chapter 31, Abraham, Isaac and Jacob are ideals of obedience and humility. A description of Abraham similar to that of Jas 2:21-22 is found in 31:2: τίνος χάριν ηὐλογήθη ὁ πατὴρ ἡμῶν 'Αβραάμ, οὐχὶ δικαιοσύνην καὶ ἀλήθειαν διὰ πίστεως ποιήσας. Whereas the emphasis in 30-31 is upon obedience, in chapter 32 Clement speaks of the gifts which God gave to Jacob and his descendants, and quotes the promise that "your seed shall be as the stars of heaven". Further, Clement's statement about the righteousness of the Christians in 32:4 has a direct parallel in what he says about the patriarchs in the preceding paragraph: "All of them therefore were all renowned and magnified, not through themselves or their own works or the righteous actions which they had wrought, but through his will".

---

[240] *Rättfärdighet och frid. En studie i det första Clemensbrevet* (Uppsala, 1960) 93.
[241] See the survey in Andrén, *Rättfärdighet och frid,* 30-44.

Andren points out that there is a change in Clement's arguments.[242] In chapters 30-31, he emphasizes that the patriarchs were justified by their deeds, but in chapter 32, he concentrates upon the gifts which they received. However, Andren's attempt to reconcile these two groups of statements is not quite successful. He introduces the example of Abraham in 1 Clem. 10 to prove that Clement has the same understanding of faith in chapters 30-31 as in chapter 32. Andren suggests that justification by faith (Gen 15:6) in 1 Clem. 10:6 is to be interpreted from its context in a way similar to 30:3: Abraham acted in such a way that he proved himself to be righteous.[243] This harmonious picture fails to investigate the reasons for the discrepancies between chapters 30-31 and 32. In these chapters, Clement is involved in a similar process of reinterpretation of tradition as in chapter 10. The foundation of his interpretation was his concept of faith as piety (εὐσέβεια) humility and obedience. The statement about Abraham in 31:2, like the rest of chapters 30-31, therefore correspond to the tradition of Abraham as an example of obedience in 10:1-2 and 7. It was this tradition that provided Clement with illustrations in his exhortations to disobedient and unruly members of the congregation in Corinth. At the same time, Clement shows knowledge of a Pauline tradition of interpretation, using the same examples from Genesis to emphasize the activity of God. In 10:3-6 as well as in 32:2-3, the idea of the promise of God is linked to the idea of justification by faith. It is this particular combination of motifs that strongly suggests that we are here dealing with the influence of a Pauline school, more than just a general Jewish or Christian tradition. Thus 1 Clement is a witness to the same tradition speaking of God's promise which we found in Acts 7 and Hebrews 11, but is also influenced by a Pauline interpretation. At the same time, however, the situation which Clement was addressing in Corinth demanded an emphasis on Abraham as an exemplary figure. Therefore it was along these lines, following another and more prominent Jewish and Jewish-Christian tradition, that Clement interpreted the tradition of the promise made to Abraham as well.

---

[242] Rättfärdighet och frid, 72.

[243] Andrén, Rättfärdighet och frid, 75-76. Cf. also J. B. Lightfoot (S. Clement of Rome 1 (The Apostolic Fathers 1, London, 1890) 96) who quotes 10:7; 31; 32; 33 as examples that Clement "combines the teaching of S. Paul and S. James on the great doctrine of salvation". Similarly Hagner, The Old and New Testament, 217.

G. *Rom* 4:13-22 *and the common tradition*

After this study of the interpretation of the promise to Abraham by Jewish and Christian authors in the first century, we can turn once more to Rom 4:13-22. Our initial question concerned the traditions behind this part of chapter 4, as well as the unity of the section as a whole. By drawing on the material we have collected from Jewish and other Christian sources, we are now in a position to establish the influence of traditional material on this latter part of Romans 4.

We first turn to the question of unity of 4:13-22. From observations of the structure of this section, we argued earlier that a strong case can be made for the unity of this paragraph on internal grounds. To these internal reasons we can now add evidence from outside sources. When Paul speaks in Rom 4:13 of "the promise to Abraham and his descendants, that they should inherit the *world* (κόσμου)" this refers to the promise of the land.[244] However, in 4:17-22, he clearly has the promise of a son in mind. There is nothing strange in this combination of motifs. The two promises were probably already connected at an early stage in the transmission and redaction of the patriarchal narratives. But the form and phraseology of Rom 4:13-22 suggest that Paul here follows a particular Jewish tradition in addition to the biblical passages. In the Jewish tradition which lies behind Acts 7:2-8 and Heb 11:8-19, the promise of the land was part of God's command to Abraham to leave the land of his ancestors. It was this revelation that initiated the Abraham story. In Hebrews the promise of a son follows in the next passage. Acts 7:5 speaks of the promise of the land and adds that at the time when he received the promise, Abraham had no son. On the whole, Acts 7:2-8 focuses more upon the promise of the land. The author of Hebrews, on the other hand, emphasizes the large posterity implied by the birth of Isaac (Heb 11:12). Similarly the series of citations in 1 *Clem.* 10:3-6 combines the promise of the land with that of descendants. Paul does not mention Abraham's departure from Mesopotamia, but to him, too, the promise was God's first act.[245] In consequence, the outline of the Abraham

---

[244] See below, 247-48.
[245] Possibly Paul combined the promise and Abraham's migration, cf. the suggestion by Berger ("Abraham", 71) that Paul in Rom 4:13 has in mind both Abraham's faith in Gen 15:6 and the promise in 15:7: "And he said to

narrative in Jewish traditions as it is contained in Acts 7:2-8; Heb 11:8-12(19) and 1 *Clem.* 10:3-6, is similar to that of Rom 4:13-22. The opening section in Rom 4:13 has parallels in the other texts we have mentioned:

Rom 4:13   ἡ ἐπαγγελία τῷ 'Αβραὰμ ἢ τῷ σπέρματι αὐτοῦ, τὸ κληρονόμον αὐτὸν εἶναι κόσμου

Acts 7:5   οὐκ ἔδωκεν αὐτῷ κληρονομίαν ἐν αὐτῇ οὐδὲ βῆμα ποδός,
καὶ ἐπηγγείλατο δοῦναι αὐτῷ εἰς κατάσχεσιν αὐτὴν καὶ τῷ σπέρματι
αὐτοῦ μετ' αὐτόν

Heb 11:8   εἰς τόπον ὃν ἤμελλεν λαμβάνειν εἰς κληρονομίαν
11:9   εἰς γῆν τῆς ἐπαγγελίας

1 *Clem.* 10:2   κληρονομήσῃ τὰς ἐπαγγελίας τοῦ θεοῦ

Although we shall see later that Paul has used traditional material in Rom 4:14-15 as well, this did not belong directly to the Abraham tradition.[246] In this context, therefore, we may describe 4:14-15 as a typically Pauline interpretation of the statement in 4:13. With 4:16, Paul is again back in the tradition connected with the promise to Abraham when he says ἵνα κατὰ χάριν, εἰς τὸ εἶναι βεβαίαν τὴν ἐπαγγελίαν παντὶ τῷ σπέρματι. That the promise must be steadfast and secure was a prominent motif in Jewish discussions of the oath of God. This was the theme of Heb 6:13-20, in which the major proof of the trustworthiness of God's promise was found in his oath, according to Gen 22:16. The comparison with Philo pointed to Judaism in Egypt as a centre for this interpretation, but it also had parallels in Rabbinic writings. When Philo spoke of the promise to Abraham, he almost invariably referred to its steadfastness (e.g., *Leg. All.* III 203, 204, 207; *Sacr.* 93; *Abr.* 273).

The parallels between Paul's interpretation and that of a Greek-speaking Jewish interpretation become more numerous as we come to 4:17-22, the very section which was regarded as specifically Pauline! In addition to Hebrews 11, we shall draw particularly on Philo's literal interpretation of Genesis 18 in *Abr.* 110-13, and include material from other of his works. The direct parallels to the predications of God in Rom 4:17 are well known. They must not be treated in isolation; rather, they should be seen in the context

---

him, 'I am the Lord who brought you from Ur of the Chaldeans, to give you this land to possess (τὴν γῆν ταύτην κληρονομῆσαι)''.

[246] See below, 254.

of the passage as a whole. A listing of the themes from this paragraph (rather than a verse-by-verse comparison) will show how closely Paul follows traditional exegesis.

a. The condition of Abraham and Sarah

The description of Abraham and Sarah is based on Gen 17:17b:

Shall a child be born to a man who is a hundred years old? Shall Sarah who is ninety years old bear a child?

Rom 4:19 ... when he considered his own body, which was as good as dead (νενεκρωμένον) because he was about a hundred years old, or when he considered the barrenness (τὴν νέκρωσιν) of Sarah's womb ...

Heb 11:11 ... even although Sarah was barren ... even though he was past the age ... [247]

11:12 ... from one man, and him as good as dead (νενεκρωμένου).

Abr. 111 For as they had passed the years of parenthood, their great age ...

Quaes. Gen III 56 Behold, our body has passed (its prime) and has gone beyond the age for begetting. ... if a centenarian and (a woman) of ninety years produce children ...

The various texts follow the literal meaning of Gen 17:17 rather closely. Both the author of Hebrews and Paul describe Abraham and Sarah with the terms νεκρόω and νέκρωσις, which are not found in the Septuagint, and in their literal meaning, are found in the New Testament only in these two instances.[248]

b. The situation of Abraham and Sarah interpreted

The assumptions implicit in the description of Abraham and Sarah are made explicit when the various interpreters comment upon their situation. The main tendency was to characterize their condition as *hopeless*;

Rom 4:18 ὃς παρ' ἐλπίδα ἐπ' ἐλπίδι ἐπίστευσεν

(Heb 11:11 παρὰ καιρὸν ἡλικίας)

Abr. 110 ... they presented him with a reward surpassing his hopes (ἐλπίδος μεῖζον).

---

[247] The translation follows Black, "Hebrews XI:11", 41; see above, 183.
[248] R. Bultmann, "νεκρόω", *TWNT* 4 (1942) 898-99.

111   . . . their great age had made them despair (ἀπεγνώκεσαν) of the birth of a son.

In other miracle stories, Philo frequently describes the situation by παρ' ἐλπίδα or similar terms.[249]

c. Abraham (and Sarah) believed in God's promise

In Rom 4:19-20, Paul reveals that he knows the discussion over Abraham's reaction in Gen 17:17: [250]

Then Abraham fell on his face and laughed and said to himself, "Shall a child be born to a man who is hundred years old? Shall Sarah, who is ninety years old, bear a child?"

In Rom 4:19, Paul describes Abraham and Sarah in terms reminiscent of Gen 17:17b, but his introduction to this description is strikingly different from that of Genesis:

He did not weaken (ἀσθενήσας) in faith when he considered his own body . . .

Similarly, in 4:20 Paul again emphatically denies that Abraham disbelieved:

No disbelief made him waver (οὐ διεκρίθη) concerning the promise of God, but he grew strong in faith as he gave glory to God (δοὺς δόξαν τῷ θεῷ).

John, too, probably was aware of this discussion over Abraham's reaction in Gen 17:17, when he rendered it in 8:56: [251]

Your father Abraham rejoiced (ἠγαλλιάσατο) that he was to see my day; he saw it and was glad (ἐχάρη).

Heb 11:11 merely states that Abraham (and Sarah) believed, without referring to the notion that Abraham doubted. Philo's exposition of Gen 17:17 in *Quaes. Gen.* III 55 contains several of the same motifs as Rom 4:20-21:

---

[249] See n. 111.

[250] Several commentators have noticed that the description of Abraham and Sarah in 4:19 represents an interpretation or even correction of Gen 17:17 (e.g. Cranfield, *Romans*, 247; Hahn, "Genesis 15:6", 104; M.-J. Lagrange, *Saint Paul épître aux Romains* (Paris, 1950) 96), but they have not realized that Paul here follows a tradition of interpretation.

[251] See H. E. Lona, *Abraham in Johannes* 8 (EHS.T 65, Frankfurt, 1976) 305-13.

Rightly did he laugh in his joy over the promise, being filled with great hope and in the expectation that it would be fulfilled, and because he had clearly received a vision, through which he knew more certainly Him who always stands firm, and him who naturally bends and falls.

In most cases Philo took Abraham's faith for granted. However, in his allegorical exposition he also bears witness to the discussion of the alleged notion of disbelief on the part of Abraham. In his interpretation of Gen 15:8 and 17:3, 17, he makes them conform to the notion that Abraham believed by using Gen 15:6 as a proof-text (cf. *Heres.* 100-101; *Mut.* 177-80). There is no doubt that Paul does the same in Rom 4:17-21, where he, too, interprets Abraham's reaction in the light of Gen 15:6.

d. Faith is faith in God

When Paul has denied that Abraham doubted, he goes on to describe his reactions as expressions of faith, 4:20-21. However, Abraham's faith is described not in psychological terms, but in theological terms, i.e., they focus upon God:

4:21 πληροφορηθεὶς ὅτι ὃ ἐπήγγελται δυνατός ἐστιν καὶ ποιῆσαι
(4:20 εἰς δὲ τὴν ἐπαγγελίαν τοῦ θεοῦ οὐ διεκρίθη)
Heb 11:11 ἐπεὶ πιστὸν ἡγήσατο τὸν ἐπαγγειλάμενον
(11:19 λογισάμενος ὅτι καὶ ἐκ νεκρῶν ἐγείρειν δυνατὸς ὁ θεός)

These expressions are linked to the Genesis narrative of the promise of Isaac, in that they are derived from the well-known statement in Gen 18:14: "Is anything too hard for the Lord?", in the Septuagint: μὴ ἀδυνατεῖ παρὰ τῷ θεῷ ῥῆμα.

Philo elaborates on this in *Abr.* 112, first quoting the text from the Septuagint and then adding: πάντα γὰρ ᾔδει θεῷ δυνατά.

That faith is faith in God who gave the promise is directly stated in Philo's version of Gen 18:12:

Yet He that promised (ὁ δ' ὑποσχόμενος) she says, is "my Lord" and "older" than all creation, and I needs must believe him (ᾧ πιστεύειν ἀναγκαῖον) (*Mut.* 166).

Behind the description of the hopeless situation of Abraham and of his faith in God, lies the familiar motif of contrast between man's lack of power and the infinite resources of God.[252] In Mark 10:27,

---

[252] Cf. Philo's use of Num 23:19, see above, 143-46. This motif runs through the Old and New Testament, cf. Mark 10:27, in Paul e.g. Rom 3:4; 9:12, 16; 2 Cor 1:9.

we find this fully spelled out in a confession similar to Rom 4:21: "with man it is impossible, but not with God, for all things are possible with God". It is only to be expected, then, that the contrast between God and man is explained in detail. Thus, the designations of God used are directly related to the description of the condition of Abraham and Sarah, or, in Heb 11:17-19, to that of Isaac.

Rom 4:17 ἐπίστευσεν θεοῦ τοῦ ζῳοποιοῦντος τοὺς νεκροὺς καὶ καλοῦντος τὰ μὴ ὄντα ὡς ὄντα.

Heb 11:19 has a similar function within Heb 11:17-19:

λογισάμενος ὅτι καὶ ἐκ νεκρῶν ἐγείρειν δυνατὸς ὁ θεός.

There is no direct parallel in Philo, but, see e.g., *Quaes. Gen.* III 56, where he combines motifs similar to those found in Rom 4:17 and 21:

> But to God all things are possible (cf. Rom 4:21), even to change old age into youth, and to bring one who has no seed or fruit into the begetting and fruitfulness (cf. Rom 4:17 and 19).

Cf. further Philo's allegorical interpretation of Abraham's complaint in Gen 15:2: "for I continue childless", in *Heres.* 36:

> For I know that Thou, who givest being to what is not and generatest all things (ὁ τὰ μὴ ὄντα φέρων καὶ τὰ πάντα γεννῶν), hast hated the childless and barren soul, since Thou hast given as a special grace to the race of them that see that they shall never be without children or sterile.

We shall later consider this appelation of God in more detail; we are primarily interested here in its function within its literary context.

e. The reversal-motif

God who is described in striking contrast to man works a complete reversal in the human situation. Thereby the power of God becomes visible in man's life:

Rom 4:20 ἐνεδυναμώθη τῇ πίστει, δοὺς δόξαν τῷ θεῷ
Heb 11:11 δύναμιν εἰς καταβολὴν σπέρματος ἔλαβεν

Quaes. Gen. III 56 (after the description of God):

> And so, if a centenarian and (a woman) of ninety years
> produce children, the element of ordinary events is
> removed, and only the divine power and grace clearly appear.

We notice that man responds to the miracle which God has worked with praise (Rom 4:20).[253] Finally, we mention briefly that in Rom 4:23: "But the words 'it was reckoned to him' were written not for his sake alone, but for ours also", Paul takes care to relate the narrative to the readers of his own time. Thus, this verse resembles the conclusion by the author of Hebrews in 11:39-40.[254]

When we consider these themes not in isolation, but as a whole, we realize that we are in fact dealing with a *miracle story*. The main intention of the story is to stress the power of God to assist and to rescue his people—here represented by the figure of the forefather Abraham. Hence the dominant position of confessions to God in every version of the story. The main motifs—*viz.* the hopeless situation of man, the confession of faith in God's power and of his faithfulness to his promise and, finally, the reversal of the situation— are typical of miracle stories. It follows that they can be applied to various situations. Philo, for example, interprets the giving of the promise (Genesis 18), the sacrifice of Isaac (Genesis 22), and the crossing of the Red Sea and other events in the desert (e.g. Exodus 14:16) according to this theological scheme. Similarly, in the *Antiquitates* of Josephus the sacrifice of Isaac and the crossing of the Red Sea serve as prototypes of a miracle. Following the same pattern, the author of Hebrews employs the promise to Abraham (11:11-12) and the sacrifice of Isaac (11:17-19) to convey the same message of trust in God. Paul, too, frequently speaks of the miracles and signs that God works,[255] and he often describes them by use of the reversal-pattern. Moreover, at times he even uses the full form of the miracle story. The closest parallel not only in form but also in content to Rom 4:13-21 is Paul's description of his trials in Asia (2 Cor 1:8-11). It contains the same motifs: 1) his situation was without hope, and he had even reconciled himself to the idea

---

[253] This conclusion is typical of a miracle story, cf. *Test. Abr.* 18: " . . . God sent a spirit of life upon those who had died, and they were revivified. Then, therefore, the righteous Abraham gave glory to God". See in the NT e.g. Luke 2:20; 7:16; 8:39; 18:43.

[254] See also the proems to treatises on the forefathers in Philo, *Abr.* 4-5; further *Vita Mos.* II 47-48, 59; Josephus, *Ant.* I 14-26; 4. Macc 17:8-10. With this praise (ἔπαινος) of the forefathers the author wants to evoke the same faith in God among his contemporaries; see *Vita Mos.* II 48; *Ant.* I 15, 24; 4 Macc 17:9.

[255] Cf. the use of δύναμις, e.g. in Rom 1:16; 1 Cor 1:18, 24; 2 Cor 4:7; 12:9; 13:4. It was God's power which was at work through Paul and the Christians; e.g. 1 Cor 2:4-5; 4:19-20; Gal 3:5 etc.

of death (1:8), 2) in order that he should not trust in himself, but in God "who raises the dead" (1:9), 3) and God *did* rescue him from death (1:10), so that Paul asks the Corinthians to join him in thanksgiving (1:11; cf. Rom 4:20: "Abraham gave glory to God").

The result is clear. In Rom 4:13-22 Paul is not just dealing with a number of disparate theological motifs or ideas; he can draw upon a coherent narrative. In particular, from 4:17 onwards, the form and terminology of his discourse have much in common with miracle stories in Philo (and Josephus). Heb 11:11-12 and 17-19 unmistakably share the same tradition of interpretation of the biblical narratives. However, there is in Romans 4 and Hebrews 11 an important theme which figures less prominently in Philo and Josephus, *viz.* the promises of descendants and of the land. The narratives in Romans 4 and Hebrews 11 share their concern over these issues with the traditions contained in Acts 7:2-8 and 1 *Clem.* 10:3-6. We may conclude, therefore, that the Abraham story as it is found in early Christian literature represents a Jewish tradition which is more directly concerned with the concrete questions of the identity of the people of God and with national eschatological expectations. Another observation confirms this. We found most of the parallels in Philo in his literal exposition of Genesis 17 and 18, e.g., in *Abr.* 110-13 and *Quaes. Gen.* III 55-56. It is here that Philo comes closest to the common Jewish tradition of interpretation, which is found both in Palestine and in the Diaspora, exemplified, e.g., by the Palestinian Targums. Thus, the fact that the closest parallels to Rom 4:13-22 are found in Philo cannot be used to revive the old debate of whether Paul was more influenced by "Hellenistic Judaism" or by "Rabbinic Judaism".

This general Jewish background is apparent also in Paul's use of πίστις. In particular, the meaning of "faith" in 4:17-21 is traditional. Its primary meaning is trust in God, that he will do what he has promised. This was noticed by Bultmann, who classified it as a general Jewish and Christian meaning of faith, a meaning not common elsewhere in Paul.[256] Bultmann found that the meaning of faith in this section differed from that in the first part of the chapter, which he considered typically Pauline. The main difference is that in *vv.* 17-21 Paul does not speak of faith in antithesis to the

---

[256] "πιστεύω", *TWNT* 6 (1959) 206-7, 219, 221; see further Sanders, *Paul*, 490-91.

law or to works. Our study of the traditions used in Rom 4:13-22 offers an explanation of the fact that faith here has a very general meaning, different from the rest of the chapter. It is typical of the miracle story that faith is best characterized as trust. It was a recurring motif in Philo's description of Abraham that he did not put his trust in anything created, but only in God himself.[257] However, most commentators on Romans 4 have failed to recognize the traditional nature of 4:17-21 and instead have ascribed the section entirely to Paul. Further, contrary to Bultmann's view, they even find in these verses a typically Pauline description of the nature of faith.[258] Thus they overemphasize the common Jewish and Christian motifs in Paul's theology and misrepresent his concept of faith by making this traditional description its centre.

The traditions contained in Rom 4:13-21 constitute the largest single block of traditional material which Paul has incorporated into his midrash on Gen 15:6. 4:18-21 in particular, follow almost directly descriptions and motifs contained in traditional material in Hebrews 11 or in Philo. We do not venture to extract the direct wording of this material from Paul's text as it now stands, but the general outline is clear:

4:13 the introduction of the promise to Abraham of the land.
4:16 The confirmation that the promise was steadfast, and that it included also the descendants of Abraham.
4:17 A confession of faith to God as a warrant for the promise.
4:18 Abraham's faith in an impossible situation is described as faith in the fulfilment of the promise of descendants (Gen 15:5; 17:5).
4:19 His faith is contrasted with a description of him and Sarah (Gen 17:17).
4:20 Abraham's faith was based on the promise of God and he was strengthened (in his faith) by God.
4:21 This faith is described as faith in God, that he is able to do what he he has promised.

We find Paul's own interpretation expressed above all in his contrast of πίστις and νόμος. Thus, the traditional introduction in *v.* 13 is bracketed by οὐ γὰρ διὰ νόμου and ἀλλὰ διὰ δικαιοσύνης πίστεως. This distinction is introduced also in *v.* 16. It is developed at greater

---

[257] See above, 160-61; further, D. Lührmann, "Pistis im Judentum", 29-32.
[258] See above, 104 n. 4.

length in 4:14-15. Another theme of particular interest to Paul is indicated by his repetition of Gen 17:5: "I have made you a father of many nations" in 4:17 and 18. Our analysis of the structure of 4:16-18 has shown that this idea was very important to him. The repetition of this promise, together with the reference to Abraham as "our father", 4:12, 16, shows that Paul has here interpreted the common motif of a great posterity in a particular way. Finally, with the quotation from Gen 15:6 in Rom 4:22 this section of Romans 4 is also put within the same framework as the rest of chapter 4.

In conclusion, we shall consider the suggestion by O. Michel, that Romans 4 was an independent midrash before Paul included it in his letter to the Romans.[259] H. J. van der Minde has developed this suggestion in his study, *Schrift und Tradition bei Paulus*.[260] He finds behind Romans 4 a midrash on Gen 15:6 which had originated among non-Jewish Christians. They used this midrash in discussions with Jewish Christians, to bolster the claim that they, too, were "children of Abraham". This is certainly an interesting suggestion. Unfortunately, however, van der Minde gives no external evidence for his reconstruction of this pre-Pauline tradition. His method is based on the assumption that one can distinguish Pauline interpretation from tradition solely on theological grounds, starting from apparent inconsistencies in the text. Thus, he establishes a pre-Pauline midrash comprising 4:3, 11, 12, 13, 16, 17a, 18c. This tradition contains the following themes: "1. der Glaube Abrahams, 2. die dadurch bedingte Vaterschaft, 3. die Adressaten der Vaterschaft, 4. die durch den Glauben erlangte Verheissung, 5. die Adressaten der Verheissung, 6. die nochmalige Erwähnung der Vaterschaft Abrahams".[261] When Paul interprets this tradition, according to van der Minde, he shifts the emphasis from the question about the children of Abraham to one of justification by faith. As a result, van der Minde attributes 4:17-21 almost entirely to Paul's interpretation of this Gentile-Christian midrash. We agree with his conclusions as far as 4:13, 16, 17a and 18c are concerned, but our study has shown that there is more traditional material than that! As a whole, van der Minde's detailed observations of the text of Romans 4 are unconvincing, since they do not consider the religious tradition of which Paul was a part. Nor is his attempt to

---

[259] *Römer*, 114.
[260] 78-83.
[261] *Schrift*, 82.

locate this midrash in a non-Jewish, pre-Pauline Christianity any more convincing.[262] It is certainly possible that traditions about Abraham had been used in such a way before Paul, but there is no evidence for this. In the synoptic tradition, which may contain information about the pre-Pauline period, we find *Christian Jews* claiming their right to Abraham against non-Christian Jews (Matt 3:7-9; Luke 3:7-9; 13:16; 19:9). Moreover, in Rom 4:13-22 we have established a Jewish Abraham tradition (also found among Christian Jews) on which Paul could build his exhortation. Therefore there is no need to insert a non-Jewish Christian tradition between this and Paul himself.

On the whole there seems to be little evidence that Romans 4 existed as an independent midrash on Gen 15:6 in anything like its present form. It is more likely that it is a composition of Paul himself, especially since its different sections correspond closely to the various questions and answers in the introduction in 3:27-31. However, Paul has followed a traditional homiletic pattern, as J. Jeremias and P. Borgen have pointed out.[263] Furthermore, he has included traditional material, in particular, in 4:13-22. We found the closest parallel to the homiletic structure of Romans 4 in Philo's *Mut.* 181-87.[264] In this text, Abraham's faith is introduced with an allusion to Gen 15:6. It is then interpreted in light of a quotation from Deut. 32:8. Philo closes his discussion with a direct quotation from Gen 15:6a. He does the same in *Mut.* 177-80, but there it is Gen 17:17 which is the principal text, quoted in the opening and alluded to in the closing, whereas Gen 15:6 is the proof-text that determines Philo's interpretation of 17:17. Therefore, although Paul was the first to write such a lengthy midrash on Gen 15:6, it is possible that he was directly influenced by contemporary Jewish exegesis in his use of this text.

---

[262] Since van der Minde fails to consider the traditions contained in Romans 4 against the background of other sources, he falls victim to his own criticism (*Schrift*, 129) of W. Koepp, "Die Abraham-Midraschimkette des Galaterbriefes als das vorpaulinische heidenchristliche Urtheologumenon", *Wissenschaftliche Zeitschrift der Universität Rostock* 2 (1952-53) *H. 3 der Reihe Gesellschafts- und Sprachwissenschaften*, 181-87. Koepp attempts to establish a pre-Pauline Gentile Christian midrash behind Galatians 3-4, much in the same way as van der Minde in Romans 4.

[263] In particular Borgen, *Bread from Heaven*, 46-51.

[264] See above, 162-63.

After this attempt to establish to what extent Paul shares material in his picture of Abraham with other contemporary interpreters, we shall in our next chapters turn more specifically to Paul's interpretation of this common material.

CHAPTER SEVEN

PAUL'S USE OF THE PROMISE THEME IN GALATIANS AND ROMANS

In this chapter, we want to establish the context for Paul's interpretation of the Abraham tradition in Rom 4:13-22. We shall start therefore with a survey of his use of this tradition in an earlier letter, Galatians 3 and 4. Then we turn to passages in Romans, in particular 1:2 and 15:8, in which Paul speaks non-polemically of the promise, apparently accepting a traditional use of it among Christian Jews. It is with this contact between Paul and an earlier tradition in mind that we finally look at 3:27-31. This section introduces chapter 4, and the dialogue-form reveals a controversy which sets the tone for Paul's use of the tradition of the promise made to Abraham.

A. *The promise as protest in Galatians 3 and 4:21-31*

Paul speaks of the promise to Abraham in Galatians 3 as well as in Romans 4, but there are marked differences in his application of the theme in the two letters. His method in Galatians 3 is not so much that of a homily as that of a carefully structured midrashic exposition, in which Paul follows Rabbinic rules of interpretation.[1] Most studies of this chapter have been concerned with strictly theological questions. This is true likewise of one of the most thorough investigations, the study by K. Berger entitled "Abraham in den paulinischen Hauptbriefen".[2] Berger shows most interest in the theological sections of Galatians 3, which he regards as a comment on the dogmatic statements in 2:15-21. The theme of justification by faith apart from the law, which is introduced in 2:16, finds its continuation in the scriptural proof in 3:6-12. In the last part of the interpretation of the Abraham tradition in 3:17-25, Paul

---

[1] See Dahl, "Widersprüche", 11-16, and *Studies in Paul*, 13-35; cf. below, 257, n. 93.

[2] For his outline of Galatians 3, see 47-48. In contrast, H. D. Betz ("Spirit, Freedom and Law", 145-60; and "In Defense of the Spirit: Paul's letter to the Galatians as a Document of Early Christian Apologetics", *Aspects of Religious Propaganda in Judaism and Early Christianity*, 99-114) pays more attention to the life situation of the congregation.

gives his view of the true function of the law. In this outline Berger
has included none of the passages which are directly related to the
situation in Galatia! Moreover, Galatians 3 cannot justly be described as a commentary to 2:15-21. The dogmatic statements in
2:15-21 are Paul's conclusions to his report of the conflict with
Peter in Antioch, rather than a starting-point for the following
sections of the letter.[3] The issue in question was table-fellowship
between circumcised and uncircumcised. Moreover, the exposition
of Gen 15:6 in Gal 3:6-12 does not primarily expand the thematic
formula in 2:16 on justification by faith apart from the law.
Rather, it represents a direct continuation of 3:1-5. In this paragraph, Paul refers to the founding period of the Galatian congregation and how they received the Spirit. Finally, the exegetical
midrash in chapter 3 leads directly up to Paul's description of the
experiences of the Spirit in the worship of the Galatian congregations (4:1-7). Contrary to the outline which Berger gives, dogmatic
statements and exegetical expositions are bracketed by passages in
which Paul speaks of experiences in the Galatian communities or
in his own missionary practice. It is in the light of this information
about the life and praxis of the Galatians that we can see more
clearly the function of the Abraham story within the larger context
of the letter.

    The large biographical section which introduces Galatians (1:10-
2:21) is directly related to Paul's argument in the following chapters.
The main issue in this introduction concerns the identity of Paul's
congregations. This question surfaces both in Paul's discussion with
the leaders in Jerusalem (2:1-10) and in the controversy with Peter
in Antioch (2:11-15). Peter had previously shared table-fellowship
with uncircumcised Christians in Antioch, but when a group of
Juidaizers arrived, he withdrew from this fellowship. Paul finds his
theological basis for his vehement criticism of Peter in "the truth
of the gospel" (2:14). Gradually, his report of the incident in
Antioch is transformed into the doctrinal statement of 2:16-21.
This conflict over table-fellowship between circumcised and uncircumcised Christians was no small matter to Paul. It raised the
question of what actually constituted religious identity and fellowship among Christians. For most Jewish Christians, their com-

---

[3] See K. Kertelge, "Zur Deutung des Rechtfertigungsbegriffs im Galaterbrief", *BZ* 12 (1962) 216-17; and F. Mussner, *Der Galaterbrief* (HTKNT 9,
2nd edition, Freiburg, 1974) 145-46.

mitment to this new group of Christians to which they belonged was apparently not yet so strong as the old ties to the Jewish community and the fellowship of Christian Jews. If at some point the problem of conflicting loyalties arose, Peter's behaviour in Antioch showed that the loyalty towards the regulations of the Jewish community, i.e. the law, was the stronger loyalty.

When Paul turns in 3:1-5 from this report from Antioch to the Galatian scene, he holds up for his readers, from their own history, a situation which resembles that of Peter in Antioch.[4] Above all, Paul points to the charismatic experiences in the founding period of the congregation. In 2:16-21, Paul spoke in theological and legal terms of the new identity which the Christians had received; in 3:1-5, he says the same by pointing to the experiences of the Spirit in their communal life. His pointed questions reveal that he regards this new religious experience as the basic factor of group identity and community fellowship.[5] That they had received the Spirit was the given fact, known by all (3:2, 3, 5). Paul's questions are phrased as antitheses, e.g. between the law (the synagogue) and faith (Christian preaching): "Does he who supplies the Spirit to you and works miracles among you do so by works of the law, or by hearing with faith?" (3:5) By his questions, Paul gives the early history of the Galatians a theological interpretation. He continues this interpretation of their situation by using the tradition about Abraham's belief and the promise made to him (3:6-29). This new section is introduced with a quotation from Gen 15:6, and Paul's interpretation of it is closely related to his defence of the charismatic community.[6] That it is the identity of this charismatic community which is at stake, becomes clear through the opening and closing statements of his exposition of Gen 15:6: "So you see that it is men of faith who are the sons of *Abraham*", (3:7), and "if you are Christ's, then you are *Abraham's offspring*, heirs according to promise" (3:29).[7] With this outline, Paul has identified the question under discussion as "who are the children of Abraham?"[8] He goes

---

[4] The accusations are similar; they have fallen away from the original freedom of the Spirit, cf. 2:12 and 3:3.

[5] See Betz, "Spirit", 151-53, and J. Jervell, "Das Volk des Geistes", *God's Christ and His People. Studies in Honour of Nils Alstrup Dahl* (ed. by J. Jervell and W. A. Meeks, Oslo, 1977) 88-89.

[6] Betz, "Defense", 107-10.

[7] Borgen, *Bread from Heaven*, 48.

[8] W. Foerster, "Abfassungszeit und Ziel des Galaterbriefes", *Apophoreta*, 139. Similarly, with more emphasis on the theological discussion of law versus faith, van der Minde, *Schrift*, 142-47.

on to qualify the identity of this community of the children of
Abraham with the help of subordinate quotations. The first one
is taken from Gen 12:3: "In you shall all the nations be blessed".[9]
What is this blessing which is promised? In two parallel clauses in
3:14 it is interpreted as the outpouring of the spirit on non-Jews:
"that (ἵνα) in Christ Jesus the blessing of Abraham might come
upon the Gentiles, that (ἵνα) we might receive the promise of the
spirit through faith". Thus, Paul has interpreted the promise made
to Abraham in such a way that it became immediately relevant to
the situation in Galatia. As a result, he sees the charismatic experiences in the congregation as fulfilment of God's promise. In this
way the Abraham tradition has served to legitimate the non-Jewish
Christians in their status as uncircumcised.

This is apparent in the extremely polemical section (3:10-13) in
which the promise of the blessing is contrasted with the curse of
the law.[10] From their previous position under the law, the believers
are now freed by Christ in his death. Those who are under the law,
however, remain under the curse. In an extremely intricate argument, Paul has combined a theological interpretation of the death
of Jesus with his own particular appropriation of the promise made
to Abraham, and finally he has made both of them bear directly
on the ethos and identity of the Galatian community. As a result,
history, theology, and praxis are all closely connected. The Galatians are exhorted to see their own identity in the light of the
promise to Abraham and the death of Jesus—and this in Paul's
version; consequently, they must reject other interpretations of
these events.

In all probability, Paul's opponents in Galatia had already used
Abraham as an example to draw the opposite conclusion, *viz.* that
non-Jewish Christians must be circumcised and had to observe the
law. C. K. Barrett places the use of the Abraham tradition by
Paul's opponents within a larger outline of their theology: "At the
heart of their theology was the concept of the people of God with
its origin in Abraham, and the divine promise which constituted it.
They probably took the view (expressly controverted by Paul in
3:17) that the Abrahamic covenant had been re-defined by the
Sinaitic. The promise was made to Abraham and his seed; and the
obligations of the seed were revealed in the law, fulfilment of which

---

[9] Hahn, "Genesis 15:6", 99.
[10] See Dahl, "Widersprüche", 12-13.

was made the necessary condition for receipt of the promised blessing".[11] Therefore, Paul faced theological opposition where the demand for circumcision was part of a careful interpretation of the promise made to Abraham. The dispute arose over the question of who were the legitimate children of Abraham.[12] This theory, that Paul faced another interpretation of the promise to Abraham, explains why he devoted such a large part of the letter to this argument. Furthermore, it gives a plausible reason why Paul included the Sarah-Hagar allegory in 4:21-29; he did this only because he had to counter the use which the Judaizers had made of this story. The literal meaning of this narrative would seem to support the Judaizers' point of view, and it is only by forced exegesis that Paul can turn the meaning round to bolster his own position.[13] This explains the extreme polemical twist which characterizes Galatians 3 and 4, above all Paul's use of antitheses (all of which include a negation of the law, and of circumcision etc.). It follows that we may accurately describe Paul's use of the promise as a *protest*. It was a protest not over differences of interpretation only, but over the demand made on the congregation in Galatia.

Compared with the use of the tradition of the promise in Hebrews 11 and Romans 4 for example, Galatians 3 is a very free adaptation. It is characterized both by Paul's explicitly christological interpretation as well as by his direct application to the actual situation in Galatia. Nevertheless, the basic structure which Paul follows in Galatians 3:6-29 is quite similar to that of Romans 4, but whereas Romans 4 contains larger blocks of traditional (haggadic) material, Galatians 3 gives a broader picture of Paul's own argument.[14] It is Gal 3:15-29 which comes closest to Rom 4:13-22. However, this paragraph is basically a repeated and prolonged parallel to 4:13-16, and Paul has not made use of the tradition from Genesis 17 and 18 (cf. Rom 4:(13) 17-21). This short résumé of the first part of Galatians 3 is sufficient to give us an idea of the relationship between

---

[11] "The Allegory of Abraham, Sarah, and Hagar in the Argument of Galatians", *Rechtfertigung*, 15.

[12] There is general agreement that Paul did not introduce the example of Abraham into the debate; rather, the question of the legitimate descendants of Abraham was raised earlier; e.g. Mussner, *Galater*, 223-24 n. 46; J. Eckert, *Die urchristliche Verkündigung im Streit zwischen Paulus und seinen Gegnern nach dem Galaterbrief* (Biblische Untersuchungen 6, Regensburg, 1971) 75-76; van der Minde, *Schrift*, 151-54.

[13] Barrett, "Allegory", 9-13.

[14] Similarly van der Minde, *Schrift*, 155-56.

theology and praxis in Paul's use of the Abraham tradition. It is not necessary for us to go through the rest of the chapter in detail, especially since we shall return later to some sections of it in a direct comparison with Romans 4.[15] However, there is one particular aspect of Paul's discussion in the remaining part of the chapter which needs to be mentioned. This concerns the relationship between the confession of faith that "God is one" and the unity of the believers.

In 3:16-17 Paul emphasizes that the promise was made to Abraham and his *seed* (τῷ σπέρματι αὐτοῦ) in the singular, not in the plural. Paul identifies this one offspring as Christ (3:17). What is his rationale behind this argument? [16] The statement that Christ is the singular seed was directed against the Judaizers. That the offspring is one, *viz.* Christ, ruled out any connection between the promise (the recipients of the promise) and the law (those who followed the law) in a chronological sense. This is made clear in the next section. *V.* 19 says that the law was valid only "till the *offspring* should come to whom the promise had been made". This notion is parallel to the one in *v.* 23: "Now before *faith* came, we were confined under the law". In consequence, the fact that the promise was made to one, i.e. Christ, implied that there was no fulfilment of the promise during the period of the law. This interpretation of Christ as the one offspring prepared the way for an understanding of the difficult passage in 3:20 as well. Commentators have always been puzzled by this verse: ὁ δὲ μεσίτης ἑνὸς οὐκ ἔστιν, ὁ δὲ θεὸς εἷς ἐστίν.[17] The section 3:19-22 as a whole clearly shows that the tenor of the argument is to prove the inferiority of the law compared with the promise. Moreover, the intermediary in *v.* 20 is Moses, the law-giver. We notice that "an intermediary is not of one" in 3:20a parallels the statements in *vv.* 19a, c and 22a, both of which speak of the function of the law, in contrast to that of the promise, *vv.* 19b, 22b. However, God is the originator of the law also, not only of the promise, and therefore the question of the relationship between

---

[15] See below, 257-58, 264-65.

[16] See V. Stolle, "Die Eins in Gal 3, 15-29", *Festgabe für K. H. Rengstorf zum* 70. *Geburtstag* (Theokratia, Jahrbuch des Institutum Judaicum Delitzschianum 2, 1971-72, Leiden, 1973) 204-13; U. Mauser, "Galater III.20: Die Universalität des Heils", *NTS* 13 (1966-67) 258-70; and Giblin, "Three Monotheistic Texts in Paul", 537-43.

[17] See the discussion in T. D. Callan, "The Law and the Mediator", (Ph.D. diss., Yale, 1976).

the law and the promise becomes a vital issue to Paul.[18] In this light, the confession from the *shema* in v. 20b: "God is one", is not to be understood in a general way; rather, it takes on a very specific meaning. That God is one, is quoted in support of Paul's claim that the true nature of God is now revealed in the promise and not in the law. In a concluding argument, Paul draws conclusions from this belief that God is one and that Christ is the one offspring of Abraham: "There is neither Jew nor Greek, there is neither slave nor free, there is neither male nor female, for you *are all one* in Christ Jesus" (3:28). Again, this unity across barriers of sex, class and ethnic borders is not put forward as a general statement. It is a conclusion describing this unity as a direct result of charismatic experiences in Christian groups,[19] in this case connected with baptism: "For in Christ Jesus you are all sons of God, through faith. For as many of you as were baptized into Christ have put on Christ" (3:26-27). Here they are all combined: God, Christ and the believers, who share in the same oneness. At the basis for this is the gift of the Spirit. The descriptions of the life of the community (3:1-5 and 4:1-7) which bracket the exposition of Gen 15:6 in 3:6-29, ascribe the charismatic gifts to an act by God: "Does the one who supplies the Spirit to you . . ." (3:5), and "Because we are sons, God has sent the Spirit of his son into our hearts". God is above all the God of the Spirit. This Spirit was the sign of the promise made to to Abraham, a promise which (in contrast to the law) expressed the oneness of God. Thus, Paul's discourse in Gal 3:1-4:7 is centred on God and the Spirit. Although Paul's interpretation of the promise made to Abraham is here (unlike Romans 4) christological, Paul stresses that it is God himself who is the agent.

The combination of Gen 15:6 and the notion that God is one, is found in Romans as well (3:30 and 4:1-25). It was an established part of the Abraham tradition, since it occurs in the third instance where Gen 15:6 is quoted in the New Testament, Jas 2:19-24, also.[20] However, when Paul interpreted Gen 15:6 exclusively in the light of the promise for all nations, this influenced his understanding of the confession that "God is one" also. This has not escaped the

---

[18] Dahl, *Studies in Paul*, 173.
[19] Cf. Betz, "Spirit", 147-51.
[20] In Jewish tradition, Abraham was praised as the first to preach monotheism, e.g. Josephus, *Ant.* I 156; *Gen. Rab.* 39; cf. *Jub.* 12. See further references in L. H. Feldman, "Abraham the Greek philosopher in Josephus", 145-46 nn. 9-10.

attention of V. Stolle and Ch. Mauser in their discussions of Gal
3:20. Stolle actually finds the notion that God is one to be the
governing idea behind Gal 3:15-29.[21] Moreover, Paul's use of this
confession shows the continuity between Christian belief and the
Old Testament in his theology. The continuity implied in the use of
this confession is particularly important since Paul elsewhere in
this chapter distances himself from many important Jewish theological conceptions, especially concerning the law. In conclusion,
Stolle says that: "Wird das Bekenntnis, dass Gott einer ist, bei
Paulus nicht zum Gegenstand expliziter Erörterungen gemacht, so
ist es doch die selbstverständliche Grundvoraussetzung seines
Denkens und der Hintergrund seiner theologischen Überlegungen".
This evaluation by Stolle represents a too static view of Paul's
theology. It is true that the belief that "God is one" was a basic
presupposition in Paul's thought; it was, so to speak, a given fact
in his theology. However, this historical continuity with the Old
Testament and intertestamental Judaism does not imply that Paul's
understanding of this confession remained unchanged. The very
fact that Paul challenged many central Jewish beliefs implies that
the Jewish understanding of "God is one" was challenged as well.
Chr. Maurer has seen this clearly: "Der Satz bleibt vielmehr
streng bezogen auf die in menschlicher Geschichte sich ereignenden
Offenbarungen von Verheissung und Gesetz. Dass Gott Einer ist,
steht in Beziehung zur Verheissung an Abraham, in der das Ver-
sprechen ruht, dass aus den Vielen eine Einheit werden wird".[22] In
consequence, formulaic confessions, whether from Jewish or from
early Christian tradition, cannot in themselves be made the
governing centre of Paul's theology. In this case, the statement
that "God is one" was part of a common set of beliefs for Paul and
his opponents. However, in Paul's theology it is understood in light
of the antithesis between promise and law. Thus, that God is one,
was not any longer an argument for the uniqueness of Israel, but
rather for the inclusion of Jews and non-Jews into one community
of all who had received the Spirit. We noticed that God is twice
explicitly spoken of as the one who gives the Spirit to the community
(3:5; 4:6). Apparently, Paul reinterpreted the traditional belief
that "God is one" in the light of Christian experience. Moreover,
this interaction between tradition and experience in Paul's thought

---

[21] Stolle, "Eins", 211-13; the quotation below is taken from 213.
[22] "Gal III.20", 269.

has its focusing point in Christ. It is in the picture of Christ crucified (3:2, 13) that the various lines of Paul's thought come together. This re-interpretation of the confession that "God is one" in the light of a common experience and of Paul's christology prepares the way for his use of "God is one" in the argument in Rom 3:30.

From Paul's allegory of Sarah and Hagar in Gal 4:21-31, we shall take up one point only, *viz.* that of the reversal motif as the key to Paul's interpretation of the narrative. We noticed that a literal understanding of the Sarah and Hagar pericopes would support the Judaizers in their claim that a descendant of Abraham born according to the promise must be circumcised. After a forced allegory, supported by the quotation from Isa 54:1, Paul draws his conclusion "Now you, brethren, like Isaac, are children of the promise" (4:28).²³ The following paragraph shows that Paul undertook this interpretation to support the non-Jewish Christians at a critical moment. They are described as being persecuted: "But as at that time he who was born according to the flesh persecuted (ἐδίωκεν) him who was born according to the Spirit, *so it is now*" (4:29). Here the Jews and the Judaizers as well are described in terms similar to those used of the Jews in 1 Thess 2:14-16, as persecutors of Christ and of the Christians.²⁴ The judgement upon them is pronounced with a citation from Gen 21:10, "Cast out the slave and her son; for the son of the slave shall not inherit (μὴ κληρονομήσει) with the son of the free woman" (4:30). Not only does Paul here exhort the Galatians to cut off all contact with the judaizing missionaries,²⁵ he even pronounces eschatological judgment upon them.²⁶ This is the final step to legitimate the non-Jewish community as true descendants of Abraham. As in the discussion in Galatians 3, the argument of the opponents is turned around. The children of Abraham are born of the barren woman! Furthermore, the claim that only the circumcised could inherit the promise to Abraham is reversed—the citation from Gen 21:10 is an extreme attack on the Judaizers.

We are now in a position to draw a conclusion. In Galatians, Paul has used the tradition of the promise made to Abraham in an

---

²³ Cf. Barrett, "Allegory", 13-16.

²⁴ See above, 62; and Michel, "Fragen zur 1 Thessalonicher 2, 14-16", 50-59.

²⁵ Cf. Mussner, *Galater*, 331: "Nicht die Juden, sondern die christlichen Judaisten sind die wahren Verfolger".

²⁶ 4:30; cf. 5:21; 1 Cor 6:9-10; 15:50.

extremely polemical way to defend the rights of non-circumcised Christians. There is an exclusive, almost negative aspect to his adaptation of this tradition which is caused by its use as a protest against social and religious pressure. The judaizing opponents of Paul are put under the curse, and there is little evidence that they are included among the children of Abraham. Apparently, the right to be considered a son or a daughter of Abraham was a burning issue among Christian Jews before Paul's time. He entered this discussion because it was necessary to counter the arguments of his opponents. Thus in Gal 3:6-29 and 4:21-31, we find Paul's version of a discussion which is also encountered in the Gospels, and which belongs to the earliest strata of gospel material.[27] Paul's interpretation of the promise is closely associated with Christian experiences of charismatic gifts. Paul here represents a trend of interpretation which is also found in Acts, in which the promise to Abraham and the forefathers consisted of the gift of the Spirit.[28] In this letter Paul employs the promise tradition in a concrete situation, and uses it to answer practical questions of the utmost importance to his congregations. Thus there is a directness and immediacy to Paul's discussion in Galatians which is lacking in Romans.

B. *Non-polemical use of the promise motif in Romans apart from chapter 4*

In his letter to the Romans Paul is more reconciliatory and less polemical than in Galatians. This change affects the way in which he speaks of the promise as well, especially in the opening and closing sections of the letter (1:2; 15:8). When Paul has introduced himself as an apostle for the gospel of God (Rom 1:1), he adds concerning the gospel: "Which he promised beforehand (ὃ προεπηγγείλατο) through his prophets in the holy scriptures" (1:2). In the conclusion to his exhortation to the Romans, Paul speaks of the example of Christ: "For I tell you that Christ became a servant to the circumcised to show God's truthfulness (ὑπὲρ ἀληθείας θεοῦ), in order to confirm the promises (βεβαιῶσαι τὰς ἐπαγγελίας) given to the patriarchs" (15:8). At first glance, one might think that Paul has thus given the letter a framework of "promise and fulfilment".

---

[27] In particular the Q-material in Matt 3:7-10 (Luke 3:7-9); this discussion is continued in Luke 13:16; 19:9; Acts 3:25; see also Joh 8:30-44; cf. below, 278, n. 159.

[28] See Acts 2:16-20, 33-35, 38-39.

However, it is necessary to take a closer look at the context of these passages.[29] Rom 1:1-7 is the opening of the letter in which Paul introduces himself and greets his readers. It is closely connected with the thanksgiving section, in 1:8-15. The function of these two introductory passages is above all to establish contact between Paul and his readers and to introduce the subject matter of the letter.[30] In 15:8, ἐπαγγελίας stands within a section (15:7-13) which concludes the long exhortation in 14:1-15:13. However, it is followed by a section (15:14-33) which is remarkably similar to 1:8-15, in that it expands on the theme from the introduction. In each passage, Paul addresses the Christians in Rome and speaks of his relationship with them. The most important question is his long awaited and delayed visit to Rome. In this way the body of the letter, 1:16-15:13, is bracketed by these two paragraphs concerning the relationship between the apostle and the Christians in Rome.[31] We may assume therefore, that the issue of Paul's visit to Rome is related to the main topic of the letter.[32] It is in the thanksgiving (1:8-15) that Paul for the first time directly addresses the question of his relationship with the Romans. In 1:9-11 he emphasizes his desire to visit them. Since his visit had several times been postponed, it was important for him to convince his readers that he was serious in his intentions of coming to Rome. Apparently, the question of his visit was a crucial issue in Paul's dealings with the Romans, and he ascribes great theological importance to it. When he invokes God as a witness to his good intentions, he also finds it necessary to give an apology for his apostolic authority and preaching: "For God is my witness, whom I serve with my spirit in the gospel of his son" (1:9). The apostolic authority which Paul claimed to have, was not independent of recognition by the churches which he served. In consequence, Paul lays great stress on the mutuality in his relationship with the Romans, when he speaks of what he has received from them (1:12-13). It is on this note that

---

[29] See the article by B. Olsson, ("Rom 1:3f enlight Paulus", 255-73) in which he undertakes a parallel study of Rom 1:1-7 and 15:7-21.

[30] W. Wuellner, "Paul's Rhetoric of Argumentation in Romans", 335-37.

[31] Michel, *Römer*, 362. For the motif of Paul's visit to his congregations, see the articles by Funk and Mullins mentioned above, 32, n. 1.

[32] Notice the importance of this theme in other letters, e.g. 1 Cor 4:14-21; 16:1-12; Gal 4:12-20; Phil 2:19-30; 1 Thess 2:17-3:13; Phlm 21-22. In 2 Corinthians, the question of Paul's visit is interwoven with his theological argument; e.g. 1:15-2:4; 8:16-23; 9:1-15; and especially in chapters 10-13; Funk, "Parousia", 253-54, 262.

Paul concludes the thanksgiving section (1:14-15) which leads naturally to the thematic statement in 1:16-17. From this evidence we draw the conclusion that the criticism levelled against Paul from some groups in Rome did not concern only his failure to visit them. Apparently, this criticism was combined with charges against his preaching and a questioning of his apostolic authority as well.[33] The concluding section in 15:14-33 leaves the same impression. His visit, now delayed by his mission to Jerusalem, is the main topic. Therefore, Paul is again concerned with his relationship with the Romans. He praises them for their faith (15:14) and asks for their support in prayer concerning his journey to Jerusalem (15:30-33). Moreover, he seeks to legitimate his bold words to the Romans by pointing to his priestly ministry to the non-Jewish nations, which he had received by the grace of God (15:15-21).

Paul based his apology for his apostolic ministry in the thanksgiving on the fact that he preached the gospel of the son of God (1:9). This motif links this section to the letter-opening in 1:1-7, in particular to the expansion of the greeting formula in 1:2-4. Paul's presentation of himself as an apostle to all nations (thereby including the Romans) starts in 1:1 and continues in vv. 5-6, followed by the greeting of the Christians in Rome in 1:7. Inserted into Paul's self-presentation is a section which describes his gospel: it is in accordance with the promise of God through the prophets (1:2); moreover, it is the gospel about the son of God (1:3-4). Paul expands upon this last motif by using a Jewish-Christian formula. Used in this position, inserted into Paul's presentation of himself, these statements serve to legitimate his position and his claims to apostolic authority.[34] When he used and interpreted an early Jewish-Christian formula in 1:3-4, it was to stress the common basis which he shared with his addressees. In the light of this, we can see more clearly the charges which were directed against Paul in Rome. It was probably argued that his gospel was an innovation, that he did not preach traditional beliefs. When Paul claimed that his gospel was in continuity with the promise which God had made to Israel, this claim was meant to counter such criticism. In con-

---

[33] Cf. Käsemann, *Römer*, 16.

[34] Olsson, "Rom 1:3f", 261; further, Wuellner, "Rhetoric", 335. This aspect is frequently overlooked—most commentators focus upon the more dogmatic aspects of these verses as introductions to the theme of Romans, e.g. P. Stuhlmacher, "Theologische Probleme des Römerbriefpräschripts", *EvT* 27 (1967) 375.

sequence, in the introduction Paul answers the same accusations
which he had to face in the body of the letter![35] In several instances,
Paul is accused of being in discontinuity with the preaching about
God and Israel as it was found in the Old Testament and in intertestamental Judaism (e.g. 3:1-8; 6:1, 15; 9:6, 14; 11:1). We may
conclude, therefore, that the argumentative situation in the introduction to the letter is similar to that in the central parts.[36] In
15:7-13, ἐπαγγελίας is found in the concluding section to Paul's
paraenesis in chapters 14 and 15.[37] However, this passage does not
deal directly with the controversy in Rome. Rather, Paul bases his
advice to the various parties among the Christians in Rome on the
example of Christ. In this way, 15:7-13 gives a theological justification for Paul's exhortation.[38] Further, it also serves as a transition
to 15:14-21 where Paul elaborates on a similar theme, his ministry
to the nations.

It follows that the references to the promise of God have their
primary function in Paul's apology for his apostolic preaching and
conduct. It was not his intention to describe his gospel as the
fulfilment of the promise. Rather, it was the gospel itself which was
his point of departure. This is apparent when in 1:16-17 he gives
what is his own interpretation of the gospel, although it is supported by quotations from the Bible as well.[39] Our interpretation
of these passages from chapters 1 and 15 within the letter to the
Romans is confirmed by a comparison with others of Paul's letters,
especially 2 Corinthians. In 2 Cor 1:15-22, there is the same com-

---

[35] I am grateful to Professor P. Stuhlmacher, Tübingen, for this observation.

[36] For the phrase "argumentative situation" see Wuellner, "Rhetoric",
333: "by which is meant the influence of the earlier stages of the discussion
of the argumentative possibilities open to the speaker". That the argumentative situation in the introduction and closing is similar to that of the body
of the letter, might imply that Paul faced similar objections in Rome and
Jerusalem (15:31). This contributes to our understanding of the situation
behind Paul's letter to the Romans. The importance of Paul's relationship
with the Romans concerning his visit to them should therefore be added to
his defence before the Jews in Jerusalem (cf. J. Jervell, "Der Brief nach
Jerusalem. Über Veranlassung und Adresse des Römerbriefs", ST 25 (1971)
61-73) as the rationale behind the letter.

[37] See above, 86-88.

[38] B. Olsson ("Rom 1:3f", 260-67) distinguishes between various uses of
the christological tradition in Rom 1:3-4. It is used within the context of
Paul's mission in 1:1-7; in a context of "soteriology and salvation history"
in 1:16-17; and finally in an "ethical-paraenetical" context in 15:7-21.

[39] Stuhlmacher, "Theologische Probleme", 378-79.

bination of themes: Paul's justification for his postponement of
travel plans and an apology for his gospel.[40] As a basis for his own
claim to dependability, Paul uses the faithfulness of God. In this
theological warrant, Paul speaks of Christ, in whom the promises
of God (ἐπαγγελίαι θεοῦ) had found their "yes" (1:20).

To Paul, the promise was always the promise to Israel. This was
something which he accepted as a fact, as a presupposition for his
thinking, e.g. in Rom 3:3 and 9:4.[41] Even in polemical contexts
Paul does not deny the Jews a special place in God's plan of salvation. Rather, he accuses them of misusing their position, and
charges that they consider it a right. In sharp contrast to this,
Paul describes it in strictly theological terms and within an antithesis: their special place was due only to God's faithfulness and
his election of them.[42] Thus, Israel's position and its fate are bound
up with God's trustworthiness to his promises. Since it was God
who made the promise to his people, Paul can point unreservedly
to it in 1:2 and 15:8. The same is true in 9:1-5. This passage is,
in several respects, similar to the opening and closing sections which
we have already discussed. In chapters 1 and 15, Paul spoke of his
relationship with the Christians in Rome; in 9:1-5 he is concerned
with the Jews.[43] They had rejected the Christians' proclamation of
Christ, and therefore their many advantages were of no help to
them: "They are Israelites and to them belong the sonship, the
glory, the covenants, the giving of the law, the worship and the
promises (αἱ ἐπαγγελίαι); to them belong the patriarchs, and of
their race, according to the flesh, is the Christ". This is the same
combination of motifs which we found in 1:2-4 and 15:7-8: Christ
came from the Jews, and the promises belonged to them. However,
whereas Paul in 1:1-4 and 15:7-8 referred to this for apologetic

---

[40] This text has been studied in the broader context of Paul's relationship
with the congregation in 2 Corinthians by S. N. Olson, "Confidence Expressions in Paul: Epistolary Conventions and the Purpose of 2 Corinthians"
(Ph.D. dissertation, Yale University, New Haven, Conn., 1976) 121-37.
See also P. Hahn, "Das Ja des Paulus und das Ja Gottes. Bemerkungen zu
2 Kor 1, 12-2, 1", Neues Testament und christliche Existenz. Festschrift für
H. Braun zum 70. Geburtstag (ed. by H. D. Betz and L. Schrottroff, Tübingen,
1973) 229-39. 2 Cor 7:1 is the only other occurrence of ἐπαγγελία in the
genuinely Pauline letters, but cf. its use in Eph 1:13; 2:12; 3:6. Here, too,
it is linked to the theme of the apostolic preaching of the gospel.
[41] Rese, "Die Vorzüge Israels in Röm 9, 4f und Eph 2, 12", 217 n. 37.
[42] See above, 37-39.
[43] See Rese, "Vorzüge", 211-22.

purposes, here it serves as an *accusation*. Unlike the other passages, in 9:1-5 ἐπαγγελία is given a typically Pauline interpretation in the following section, 9:6-13.[44] In this paragraph, Paul speaks antithetically of the promise, and with an emphasis on the election of Israel as an act of God alone. Even so, Paul is markedly less polemical than in Gal 4:21-31, to which Rom 9:6-13 is, so to speak, the positive counterpart. In each case, Paul uses the two sons of Abraham, one born of Sarah, the other of Hagar, to illustrate his thesis. However, whereas in Gal 4:21-31 Isaac prefigures the uncircumcised Christians, in Rom 9:6-9 he represents the true Israel. In Galatians, the midrash leads up to exhortations which are directly related to the conflict in Galatia; Paul is concerned with attitudes towards competing missionaries and the ethos of the community (4:30; 5:1). In contrast to this, in Rom 9:6-13 it is the identity of Israel which Paul interprets in light of his theology.

In all the passages we have discussed so far, Paul has used formulations which are close to earlier Christian tradition. In Rom 1:1-7, Paul built on a traditional christological formula in *vv.* 3-4. Moreover, the combination of this and the promise motif in *v.* 2 was probably also part of tradition, as Rom 9:4; 15:8; 2 Cor 1:19-20 share a similar structure.[45] The main motifs of this tradition were the promises to the forefathers now confirmed (or fulfilled) in Jesus, the son of David, and his resurrection as the sign of this. Acts 3:25-26 bears witness to this tradition which originated among Christian Jews. The blessing promised to all nations in the seed of Abraham in Gen 12:3 is here interpreted as the blessing of God's servant whom he "raised up". This is a christological interpretation of the promise to Abraham, and it is primarily proclaimed to the Jews. Paul built on this traditional material in Galatians 3 as well.[46] He, too, found that the promise in

---

[44] See above, 45-47.

[45] For the early Jewish Christian tradition contained in particular in Acts 2:22-24 and 13:32-39, see H. Schlier, "Zu Röm 1, 3f", *Neues Testament und Geschichte, O. Cullmann zum 70. Geburtstag* (ed. by H. Baltensweiler and B. Reicke, Zürich, 1972) 213-15. However, Schlier fails to see the link to 3:25-26; but see G. Delling, "Israels Geschichte und Jesusgeschichte nach Acta", *Neues Testament und Geschichte*, 195-97, esp. 197; "Lukas wird durch diese Verbindung von Geschichte Israels und Jesusgeschehen noch nicht als Paulusschüler ausgewiesen (sie dürfte bereits vorpaulinisch sein); aber es ist nicht zu übersehen, dass sie bei Paulus ebenfalls in einer besonderen Weise sichtbar wird (s.z.B. Röm 9, 4f; 11, 28b; 15:8b)".

[46] See Lindars, *New Testament Apologetic*, 207-9.

Gen 12:3 was fulfilled through Christ (Gal 3:8, 13-14, 16). However, his application of Gen 12:3 was strikingly different, in that he proclaimed the promise to the nations.

Unlike Galatians 3 and 4, in Rom 1:1-7 and 15:7-13 Paul's style is markedly non-polemical. Moreover, the antithesis between promise and law is absent from these texts (although it may be implied in the contrast between κατὰ σάρκα and κατὰ πνεῦμα in 1:3-4). We suggested that the reason was Paul's desire to establish contact with his readers. However, the conclusions he draws are no different from the conclusions drawn when he speaks in a conflict situation of the promise: he proclaims the gospel for the nations, i.e. the non-Jews, as well as the Jews. It was in the service of the gospel, which God had promised beforehand, that Paul received his apostolic mission "among all the nations" (1:5). Similarly in 15:8-9, Paul wants to make Jews and non-Jews unite in the worship of God. In Rom 1:1-7 and 15:7-13, therefore, Paul proclaims the same central message as in the rest of the letter, but without using the antithesis. Instead, he attains the same end by emphasizing the theological character of the promise: it was given by God who was faithful to his promise. On the whole, *God* is in the centre of the passages where Paul uses ἐπαγγελία. God is the subject and the agent in the opening (1:1-7),[47] and it is his trustworthiness and the praise rendered to him which is the focus of 15:7-13. This is even clearer in 9:6-13. In this short paragraph, Paul bases his argument on the words of God in the promise (9:7, 9, 13) and on the description of him in antithesis to man (9:11-12).

This short survey of the use of ἐπαγγελία in Romans apart from chapter 4 has pointed out that it is found primarily in Paul's apologetic for his missionary preaching. Thus, it is related to the use he made of it in Galatians 3 and 4, where he used it to defend the congregations he had founded among non-Jews. However, whereas in Galatians he was strongly attacking the Judaizers, in Romans he is engaged in a dialogue with Jewish Christians.[48] An additional use of it is in accusations against the Jews (9:4)—although Paul did not deny the Jews their right to the promise. The promise was a given fact in Paul's theology. However, his own view of the promise is most clearly stated when he has to face the arguments from his

---

[47] Also noticed by Olsson, "Rom 1, 3f", 263 n. 22.
[48] See Jervell, "Brief", 68-69, for a succinct evaluation of the differences in viewpoint in the two letters, caused by different situations.

Jewish-Christian opponents directly. This is the situation in Romans 4, which is not so much a proof from scripture for Paul's thesis in 3:21-26, as a continuation of the discussion in 3:27-31.

C. *Rom 3:27-31 as an introduction to chapter 4*

Despite many differences between Galatians and Romans in Paul's interpretation of the Abraham tradition, the position of the story within the structure of the letters is remarkably similar. In each letter it is associated with a rather dogmatic statement (Gal 2:15-21; Rom 3:21-26), in which Paul sums up the report of historical events or the discussion in the first part of the letter. However, between this dogmatic section and Paul's adaptation of the Abraham tradition, there is a short paragraph in dialogue style (Gal 3:1-5; Rom 3:27-31). In this section Paul raises questions of a practical nature, related to the concrete situation of his addressees or to the discussions in which he is involved. This section serves as a transition between the dogmatic statement and the Abraham example, and therefore it gives information about the situation in which Paul uses the tradition of the promise to the patriarch.

Earlier in this study, we have glanced at the structure and content of Rom 3:27-31, and we shall here repeat some of the conclusions only.[49] Here Paul addresses the problem of divisions between Jews and non-Jews within Christian communities. Concerning Paul's argument in 3:30, which he based on the statement that "God is one", we noticed that this was an example of God—language applied to the question of the identity of a religious community. In this context, "God is one" served as an argument for the inclusion and co-existence of both Jews and non-Jews in the same community, on the basis of faith. Paul is here primarily concerned with the unity of the two groups. When he says that God "will justify the circumcised on the ground of their faith and the uncircumcised through their faith" (3:30), this is more than a rejection of the idea that Jews and Jewish Christians had a privileged position (cf. 3:27-28). Rather, it amounts to a conscious effort to include them. It was necessary for Paul to stress this in face of the arrogant attitude from many non-Jewish Christians. When Paul spoke of the circumcised whom God will justify through faith, he had in mind Christian Jews. They were in themselves a sign that

---

[49] See above, 40-41.

all of Israel should be saved (11:25-32). Therefore their inclusion into Christian congregations was so important for Paul, for they were the very proof that God was faithful to his people and to his words to them. Paul argued for the fellowship of circumcised and uncircumcised Christians in an attempt to create a new solidarity. Moreover, he gave this unity and solidarity a theological justification. The confession that "God is one" was meant to serve as a bond of unity between Christians. However, when Paul argued that faith in Christ could not be reconciled with observance of the law, large groups of Christian Jews protested. Their criticism focused on Paul's attitude to the law. This criticism and Paul's answer to it is contained in 3:31: νόμον οὖν καταργοῦμεν διὰ τῆς πίστεως; μὴ γένοιτο, ἀλλὰ νόμον ἱστάνομεν. This is the last exchange of objections and answers within the dialogue in 3:27-31, and it makes a transition to the midrash in chapter 4.[50] In particular, it is related to 4:13-22, and for that reason also we shall look at this verse more closely.

The accusation in Rom 3:31a is directed against Paul's theology at a crucial point. The questions from his opponents did not only deal with individual commandments in the law, or with its new function after the revelation of God's righteousness in Christ,[51] they raised even more fundamental issues. The accusations in 3:31 imply that Paul's preaching threathened the belief that God had revealed himself to Israel in the law.[52] As in 3:5, 7, 8 etc. the rhetorical question in 3:31a is based on the argument from Paul's opponents. We must understand νόμος here in a broad sense. Paul refers to many aspects of the Jewish view of the law in 3:27-4:25: it implied that which made Yahweh the God of Israel and Israel his people (3:29), it was contained in the *shema* (3:30), in circumcision (4:9-12), and in the commandments of the law (3:27;

---

[50] E.g. Käsemann, *Römer*, 98-99; Jeremias, "Gedankengang", 51-52; against e.g. Cranfield, *Romans*, 223 (conclusion to 3:27ff); Luz, *Geschichtsverständnis*, 171-73 (preparing 8:3f); see Luz for a survey of various viewpoints.

[51] In her study of the μὴ γένοιτο argument in Paul and in Jewish writings, A. C. Wire ("Pauline Theology", 151-54) finds that it is often used to voice an objection to statements which blaspheme Israel's most sacred traditions and the relationship between God and Israel; cf. e.g. R. Simeon b. Yohai (c. 150) *Sabb* 138b; Elisha b. Abuja (c. 120) *Hag.* 15a; also Luke 20:16.

[52] For the discussion of Paul's understanding of the law, touching on many of the texts we are using, see F. Hahn, "Das Gesetzesverständnis im Römer- und Galaterbrief", *ZNW* 67 (1976) 26-63.

4:2-6). In short, ὁ νόμος represented God himself in his dealings with his people throughout its history, as it was recorded particularly in the Torah, both in its stories and in its commandments.[53] To Paul as well νόμος above all meant the Pentateuch, or the Old Testament in general. It is in this general sense that he claims to have the true interpretation of the law. In 3:31, he employs vocabulary from Rabbinic exegetical discussions when, to the charge that his doctrine abolished (καταργοῦμεν) the law, he answers that he upholds (ἱστάνομεν) it.[54] In a broad sense, Paul and his opponents mean the same by νόμος. But this is in a broad sense only: it is the context which must decide the nuances in Paul's view. On the basis of consistency in Paul's thought, U. Luz argues that νόμος must have the same meaning throughout 3:27-31.[55] However, he fails to recognize the dialogue style of this paragraph. When Paul answers the objection with μὴ γένοιτο, ἀλλὰ νόμον ἱστάνομεν, the conception of νόμος implied in this answer is not necessarily identical with that of the objection. In several passages where he uses the μὴ γένοιτο argument it implies a reinterpretation of the concept under discussion.[56] The question and answer in Rom 3:31 follow a common rhetorical form in Romans.[57] This often starts with an introduction, e.g. τί οὖν ἐροῦμεν? In 3:31, Paul starts directly with

[53] See J. A. Sanders, "Torah", *IDBSupp* (1976) 909-11; and "Torah and Paul", *God's Christ and His People*, 132-40.

[54] The terms used are ביטל and קיים, see B. Gerhardsson, *Memory and Manuscript. Oral Traditions and Written Transmission in Rabbinic Judaism and Early Christianity* (Acta Seminarii Neotestamentici Upsaliensis 23, Uppsala, 1961) 287, and D. Daube, *The New Testament and Rabbinic Judaism* (London, 1956) 60-61. Notice e.g. several instances of קיים in *Mekh.* to Exod 14:29.

[55] *Geschichtsverständnis*, 171-72.

[56] Wire ("Pauline Theology", 151-222) holds this argument to be one of the basic elements of Paul's theology. She discusses various passages in Romans in which it is used with a view to the transformation of the understanding of God implied. Our own conclusions reached independently from a more summary study are similar to Wire's.

[57] Cf. similar features in the following examples:

	3:3-4	3:5-6	3:31	6:1-4	6:15-16	7:7-8	9:14	11:1	11:11
Introduction	x	x		x	x	x	x	x	x
Question	x	x	x	x	x	x	x	x	x
μὴ γένοιτο	x	x	x	x	x	x	x	x	x
Answer	x	x	x	x		x			x
Warrant:									
Scripture	x		Rom 4			x	x	x	
experience			x	x					
other									x

See further Wire, "Pauline Theology", 151-52, and above, 59, nn. 9-11.

the question, which is normally short. It is rejected with μὴ γένοιτο, followed by a short answer (e.g. 3:4a; 6:2). Paul frequently adds a warrant or a further explanation to the answer. This can take the form of a scriptural quotation (e.g. 3:4; 9:15). He can also refer to some other authority, for example a common experience in the life of the congregation (e.g. 6:3-4), or another well-known situation (6:16). These dialogues give typical examples of Paul's use of the Bible, or early Christian tradition, and of common experiences, in a polemical situation. He counters objections from his opponents by an appeal to a known and accepted authority. Then he gives his own interpretation, which disposes of the claims made by his adversaries. In some instances, the concept held by his opponents is shown to be absurd or completely damnable (e.g. 3:5; 6:2). The exchange in 3:31 belongs to a group of texts in which the answer is introduced with ἀλλά (7:7, 13; 11:11).[58] Furthermore, the major word or concept of the question is repeated in the answer. Thus the idea in the objection is not outright rejected. Rather, it is interpreted so that "a consequence different from that proposed in the question is established".[59] In Rom 3:31, this is achieved by help of πίστις. When Paul says that he upholds the law, he speaks of the law as interpreted in the light of faith in Christ Jesus. However, it is still the Torah which Paul has in mind. Consequently, the dialogue in 3:31 is similar to his almost paradoxical statement in 3:21 that the righteousness of God is revealed apart from the law, although the law and the prophets bear witness to it. Here, too, Paul counters Jewish interpretation and praxis concerning the Torah. Similarly, in 7:7 and 13, Paul says that it was not the law itself, but the use made of it by sin which brought death.[60] This is not an observation of human psychology, but an argument from history similar to 2:17-29 and 5:12-21.[61] That it was sin, and not

---

[58] 7:7, 13; 11:11; see n. 60.

[59] Wire, "Pauline Theology", 152.

[60] Paul rejects the idea that the law is sin (7:7) or that it leads to death (7:13), but there still remains a relationship between law and death which needs explanation. When he bases his answer on the effect of sin, this means that *law* has now been more strictly defined, its relationship with death being explained, see G. Bornkamm, "Sünde, Gesetz und Tod", *Das Ende des Gesetzes; Gesammelte Aufsätze* 1 (BEvT 16, 5th edition, Munich, 1968) 53: "Eins ist dem Apostel so wichtig wie das andere: die *Unterscheidung* von Gesetz und Sünde . . . zugleich aber die eigentümliche *Verbindung*, die Gesetz und Sünde gleichwohl miteinander eingegangen sind" (Bornkamm's italics).

[61] Cf. Käsemann, *Römer*, 184-85; and Jervell, *Gud og hans fiender*, 126-33.

law which brought death upon them was no excuse. Rather, it was an accusation that the Jews had utterly perverted the meaning of the law. It was this meaning, i.e. God's righteousness, which was now made manifest through faith in Christ. From this standpoint, Paul regarded any interpretation or practice of the Torah which rejected Jesus as an aberration.

The closest parallel to Rom 3:31 in Paul's letters is his introduction to the Sarah-Hagar allegory in Gal 4:21: [62] "Tell me, you who desire to be under law (ὑπὸ νόμον), do you not hear the law (τὸν νόμον)?" His question to the Galatians is ironic when he describes them as "you who desire to be under law", i.e. as inclined to follow the Judaizers, to accept circumcision and to observe all the regulations of the law. In the context of the letter, νόμον in 4:21a means a misconstrued use of the Torah. In contrast to this, Paul speaks of the true meaning of the law when he asks: "do you not hear the law?" Following this question, he introduces the example from Genesis with γέγραπται γάρ (cf. Rom 4:3: τί γὰρ ἡ γραφὴ λέγει;). Despite its intricate argument, the main points in the allegory in Gal 4:21-31 emerge clearly: the legitimate descendants of Abraham are born according to the promise (4:23, 28), of the free woman (4:26, 28); they have the Spirit (4:29). Thus the Torah is characterized by its main content; "to hear the law" unmistakably means to hear the promise of the Spirit! Paul's use of the patriarchal narrative from Genesis as his proof clearly shows that for him as well as for his opponents the divine will was found in the Torah. However, he claimed that it was found in God's *promise* to the forefathers, not in the commandments. Furthermore, the Torah was not "scripture" in an abstract sense, but rather it recorded God's dealings with his people. In consequence, Paul's arguments from scripture should rather be called arguments from Israel's experiences in the past. Therefore, when Paul asks "do you not hear the law?", τὸν νόμον refers to God's intentions as they were revealed in the life and the history of Israel, written down in the scriptures and relevant for the contemporary situation. It is impossible to find a unified concept of νόμος in Paul's letters; it must always be analysed in the light of the context. An attempt to come to terms with Paul's use of νόμος must bear in mind that it is used in a dialogue situation where Paul interprets and corrects

---

[62] This has gone unnoticed in most commentaries, but see Wire, "Pauline Theology", 171.

traditional views. However, in Rom 3:21-4:25; 9:6-13; Gal 3 and 4:21-31, there is a remarkable unity in Paul's interpretation: in each text he finds the original intention of the Torah in the promise.[63]

In Romans 4 Paul "upholds the law" first of all by emphasizing the promise (4:13-22). Against the view that Rom 3:31 introduces chapter 4, it has been argued that 4:1 represents a new beginning, since it has a new introductory formula, τί οὖν ἐροῦμεν.[64] This difficulty is solved, however, when we realize that chapter 4 corresponds to and develops themes from various sections of 3:27-31.[65] It is not a proof from Scripture for one concept only. Even if the structure of Romans 4 is first of all determined by the use of Gen 15:6, both in terminology and in the issues which it addresses it follows 3:27-31 closely.[66] The issue raised in 3:27 concerned boasting (καύχησις), which could not be excluded by νόμος ἔργων but only by νόμος πίστεως. It is this same question which opens the discussion in 4:2: "For if Abraham was justified by works, he has something to boast about". The contrast in this first section (4:1-8) is between ἐργάζομαι and πιστεύω. In 3:29-30, Paul directly addresses the question of God and his people; he speaks of God who will justify the circumcised as well as the uncircumcised through faith. We find the same missionary interest when Paul speaks of circumcised and uncircumcised in 4:9-12. That God reckoned Abraham his faith to righteousness before he was circumcised was an argument which itself could be applied to various questions. Here, Paul applies it explicitly to the missionary situation, to the question of the inclusion of non-Jews and their co-existence with Christian Jews. His arguments in 4:1-8 and 9-12 are rather summary. For example, he introduces the antithesis between "work" and "faith" without any further explanation. Likewise he takes

---

[63] Hahn, "Gesetzesverständnis", 41 n. 39.
[64] Cranfield, Romans, 223.
[65] See Hahn, "Gesetzesverständnis", 38-40.
[66] This table shows the correspondence between the most important terms, apart from πιστεύω, which is used in all sections.

	3:27-31	4:1-8	4:9-12	4:13-22
ἔργον, ἐργάζομαι	3:27, 28	4:2, 4, 5, 6		
περιτομή, ἀκροβυστία	3:30		4:9, 10, 11, 12	
νόμος	3:27, 28, 31			4:13, 14, 15, 16
ἐπαγγελία				4:13, 14, 16, 20, 21

for granted that λογίζομαι has the inherent meaning of κατὰ χάριν. Moreover, he touches only upon some aspects of the Torah understood as law, namely works and circumcision.

This leaves 3:31 as the parallel to 4:13-22, and it is here that we find a more explicit discussion of νόμος. First of all, it is only in 4:13-16 that νόμος is mentioned in chapter 4. Clearly, it is ἐπαγγελία which is the main theme in 4:13-22, as in Galatians 3 and 4:13-22. Therefore νόμος is used in contrast to ἐπαγγελία. It is expressed as a conflict between two powers, the terminology used, καταργέω (4:14) and βέβαιος εἰμί (4:16) is similar to that of 3:31,[67] where καταργέω stands antithetically to ἱστάνω. This shows that behind 4:13-16 lies a situation of dialogue and confrontation similar to that in 3:31.[68] The antithesis between νόμος and πίστις is not a subordinate idea: in 4:13-16 it is for the first time in this chapter spelled out in detail. Paul here splits up the traditional unity of promise and law in the Torah—he can only speak of them antithetically. This is the re-interpretation of νόμος which is implied in Paul's argument in 3:31. He can uphold the law only by speaking of it in contrast to the promise. It is significant that this happens in a section where Paul is dealing with the promise to Abraham to become a father to all nations. It was on this issue, central to missionary practice in the first Christian communities, that the confrontation over the understanding of the law became most acute. In each case (Gal 3; 4:21-31; Rom 4), Paul answers objections from Christian Jews who argue that the Torah, understood as the commandments of God, must be the foundation for the people of God. Paul's emphasis on the promise as the real intention of the Torah is a result of this constant confrontation with Christian and non-Christian Jews.

Our analysis of the structure of 4:13-22 showed that the designation of God in 4:17 holds a central position in this passage. In fact, it is Paul's main warrant for his argument that the promise made to Abraham and his seed of Jews and non-Jews is steadfast. Thereby this concept of God as the one "who gives life to the dead and calls into being that which does not exist" is placed in opposition to the very law which was given by God. Apparently, the conflict between the promise and law in the Scriptures implies a

---

[67] The connection between the two terms are often overlooked, but see Berger, "Abraham", 70.

[68] See below, 254-56; cf. also Michel, (*Römer*, 122) on Rom 4:15.

conflict over the understanding of God himself. Using a term from systematic theology we may speak of the problem of "God against God" in Paul's theology.[69] It is to this problem of the function of the designation of God in 4:17 within the context of 4:13-22 that we now turn.

---

[69] See G. Ebeling, "Existenz zwischen Gott und Gott", *Wort und Glaube* 2 (Tübingen, 1965) 279-86.

CHAPTER EIGHT

GOD "WHO GIVES LIFE TO THE DEAD"

Rom 4:17 and Paul's interpretation of the promise in 4:13-25

Paul's use of ἐπαγγελία was always linked to the question of the identity of the Christian community. Even when he spoke non-polemically of the promise, he used it to argue that non-Jews as well as Jews should be included in his congregations. In the conflict between Paul and Christian Jews over this issue, both parties used the same authority, God's promise to Abraham. Thus Paul and his opponents shared some fundamental beliefs in God: his promise was steadfast (Rom 4:16) and he was able to do what he had promised (4:21). Despite these similarities, Paul's theology (as it was expressed in Romans 4) was actually very different from that of his Jewish-Christian adversaries. His position, especially in 4:11-12, 16, 18, implied a completely different view of the relationship between God, Israel and the rest of the world. Within the framework of the promise tradition Paul used the confession of God in Rom 4:17 to argue for this change of view. With the help of the phrase "God who gives life to the dead", Paul interpreted the promise to Abraham within the reversal (or transfer) scheme "from death to life". Almost paradoxically, it is a traditional formula which appears to be at the centre of Paul's drastic reinterpretation of tradition. It is therefore by studying Paul's use of this phrase in its context that we shall see how he actually transforms the traditional understanding of God.

Too often the only question which has been addressed in Romans 4:17 has been the historical one: how did Paul picture Abraham's faith? K. H. Schelkle's study of the interpretation of Romans by the Early Church fathers shows that most of the various modern suggestions concerning Rom 4:17 were made already at that time.[1] The verse was frequently understood to refer to the birth of Isaac,[2]

---

[1] K. H. Schelkle, *Paulus, Lehrer der Väter* (Düsseldorf, 1956) 136-38.
[2] E.g. Ephraem Syrus, *Commentarii in epistolas D. Pauli* (a Patribus Mekitharistis translati, Venedig, 1893) 13; another interpretation, see n. 3. Ambrose, *Comm. in epistolam ad Romanos*, PL 17, 86.

or in some cases to his rescue from the sacrifice (the Akedah).[3] Furthermore, it was generally held that Rom 4:17 concerned creation.[4] Among the most ancient solutions is one which Schelkle criticises for overlooking the obvious meaning in search of a deeper one. He quotes 2 Clement and Origen,[5] among others, who applied Abraham's faith in resurrection and creation allegorically to conversion of sinners and to mission among unbelievers. More typical of modern interpretation, however, is the emphasis on the similarity between Abraham's faith in 4:17 (resurrection and creation) and that of the Christians in 4:24 (the resurrection of Christ).[6] This emphasis is at least partly a result of the modern discussion concerning the relationship between the Old and the New Testament. Consequently, although this suggestion answers a question from our own time, it misses the point in Paul's conjunction of the two expressions of faith.

As already mentioned, the most recent discussion of Rom 4:17 has focused on the question of creation and righteousness. Käsemann and others have used Rom 4:17 to prove that in Romans 4 the righteousness of God is an expression of his action as creator.[7] The attempt by Berger to counter this thesis in his discussion of Rom 4:17 is quite unconvincing.[8] He fails to consider this expression of faith in its context, and it therefore remains an abstract belief in God as creator. Käsemann and his followers were right to consider

---

[3] E.g. Ephraem Syrus, *Commentarii*, 12; *et sicut Isaac vocavit ex eo quod non erat, sic ab altari illum eripiebat*. This interpretation, which corresponds to the Rabbinic use of the second benediction from the Shemoneh Esreh (above, 187, n. 225), has been suggested in recent times as well, e.g. by Cavallin (*Life after Death*, 122, 126, n. 34) and Le Déaut (*La nuit pascale*, 205-6), but see n. 43.

[4] Origen (Rufinus), *Comm. in Rom.*, PG 14, 978-79; *Const. App.* V 7, 16; Theodoret of Cyr, *Rom.*, PG 82, 93.

[5] E.g. 2 *Clem.* 1:8; Origen (Rufinus), *Comm. in Rom.*, 977-8; Origen, *Comm. in Rom.*, frg. 25 (ed. H. Ramsbotham, *Journal of Theological Studies*, 13 (1912) 360-61); *Sel. in Ps.*, PG 12, 1410.

[6] Cf. a few of the suggestions: the Christian faith is identical with the faith of Abraham; Käsemann, "Glaube Abrahams", 166-67; it relates to Abraham's faith as fulfilment to promise; Wilckens, "Rechtfertigung", 125-26; Christian faith represents a "Steigerung" compared with the faith of Abraham, L. Goppelt, "Apokalyptik und Typologie bei Paulus", *TLZ* 89 (1964) 333.

[7] Cf. above, 105.

[8] "Abraham", 72 n. 50; cf. the response by Käsemann, *Römer*, 116. The criticism by Luz (*Geschichtsverständnis*, 169 n. 128) in particular of Stuhlmacher's *Gerechtigkeit Gottes*, is more pertinent.

4:17 within its context in Romans 4. Their emphasis on the identity of creation and righteousness as actions of God represents a necessary correction to Bultmann's position. However, this is not the point for which *Paul* is arguing. Rather, he takes for granted the similarity between God's actions in creation and in justification, so that his main concern lies elsewhere. As we have already noticed, Paul's use of Rom 4:17 is primarily directed towards the inclusion of non-Jews also among the children of Abraham.[9]

In this chapter we shall look at the options which were open to Paul when he used the phrase "God who gives life to the dead" (Paul's "background" or "tradition"). Thereafter, we shall study Paul's use of this phrase especially in light of his criticism of the law in 4:13-16. Our main question when we compare tradition and interpretation in Romans 4, concerns the *centre* of Paul's understanding of God. What are his criteria when he applies a traditional formula to a new situation, and how does it change his understanding of God?

For the sake of brevity, in the following, "God who gives life to the dead" refers to both parts of the designation in 4:17 (also to "who calls into existence the things that do not exist") unless it is clear from the context that the first part only is intended.

A. *Rom 4:17 and resurrection and creation in the Old Testament and in the Shemoneh Esreh*

It is well-known that Paul makes use in Rom 4:17 of a liturgical formula which is best known from the second benediction of the Shemoneh Esreh: [10] "Blessed are You, Lord, who revive the dead

---

[9] Cf. van Unnik, *Foi et salut selon S. Paul*, 65. This is noticed by Käsemann, Stuhlmacher and Müller as well. However, as a result of the discussion with the followers of Bultmann, the creation motif is overemphasized, cf. above, 79, n. 3 and below, 286.

[10] A useful collection of texts and studies of the Shemoneh Esreh is now available in J. J. Petuchowski, *Contributions to the Scientific Study of Jewish Liturgy* (N.Y., 1970). In the following, references to articles reprinted in this collection are given in parenthesis. Texts of the Palestinian version of the Shemoneh Esreh: S. Schechter, "Geniza Specimens", *JQR* OS 10 (1898) 654-59 (373-78); L. Finkelstein, "The Development of the Amidah", *JQR* NS 16 (1925-26) 130-70 (137-77); translations in C. W. Dugmore, *The Influence of the Synagogue upon the Divine Office* (Oxford, 1945) 114-27. Cf. the following studies of the Shemoneh Esreh: I. Elbogen, *Der Jüdische Gottesdienst in seinen geschichtlichen Entwicklung* (3rd revised edition, Frankfurt, 1931) 27-60; K. Kohler, "The Origin and Composition of the Eighteen Benedictions with a Translation of the Corresponding Essene Prayers in the Apostolic Constitutions", *HUCA* 1 (1924) 387-425 (52-90).

(מחיה המתים)". This reference to God's power in resurrection has not always been a part of the second benediction, which was originally concerned with God's creation and his sustenance of the world. At a later stage, perhaps in the first century B.C., this direct reference to the resurrection was added.[11] This was probably due to Pharisaic influence as a result of their discussions with the Sadducees over the resurrection of the dead. Although the historical development of the second benediction is not altogether clear to us, the outcome of the process is certain. The confession of God "who revives the dead" now stands in a context which speaks of God as creator. We quote the second benediction from a Geniza fragment which contains an early form of the Shemoneh Esreh: [12]

> Thou art mighty, who bringest low the proud, strong and
> He that judgeth the ruthless, that liveth for ever, that raiseth the dead,
> that maketh the wind to blow, that sendeth down the dew,
> that sustaineth the living, that quickeneth the dead;
> in the twinkling of an eye Thou makest salvation to spring forth for us,
> Blessed art Thou, O Lord, who quickenest the dead.

God's saving acts are here described in accordance with the reversal scheme which is well-known from the Old Testament. This particular benediction, as well as the Shemoneh Esreh in general, draws heavily on the Old Testament psalms.[13] The hymnic ascription מחיה המתים is not found in the Old Testament, but there are similar formulae in passages which bear resemblance to the second benediction as a whole. The most significant ones are I Sam 2:6; Deut 32:39 and 2 Kgs 5:7.[14] In the hymnic confessions in these texts, it is said of God that יהוה ממית ומחיה.[15] Normally this is one motif in a long list of acts ascribed to God:

---

[11]. Elbogen, Gottesdienst, 29-30; Finkelstein, "Amidah", 122-23 (112-13); against M. Liber, ("Structure and History of the Tefillah", JQR 40 (1949-50) 338) who argues that resurrection was always a part of this benediction.

[12] Dugmore, Influence, 114-15; translated from Schechter, "Geniza", 656, (375).

[13] E.g. Pss 145:14-20; 146:7-9. Notice in particular the similarities between Shemoneh Esreh and the Hebrew psalm inserted between Sir 51:12 and 13; cf. T. Vargha, "De psalmo hebraico Ecclestiastici c. 51", Antonianum 10 (1935) 9-10.

[14] Other similar passages include Job 36:5-12; Isa 26:7-19; Dan 12:1-4.

[15] I Sam 2:6; Deut 32:39 and 2 Kgs 5:7 have other grammatical constructions; common for all is their formulaic, confession-like character and

The Lord kills and brings to life,
he brings down to Sheol and raises up.
The Lord makes poor and makes rich;
he brings low, he also exalts.
He raises up the poor from the dust;
he lifts the needy from the ash heap,
to make them sit with princes,
and inherit a seat of honour (1 Sam 2:6-8).[16]

The hymn in 1 Sam 2:1-10 is in praise of God who intervenes and brings about a reversal in a situation of injustice. God assists and helps the poor and the meek, but he judges the rich and the proud. In the Old Testament "rich" and "poor" are terms which express both cultic and social values. The poor and the needy are the same as the righteous: they belong to the people of God. God undertakes this radical reversal for the benefit of his people. He is the judge of the world and therefore he gives the righteous their due, but he condemns their enemies and oppressors. This theme originally belonged to the national lamentations and thanksgiving psalms (or even hymns). Here God was urged to help his people, or praised for his assistance. Quite often, it was the conflict between Israel and her enemies which provided the setting for these psalms.[17] In Israel's religious poetry this political conflict found its theological expression in the confession of Yahweh as the only powerful God:

There is none holy like the Lord,
there is none besides thee;
there is no rock like our God (1 Sam 2:2).

This confession of Yahweh is common to the hymnic style. Apart from the Psalms, it is used in Deuteronomy and in Deutero-Isaiah in particular.[18] The cultic setting gives this confession of God a

---

their emphasis on Yahweh as the only God; see K. Seybold, *Der Gebet der Kranken im Alten Testament* (BWANT 99, Stuttgart, 1973) 42.

[16] Cf. Ps 113:7-9; for the following see H. J. Stoebe, *Das erste Buch Samuelis* (Kommentar zum AT 8/1, Gütersloh, 1973) 100-7.

[17] Cf. G. Ernest Wright, "The Lawsuit of God: A Form-Critical study of Deuteronomy 32", *Israel's Prophetic Heritage. Essays in honor of J. Muilenburg* (ed. by B. W. Anderson and W. Harrelson, London, 1962) 26-67, esp. 56-58.

[18] Cf. Pss 18:32; 32:10; 71:19; 77:14; 86:8; see H. J. Kraus, *Die Psalmen* I (Biblischer Kommentar: Altes Testament 15/1, Neukirchen, 1960) XLIV-XLV. See also Isa 44:6; 45:5, 22 etc.; Deut 4:35, 39, etc. This is a variation of the much used self-presentation form "I am Yahweh"; see W. Zimmerli, "Ich bin Yahweh", *Gottes Offenbarung. Gesammelte Aufsätze* (TBü 19, Munich, 1963) 11-40.

wider perspective than a particular crisis or act of deliverance. The hymns in Deuteronomy 32 and 1 Samuel 2 are characterized by a combination of cosmic, national and individual motifs. Therefore they can be ascribed to individuals as well, for example to Hannah in 1 Samuel 2 and to Mary in a similar hymn in Luke 1:46-55.[19] However, Hannah and Mary are both figures of symbolic importance and thus their praise transcends their own particular situation. In each case the son who is born introduces a new period of salvation for Israel. The concept of God who gives life and kills in these texts is not combined with the idea of resurrection from the dead.[20] Rather, it is a way of speaking of God's acts as creator and judge towards his righteous people or towards individual Israelites. This is a prominent motif also in later texts in the Old Testament as well as in the intertestamental literature. In some instances these writings bear witness to the rise of faith in a resurrection from the dead or some other concept of future life, for example immortality.[21] In several texts, the resurrection motif functions within a reversal scheme: God vindicates the martyr or the oppressed and punishes the persecutor or the oppressors (e.g. 1 *Enoch* 92-105; 2 Macc 7).[22] The political and religious conditions in Palestine in the last two centuries B.C. were conducive to the development of a theology of this kind. Belief in a resurrection of the dead was not a self-contained idea, but belonged to the wider context of trust in God's power to assist his people.

It is within this larger context of the reversal and judgment theme that we find the blessing of God who revives the dead in the second benediction of Shemoneh Esreh as well. This particular confession parallels other expressions of God's assistance to his faithful: "who bringest low the proud, strong, and He that judgeth the ruthless". These acts are all part of God's merciful dealings as creator: "that maketh the wind to blow, that sendeth down the dew". God the creator was at the same time the God of Israel; in

---

[19] H. J. Stoebe, *Das erste Buch Samuelis*, 106-7; notice the similarity with Rom 4:17 and Heb 11:11 as well.

[20] However, later interpreters found here a reference to resurrection; cf. the use of Deut 32:39 in 4 Macc 18:19 and *b. Sanh.* 91b.

[21] See Nickelsburg, *Resurrection, Immortality, and Eternal Life in Intertestamental Judaism*; also H. C. C. Cavallin, *Life after Death. Paul's Argument for the Resurrection of the Dead in 1 Cor 15. Part 1: An Enquiry into the Jewish Background* (ConBNT 7/1, Lund, 1974).

[22] See Nickelsburg, *Resurrection*, 93-130.

the first benediction he is addressed as the "God of the fathers" and blessed as "the shield of Abraham".[23] Outside of the Shemoneh Esreh, the formula "Blessed be God who revives the dead" is not often found except in written sources of a later period.[24] However, the central position which the Shemoneh Esreh occupied in Jewish life makes it certain that this benediction was well-known. Likewise, belief in a resurrection of some kind became increasingly important, in particular among Pharisaic groups. The way in which the second benediction speaks of resurrection is typical of most Old Testament and intertestamental Jewish sources: it focuses on God and on his power to bring about an act of salvation. There was here a set of ideas which were part of the religious heritage of Christian Jews as well, and early Christian writings show that it was the idea of resurrection, rather than any other form of afterlife, which was most widespread.[25] God's power to give life to the dead was part of his work as creator and sustainer of the world and of his people. Against this background the double designation of God in Rom 4:17 is easily understandable: "who gives life to the dead and calls into existence the things that do not exist (καλοῦντος τὰ μὴ ὄντα ὡς ὄντα)". This last ascription also has many parallels in Jewish literature. H.-F. Weiss has provided the most useful survey of this material for our purpose in his study *Untersuchungen zur Kosmologie des hellenistischen und palästinischen Judentums*.[26] Here he finds that Rom 4:17 is part of a tradition within Judaism which is represented above all by 2 *Apoc. Bar.* 48:8; 2 Macc 7:28 and *b. Sanh.* 91a.[27] Cosmology as such is not a dominant theme in these texts. The statement that God has created the world out of nothing is first and foremost a confession of God or an exhortation to trust in

---

[23] Cf. A. Spanier, "Die erste Benediktion des Achtzehngebetes", *MGWJ* 81 (1937) 71-76.
[24] *b. Ketub.* 8b; *b. Ber.* 58b, 60b; *b. Sanh.* 108a; *Pirqe R. El.* 34; *JosAs* 20:5 (rec. A); see the edition by P. Batiffol, "Le Livre de la Prière d'Aséneth", *Studia Patristica* 1-2 (Paris, 1889-90) 76.
Notice in particular the connection between resurrection and creation in the Christianized version of the second benediction in *Const. App.* VII 34; and in the burial Kaddish; see b. de Sola Pool, *The Jewish-Aramaic Prayer the Kaddish* (Leipzig, 1909) 79-83; cf. further above, 187, n. 225.
[25] But see the idea that the faithful shall be together with God immediately after death: e.g. Luke 16:19-31; 23:43; Phil 1:23; Joh 14:3.
[26] 139-45.
[27] Continuing a Jewish tradition are further *Const. App.* VIII 12, 7; Hermas, *Mand.* I 1; *Vis.* I 1, 6.

him.[28] Particularly noteworthy in this respect is 2 Macc 7, a text which we mentioned earlier as an example of resurrection used within a reversal scheme. Here, the belief that God has created man is combined with the trust that he will also give him new life. Both ideas are used for paraenetic purposes in the exhortation of the mother to her sons facing martyrdom: [29] "Therefore the Creator of the world, who shaped the beginning of man and devised the origin of all things, will in his mercy give life and breath back to you again, since you now forget yourselves for the sake of his laws" (7:23). The mother's appeal to her youngest son in 7:28-29 like-wise combines creation and resurrection,[30] and this time it is explicitly stated that "God did not make them out of things that existed (οὐκ ἐξ ὄντων)". Philo as well speaks frequently of God who creates by bringing into being that which has no being.[31] We find the closest parallel to Rom 4:17b in *Heres*. 36. This passage is part of Philo's exposition of Abraham's question in Gen 15:2, concerning the promise from God: "For I know that Thou, who givest being to what is not and generatest all things (ὁ τὰ μὴ ὄντα φέρων καὶ τὰ πάντα γεννῶν) hast hated the childless and barren soul, since Thou hast given a special grace to the race of them that see, that they should never be without children or sterile". As in *Spec. Leg.* II 2, 225, 229, τὰ μὴ ὄντα in *Heres*. 36 probably refers to unborn children who have not yet been created by God.[32] The use of καλοῦντος with τὰ μὴ ὄντα in Rom 4:17 is of special importance. In the Old Testament it is by his word that God creates; he calls into being.[33] This expression is typical of Deutero-Isaiah; moreover, it is not only the

---

[28] Cf. 2 *Apoc. Bar.* 14:17; 21:4; 48:8; 2 Macc 7:28; see Weiss, *Kosmologie*, 73-74, 125-26.

[29] Weiss, *Kosmologie*, 73. Notice the development of the story of the seven sons in 4 Macc. However, 4 Macc speaks of immortality, not of resurrection, and creation is not any more a guarantee for resurrection. Cf. 2 Macc 7:23, 28-29 with 4 Macc 16:18-20; see Nickelsburg, *Resurrection*, 110.

[30] This is the same combination of motifs as in Rom 4:17; Weiss, *Kosmologie*, 141 n. 4. See further O. Hofius, "Eine altjüdische Parallele zu Röm. IV 17b", *NTS* 18 (1971/72) 93-94; and H. Schwantes, *Schöpfung der Endzeit* (Arbeiten zur Theologie I/12, Stuttgart, 1962) 56-57.

[31] Cf. the reference to God's creation from nothing and Abraham's faith in Gen 15:6 in *Migr*. 44 (quoted above, 155). Cf. further *Somn*. I 76; *Spec. Leg.* II 2, 228-29, IV 187; *Op*. 81; *Vita Mos*. II 259-69; etc.; see Weiss, *Kosmologie*, 59-72.

[32] In *Spec. Leg.* II 225, 229, the role of parents is compared with that of God in creation; Weiss, *Kosmologie*, 68-69.

[33] E.g. Pss 33:6; 147:15-20; 148:5; Amos 5:8; 9:6 etc.

world which God creates, he also calls his people into being.[34] The same motif is found in later Jewish texts as well, for example 2 *Apoc. Bar.* 48:8, Wis 11:25, Philo's *Spec. Leg.* IV 187.[35]

Although we have given only an outline of the use of statements about God as creator and reviver of the dead, we have become increasingly aware of the need to see these statements in their context. They are always used with a purpose related to the main issue of the text itself. We shall therefore in our next paragraphs address the question of their function within Paul's argument in Romans 4.

B. *God as a healing God*
Rom 4:17 and 19

In its context, "God who gives life to the dead" in Rom 4:17 corresponds most directly to the description of Abraham and Sarah in 4:19: "When he considered his own body, which was as good as dead because he was about a hundred years old, or when he considered the barrenness (τὴν νέκρωσιν) of Sarah's womb". The power of God to give life to the dead became manifest in his giving new strength to the bodies of the patriarch and his wife.[36] This interpretation is known from Rabbinic writings; the idea is that God gives life in a physical sense by renewing sexual potency.[37] In his literal exposition of Gen 17:17 in *Quaes. Gen.* III 56 Philo bears witness to this view: "To God all things are possible, even to change old age into youth and to bring one who has no seed into fruitfulness and begetting". However, in the allegorical interpretation of this and similar events, the miracle is performed solely by God, in a spiritual manner, without Abraham or any other man playing a part.[38] M. Dibelius suggested that Paul knew this interpretation of the "miraculous childbirth" and that he used it in

---

[34] E.g. Isa 41:8-10; 43:1; 44:1; 48:12-13; see R. Rendtorff, "Die theologische Stellung des Schöpfungsglaubens bei Deuterojesaja", *ZTK* 51 (1954) 3-13; esp. 11-12.

[35] Delling, "Gottesprädikationen", 31 nn. 2-4.

[36] Cf. Kuss, *Römer*, 192; and, grossly overstated, Barth, *Foi et salut selon S. Paul*, 59-63.

[37] See above, 150, nn. 100-103.

[38] Philo speaks of Sarah, Leah, Rebeccah and Zipporah in this way; cf. *Cher.* 44-47; *Mut.* 134, 138; *Leg. All.* III 180, 217-19; etc.; cf. R. A. Baer, Jr. *Philo's use of the Categories Male and Female*, 61-62 n. 2.

Gal 4:21-31.[39] In this text there is no mention of Abraham, and the son of the promise is born by the power of God.

The connection between the description of God as the giver of new life to the dead and that of old and worn bodies corresponds to the Old Testament way of speaking about illness as death.[40] The formula "God who kills and makes alive" in 2 Kgs 5:7 is used in this sense: it is related to the healing of a leper. In the Psalms, to suffer from illness is frequently described as being in the snares of death or Sheol.[41] In the same manner, God's assistance and help is described as deliverance from death, from Sheol. The particular ascription that God gives life to the dead is not found in the Old Testament. However, in Assyrian and Babylonian religious texts "God who gives life to the dead" is a frequent title for a healing God, for example Marduk.[42]

The parallel between the appellation of God in 4:17 and the picture of Abraham and Sarah in 4:19 represents a concrete way of thinking about creation and resurrection. In the Old Testament and in intertestamental Jewish tradition, the miracle of renewed life was given added significance by the fact that the child who was born was Isaac. He represented in his own person the promised offspring which was to become Israel. Thus, even taken in the literal sense the correspondence between Rom 4:17 and 19 has great theological significance. However, most commentators have rightly seen that Paul has thoroughly reinterpreted this motif. The actual physical renewal of Abraham and Sarah plays no role. Rather, Paul precludes this notion in *v.* 20 when ἐνεδυναμώθη is

[39] Cf. M. Dibelius, "Jungfrauensohn und Krippenkind", 30-33; however, Dibelius fails to see that Paul's real intention with this passage is to emphasize the gift of God in the promise versus the flesh. See the criticism of Dibelius's thesis by O. Michel and O. Betz, "Von Gott gezeugt", 18-19; and Mussner, *Galater*, 319.

[40] See Ch. Barth, *Errettung von Tode* (Basle, 1947); and more recently K. Seybold, *Gebet*, 31-48.

[41] E.g. Pss 30; 38; 39; 41; see Seybold, *Gebet*, 98-146.

[42] See the description of Marduk in an Akkadian prayer: "who is seizing the hand of the fallen, who is unloosing the bound, is restoring the dead to life (*mu-bal-lit(amel) miti)*", KAR I no. 23, 20-21. Translation from G. Widengren, *The Accadian and Hebrew Psalms of Lamentation as Religious Documents* (Stockholm, 1937) 46; text in E. Ebeling, *Die Akkadische Gebetserie "Handerhebung"* (Deutsche Akademie der Wissenschaften zu Berlin, Institut für Orientforschung, Veröffentlichung 20, Berlin, 1953) 12-13. See further examples pp. 8-9, 66-67, 94-97, 110-11, 136-37. For the same motif in names derived from a god, see J. H. Stamm, *Die Akkadische Namengebung* (Leipzig, 1939) esp. 153-55, 187-88, 239-41.

qualified by τῇ πίστει. Furthermore, the birth of Isaac is not even mentioned: τῷ σπέρματι in 4:13 and 16 is applied directly to Paul's contemporary situation.[43]

C. God as the creator of a new community
Rom 4:17 and 16-18

With the predication of God in 4:17 as well as with the description of Abraham and Sarah in 4:19, Paul has put the last part of chapter 4 (especially 4:17-22) under the scheme of a transfer "from death to life". Moreover, the citations of the promise to Abraham in 4:17a and 18 tell us that this soteriological scheme "from death to life" is applied to the question of the identity of the children of Abraham. It is the quotations of this promise in 4:17a and 18 which form the immediate context for the designation of God in 4:17b. However, this widening of the perspective for Paul's use of the designation was already prepared by Jewish interpretation.

In the allegorical exegesis of Philo, God's power to renew old people and to make the barren give birth is a symbol of his power to create faith. In *Quaes. Gen.* IV 17, the birth of Isaac is interpreted in this way: "a new act shall be sown by God in the whole soul for the birth of joy and great gladness". The promise of Isaac is only one out of several events which Philo interprets to speak of God's ability to create faith when man is in a position of no hope. A typical situation from the life of Abraham was his reaction when

---

[43] The underlying theme which Paul interprets is that of the creation of the people of God through the birth of Isaac. The use of "God who gives life to the dead etc.", in 4:17 does not prove that Paul has in mind Genesis 22. In Hebr 11:17-19, however, the promise of a large offspring and this confession of God were linked to the Akedah tradition. Thus, both the birth of Isaac and his return to life could be used as examples of God's fulfilment of his promise through an act of creation (cf. Heb 11:11-12). There is a similar combination of texts and motifs in *Tg. Neof.* and *Frg. Tg.* Ex 12:42, in the description of the nights of the passover. The theme of the first night is God's creation of the world. The second night combines Genesis 15 (God appeared to Abraham between the pieces; only in the *Fragmentary Tg.*) with Gen 17:17 (the promise to Abraham and Sarah in their old age) and Genesis 22. See Le Déaut, *La nuit pascale*, 133-39, 205-6. However, although any use of Genesis 22 by Paul is often too summarily dismissed, the Akedah theme does not seem to play a part in Paul's argument here. If it is alluded to at all, it is not in 4:17-21, but rather in 4:25; cf. the use of παρεδόθη with παρέδωκεν in 8:32. In the latter text it is possible that Paul alludes to the Akedah, but allegorically: *God* is the father who gives up his son: cf. N. A. Dahl, "The Atonement—an adequate Reward for the Akedah? (Ro 8:32)", *Neotestamentica et semitica*, 15-29.

he received the promise from God: he fell down and confessed that
he was in himself nothing; but then God raised him up again.[44]
The terms used are πίπτω and ἀναγείρω/ἀνίστημι. They indicate
that Philo is here describing a conversion, similar to passages where
Philo speaks of God creating new life. In *Migr.* 122, these two
motifs, the giving of new life and raising up, are combined in an
allegorical exposition of Abraham's prayer for Sodom and Gomorrah
in Genesis 18. Philo introduces this section (118-126) with a quotation from Gen 12:3: "In you all the families of the earth shall be
blessed". Abraham is an example that for the sake of the virtuous
man God will show mercy to his surroundings: "for the sake of
this little piece He looks with pity on the rest also, so as to raise up
fallen things (πεπτωκότα ἐγείρειν) and to quicken dead things
(τεθνηκότα ζωπυρεῖν)". The context of this statement indicates that
Philo is here thinking of conversion, maybe even more directly of
the acceptance of proselytes into the Jewish synagogue.[45]

In another first-century document, *Joseph and Asenath*, the
confession of God as the creator is even more directly applied to
mission and proselytizing. This has most recently been pointed out
in an article by K. Berger.[46] This novel or romance probably
originated in the Alexandrian Jewish community, in circles which
were open towards non-Jews and their cultural influence.[47] However, they had at the same time a strong desire to preserve a Jewish
identity. This was attained by an emphasis on mission and acceptance of proselytes into the community through conversion. It is
particularly in 8:10-11 and 15:3-4 that statements about God as
creator and reviver are related to conversion. The first of these passa-

---

[44] *Mut.* 155-56, 175-76.

[45] Cf. K. Berger, "Jüdisch-hellenistische Missionsliteratur und apokryphe
Apostelakten", *Kairos* 17 (1975) 233. Similarly in the texts from Qumran
"to stand" or "to be raised up" (e.g. כון, עמד) frequently refers to the
inclusion in the sect or to living in the sectarian community; e.g. IQH IV
21-22; X 6; XI 11, 14. See W. Grundmann, "Stehen und Fallen im qumranischen und neutestamentlichen Schrifttum", *Qumran-Probleme* (ed. R.
Bardtke, Deutsche Akademie der Wissenschaften zu Berlin, Schriften der
Sektion für Altertumswissenschaft 42, Berlin, 1963) 147-53.

[46] "Missionsliteratur", 232-48. Berger finds striking parallels between
conversion texts in JosAs and in the apocryphal Acts of the Apostles, in
particular *A. Phil.* 115-117. However, a comparison with this literature from
a much later period will take us too far from our present study.

[47] H. C. Kee, "The Socio-Religious Setting and Aims of Joseph and Asenath", *SBL Seminar Papers* 10 (ed. G. MacRae, Missoula, Mont., 1976) 188-90;
but see M. Philonenko, *Joseph et Asénath*, (SPB 13, Leiden, 1968) 48-52.

ges is Joseph's prayer to God for Asenath, the second is the message delivered by the angel after her conversion. There are many parallel expressions in these paragraphs, as well as between Joseph's prayer in 8:10-11 and that of Asenath in 12:2-11. Each prayer is inserted at a crucial point of the narrative to give a theological interpretation of the events. Philonenko suggests that these texts are related to a liturgy used when proselytes were received into the synagogue.[48]

The introduction to Joseph's prayer describes Go l in typical Hellenistic terms, emphasizing his activity as creator:

Lord, God of my father, Israel,
Most High, Powerful One
Who makes all things to live (ὁ ζωοποιήσας τὰ πάντα)
Who calls out (καλέσας) of darkness into light
and from error to truth,
from death to life (8:10).[49]

These expressions are used of God as creator of the world. However, when they are repeated in Joseph's intercession, they are now directly applied to the conversion of Asenath:

You indeed are the Lord,
make alive (ζωοποίησον)
and bless this virgin.

Asenath's conversion is identical with God's giving her new life. As an idolatress she was earlier "dead", since she worshipped dead and mute idols (8:3). The following part of Joseph's prayer is therefore characterized by terms for renewal: [50]

Renew her by your Spirit,
Reform her by your hidden hand,
Restore her to your life,
and let her eat the Bread of Life
and drink the Cup of Blessing,
she whom I chose before her birth,
and let her enter into your rest
which you prepared for your Elect Ones (8:11).

---

[48] Joseph, 54-55, 158. In these texts μετάνοια is a technical term for conversion, cf. 15:6, 7, 8; there is also frequent use of terms which indicate transition e.g. "from darkness to light", 8:11; 12:10-11; 15:13. Cf. further 12:17 and 27:8. See in the NT e.g. Acts 26:18; 2 Cor 4:6; Eph 5:8; 1 Pet 2:9; further references in Berger, "Missionsliteratur", 234.

[49] The translation of 8:10-11 (except for the next quotation) is taken from Kee, "Setting" 188-89; I have given my own translation of other passages.

[50] Both in 8:11 and in 15:4, we find ἀναζωοποιέω, ἀνακαινίζω, ἀναπλάσσω, terms for "new birth"; Philonenko, Joseph, 185.

Here the "creation" of Asenath is attributed to the Spirit of God. The prayer that she might partake in the commúnual meal and in the rest for the elect point to a background in Jewish mysticism.[51] After Asenath's long confession in chapter 12, a messenger angel describes her initiation into true faith in terms identical with that of Joseph's prayer: "See, from today you are renewed, reformed and restored to life, and you shall eat the Bread of Life and drink the Cup of Immortality" (15:4). In Asenath's reply to this message, expressions from the hymnic introduction to Joseph's prayer come up again: "Blessed be the Lord, God, who sent you to rescue me from darkness and lead me to the light" (15:13).

This new creation and new life which were given to Asenath were not restricted to her alone. The importance of this event for other idolaters as well is emphasized by the new name which the angel gives her: "You shall not be called Asenath any more, but your name shall be City of Refuge, for in you shall many nations find refuge, and under your wings shall many people find shelter and within your walls shall they who turn to God in repentance be protected" (15:6). There are similarities here to Philo's description of the change of name for Abraham, which was also an act of great consequence.[52] The "many people" who shall find refuge in the City of Refuge are identified as οἱ προσκείμενοι, which is a term for proselytes.[53] Conversion from idolatry to true faith is described in different images. Common to all of them, however, is that they are related to terms used of creation. For example, in the use of καλέω in 8:10 there is a gliding transition from its use for God's act in the creation of the world to its designation of a spiritual creation: "who makes all things to live, who calls (καλέσας) out of darkness into light, and from error to truth, from death to life".[54] Thus creation imagery is applied to conversion, so that initiation into the Jewish faith was described as a new creation for the proselyte. At a later stage of this tradition, καλέω used of creation is similarly attributed to the calling of believers, (e.g. 1 Pet 2:9; 1 Clem. 59:2; 2 Clem. 1:8; Const. App. VII 39:3). These texts exhort the Christians

---

[51] See Sanders, "The Covenant as a Soteriological Category", 24-26.

[52] See above, 131. Notice that Philo describes Abraham as a city and a refuge, Quaes. Gen. IV 120; Philonenko, Joseph, 55.

[53] Philonenko, Joseph, 183. The use of the Old Testament image of "city of refuge" here indicates that the group behind Joseph and Asenath considered itself an "inclusive religious community"; Kee, "Setting", 184.

[54] Delling, "Gottesprädikationen", 31 n. 4.

to look back upon their call from God. Thus a motif which was originally part of missionary preaching is reflected in paraenesis and anamnesis.

In his study, Berger has succeeded in identifying a pattern of missionary preaching in which there are several recurring motifs. They are clustered around the designation of God as the one who calls from death to life and who gives life. Before he goes on to draw implications for the New Testament, Berger concludes: "Schliesst man sich dieser Annahme an, dann liegt in dieser Gottesprädikation ein jüdischer Beleg für die Verbindung von Bekehrung, Geistempfang (Erneuerung des Geistes) und Empfang des neuen, ewigen Lebens vor".[55] Thus Berger has pointed to a possible parallel tradition to the Pauline scheme "from death to life" which is so dominant in Romans 5-8. However, the material which Berger presents from Hellenistic-Jewish mission literature is not eschatological in character in the same way as Paul's writings. Moreover, even in this material Berger seems to neglect the collective aspect of Asenath's conversion. The positive intentions towards the Greek or Egyptian surroundings were visible in the description of Asenath as a "City of Refuge" for all who turn to God in repentance. When Berger looks for parallels in Paul he finds them in Romans 6 in particular, whereas he pays scant attention to chapter 4.[56] However, it is Romans 4 which has the same designation of God as *Joseph and Asenath*, and it is here related to Abraham, who as the father of the proselytes is, so to speak, a parallel figure to Asenath.[57] Furthermore, when Paul in 4:16-18 speaks of the inclusion of Jews and non-Jews into the offspring of Abraham, his proof-text is Gen 17:5, God's promise to Abraham after his change of name. Still, a direct link between the Hellenistic tradition which Berger delineates and Paul is unlikely. Paul's religious system is very different from Hellenistic religiosity. For example, the concept of μετάνοια, which is so central to the latter, plays no role in Paul's thinking.[58]

---

[55] "Missionsliteratur", 248.
[56] Ibid.
[57] Philonenko, *Joseph*, 55; Ch. Burchardt, *Untersuchungen zu Joseph und Asenath* (WUNT 8, Tübingen, 1965) 120.
[58] The noun is found in Rom 2:4 only, the verb in 2 Cor 12:21. Furthermore, *Joseph and Asenath* shows no interest in the question of Israel or resurrection, themes which are of vital interest to Paul. The list of corresponding motifs between *Joseph and Asenath* and Paul in C. Bussmann

Some of the texts from *Joseph and Asenath* were already used to illuminate the concept of a new creation in Paul in an article by P. Stuhlmacher in 1967.[59] However, he added material from Qumran (and apocalyptic writings), and was thereby able to explain the apocalyptic side of the idea of a new creation in Paul also. Although the specific designations of God "who revives the dead" are not found here, this material is of obvious relevance to our question. In the Qumran Hodayot deliverance from enemies is described in terms similar to the Old Testament psalms. Moreover, it is directly related to the entry into the Qumran community, especially in IQH III 21-23 and XI 11-14.[60] There is a major difference between Qumran and other Jewish groups in their view of Israel and the covenant. To the sectarians, one entered the covenant individually, and those outside were sinners, awaiting destruction.[61] Thus the transition from "outside" to "inside" was much more real than in other Jewish groups where the Jews were regarded as included in Israel by birth. Moreover, when the idea of a new creation was used of proselytes at their conversion, within Rabbinic Judaism this often remained a mere metaphor.[62]

Thus, Paul's use of God" who gives life to the dead and calls into existence the things that do not exist" in Romans 4 is his version of a traditional motif which was developed in various ways. The common basis was the Old Testament, and in particular the later writings in which the concept of God as creator became increasingly important. God's assistance and help to his people were frequently described in terms of sustenance of his creation. Not surprisingly, this terminology was also attributed to the proselytes who were added to the Jewish community. Their conversion meant that they were included in this realm of God's care and providence. In

---

(*Themen der paulinischen Missionspredigt auf dem Hintergrund der spät-jüdisch-hellenistischen Missionsliteratur* (EHS.T 3, Frankfurt, 1971) 160-62, must be read in the light of his caution remarks on p. 192. For a comparison between the religious system of Paul and that of Hellenistic Judaism, see above all Sanders, *Paul*, 500-1.

[59] "Erwägungen zum ontologischen Charakter der καινὴ κτίσις bei Paulus", *EvT* 27 (1967) 1-35, esp. 17-19; but see the criticism by J. Baumgarten, *Paulus und die Apokalyptik* (WMANT 44, Neukirchen, 1976) 164-79.

[60] Stuhlmacher, "Erwägungen", 12-14; E. Sjöberg, "Neuschöpfung in den Toten-Meer-Rollen", *ST* 9 (1955) 131-36.

[61] See Sanders, *Paul*, 269-70, 276-7, 317.

[62] E. Sjöberg, "Widergeburt und Neuschöpfung im palästinischen Judentum", *ST* 4 (1951-52) 50, 54.

consequence, since they were not, like the Jews, already a part of God's creation, their inclusion was described as a transfer from "darkness" to "light", or from "death" to "life". Moreover, it was only God who could make this transfer possible; it was therefore ascribed to God "who gives life to the dead" and "who calls from darkness to light". The character and identity of a religious group probably determined the particular development of this tradition. Groups with strong apocalyptic expectations (Qumran) or mystical (*Joseph and Asenath*) or charismatic experiences (early Christians) were more likely to use creation imagery in a *real* sense to express their identity than were groups of a less ecstatic religious type (Rabbinic Judaism).[63] In Paul, materials from various traditions have been blended. We found many of the parallels to Rom 4:13-22 in Philo and other texts from the Jewish Diaspora where eschatology was relatively unimportant. It is possible that Paul's own background as a "Diaspora-Pharisee" contributed to his integration of material from various sources.[64] However, he incorporated it into an eschatological framework.

The eschatological setting for Paul's use of the Abraham tradition is signalled in Rom 4:13. Here the promise to Abraham and to his offspring is described as his becoming "heir to the world". The interpretation of τὸ κληρονόμον αὐτὸν εἶναι κόσμου has caused commentators many difficulties.[65] The expression itself is not found in the Old Testament. As it now stands, the formula is the result of a long history of interpretation of the promise of the *land*.[66] Within Paul's appropriation of the promise to Abraham in Rom 4:13-22 this motif is parallel to Acts 7:5, and in particular to its eschatological interpretation in Heb 11:9-10. In the interpretation of this phrase, we face the additional difficulty that nowhere else in Paul's letters does κόσμος have the connotation of a future, eschatological world. It is generally used of the created world or of all the people

---

[63] Cf. Sanders, "The Covenant as a Soteriological Category", 42-44.

[64] Weiss, "Zur Frage der historischen Voraussetzungen der Begegnung von Antike und Christentum", 318-19.

[65] See e.g. Kuss (*Römer*, 187-88) who suggests three alternatives; Käsemann (*Römer*, 113); Michel (*Römer*, 121); Cranfield (*Romans*, 239-40) each offers a different solution.

[66] Cf. *Jub.* 19:21; 22:14; Sir 44:21; 1 QAp Gen 21:8-14; it is used of Moses in Philo, *Vita Mos.* I 155. The most thorough study of the history of interpretation of this theme is Davies, *The Gospel and the Land.* However, in his section on Romans 4 (168-79), he does not explicitly discuss the phrase "heir to the world" in 4:13.

on the earth.[67] This suggests that an interpretation of Paul's use of this traditional formula ought to start from κληρονόμος, since this term occurs both in the Abraham tradition and elsewhere in his letters. Although it is used only twice in Romans 4, it is indirectly qualified by other similar terms in this chapter as well as in Galatians 3 and 4. There is in these chapters a group of related terms which express various facets of what it meant to belong to the new community, for example "sons of Abraham", "offspring", "sons of God".[68] In Galatians 3 and 4, Paul applied the promise to Abraham directly to the charismatic experiences of the community. Thus "heirs" became a title for the charismatic community. It is this same experience which Paul refers to in Rom 8:12-17 when he speaks of the outpouring of the Spirit on the children of God, who are also the heirs (8:17). In the following section, 8:18-31, Paul draws on pictures from the created world (ἡ κτίσις) to support his thesis that the gift of the Spirit guarantees the final consummation of the promise of sonship.[69] In Romans 4, the final clauses in vv. 11-12 and 16-18 show that the main emphasis in Paul's use of the theme "heir to the world" is on the universality of the promise. At the same time, Paul holds up an eschatological perspective to the community which he addresses in his letter.

To be heirs of the earth or of the Kingdom (of God) was a motif which was frequently used in early Christianity to express the identity of the believers. It found its most characteristic expressions in the beatitudes in the Gospels: [70]

Blessed are the meek,
for they shall inherit the earth.

Blessed are the peacemakers,
for they shall be called sons of God (Matt 5:5, 9).

The main point in these beatitudes is similar to that of Matt 3:7-10: God can raise up children for Abraham from the stones. That is,

---

[67] Cf. H. Sasse, "κόσμος", *TWNT* 3 (1938) 882-96, esp. 888.

[68] σπέρμα, Gal 3:29, Rom 4:13, 16; υἱοὶ Ἀβραάμ, Gal 3:7; Abraham is father (πατήρ), Rom 4:1, 11, 12, 16, 17, 18; κληρονόμος, Gal 3:29; 4:1, 7; Rom 4:13, 14; 8:17; υἱοὶ θεοῦ, Gal 3:26; Rom 8:14; cf. 8:16.

[69] See J. Baumgarten, *Paulus und die Apokalyptik*, 170-79.

[70] J. Dupont (*Les Béatitudes* 3. *Les Evangélistes* (New edition, Paris, 1973) 475-86) stresses the connection between Matt 5:5 and the promise to Abraham in Jewish tradition and in Paul. See further Jas 2:5; cf. M. Dibelius (*Der Brief des Jakobus*, (MeyerK 15, 11th revised edition by H. Greeven, Göttingen, 1964) 58-66) for the social setting of this beatitude.

God gives the disinherited a share in the kingdom. As an aspect of the reversal motif from the Old Testament it was adopted and used polemically by the Christians to speak of themselves as the eschatological community. The similarity between τὸ κληρονόμον αὐτὸν εἶναι κόσμου in Rom 4:13 and αὐτοὶ κληρονομήσουσιν τὴν γῆν in Matt 5:5 has often been noticed. Moreover, we should also consider whether Rom 4:6-9 belongs to this same group of sayings. Each verse in the quotation from Ps 32:1-2 in Rom 4:7-8 starts with μακάριοι and Paul has bracketed the quotation with phrases characterizing it as ὁ μακαρισμός (4:6-9). Thus Rom 4:6-9 as well as *v.* 13 can be said to belong to the beatitude form.[71] In consequence, Paul's words about the "heirs", in particular "heirs to the world", is part of his adaptation of the Kingdom of God motif.[72]

When Paul introduces the phrase "heir to the world" in Rom 4:13, it refers to the charismatic community, viewed from an eschatological perspective. He does not go into details about the future hope, which is introduced merely as a phrase with which his readers would immediately associate their concept of themselves as "heirs". It is the structure and identity of the community of "heirs to the world" with which he is concerned. The following verses show that Paul uses this eschatological motif to introduce his argument that both Jews and non-Jews are children of Abraham. This corresponds to the function of "God who gives life to the dead" in 4:16-18, so that it becomes clear that Paul applies creation language to his claim for the universal fatherhood of Abraham. It is significant that the main emphasis in Paul's use of quotations from the Genesis is not merely upon many descendants, but more specifically upon Abraham as the *father* of many nations.[73] This was a much more controversial question than the extension of Israel's blessings to the nations, and probably reflects the discussion whether proselytes could properly be called children of Abraham.[74] Paul argues that not only proselytes, but even uncircumcised

---

[71] See the suggestion that Gal 3:28 belongs to a similar form of macarisms; Betz, "Spirit", 147-50.

[72] W. G. Kümmel (*Theologie des Neuen Testaments*, 126-128) argues that the notion of the Kingdom of God is the foundation for Paul's theology as well as for that of the Synoptics.

[73] Berger, "Abraham", 73 n. 83; cf. above 46, n. 41.

[74] Foerster ("κληρονόμος", *TWNT* 3 (1938) 784) argues that the Christian Judaizers in the controversy in Galatia were ready to accept proselytes into the sonship of Abraham, provided they observed the law. The Rabbis, on their part, did not regard the proselytes as sons of Abraham, cf. *m. Bik.* 1, 4.

converts had Abraham as their father! This is related to the reversal scheme which underlies Rom 4:16-19. In Jewish mission literature, non-Jews could only be included in the community of believers through a transfer from "death" to "life", from "far away" to "close by", from "non-being" into "being".[75] However, when this transfer language is introduced in the designation of God in 4:17, Paul applies it not only to non-Jews, but to Jews as well. When used in a mission context, this was offensive to Jews. That God gave life to the dead and created out of the non-existent was used of *proselytes only*—Jews already possessed life.[76] Now Paul turns this completely around. The formula in 4:17 which the Jews themselves used to show that God reverses the order of the world, Paul now used to argue for a radical reversal in the relationship between Jews and non-Jews. He brought this traditional benediction down with full force upon the Jews themselves: it implied that they were "dead" and that only by an act of God could they become Abraham's offspring.[77] As in the earlier chapters of Romans, Paul uses this traditional confession to counter the Jews with God's judgment in an unfamiliar way. In the context of a letter, as a means of exhorting and convincing, Paul asks of his Jewish readers that they accept a complete change of religious identity, and consequently, adopt a new understanding of God. These are the implications when Paul relates "God who makes life to the dead" in the same way to "all the offspring of Abraham", both Jews and non-Jews.

The explanation which Paul gives of παντὶ τῷ σπέρματι in 4:16 has prompted many explanations. The immediate reaction is often that Paul cannot possibly mean what he seems to be saying: "not only the adherents of the law but also to those who share the faith of Abraham". Most commonly οὐ τῷ ἐκ τοῦ νόμου μόνον is taken to refer to the Christian Jews only, whereas τῷ ἐκ πίστεως 'Αβραάμ speaks of non-Jewish Christians.[78] This would seem to correspond with the most probable reading of 4:11-12, and it also takes into account that Paul's controversies in Romans are mostly with Christian Jews. However, this interpretation is based on the presupposition that Paul would deny the Jews their claim to be

---

[75] See nn. 45, 48; cf. also the allusions to Isa 57:19 in Eph 2:13; Acts 2:39; see Lindars, *Apologetic*, 36, 38.

[76] Sjöberg, "Widergeburt", 45.

[77] Similarly Käsemann, *Römer*, 116.

[78] E.g. Cranfield, *Romans*, 242-43; Davies, *Gospel*, 177; Käsemann, *Römer*, 113; Schmidt, *Römer*, 85.

the offspring of Abraham. In Galatians Paul apparently argued thus, but this is not the case in Romans, where he is more intent on re-interpreting the meaning of this sonship. Moreover, we should also take into account that Paul discusses this issue from a *theological* perspective. To Paul, the question of Abraham's offspring is related to the question of the promise. Against the accusation that his preaching destroyed the trustworthiness of the word of God, Paul argued that the promise of God was steadfast. This meant that it included non-Jews, but it was equally important to Paul that it should also include the Jews.[79] Moreover, Paul's thesis is here oriented towards the future, and it points towards the inclusion in the eschaton of Israel as a whole (ch. 11). Paul brings his readers face to face with the God of creation and resurrection. He does not withdraw from his position that participation in the promise and inclusion among the children of Abraham is by faith and not through the law. It is typical of Paul's paradoxical language that he contrasts the absolute rejection that οἱ ἐκ νόμου were heirs, in 4:14-15, and the inclusion of τῷ ἐκ νόμου in the offspring of Abraham, in *v.* 16.[80] This paradox is stated again and again, particularly in Romans 11 (e.g. 11:25-26; 28, 31). In each instance, Paul concludes the paradox with a statement about God (11:26-27; 29; 32), and the solution is found in an eschatological salvation where Israel is included (11:26; 32b). In chapter 4, Paul speaks from the new situation of salvation, the appearance of the righteousness of God, but at the same time the final appearance of God's righteousness is still in the future (3:30; 4:24). This way of speaking, in part in the present, in part in the future tense, reveals how Paul's argument in Romans 4 is related to the contemporary situation. He is defending a new community, and argues for the inclusion of hitherto separate groups. In this new community of small, ethnically integrated groups he sees the promise coming true—they represent a vision of the future. In this vision, Paul sees at work the God "who gives life to the dead"—and therefore the Jews must be included as well.

We find a similar argument in 9:22-29, a section where καλέω is a key term as in 4:17.[81] Paul describes how God wanted to show his

---

[79] Cf. Rom 3:3; 11:1-2, 28-29; 15:8.

[80] Luz (*Geschichtsverständnis*, 176), who suggests that Paul uses νόμος in two different meanings in 4:13 and 16, fails to see the paradoxical nature of Paul's polemics.

[81] See above, 47.

glory to the "vessels of mercy" (9:23). In the following verse they are identified: "even us whom he has called (ἐκάλεσεν) not from the Jews only but also from the Gentiles". It lies close at hand to interpret the quotations from Hosea in 9:25-26 so that they are applied to both groups, Jews and non-Jews: [82]

Those who were not my people
I will call (καλέσω) my people (Hos 2:25ba)
and her who was not beloved
I will call 'my beloved' (Hos 2:25ab).
And in the very place where it was
said to them, 'You are not my people'.
They will be called 'sons of the living God' (Hos 2:1b).

In the quotation from Hos 2:25: "Those who were not my people I will call my people", Paul has changed the introductory ἐρῶ to καλέσω. Thus the citation connects immediately with ἐκάλεσεν in 9:24, and with the use of this important term in 9:7 and 12. Paul applies this word from Hosea in the same way as he interpreted the promise to Abraham in Romans 4: from the begin-

---

[82] N. A. Dahl, *Studies in Paul*, 145-47. Most commentators take the quotation from Hosea in Rom 9:25-26 to refer to the Gentiles in 9:24 only; whereas the quotation from Isa 10:22-23 and 1:9 in vv. 27-29 refers to those who were called from the Jews; e.g. Dodd, *Romans*, 160; Michel, *Römer*, 246. This assumption is based on the presupposition that Paul disregarded the fact that the text in Hosea was originally addressed to Jews, and that he applied it instead to non-Jews. According to Käsemann, *Römer*, 264-65, it is in this way that Paul's usage is polemical against the Jews. However, this interpretation fails to see that Paul is concerned with the unity of Jews and non-Jews, both as "not my people" and as "called". Thus, the polemic implied in Paul's use of the quotations from Hosea is that he uses them of the Jews as well, and thus he retains the original intention of the text; at the same time he widens them to include the non-Jews; see E. E. Ellis, *Paul's Use of the Old Testament*, 138.

The common interpretation fails at another point also. The quotation from Isaiah in 9:27-29 (introduced with "And Isaiah cries out concerning Israel") does not refer to the elect from Israel in v. 24, as one would expect if the Hosea quote was used of the Gentiles in v. 24 only. Vv. 27-29 are not a promise of election, but rather a threat of destruction from which only a remnant shall be saved. Consequently, vv. 27-29 represents a contrast to vv. 24-26, and continues the line from 9:22, concerning the "vessels of wrath". Käsemann (*Römer*, 265-66) has seen this, but has not drawn the consequences of this insight in his interpretation of 9:24-26. Thus, instead of the two groups of Jews and non-Jews in 9:24-29, Paul speaks on one group of "called", consisting of Jews and Gentiles, versus another group consisting of the unbelieving Jews. His argument about the two vessels in 9:22-24 and the prooftexts in 25-29 actually follows a chiastic structure: a (22), b (23-24), b¹ (25-26), a¹ (27-29).

ning it included both Jews and non-Jews. Thus, he reminds the Jews that Hosea called them τὸν οὐ λαόν μου. In Paul's argument this term is similar to τὰ μὴ ὄντα in 4:17, a description which the Jews reserved for Gentiles! [83] With this quotation Paul wanted to prove that when God called forth "the vessels of mercy" he made no distinction between Jews and non-Jews.[84]

In Rom 4:16-18 Paul turns the designation that God gives life to the dead against the Jews when he says that God united Jews and non-Jews in a new community of faith. When he brings the description of God as creator and lifegiver to bear upon the identity and unity of the Christian community, he pictures this community as a result of the new creation. This unity existed only in its beginning. It was constantly threatened, and therefore Paul depicts its consummation in an eschatological perspective. The end of the world and the resurrection of the dead will not take place until the Jews have been included: "For if their rejection means the reconciliation of the world, what will their acceptance mean but life from the dead" (ζωὴ ἐκ νεκρῶν, 11:15). Here, the "life and death" symbolism turns up again, once more at an important juncture in Paul's argument. As in Rom 4:17-19, in chapter 11 it is applied to the issue of the identity of the new community. Not only will the conversion of all Israel mean new life for them, further, this complete unity between Jews and non-Jews signals the parousia. In this way Paul has bound Israel and the church, in their history from Abraham to the resurrection, to an existence under "God who gives life to the dead".

D. *The grace of God and Paul's criticism of the law*
Rom 4:17 and 13-16

In the haggadic tradition of the promise to Abraham in Heb 11:8-19, the author inserted his own comments in *vv.* 13-16. It was in this section that his own intentions were most clearly expressed. The situation in Rom 4:13-22 is similar. Here, the promise to Abraham is introduced in 4:13 and continues with traditional motifs in 4:16-21. However, after his introduction, Paul inserts a

---

[83] Cf. the use of Isa 40:17, "all the nations are as nothing before him", in Jewish polemics. It is attributed to various authorities, e.g. R. Jehuda b Elai, c. A.D. 150, *t. Ber.* 7, 18; see M. Hengel, *Juden, Griechen und Barbaren* (SBS 76, Stuttgart, 1976) 110-11.

[84] See n. 82.

small section which is different in style from the rest of the passage. It is inserted almost parenthetically into the text: Paul connects *v.* 16 directly with the introduction in *v.* 13 by repeating his thesis: διὰ τοῦτο ἐκ πίστεως. However, the problem he faces in this parenthesis is the same as in the passage at large. In 4:16-21, he was directly involved in the defence of his missionary praxis and of the unity between Jewish and non-Jewish Christians. When addressing this situation he used the common mission terminology "from death to life". Thus Paul attempted to legitimate his highly controversial praxis. But this adaptation of the Abraham tradition was not sufficient to answer his critics. Their criticism was directly theological, and first of all concerned with what consequences his praxis had for the law. It was this criticism which prompted Paul's justification of his praxis in more explicitly legal and dogmatic language.[85]

Paul was accused of destroying the law and of rendering the word of God void. In Romans 4 and 9:6-13, these accusations prompted his exposition of the promise of God. In his replies, Paul emphatically states that the word and the promise of God are steadfast. Paul followed a traditional pattern in his argument, for example with the antithesis between πίπτω and μένω in Rom 9:6-12:[86] "But it is not as though the word of God had failed (ἐκπέπτωκεν 9:6)" . . . "in order that God's purpose of election might continue (μένῃ, 9:11)". Another example is the exchange in 3:31 with its antithesis between καταργοῦμεν and ἱστάνομεν. We argued earlier that 3:31 not only introduced chapter 4 in general, but more particularly the section 4:13-22. As in 9:6-13 and Gal 4:21-31, when Paul says that he upholds the law, he does it through a drastic re-interpretation. In Rom 4:14-16, Paul even reverses the pattern of accusation and response. When he says in 4:16 that "the promise shall be steadfast" (εἰς τὸ εἶναι βεβαίαν), this was part of the traditional description of the promise of God.[87] Here, it also serves as Paul's explanation of his claim in 3:31, that he upholds the law through his preaching. In Rom 3:31, Paul's opponents claimed that his preaching destroyed the law. In 4:14-15, Paul turns the argument around and claims

---

[85] This difference in language is noticed by several commentators, e.g. Luz, *Geschichtsverständnis*, 184 n. 157.

[86] This form goes back to a rhetorical formulation in the Septuagint, see above, 57, n. 4.

[87] See above, 196.

that it is the law which threatens to destroy faith and the promise of God. Thus, 4:14-16 follows the same pattern of argument as 3:31: the law (or the promise) is being attacked, but it is upheld (guaranteed). What then, is the difference between these two passages? Paul apparently sees the situation in the same way as did his opponents in 3:31: the people of God meets with experiences which totally contradict the promises, and the evil forces of the world seem to destroy them. To fit this picture, Paul uses mythological language. Law, promise and faith are almost hypostatized and involved in a cosmic power-struggle.[88] However, Paul sees the threat to the promise and the word of God as coming from a different quarter than did his opponents. It is in his answer to this dilemma that Paul differs radically from his fellow Jews, even from the Christians among them. He sees the threat to the promises coming from the law—that is, God's law! This is the drastic conclusion of what Paul says in 4:14: εἰ γὰρ οἱ ἐκ νόμου κληρονόμοι, κεκένωται ἡ πίστις καὶ κατήργηται ἡ ἐπαγγελία. This statement puts Paul's use of tradition in 4:13-22 in a new light. In 4:16-21 too, he had altered the tradition by applying the promise to Jews and non-Jews alike, but his interpretation was always warranted by traditional statements about God. In 4:14-15, however, the promise which he preached is portrayed in absolute conflict with the law, the very basis for Jewish tradition. This conflict is introduced first in 4:13 when Paul establishes the antithesis between νόμος and πίστις, an antithesis which was unheard-of in Jewish theology. It is partly this antithesis which Paul expands on in legal and apocalyptic terms in 4:14-15. Through the distinction between promise and law, as well as between faith and law, Paul has split Jewish tradition, and set one part up against the other. Thus, the controversy in which Paul is involved cannot be solved by mere recourse to tradition. Therefore his real answer lies in the final clauses in v. 16: "That is why it depends on faith, in order that (ἵνα) the promise may rest on grace and (εἰς τό) be guaranteed to all his descendants". In this first part of the verse, three different phrases are combined in one stream of thought. "That is why it depends on faith", refers

---

[88] The term καταργέω in 4:15 is frequently used of an eschatological conflict, most often of the destruction of cosmic enemies by God or Christ, e.g. 1 Cor 15:24; 2 Cor 3:7, 11, 13-14; see J. Cambier, "Paul. L'eschatologie", DBSup 7 (1966) 378-79. For the concept of the law as a cosmic power see R. Leivestad, Christ the Conqueror. Ideas of Conflict and Victory in the New Testament (London, 1954) 84-138, esp. 95-96, 104-7.

back to the antithesis between law and faith in 4:13 and summarizes Paul's view: the law is excluded! This is grounded in the two following final clauses.[89] The last one, εἰς τὸ εἶναι βεβαίαν τὴν ἐπαγγελίαν παντὶ τῷ σπέρματι, is an argument from Paul's missionary praxis. To Paul the unity of Jews and non-Jews in one fellowship represented the aim of God in his dealings with the world, and therefore it meant the fulfilment of history.[90] The central position in v. 16a is held by the short, easily overlooked phrase, ἵνα κατὰ χάριν.[91] This phrase warrants the theological antithesis in v. 13 and its practical applications in 4:16-18. Within tradition, the promise to Abraham and to his descendants could be extended to such new groups as the proselytes. However, tradition could not be used as an argument for Paul's antithesis between law and faith. Therefore, just at the point at which he departs from Jewish or Jewish Christian tradition, Paul continues his argument with two final clauses. They represent his deepest convictions; they are almost prophetic in their vision of the eschatological goal which Paul sees in history. When the antithesis in 4:13 is interpreted with the help of ἵνα κατὰ χάριν, it becomes clear that this antithesis is not between man's works of law and his faith. Rather, it is *theo*-logical in character. When Paul speaks of χάρις in Romans, it is most often in discussion of Israel or of the Christians on the threshold between "old" and "new", that is, when he is involved in questions concerning the law. As in Rom 3:24 and 4:4, in 4:16 χάρις characterizes an act of God in contrast to the law. The antithesis in 4:13 actually says that *God* gives his promise not through the law, but through faith![92]

---

[89] From the importance that Paul attaches to the second clause in his argument it follows that this, too, is final, not merely consecutive; Michel, *Römer*, 123; contra Käsemann, *Römer*, 114.

[90] See Rom 11:32; cf. Luz, *Geschichtsverständnis*, 298-300; and passages where Paul speaks of separate groups united in the praise of God, e.g. Rom 15:8-12; 2 Cor 1:11; 4:15; 9:12-15.

[91] Käsemann (*Römer*, 114) and Dodd (*Romans*, 69) do not even mention χάρις in their comments upon 4:16; more satisfactory is Michel, *Römer*, 123. See the suggestive article by D. J. Doughty ("The priority of χάρις", 163-80) in which he shows how Paul's use of χάρις structures his argument. However, Doughty does not mention the function of the antithesis between grace and wrath.

[92] Doughty, "Priority", 169-72; cf. E. Lohmeyer, *Grundlagen paulinischer Theologie* (BHT 1, Tübingen, 1929) 116-18; further J. J. O'Rourke ("Pistis in Romans", *CBQ* 35 (1973) 188-94), whose attempt to distinguish between passages where faith belongs to God and others where it belongs to man is too schematic.

With the use of χάρις Paul proclaims God without using tradition, and thus re-interprets traditional concepts of God. We noticed that the terminology of 4:13-16 is similar to that which Paul used in apologies. However, this passage represents a reversal of this rhetorical form, since Paul is here making accusations, rather than defending his gospel. When he claims that the law is a threat to the promise, he turns the accusations against the proponents of Jewish tradition. It follows therefore that the style of this particular passage is much closer to that of Galatians. In that letter, this polemical form, where Paul is the accuser, is more common. By comparing Rom 4:13-16 with other passages, especially in Galatians, we shall try to identify the setting in Paul's life of this particular polemic form.

The statements in Rom 4:13-16 repeat in summary form the discussion in Gal 3:15-22.[93] Paul starts with an example from Jewish legal practice in 3:15-18. When a will is ratified, nobody can alter it or make additions to it. The comparison with the promise of God to Abraham in 3:(15)16 is based on an argument *a minore ad majus*: when this is true of a human covenant, how much more then of God's covenant! Paul concludes in 3:17 that the law, given 430 years later, could not annul the covenant with Abraham or destroy the promise (εἰς τὸ καταργῆσαι τὴν ἐπαγγελίαν).[94] Thus, Paul has concluded a correct Rabbinic argument and proved that the promise has priority over the law.[95] Moreover, Paul argues that the law cannot in any way be added to or combined with the promise. This last point was of particular importance in the Galatian controversy where Paul's opponents claimed that the lifestyle and faith of the Galatians needed to be supplemented by circumcision. So far Paul has argued against tradition by help of tradition, but here, too, his final argument is not drawn from tradition: "For if inheritance is by the law, it is no longer by promise; but it was given (κεχάρισται) to Abraham by a promise". This is an argument of a type similar to those in Rom 4:4 and 16. Paul's dismissal of the law

---

[93] To the following, see in particular E. Bammel, "Gottes διαθήκη (Gal III 15-17) und das jüdische Rechtsdenken", *NTS* 6 (1959-60) 313-19; and K. Müller, *Anstoss und Gericht* (SANT 19, Munich, 1969) 114-19.

[94] In this paragraph Paul states the contrast between "uphold" and "destroy" with negative terms: οὐκ ἀκυροῖ versus εἰς τὸ καταργῆσαι, 3:17.

[95] According to Rabbinic reasoning the temporal priority of the promise meant that it was also superior to the law; Mussner, *Galater*, 241.

is in fact based on this faith-judgment, on the experience that God's gift by χάρις excludes the law.[96]

We find more examples of the fact that Paul's main argument is not drawn from tradition when we look at his use of this conflict terminology in other passages.[97] Gal 5:11 is the closest formal parallel to 3:17 and Rom 4:14 when Paul says: "But if I, brethren, still preach circumcision, why am I still persecuted? In that case the stumbling block of the cross has been removed (ἄρα κατήργηται τὸ σκάνδαλον τοῦ σταυροῦ)".[98] The suggestion that Paul should join the Judaizers and preach that faith must be accompanied by circumcision is negated by a dogmatic statement: then the cross would have ceased to be an obstacle. This is the central theme in each one of Paul's arguments against the law in Galatians. The phrases, "the cross" or "the death of Christ" are, in short form, the essence of Paul's gospel.[99] These expressions are firmly rooted in Paul's own experience and in that of his congregations. In this letter, the death of Christ (the cross) and the suffering of the apostle and of the community belong inseparably together (5:11; 6:12; cf. 4:29). Paul finds the theological justification for this in the suffering and death of Christ, upon which the life of the Christians is modelled. The Judaizers on the other hand (who are not being persecuted, 6:12), are condemned because their message would empty the gospel of its meaning. Paul therefore proclaims judgment upon them (5:12).[100] The hypothetical clause in 2:21 is

---

[96] Bammel, "διαθήκη", 317-18.

[97] Since Paul is the accuser, the positive terms like "uphold" are not much used in polemical passages; instead he speaks of the threat against the gospel with terms like κενός, κενόω, 1 Cor 1:17; 15:10, 14, 58; 2 Cor 6:1; Gal 2:2; Phil 2:16; and καταργέω, Gal 5:4; 11; cf. 1 Cor 13:8, 10; 2 Cor 3:11. See Carl J. Bjerkelund, " 'Vergeblich' als Missionsergebnis bei Paulus", *God's Christ and His People. Studies in Honour of N. A. Dahl* (ed. by J. Jervell and W. A. Meeks, Oslo, 1977) 175-91.

Paul frequently uses the positive term from the conflict in Rom 4:13-16, βέβαιος, βεβαιόω, in the introduction to his letters when he speaks of how the gospel was confirmed among the Christians by the grace of God; 1 Cor 1:6-8; Phil 1:7; cf. 2 Cor 1:7, 21.

[98] Was Paul faced with the accusation of being inconsistent, in that he preached circumcision elsewhere, but not in Galatia? Cf. J. Bligh, *Galatians*, (London, 1969) 431-32. N. A. Dahl makes similar suggestions in his paper on Galatians to the SBL Paul seminar, 1973.

[99] E.g. 1 Cor 1:18, 23; Gal 3:1; cf. also Paul's use of the death of Christ as his main argument in Gal 2:21; 5:11; 6:12; see Sanders, *Paul*, 444-46.

[100] By castrating themselves they would be manifestly excluded from the kingdom of God; cf. Deut 32:2; Müller, *Anstoss*, 117.

another example of the "destroy/uphold" scheme: "I do not nullify the grace of God; for if justification were through the law, then Christ died to no purpose".[101] It is not by the help of logical arguments that Paul rejects the hypothetical clause εἰ γὰρ διὰ νόμου δικαιοσύνη. Rather, he shows it to be incompatible with the following statement: ἄρα Χριστὸς δωρεὰν ἀπέθανεν. Here χάρις and the death of Christ clearly belong together and refer to the same event; moreover, they are both antithetical to the law. It follows, therefore, that the death of Christ is the event which Paul interprets in theological terms as grace. Moreover, this is a *God-event*, Paul consistently describes it as an act of God.[102] This is illustrated also by Rom 3:19-26. Here, too, it is God's action in the death of Christ, as an expression of his grace (3:24), which excludes justification through the law (3:20).[103] This emphasis upon Christ the crucified as the centre of Paul's understanding of the grace of God goes back to his conversion or calling experience.[104] In Gal 1:15-16, he describes how God called him by his grace and revealed his son to him. Furthermore, in 1:6 and 3:1, he reminds the Galatians that they themselves have had similar experiences. Called by God to grace in Jesus Christ crucified—this is how Paul summarizes his message and the initial experiences both of himself and of the Galatians. It is this historical experience which is interpreted when Paul speaks of "the grace of God". This is apparent also in Galatians 5:1-4, to mention briefly a last example from that letter. In 5:1, he exhorts the Galatians to stand firm (στήκετε) in the freedom which they have in Christ. If they do not listen to his command, they will be destroyed: "You are severed (κατηργήθητε) from Christ, you have fallen away (ἐξεπέσατε) from grace" (5:4). This is the opposite of their inclusion in Christ and in his grace by the call of God.[105] With this drastic description, Paul brings divine judgment down upon those who fall away from their first experience.[106]

---

[101] The terms for "uphold" here is οὐκ ἀθετῶ, cf. 3:15.

[102] Cf. 1:1, 15; see further the important role of "God is one" in chapter 3; cf. above, 212-15.

[103] Doughty, "Priority", 169-70.

[104] A most thorough study of this question has now been made by S. Kim, "An Exposition of Paul's Gospel in the Light of the Damascus Christophany" (Ph.D. dissertation, Manchester University, 1977).

[105] Grundmann, "Stehen und Fallen", 158-59.

[106] E. Käsemann, "Sätze heiligen Rechtes im Neuen Testament", *Exegetische Versuche und Besinnungen* (3rd edition, Göttingen, 1970) 73.

We shall only mention one more example of Paul's use of terms for "destroy, empty" in polemics, this time from 1 Corinthians. This shows that Paul's use of this terminology was not restricted to controversies over the law only, but that he used it whenever his gospel was threatened.[107] He sees the schism in Corinth as a threat to the very centre of the gospel: "For Christ did not send me to baptize but to preach the gospel, and not with eloquent wisdom, lest the cross of Christ be emptied (κενωθῇ) of its power" (1:17). In 15:14 he uses a similar argument concerning the resurrection of Christ. In chapter 1, Paul describes how the revelation of God through "the cross of Christ" meant a complete reversal of traditional belief in God (1:21, 22-24, 25, 26-31). The terminology is different from that in Romans and Galatians: the antithesis is between σοφία and κήρυγμα (1:21; 2:4), not between law and faith. In his polemics in the various letters, Paul can therefore build on a common pattern which could be used in different situations.

This brief survey has shown that the conflict terminology used in Rom 4:14-16 had its origin in Paul's controversies with his opponents over the fundamental themes of his missionary preaching. It was his gospel which was the central issue. In several instances this gospel was described as the grace of God, so that to Paul, χάρις was always christologically determined. Unlike many apologetic passages in Romans where Paul defends his preaching, in these texts he accuses his opponents or his congregations of leaving the true faith. Most of his arguments are drawn from Christian experience, and it is this experience interpreted in the light of the death of Christ which is Paul's last word. When he uses this form in an interpretation of scripture and therefore argues within a traditional framework, his final argument moves beyond tradition. As in Gal 3:17, so also in Rom 4:16: the conflict between law and promise could only be resolved by an act of God's grace.

The historical background to this argument is Paul's interpretation of the death of Jesus. His death was a death without honour, brought upon him by the lawabiding leaders of Israel. All New Testament authors had to face this puzzling fact, and every effort to explain his death recognized, at least implicitly, this confrontation with the law. Paul made this implicit conflict with the law into

---

[107] Müller, *Anstoss*, 117-18.

a direct confrontation: it is over the issue of the death of Christ that he sees the split in Israel's tradition occur.[108]

The seemingly insignificant phrase: ἵνα κατὰ χάριν, turned out to be of vital importance in Paul's argument in Rom 4:13-16. Although it is not here christologically qualified, Paul's use of it in this familiar polemical pattern proved that he referred to God's dealing with the world in Christ. In a short form, therefore, it conveyed the centre of Paul's understanding of God which was completely dominated by the Christ-event. Moreover, χάρις has a function similar to the designation of God in 4:17, and therefore it clarifies Paul's meaning with the traditional formula "God who gives life to the dead". Both serve as warrants for Paul's extension of the promise to non-Jews as well as to Jews. Within the traditional, haggadic part of Rom 4:13-22, "God who gives life to the dead" was a guarantee that both Jews and non-Jews were included in the offspring of Abraham. Although in itself traditional, it became a suitable expression for Paul's position when it was applied to his missionary practice. Within the polemical section in 4:14-16a, this practice was given a theological justification through the antithesis between law and faith. This antithesis was grounded in the grace of God. In a much briefer form, the mention of χάρις in Rom 4:16 represents an interpretation of the Abraham-tradition in the light of the death of Jesus, similar to that in Gal 3:10-14. Thus, "God who gives life to the dead" is in Paul's use modified through χάρις, a term which came out of Christian experience.

E. *"God gives life to the dead" versus "the law brings wrath"*
Rom 4:17 and 15

We started our study of Rom 4:13-16 with *v.* 16, in order to follow the logic of Paul's own argument, which starts with the saving acts of God as they were expressed in the final clauses of 4:16. We now turn to 4:14-15 to have a closer look at the function of statements concerning the law within this polemical context. First, we shall give an outline of the features typical of this polemic.[109]

---

[108] That life was given in Jesus and in no other "place" was the main reason for Paul's rejection of the law, cf. Gal 3:10-14: it was not a result of an analysis of the human situation. See the discussion by Sanders (*Paul*, 474-97) against e.g. Bultmann (*Theologie*, 187-270).

[109] The pattern of Paul's arguments in polemic is in need of a thorough study. This theme is often neglected in commentaries; see, however, Schneider, *Die rhetorische Eigenart der paulinischen Antithese*, esp. 87-89; and Müller

Within this outline we can identify four successive steps in Paul's argument.

1) Paul first summarizes the view of his opponents. He often renders it with a hypothetical clause: "If this view is true, then . . .". His rendering is polemical, so that we do not get a clear impression of the view he is arguing against.

2) He then proceeds to show that the view of his opponents is in absolute opposition to the gospel which he proclaimed and which the congregation received at their calling. Paul frequently uses words like "destroy, empty", etc., thereby invoking the idea of a demonic power fighting against the true gospel. Paul's gospel is referred to in a summary way; with terms like "the cross", "the death of Christ", "the gospel", etc.[110]

3) Most passages contain some form of judgment on Paul's adversaries, for example that the law which they are proclaiming actually brings punishment and death upon them. When Paul has defended the superiority of his own preaching (step two), this motif represents the reversal of his opponents' viewpoint. Paul contends that their claim that the law brings life, is untrue; on the contrary, they are on their way to damnation.[111]

4) Paul's polemic is tempered by a final phrase in which he emphasizes his positive intentions. When he rejected so vigorously the view of his opponents, it was in order that the grace of God, his promise, etc. should be steadfast and visible. Paul can phrase this last motif in various ways, for example with a final clause or with a quotation from the Bible. In each case this final statement is dogmatic or prophetic, i.e., without any further argument or warrant.

The following table shows some examples of Paul's use of this polemical argument: [112]

(*Anstoss*, esp. 84-120), who studies one group of polemical passages concerned with σκάνδαλον. Very stimulating is Sanders, *Paul*, 474-97; cf. also the suggestions in Michel, "Polemik und Scheidung", 193-95. See the suggestions for a methodology of such a study in J. A. Fischer, "Pauline Literary Forms and Thought Patterns", *CBQ* 39 (1977) 209-23.

[110] Michel, "Polemik", 193-94; Sanders, *Paul*, 482-85, 549-52.

[111] This reversal of the opponents' argument is typical for polemic within a group or between closely related groups; cf. Michel "Polemic", 194; and above, 56-77.

[112] Other texts have some parts of the argument; cf. Rom 4:2; 1 Cor 15:12-15, 16-19; Gal 2:21; cf. also the μὴ γένοιτο argument, see above, 225-26.

	Romans	Galatians	1 Corinthians
1)	4:14a	3:18a 3:21a 5:11a	1:17a
2)	4:14b	3:18b 3:21b 5:11c	1:17b
3)	4:15	3:22a (5:12)	1:18a
4)	4:16a	3:18c 3:22b	1:18b

As part of Paul's accusations against his opponents, his statements in Rom 4:14-15 are brief and summary. It is not their function to explain or to develop a thesis, but rather to attack his adversaries at what he considers their weakest point. That it is this polemical situation which accounts for the style of Romans 4:14-15, has not been sufficiently recognized. It is frequently observed that Paul here merely states his position without elaborating on it, but it is often regarded as an introduction of a theme which he treats in detail later (5:12-21 and 7:7-25).[113] However, the function of 4:15 is to be found primarily in the context of Paul's rhetorical argument in 4:13-16.

It follows that 4:15, "For the law brings wrath, but where there is no law, there is no transgression", is Paul's rejection of a Jewish claim concerning the law. It was a basic presupposition for every Jew that God's power to give life was closely connected with the law.[114] It was through the law he gave and preserved life; moreover, the law was a barrier against the destructive powers of sin and evil. Paul's rejection of this claim lies at the very centre of his polemics against Jews and Judaizers. Thus, he mentions it frequently and at least on two occasions he goes directly into the discussion of the biblical evidence for this view. It was found in Lev 18:5; "You shall therefore keep my statues and my ordinances, by doing which a man shall live: I am the Lord".[115] In each case, Paul counters it with another text from the Bible, in Rom 10:5-8 with Deut 30:12-14; in Gal 3:10-14 with Hab 2:4: "the righteous shall live by his faith". In Galatians 3, it is in the exposition of Gen 15:6 that Paul discusses the contrast between Lev

---

[113] E.g. Hahn, "Gesetzesverständnis", 41-42; Luz (Geschichtsverständnis, 187) regards Rom 4:15 as a maxim ("einen allgemeinen Grundsatz"). This dogmatic position is characteristic for Luz, who in his otherwise magisterial study of Paul's theology pays little attention to the rhetorical or historical situation of his letters.

[114] Sir 17:11; Bar 4:1; Pss. Sol. 14:2; etc., see the large collection of texts in Billerbeck 3, 129-31.

[115] For this discussion, see Lindars, Apologetic, 228-32; and Sanders, Paul, 483.

18:5 and Hab 2:4. Thus, Abraham is Paul's example of the righteous man who shall live by faith. Third in this group of texts, we find Paul's polemical interpretation of Ps 143:2: "For no human being will be justified in his sight by works of the law" (Rom 3:20; Gal 2:16). In Galatians these texts are clustered together. They are found in 2:16 (Ps 143:2), 3:6 (Gen 15:6), and 3:11 (Hab 2:4). In Romans they are more widely scattered, but all are situated at important points in the letter: 1:17 (Hab 2:4), 3:20 (Ps 143:2), 4:3 (Gen 15:6). In each case the connection, indeed, the virtual identity between *righteousness* and *life* is presupposed (cf. Gal 3:21).[116] The Judaizers in Galatia must have claimed Abraham as an example that righteousness and life came through the law. It is this claim to life through the law which Paul rejects, both in Gal 3:10-14 and 21-22. In each case, he answers with his definition of "life": it is identical with receiving the Spirit (3:14, 22).

The closest parallel to Rom 4:14-16 is Gal 3:21-22, where Paul answers the objection that the law appears to be against the promise.[117] Here he refers directly to the claim that God had intended to give life through the law: "if a law had been given (ἐδόθη) which could make alive" (3:21b, cf. Rom 4:14a). The connection between life and righteousness is expressed when Paul rejects this claim on the ground that then righteousness would be (not through faith but) through the law: "then righteousness would indeed be by the law" (3:21c, cf. Rom 4:14b). When he has rejected this false claim, Paul goes on to point out the actual result of the law: "But the scripture consigned all things to sin" (3:22a, cf. Rom 4:15a).[118] Finally, he comes to his positive goal, in a ἵνα-clause, when he asserts that God has made life available in faith: "that what was promised to faith in Jesus Christ might be given to those who believe" (3:22b, cf. Rom 4:16a). This last clause signals that Paul even in his polemics is primarily concerned to reassure the Galatians that the promise is fulfilled in their lives.

---

[116] See Sanders, *Paul*, 503-8 and 493-95, where he modifies his view from "Patterns of Religion in Paul and Rabbinic Judaism", *HTR* 66 (1973) 470-74, that the "real" meaning of righteousness is "life". Cf. also H. Binder, *Der Glaube bei Paulus* (Berlin, 1968) 41.

[117] The arguments in 3:19-20, 21-22 and 23-24 run parallel, but with different structure and imagery. For 3:19-20 see above, 212.

[118] The use of γραφή (cf. 3:8) probably points to the subordinate position of the law; it was Scripture which put men under the law until the promise was given by faith, 3:22b; cf. Dahl, "Widersprüche", 15.

It is within the context of this positive intention that we must consider Paul's polemics as well. He speaks directly about God, and contrasts two different views of God's dealings with his people: one is that God has given the law power to give life, the other, which excludes the former, is that it is by *faith* that he has given the promise to the believers. In his defence of this latter view (which is his own starting point), Paul goes to the extreme. He confirms the Jewish view that the law is given by God—but not to make alive. Rather, he points out the disastrous effects the law has had in the lives of his opponents and in the history of Israel in general. This attack borders on the blasphemous, since Paul insists that it is *God* who has given the law which has had this effect. The law was willed by God, but only until the arrival of Christ.[119] Therefore, the law belongs to the past. It has served its role—it was an episode in the history of God's dealings with man. There is an historical realism in Paul's view here: his views are determined by the new experience of God who gives life through the Spirit. Paul claimed that the Judaizers who wanted to combine this experience with the law, were dragging the past into the present! This conflict influenced Paul's view of the history of Israel as well. It is not the case that the law at one point was life-giving by God's will, and that it has now been superseded by the promise. Paul's interpretation is much more drastic: it was never God's plan to give life through the law, even though it was the law of God! Paul here rejects the more easily acceptable view that the law was God's plan of salvation, but that Israel was not able to fulfil it (Acts 13:38-39). To Paul, there was no peaceful transition from law to promise: the law did not quietly give way. Quite the opposite—the law is still active, but it leads to death, because it is taken over and dominated by sin. Paul's view of the law in Galatians is much more negative than in most parts of Romans.[120] However, Rom 4:14-15 has the same polemical note as Galatians 3.

In Rom 4:13-22, Paul encounters the claim that the law gives the inheritance, that the adherents of the law are heirs to the promise. This is another way of speaking of "life" (cf. 8:12-17, where to live, to receive the Spirit and to be heirs are parallel

---

[119] Paul is here concerned with the unity of the acts of God; both the promise and the law were given by him; Dahl, "Widersprüche", 14-16; Bammel, "διαθήκη", 317.

[120] Hahn, "Gesetzesverständnis", 58-60.

terms). Paul rejects this claim categorically when he says that the law does not bring life, but rather the wrath of God upon those who adhere to the law.[121] This saying is almost formulaic, but within the rhetorical form of Paul's argument it is directly related to the situation which he faces. It is a judgment on those who held that only the law gave participation in the promise (4:14a). In 4:14b Paul claims that this is a fundamental distortion of the gospel, and he continues in *v*. 15: "(Don't you see that) the law brings the wrath (of God over you who adhere to it)!" This statement is similar to Paul's proclamation of the judgment of God over sinners and blasphemers earlier in the letter (3:8; 2:3 etc.).[122] The wrath of God is identical with judgment and death (cf. 2:7-8), and in 4:15b Paul emphasizes that it is linked to the law and to the transgressions provoked by the law.[123] After this judgment Paul can continue with his positive message: "This is why it depends on faith, in order that the promise may rest on grace and be guaranteed to all his descendants". With his polemics Paul brings God's judgment down upon those who are "of the law", in order to proclaim that the grace of God is revealed in the promise, for everybody to believe. It is this grace of God which expresses the divine purpose in history, and it is from this experience of grace that Paul preaches and develops his argument.

In this controversy in Romans 4 over the identity of the Christian community as children of Abraham, Paul most probably has Christian Jews in mind. However, Paul gives expression to this conflict in drastic terms: it is a choice between total acceptance or total rejection of the gospel. In 4:14-16, Paul speaks of law, transgression and wrath versus promise, with faith and grace almost as hypostatized powers.[124] He speaks in a similar manner in the conclusion to the "from Adam to Christ" pericope in 5:20-21 and in chapter 7. In these texts, he explains how it was possible that the law could bring the wrath of God. It was because of sin that "the

---

[121] Paul speaks of the *wrath of God* and not of "an inevitable process of cause and effect in a moral universe"; Dodd, *Romans*, 23. Against Dodd and others, see U. Mauser, *Gottesbild und Menschwerdung*, 144-62.

[122] See above, 59-62.

[123] 4:15b: "where there is no law, there is no transgression", serves to emphasize that the law provokes sin; see 5:13, 20; 7:7-11; Hahn, "Gesetzesverständnis", 41-44; against Käsemann (*Römer*, 114) who at this point fails to see the rhetorical situation in 4:13-16 and regards 4:15b as a general truth.

[124] Michel, *Römer*, 123.

very commandment which promised life proved to be death to me"
(7:10). Paul does not reflect on why God did not prevent sin from
perverting the law, but he emphasizes that the law was without
power to rescue men from sin (8:3). Only God could do this by
sending his son with the Spirit of life (8:2, 3-4). Here there is a
similar contrast between the law, which is weakened by sin so that
it resulted in death, and God's power to make alive, as we found in
4:15-17. But there is a marked difference in style. In chapter 7,
Paul is defending his preaching against the suspicion that he
destroys the law; in 4:14-15, his polemics are directed against the
proponents of the law. Therefore, whereas in chapter 7 he emphasizes
that the law is holy and good (7:12) and that it is from God, in 4:15
he charges that God is behind the work of the law to destruction also.

To the Jews, Paul's polemic was blasphemous, and modern
readers could find here a doctrine of predestination. However,
predestination is not what Paul is arguing for,[125] and his polemic
reveals a deeply-felt theological concern. With his accusations he
puts the Jews in a position where they cannot hide from God. Even
the destructive effect of the law, to bring wrath down upon them,
cannot escape the will of God to give salvation (4:16a). This is a
theme which returns frequently in chapters 9-11, and reaches its
paradoxical climax in 11:32: "For God has consigned all men to
disobedience, so that he may have mercy upon all". Paul's polemic
in 4:14-15 has an ultimately positive intention: to make his
opponents accept his interpretation of the promise to Abraham. In
chapter 1 also, it is the gospel which is Paul's starting point. God's
righteousness is revealed as a source of life for the believers, but,
as a result, the wrath of God over the wicked is revealed as well.[126]
The wrath of God brings death (1:32), Paul says, so that from the
beginning of the letter wrath, sin and death are related terms, as
are righteousness, faith and life. Thus the combination of "life/
death" symbolism and of the legal language (linked to Paul's
explanation of righteousness) later in the letter is prepared here.
In 4:13-22, Paul makes this combination explicit when he contrasts
v. 15: the law brings wrath (and death), with v. 17b: God who gives
life to the dead.[127] When Paul uses this designation in his discussion

---

[125] Cf. Sanders, Paul, 446-47.
[126] See now G. Harold, Zorn and Gerechtigkeit Gottes bei Paulus. Eine
Untersuchung zu Röm, 1, 16-18 (EHS.T 14, Frankfurt, 1973).
[127] This contrast is also noticed by Müller, Gottes Gerechtigkeit, 94.

of the inclusion in the sonship of Abraham of both Jews and non-Jews, it meant that the Jews had to accept that they also were "dead", as it were "non-existent" in the eyes of God. Therefore life had to be *given* to them. In the polemics in 4:14-16 Paul says the same in theological terminology: the law does not bring life, but the wrath of God. It is only the grace of God which gives share in the promised inheritance, in life. Thus both the judgment and the proclamation of grace are brought to bear on "God who gives life to the dead", to clarify Paul's intention by using this traditional statement about God.

Consequently, the grace of God and his wrath are primarily hermeneutical terms used to explain the relationship between God and Israel (and the world), not to describe the nature of God. This "historical" use of the terms wrath and grace is paralleled in the Pauline antithesis between letter and Spirit in 2 Cor 3:6: "the letter kills, but the Spirit gives life".[128] This antithesis is likewise applied hermeneutically to his understanding of Scripture, that is, to the use made of it by the congregation in Corinth. The main point in the comparison between the two covenants is not that the old was imperfect whereas the new is perfect. Paul emphasizes that both covenants are from God, and only in Christ is it revealed that the old does not bring life, but kills! God is found as the giver of life only in Christ and in the Spirit; if the Corinthians attempt to find him in the law, they will discover that the law brings death. Thus death-versus-life and Spirit-versus-letter are theological terms whereby Paul distinguishes between synagogue and church, between judaizing Christians and his own followers.

A comparison with Galatians 3:21-22 and 2 Cor 3:6 reveals that Paul uses "death/life" language in Rom 4:17 for a somewhat different purpose. The polemical section in 4:14-15 excludes those who adhere to the law, who are under the wrath of God. However, in 4:16-18 χάρις and "God who gives life to the dead" are used to *include* "all the offspring" of Abraham. Consequently, Paul does not only use this designation of God polemically; he also intends to convince his readers. He points out to them that to confess God "who gives life to the dead" implies acceptance of judgment on their life under the law. As in 3:24-26, 4:7-8 and 4:24-25, Paul's

---

[128] To this verse see U. Luz, "Der alte und der neue Bund bei Paulus und im Hebräerbrief", *EvT* 27 (1967) 318-28; and E. Käsemann, "Geist und Buchstabe", *Paulinische Perspektiven*, 237-85.

theology here consists of a re-interpretation of tradition. In this case, Paul draws radical implications from a liturgical formula! He sees the Christian community as a congregation of newly-created members where all were given over to death and needed to be created anew. Thus Paul has excluded the possibility that this confession of God should become an expression of self-confidence for the Jews (cf. 3:27; 4:2). In this perspective, God's power in the resurrection of the dead is not a guarantee that justice will be done to Israel in the end (cf. 2 Macc 7). On the contrary, the Jews do not partake in the resurrection of the righteous, but of the sinners. With the interpretation of the designation in Rom 4:17 through ὀργή and χάρις in 4:14-16, Paul has given the traditional liturgical formula a meaning similar to the radical expression in 4:5, that God justifies the ungodly.[129] Thus it has become almost a paradox: Paul has pushed it close to the limit of what language can meaningfully convey.

F. *"God who gives life to the dead" and "God who raised from the dead Jesus our Lord"* 4:17 and 23-25

The full meaning, both of the designation of God in 4:17 and of chapter 4 as a whole, can be grasped only when seen together with Paul's conclusion in 4:23-25. In this section, Paul identifies the basis of his argument in the previous parts of the chapter. Here he speaks directly to his readers about their faith in God, who has acted by raising Jesus from the dead. This event marks the "new" situation from which Paul speaks even when he does not specifically mention Christ. However, 4:23-25 is couched in traditional language, so it is necessary here, too, to distinguish between commonly-held beliefs and the specific points which Paul is making.[130] Furthermore, this section has frequently been studied with a view to the broader issues raised by systematic theology, like the relationship between the Old and the New Testaments and Paul's use of typology,[131] which is why it is necessary to concentrate on the

---

[129] Stuhlmacher, *Gottes Gerechtigkeit*, 226-27. Thereby the traditional language about the community, e.g. in terms of creation or Abraham's offspring, is interpreted in light of Rom 4:5 as well; see W. Klaiber, "Die Bedeutung der justificatio impii für die Ekklesiologie des Paulus" (Diss. Tübingen, 1971).

[130] See the detailed discussion by van der Minde (*Schrift*, 89-99), but cf. no. 140.

[131] The broad treatment of these questions by Käsemann (*Römer*, 119-22, further literature there) bears witness to their importance for a theological

meaning of this passage for Paul's contemporaries and in this particular context. Therefore we shall first consider ideas and beliefs which were common to Paul and his Christian readers.

1) The combination of faith in God who gives life to the dead *v.* 17, and faith in God who raised Jesus from the dead, *v.* 24, suggests that among early Christians, faith in a general resurrection of the dead was used as an argument for the resurrection of Jesus.

2) This faith in God was combined with faith in Jesus: *v.* 25 mentions the basic facts of this faith, his death and resurrection.

3) The example of Abraham and God's acts towards him did not belong to the past only, but applied to the contemporary situation also.

The confession that God raised Jesus from the dead is found in two principal forms.[132] The participial construction in 4:24 is the one more frequently used. It is found with slight variations eight times in the Pauline corpus. In another version of this confession, God was the subject for a finite verb, cf. e.g. Rom 10:9: "and believe in your heart that God raised (ἤγειρεν) him from the dead". God is the implied subject for ἐγείρω even when the verb is used in the passive, as in Rom 4:25 when Paul says that Jesus "was raised from the dead". Only exceptionally is it said that Jesus "died and rose again", e.g. 1 Thess 4:14.[133] This emphasis upon the resurrection as an act of God is significant. This was the truly *new* act which the Christians ascribed to him. When this belief was made into a confession it gave formal expression to the conflict between Christian and Jewish understanding of God.[134] The earliest interpretation of the death and resurrection of Jesus focused upon the vindication theme, that God has vindicated Jesus against his

---

interpretation of Paul. In contrast, these issues are barely touched in Michel, *Römer*, 127-28; or Cranfield, *Romans*, 250-52.

[132] See J. Becker, "Das Gottesbild Jesu und die älteste Auslegung von Ostern", 118-23. The discussion of the development of this formula has not yet reached definite answers, despite a large number of studies in recent years. See the survey by M. Rese, "Formeln und Lieder in NT", *VF* 15/2 (1970) 87-95; and the literature listed in the thorough study by B. Rigaux, *Dieu l'a ressuscité* (Studii biblici franciscani analecta 4, Gembloux, 1973) 106-46.

[133] The word used is ἀνέστη. The power to "raise up" and to give life is attributed to Jesus in the Gospel of John, e.g. 5:21, 26; 6:39, 54. The tendency to attribute this power to *Jesus* instead of to God is brought to completion in the apocryphal Acts of Apostles, where Jesus is frequently spoken of as "God who revives the dead", e.g. *A. Phil.* 29; 84; *A. Jo.* 46.

[134] Cf. Berger, "Gottesbild", 120-24.

accusers.[135] Thus Jesus' controversial preaching of God was vindicated as well, and God had sided with him who died under the curse of the law. The death and resurrection of Jesus formed a main topic in the controversy between Jews and Christians. In this controversy the Christians claimed that, by raising Jesus, God had given them their right. Therefore, this belief in God, that he had raised Jesus, at the same time expressed the identity of the Christians. In this way, the resurrection of Jesus was related to the notion that God created a people.[136] This theme was developed in various ways, by Paul and other writers, but it was implied from the beginning in the confession of God who raised Jesus from the dead. Luke gives an illuminating example of this in the defence speeches of Paul in the last chapters of Acts. Here Luke combines the promise to the fathers and the resurrection of Jesus. The promise to the fathers, or the hope of Israel, are phrases which refer to the resurrection from the dead (23:6-10; 24:15-21; 26:6). Paul argues in his speeches that the resurrection of Jesus is the fulfilment of this hope in Israel. Therefore, if the Jews believed in a resurrection of the dead, it followed that they should also accept the claim that God has raised Jesus from the dead (26:8). These examples from Acts show that the claim that the resurrection of Jesus follows from a general belief in resurrection was part of Christian apologetic or polemic.[137] Paul accepts and presupposes this common Christian scheme, but his own argument is different. He does not see the resurrection of Jesus primarily as the fulfilment of a hope of a general resurrection from the dead. Paul writes to Christians who believed that the promises were fulfilled, but he qualifies this notion by the way in which he speaks of the promise. In Romans 4 (as well as in 9:6-13, and Galatians 3 and 4), Paul never speaks of

---

[135] Cf. the scheme in many speeches in Acts: "you killed—God raised him up", e.g. 2:22-24; 3:13-15; 4:10; 5:30-31; 10:40-41; see J. Roloff, "Anfänge der soteriologischen Deutung des Todes Jesu (Mk X. 45 und Lk XXII. 27)", *NTS* 19 (1972-73) 38-39.

[136] Rigaux, *Dieu*, 378-91; Delling, "Gottespredikationen", 34-35.

[137] P. Stuhlmacher ("Das Bekenntnis zur Auferweckung Jesus von den Toten und die Biblische Theologie", *ZTK* 70 (1970) 365-403) emphasizes the continuity between the Jewish faith in the resurrection and the definition of this faith among the Christians as belief in the resurrection of Jesus. However, Stuhlmacher does not make it clear enough that this continuity is a controversial question. The NT bears witness to this continuity in a context of controversy. It seems that both Luke and Paul, in 1 Cor 15:12-18, use this common faith in resurrection for polemic purposes. They are concerned with the appropriation of a common tradition.

"promise and fulfilment", but of the promise in contrast to the law.[138] It is this antithesis between law and promise which is Paul's main concern.

In Rom 4:25 Paul adds a christological formula to the confession that God raised Jesus from the dead: "who was put to death for our trespasses and raised for our justification". This two-part formula has been much discussed.[139] It is a traditional form, but Paul may have made alterations to it.[140] In particular the second part, ἠγέρθη διὰ τὴν δικαίωσιν ἡμῶν, goes well with the terms δικαιόω and δικαιοσύνη which are prominent in this part of Romans. It is indeed, possible that the combination of a theological and a christological formula in 4:24-25 was part of a tradition. However, the emphasis upon God, followed by a statement about Jesus, is typical of Paul's style (cf. Rom 1:1-4; 3:21-26, and in particular Gal 1:1-4). This double formula, with v. 25 actually repeating what is said about God in v. 24, underlines the importance of Christ for Paul's thinking about God.

In order to relate the Abraham example to his readers, Paul says that "it was written not only for him, . . . but also for us". Paul was convinced, as were all Jews, that Scripture had immediate relevance to the contemporary generation. In his introduction to the *De Abrahamo*, Philo describes the relevance of the patriarchs as examples for his contemporaries in similar terms.[141] However, there are variations in the use of this common hermeneutical principle. Within Philo's religious system, the praise of the fathers functions as an exhortation to his contemporaries to study and to follow their example. In Qumran and among the first Christians, there was an eschatological fervour to the use of scripture, which they regarded

---

[138] Rom 4:13, 14; Gal 3:17, 18, 21, 22; cf. further Rom 9:8; Gal 4:28-29; see Schniewind/Friedrich, "ἐπαγγελία", *TWNT* 2 (1935) 578-79.

[139] See the summary and discussion of some important recent studies (Kramer, *Christ, Kyrios,Gottessohn*; and R. Popkes, *Christus traditus* (ATANT 49, Zürich, 1967)) in van der Minde, *Schrift*, 90-99. Mussner (*Galater*, 50 n. 38) gives an extensive bibliography to the first part of the formula.

[140] The parallelism between the two parts, which is an integral part of the structure of the formula, speaks against the suggestion by van der Minde (*Schrift*, 94-95) that the second part is formed by Paul himself.

[141] Cf. *Abr.* 4: "These are such men as lived good and blameless lives, whose virtues stand permanently recorded in the most holy scripture, not merely to sound their praises but for the instruction of the reader and as an inducement to him to aspire to the same (οὐ πρὸς τὸν ἐκείνων ἔπαινον αὐτὸ μόνον, ἀλλὰ καὶ ὑπὲρ τοῦ τοὺς ἐντυγχάνοντας προτρέψασθαι καὶ ἐπὶ τὸν ὅμοιον ζῆλον ἀγαγεῖν).

as fulfilled among them.[142] Paul shared this view, and therefore we must ask what conclusions he draws from the Abraham story. Throughout chapter 4, he has emphasized God's actions towards Abraham, and consequently it is this motif which he summarizes in 4:23 as well: "But the words 'it was reckoned to him (ἐλογίσθη αὐτῷ)' were written not for his sake alone, but for ours also". It was not necessary for Paul to convince his readers that the Abraham example was valid for them too: however, this chapter and Galatians 3 show that Paul had to convince them that it had a meaning different from the generally accepted one. In Romans 4, Paul argued that the righteousness of God revealed through faith resulted in the inclusion of Jews and non-Jews in the sons of Abraham. It is these same consequences which Paul wants to point out in his hermeneutical application in 4:23-25.[143] The inferences which Paul drew from the righteousness reckoned to Abraham in 4:11-12 and 16-18 are present in 4:23-24 as well, when he speaks of the Christians as οἷς μέλλει λογίζεσθαι. This righteousness which shall be reckoned to them through their faith is not here suddenly an abstract notion, unrelated to Paul's former arguments in chapter 4.[144] With this statement, he brings God's act of righteousness in the present and the future down upon them.[145] In chapters 9-11 in particular, Paul has spelled out the future implications of this righteousness: the complete unity between Israel and the rest of the world through God's final act of salvation.

Judged from the structure of this chapter only, 4:23-25 appears to be its conclusion, with a new reference to tradition. However, by his interpretation of the traditional material in this part as well, Paul once more confronts his readers with a new understanding of accepted Christian beliefs. As in Rom 3:21-26 and Gal 3:10-14, Paul's emphasis on justification by faith is centred in the death and resurrection of Christ.[146] Thus the christological formula of v. 25 in

---

[142] Cf. Lindars, *Apologetic*, 282-83.

[143] This is not sufficiently emphasized in most commentaries on Rom 4:23-25, but see the suggestive remarks by Luz, *Geschichtsverständnis*, 115.

[144] Cf. e.g. Cranfield, *Romans*, 250, where "justification" in 4:24 is a motif unrelated to Paul's previous argument.

[145] μέλλει λογίζεσθαι is best understood as referring to the future parousia; however, its effects are already present, similarly 2:6, 12, 13, 16; 3:30; cf. Käsemann, *Römer*, 121; and Schmidt, *Römer*, 88; against among others Luz, *Geschichtsverständnis*, 133 n. 367.

[146] Käsemann (*Römer*, 122) emphasizes that the christology is the foundation of Paul's teaching of justification; against Stuhlmacher (*Gerechtigkeit*

Paul's usage qualifies the confession of faith in God in *v.* 24. In Paul's interpretation, the phrase that Jesus "was put to death for our trespasses and raised for our justification" describes God in the same way as χάρις in *v.* 16. In consequence, through 4:24-25 Paul has modified the statement that "God gives life to the dead" in 4:17 in such a way that it has the same meaning as "God who raised Jesus our Lord from the dead" in *v.* 24. However, they are not identical; the work of God in creation and resurrection are fully understood only in light of the Christ-event.[147] It is Paul's interpretation of this event which underlies the previous sections of the chapter also. The transfer from death to life which was implied in 4:17 is interpreted in the light of faith in Jesus who died and was raised by God. From now on God is known as the God of Jesus, the God who raised Jesus from the dead.

In Rom 4:23-25, Paul has described the faith of the Christians as directed towards God who raised Jesus and who will reckon their faith to them as righteousness. Thus he has emphasized the characteristic elements of faith, that which distinguished it from the law.[148] That means that Paul does not intend Romans 4 to be a full discussion of the nature of faith; rather, he wants to stress the distinctive aspects which followed from his preaching. We noticed as a part of the midrashic structure of Romans 4 that faith was primarily characterized by descriptions of God.[149] It follows that with his interpretation of "God who gives life to the dead" (and the implications for the relationship between God, Israel and the world) Paul has altered the meaning of "faith" as well. The traditional language of faith in 4:17-21 is interpreted in the light of the antithesis between faith and law in 4:13-16 and of Paul's concluding comment in 4:22: "That is why his faith 'was reckoned to him as righteousness' ". Faith remains the same, it is still trust in God, hope against hope, a looking towards the future, etc.; but now Paul draws conclusions which were previously unknown. Paul accepts and makes use of traditional descriptions of faith, but he is primarily interested in the consequences of this faith. That Abraham

---

Gottes, 207-10), who stresses that Paul uses justification as an interpretation of christology.

[147] Cf. H. Schwantes, *Schöpfung der Endzeit*, esp. 62-67.

[148] See in particular Sanders, *Paul*, 490-91; further Käsemann ("Der Glaube Abrahams in Röm 4", 140-77) who interprets the traditional notions of faith in the light of Paul's teaching of righteousness.

[149] See above, 109.

believed in hope against hope (4:18) is not a statement which sets forth an ideal of Christian faith in general terms. The subject of Abraham's hope was that he should become a father to all nations. This was the truly impossible goal towards which his faith was directed. God had promised that Abraham and his offspring should inherit the world (4:13), and it was towards this goal that Abraham looked in faith, trusting that God was able to do what he had promised (4:21). These were the very goals towards which Paul was working in his missionary practice, against opposition from Jews and Jewish Christians! Finally, in 4:23-25, Paul uses the most central parts of the Christian faith as support for his position. Thus Paul has brought together the various notions of faith in chapter 4. They are united, not in any one concept of faith, but in their dependence on the righteousness of God. It is the unifying characteristic of faith that it is contrasted with the law, or, in line with this contrast, that it results in mission to Jews as well as non-Jews! Throughout Romans 4, these are the two major points which Paul wants to make. There is a simplicity to his argument which is easily confused when the haggadic section in 4:17-21 is treated as an anatomy of faith and dissected to identify its various components. Although "faith" in itself is a term common to Jews and Christians, Paul has here appropriated this traditional language and turned it against the Jews.[150] However, they can re-enter this faith, but it is now qualified as faith in God who raised Jesus from the dead!

With this re-interpretation of tradition in chapter 4, Paul has laid a foundation for his argument in the following chapters, not only for 9-11 but for 5-8 as well. It has been noticed, for example by R. Scroggs and N. A. Dahl,[151] that the Christological statement in 4:23-25 serves as a transition from chapters 1-4 to 5-8. However, even 4:13-22 prepares the following section through the introduction of the "life/death" language in 4:17 and 19. Here the "life/death" terminology is used of God's creating a new community.

---

[150] See Sanders, *Paul*, 490-91.

[151] Scroggs, "Paul as Rhetorician", 288-289; Dahl, "Two Notes on Romans 5", *ST* 5 (1962) 40. Dahl notices that 4:23-25, where Paul uses first-person plurals, serves as a transition from chapters 1-4, held mostly in the third person, to the dialogue style with first and second person in chapters 5-8. However, the phrase "our father Abraham" in 4:(1), 12, 16 has a function similar to the first person plural in 4:23-25, and thus prepares the transition to chapters 5-8.

This "life/death" language is the main characteristic of chapters
5-8, and it is here always used in a specifically Christian context.[152]
In these chapters, Christian life is described in a "new" language;
it is life "in Christ" and a result of dying and rising with him.[153]
These are terms closely connected with baptism, which represents
a transfer situation similar to the one in 4:17. The contrast between
4:15 (the law brings wrath) and 4:17 (God gives life) is paralleled
in phrases referring to Christ (e.g. 6:23; 7:4; 8:2). In Romans 5-8
Paul speaks in general terms, so that the conflict is not only between
the law and God's power to give life, but between "flesh" and
"Spirit" as well (e.g. 8:6, 13). The Christians are addressed as
"men who have been brought from death to life (ἐκ νεκρῶν ζῶντας)"
(6:13). This transfer is performed by God "who raised Christ Jesus
from the dead" (8:11).[154] The links are particularly strong between
4:13-25 and chapters 5:1-11 and 8.[155] In chapters 5 and 8, Paul
deals with Christian hope in the plights of the contemporary world.
This hope concerns the sonship of God, which was implied in the
promise that Abraham and his offspring should become heirs to the

---

[152] Cf. A. Feuillet, "Les attaches bibliques des antitheses pauliniennes dans
la première partie de l'épître aux Romains (1-8)", *Mélanges bibliques en
hommage au R. P. Beda Rigaux* (ed. A. Deschamps, Gembloux, 1970) 323-49,
esp. 333-40; also J. Nelis, "L'antithese litteraire ΖΩΗ — ΘΑΝΑΤΟΣ dans
les épîtres pauliniennes", *Ephimerides theologicae lovanienses*, 20 (1943) 18-53.
However, Feuillet and Nelis are more interested in the origin and background of this antithesis, and Scroggs is the first to draw such wide-reaching
conclusions from his observations. He suggests that Romans 1-4 and 9-11
originally formed a separate homily, dealing with the history of Israel.
Chapters 5-8 formed another, more Christ-centred homily of Hellenistic
type. Scroggs (283-84) finds a total of 69 words for life and death in Romans
5-8, against only 4 in chapters 1-4 and 9-11. However, he fails to include
νεκρός, νεκρόω etc. in 4:17, 19a-b, 24. When ζῳοποιέω in 4:17 and ἐγείρω
in 4:24-25 are counted as well, it becomes obvious that 4:(13)17-25 must be
included among the "life/death" passages.
[153] See R. C. Tannehill, *Dying and Rising with Christ* (BZNW 32, Berlin,
1967).
[154] Notice that both 6:13 and 8:11 are qualified by antitheses similar to
those of 4:13-16; in 6:14 with νόμος versus χάρις; in 8:9 with πνεῦμα versus
σάρξ. 6:13-14 in particular reflects a rhetorical-polemical situation similar
to 4:13-16; cf. the question in 6:15; Käsemann, *Römer*, 170.
[155] For the thematic connection between Romans 5:1-11 and chapter 8,
see Dahl, "Two Notes on Romans 5", 37-42; and Scroggs, "Rhetorician",
285-88. Notice the correspondence in terminology between 4:13-25; 5:1-11
and 8: ἐλπίς, ἐλπίζω: 4:18; 5:2, 4, 5; 8:20, 24, 25. κληρονόμος: 4:13, 14;
8:17a, b. Notice further the connection between κληρονόμος and πνεῦμα,
8:15-17, cf. the use of πνεῦμα in 5:8.

world. In each instance this promise or hope has not been fully realized, consequently, Paul needs to emphasize that it rests on a secure foundation. In 5:1-11 and 8:18-39 Paul finds this secure basis in God's actions with Christ,[156] and this is typical of chapters 5-8 as a whole. Paul's christological descriptions here are partly parallel to the strictly *theo*logical ones in chapter 4.

The function of chapter 4 in Romans can also be compared with that of 1:26-31 in 1 Corinthians.[157] In each letter, Paul has to face the question of the identity and unity of the Christian community. In Corinth the issue is restricted to that particular congregation or to groups of congregations, but in Romans Paul also deals with the question more in general terms. The theological foundation for his discussion is the central message of his gospel: in Christ, God has made himself known in a way which contradicts both Jewish law and human expectations (Rom 3:21-26; 1 Cor 1:18-25). As a further warrant for this theological basis, Paul has recourse to the past. In 1 Cor 1:26-31, he can point to an experience he shared with the Corinthians: "For consider your call, brethren ... " (1:26). In Romans, where there was no such mutual experience, Paul speaks of the history of which they were a part: "What then shall we say about Abraham, our forefather according to the flesh?" (4:1; cf. 4:12, 16, 23-25). Paul uses this example from the founding period or from history in a similar way in Romans and 1 Corinthians. In each letter the great threat against unity is boasting (καύχησις) since this attitude opened the way for factions and powerstruggles. Paul explains it in theological terms as a threat against the supremacy of God himself (Rom 3:27; 4:2; 1 Cor 1:29). In marked contrast to this, he describes God as the one who chooses and calls that which is nothing (τὰ μὴ ὄντα) (Rom 4:17; 1 Cor 1:28). He reminds his readers that they were brought into being and given life by God

---

[156] The conclusion to each sub-section of Romans 5-8 emphasizes the victory of God in Christ over death; 5:10-11; 5:21; 6:11; 6:23; 7:6; 7:24-25; 8:11; 8:29-30; 8:39; see Scroggs, "Rhetorician", 282-83.

[157] Most commentators mention the similarity between καλοῦντος τὰ μὴ ὄντα ὡς ὄντα in Rom 4:17 and ἐξελέξατο ὁ θεός, τὰ μὴ ὄντα in 1 Cor 1:28, but without drawing any conclusions for the wider context of the two phrases. This holds true also for G. Bornkamm ("Der Römerbrief als Testament des Paulus", *Geschichte und Glaube* 2, 131-132) who in addition notices the similarity between Rom 3:27 and 1 Cor 1:29-31 concerning boasting. That Romans 4 comes much later in the letter than the corresponding section 1 Cor 1:26-31 is a result of a different letter-structure. However, in Rom 1:18-3:20 Paul expands the themes from 1 Cor 1:18-25.

through his reversal of the structures of this world.[158] Thus, God broke down the divisions between rich and poor, wise men and fools, and even between Jews and non-Jews. In each letter, this act of God is identified by a christological conclusion: this reversal took place through faith in Christ (Rom 4:23-25; 1 Cor 1:30-31). In consequence, with Romans 4 and 1 Cor 1:18-31, Paul has established a basis for unity through a theological foundation of the Christian community. Furthermore, this basis could now be used to criticize their contemporary situation.

In Romans 4, Paul's criticism was directed primarily against Jews, Christian and non-Christian, when he confronted them with God "who gives life to the dead". In so doing, he elaborated on a polemical theme from the early Christian mission among Jews. The same theme is found in an early form in Matt 3:7-10 (Luke 3:7-9), in an exhortation attributed to John the Baptist.[159] It belongs to Q and is therefore roughly contemporary with Paul.[160]

> But when he saw many of the Pharisees and Sadducees coming for baptism, he said to them "You brood of vipers! Who warned you to flee from the wrath to come? Bear fruit that befits repentance, and do not presume to say to yourselves 'We have Abraham as our father', for I tell you, *God is able from these stones to raise up children to Abraham*" (Matt 3:7-10).

Here the polemic and critical use of theology is predominant. The statement that God was able to raise up children to Abraham from stones was a threat to the Jews: they could be replaced as the people of God! Unlike Rom 4:16-18, there is no description of the new people being raised up. By implication, however, we may here see a reference to the community behind Q. This was a group which

---

[158] The idea behind 1 Cor 1:28 is more that of God's reversal of the structures in the world, at the time of the eschatological salvation, (H. Conzelmann, *Der erste Brief an die Korinther* (MeyerK 5, 11th edition, Göttingen, 1960) 67 n. 23), than of creation (Stuhlmacher, *Gerechtigkeit Gottes,* 208).

[159] For the setting of this pericope within Jewish Christian mission and polemic, see C. H. Dodd, "A l'arrière-plan d'un dialogue johannique"; and Schürmann, *Lukas* 1, 162-83, esp. 180-83.

[160] See the following surveys of recent literature to Q: M. Devisch ("Le document Q. source de Matthieu. Problématique actuelle", *L'Evangile selon Matthieu* (ed. M. Didier, BETL 29, Gembloux, 1972) 71-97) gives a good bibliography and discusses several unpublished works also; further U. Luz, "Die wiederentdeckte Logienquelle", *EvT* 33 (1973) 527-33.

consisted primarily of Christian Jews, and Matt 3:7-10 therefore presents us with an example of polemic within the larger Jewish community. This criticism from Christian Jews was directed against other Jews (in fact, most of the Jews) who did not accept the radical reinterpretation of the Torah through Jesus. Although the polemic in Q is much more sarcastic in tone than is Paul in Romans 4, the actual position argued for is less radical. There is no mention of people outside Israel being included among the children of Abraham,[161] and the law is sharpened rather than criticized.

However, this sermon puts the theological question about the children of Abraham within a framework of typical themes from early Christian missionary preaching. Similar motifs are found in the outline of Romans 1-3,[162] leading up to the idea of children of Abraham being raised up by the power of God in Rom 4:16-18. It is therefore probable that Paul built Romans 1-4 on themes from a typical missionary sermon to Jews.[163] However, in his version this Jewish-Christian scheme has been modified.[164] It is preceded by the announcement of the righteousness of God in Christ (1:16-17), and this theme is repeated in 3:21-26 and in 4:23-25. Thus the preaching of the wrath of God and the polemic against the Jews is bracketed by Paul's message of salvation. It corresponds with this positive intention that with the phrase "God who gives life to the dead" Paul includes the Jews as well.

In 2 Corinthians, too, Paul describes the life of the Christians as founded on faith in God "who raises the dead" and "who raised the Lord Jesus". Unlike Matt 3:9 and Rom 4:17 where God "raised up" a new community of believers, in 2 Cor 1:9 the designation is applied to Paul in his role as an apostle. However, he is in his own person a type of the church as well.[165] As part of the introduction to his letter he describes his trials in Asia:

---

[161] R. Walker, *Die Heilsgeschichte im ersten Evangelium* (FRLANT 91, Göttingen, 1967) 87.

[162] Cf. the warning of the wrath of God, Matt 3:7, with Rom 1:18-2:16, esp. 2:3; the demand for fruit of repentence, Matt 3:8, with Rom 2:4; criticism of false security, Matt 3:9, with Rom 2:17-27 and 3:1-20. Notice also the similarity between the main themes in Romans 1-4 and 1 Thess 1:9-10.

[163] Scroggs, "Rhetorician", 281; cf. further G. Schrenk, "Der Römerbrief als Missionsdokument", *Studien zu Paulus* (ATANT 26, Zürich, 1954) 81-106; Bornkamm, "Der Römerbrief als Testament des Paulus", 120-29.

[164] Similarly Demke, "Ein Gott und viele Herren", 474.

[165] Dahl, *Volk Gottes*, 234-36.

For we do not want you to be ignorant, brethren, of the affliction we experienced in Asia; for we were so utterly, unbearably crushed that we despaired of life itself. 9. Why, we felt that we had received the sentence of death; but that was to make us rely not on ourselves, but on God who raises the dead; 10. he delivered us from so deadly a peril, and he will deliver us; on him we have set our hope that he will deliver us again. 11. You also must help us by prayer, so that many will give thanks on our behalf for the blessing granted us in answer to many prayers (2 Cor 1:8-11).

With this paragraph Paul intends more than merely to inform the Corinthians about recent events. The narrative is couched in traditional language of lamentations from righteous sufferers in the Old Testament.[166] This helps us to understand the function of 2 Cor 1:8-11 within Paul's apologetic in the letter. In Corinth he was accused of being weak and without power, and, consequently, not a true apostle.[167] Now Paul can claim that God rescued him from his sufferings and thus vindicated him against his accusers. When Paul here confesses his trust in "God who raises the dead", he appropriates this confession to himself and turns it against his opponents. The phrase "not to trust in oneself, but in God" reflects a common idea in Jewish and Christian religion, but in this context it receives a very special meaning. It introduces an apologetic motif in this letter where Paul frequently accuses his opponents of trusting in their own strength (e.g. 10:12, 18; 11:18). In contrast, Paul claims that in his weakness he is vindicated by the power of God (e.g. 11:30; 12:9; 13:3-4).

The passage from 1:8-11 with its strictly theological language has a parallel in 4:7-15. With its Christocentric language this paragraph serves almost as an interpretation of the earlier one (cf. Rom 4:17 and 23-25):

---

[166] Cf. in particular Pss LXX 21 and 33 (all references in this note are to the LXX). Similar motifs are: the description of suffering, e.g. 21:12-16; 31:4; 114:3-4; and of deliverance, 21:2; 32:19; 33:5; 55:14: expressions of confidence, 21:5-6; 33:19-21. God's deliverance meant vindication for the righteous sufferer, 33:6, 8, 10 etc.; cf. C. Westermann, "Strukturen und Geschichte der Klage im Alten Testament", *ZAW* 66 (1954) 44-80.

[167] See the recent study of this theme by J. Jervell, "Der schwache Charismatiker", *Rechtfertigung*, 185-98.

always carrying in the body the death of Jesus, so that the life
of Jesus may also be manifested in our bodies. 11. For while we
live we are always given up to death for Jesus' sake, so that the
life of Jesus may be manifested in our mortal flesh. 12. So death
is at work in us, but life in you. 13. Since we have the same spirit
of faith as he who wrote, "I believed, and so I spoke", we too
believe, and so we speak, 14. knowing that he who raised the
Lord Jesus (ὁ ἐγείρας τὸν κύριον 'Ἰησοῦν) will raise us also with
Jesus and bring us with you into his presence. 15. For it is all
for your sake, so that as grace extends to more and more people
it may increase thanksgiving, to the glory of God (2 Cor 4:10-15).

Here it becomes clear that Paul's afflictions are sufferings "in
Christ",[168] and the conflict with the Corinthians is also directly
spoken of. In this conflict, his hope of new life is based on God
"who raised the Lord Jesus". This transfer scheme "from death to
life" applied to all Christians, but it was visible at that time in
Paul only. Therefore God "who raised the Lord Jesus" was now
on the side of Paul in his conflict with the Corinthians. But here,
too, it is Paul's ultimate hope to be reconciled with the Corinthians,
to the glory of God. Throughout the letter, statements about God
as creator and reviver of the dead are applied to Paul and his
calling as an apostle (4:6, 14; 7:6; 12:9; 13:3-4; etc.). The polemical
use of this creation terminology is seen most clearly in 2 Cor 3:4-18,
in the antithesis between the letter and the Spirit: "the letter kills,
but the Spirit gives life" (3:6).[169] This antithesis is applied to
Moses in the old covenant versus Paul in the new. Once more Paul
has appropriated God's power to give life for his gospel, whereas his
opponents are left only with the wrath of God in his law.

That God gives life to the dead, and calls the non-existent into
being, are themes connected with the founding of Christian communities. Paul could even use this language of himself, since by
his preaching he actually carried out God's work in creation. This
is a use of creation and resurrection language which is well-known
from Jewish and early Christian mission. Paul describes God's
appearance as creator and reviver of the dead as an act with two
sides: it is both salvation and judgment, life and death, wisdom and

---

[168] See W. Schrage, "Leid, Kreuz und Eschaton", *EvT* 34 (1974) 141-75,
esp. 160-75.
[169] See above, 268 n. 128.

folly. This antithetical way of speaking of God "who kills and makes alive" is similar to Old Testament usage. However, the criterion for this antithesis is genuinely Pauline: it is found in his preaching of Christ, who was crucified in weakness and raised by the power of God. Therefore the antithesis between death and life now corresponds to the hermeneutical antitheses which Paul developed in controversies over his gospel: law and faith, wrath and grace, letter and Spirit. Thus the single phrase "God who gives life to the dead" or "who calls into existence the things that do not exist" has the function of an antithesis when Paul applies it to the identity of his congregations in apologetics or paraenesis.

FINAL REMARKS

The title of our study was "Theology in conflict", and we have
dealt with various aspects of conflict as they are reflected in Paul's
letter to the Romans. Our study of Rom 4:13-22 has confirmed
the findings from part one, where we looked at Paul's use of God-
language in Romans 1-4 and 9-11 in general.[1] The main conflict
which Paul experienced at the time of writing was between himself
and his "integrated" congregations of Jews and Greeks on the one
hand, and his opponents among Jews (Christian and non-Christian)
on the other. This was a conflict primarily over missionary praxis,
and it involved questions of group identity and foundation, group
binding etc. In addition there was the question (which we did not
deal with in this study) of conflicts between the "weak" and the
"strong" among the Christians in Rome. Paul and his opponents
faced these conflicts as theological issues; differences in praxis and
expressions of identity reflected different views of God. Typical of
a conflict within a group or between closely related groups, it took
the form of a controversy over the legitimate right to a common
tradition. This was reflected in the use of a common language, e.g.
in statements about God or terms like law, promise, faith and even
larger parts of tradition. Rom 4, with the promise to Abraham and
the question of legitimate descendants is an example of such a
tradition. At its centre was the double designation of God "who
gives life to the dead and calls into existence the things that do not
exist". This belief in God as creator and reviver of the dead was
applied in Judaism and early Christianity to proselytizing and
mission. To a large extent Paul followed common use, but he
radicalized it, when he saw this belief in God given visible expression
in his own congregations of the uncircumcised. In consequence,
when God related in a new way to the uncircumcised, the understanding of God implied in the designation in 4:17 changed. This
was a break with Jewish belief in God and had direct consequences
for the conflict between Christian and Jewish groups. Thus Paul's
mission to the non-Jewish world and the understanding of God

---

[1] In particular concerning the antithetical way of speaking of God, and
the unity between Jews and non-Jews as the context for discourse about
God; see above, 97-99.

which legitimized his praxis belong inseparably together. His frequent use of God-language in Romans which centred on this question shows his continuing theological reflection on issues which arose from his missionary activity. Thus the new community is not a topic of its own in Paul's thinking, separate from God or from the question of justification by faith. Rather, what Paul says about the community of believers is an aspect of theology, an extension of statements about God in the world. Similarly, Paul cannot speak of God in isolation from the world of Jews and Greeks. However, except for Rom 4:5, he does not express his theology in a new language about God. As a result traditional statements and new conclusions stand side by side and interpret one another. It is Paul's way of speaking antithetically of God which above all characterizes his theology. Therefore, in Rom 4:13-16 Paul explains his use of "God who gives life to the dead" in 4:17 with the help of the antitheses law-versus-faith and wrath-versus-grace.

Here we have reached a third stage of the conflict between Paul and his opponents. There seems to be a conflict within Paul's theology between the grace of God and the wrath of God. Paul's position at this point does not lend itself easily to systematisation. He contrasts traditional beliefs and radical interpretation in an antithetical structure. As with faith, Paul can speak of God only in antitheses! The designation "God who gives life to the dead" was in itself traditional. Moreover, it could be used as an argument by Paul's opponents, claiming that God raised the proselytes to new life in *the law*. Therefore Paul must say that through the law, God works wrath only. In this way he contrast God who kills through the law, and God who gives life through faith! This was the ultimate theological result of Paul's deliberations over the conflict *and* the unity between Israel and the Christians. It is, in particular, when he is concerned with Israel or with the demands made upon Christians by the law, that Paul speaks of God antithetically. This is prompted by his proclamation of God's righteousness, or more often his grace, characterizing his actions with the world through Jesus. This leaves behind Israel and those who persist in the law. However, this cannot mean that the Jews were outside God's realm, that they were no longer his people. That would be an impossible thought for Paul. Israel was still God's people, but now under his wrath, provoked by the very law which God gave them. Even when he is at his most polemical, Paul speaks of Israel's history under God. However, in this history, which continues into the contemporary situation, Israel was now confronted with the law (the letter) which brings death (2 Cor 3:6). It was in Paul's preaching only that men met God in the lifegiving Spirit. His preaching revealed this conflict in Israel's relationship with God, a conflict which became visible only when Christ was revealed (2 Cor 3:14). Until then, the Jews had unknowingly been under the death-sentence of the letter. Paul does not develop a system in which he speaks of grace and wrath as parts of God's nature; rather, these terms express relations between God and Israel and the world. Therefore, this antithesis on the part of God corresponds to terms which describe Israel or man in general: faith versus disbelief or disobedience. Paul's way of speaking antithetically about God is part of his interpretation of scripture, when he brings it to bear on the contemporary situation. He finds in scripture both faith and the promise of life, but also the law which could not bring life. Since Paul insisted that the law was given by God, he was brought to speak antithetically not only of faith versus the law, but also of God versus God!

Thus, Paul's way of speaking antithetically about God does not imply that God is irrational or that he predestines men. Rather, it means that Israel—and the rest of the world—encounter God in Jesus, and that this is an encounter with God which leaves them without excuse if they reject it. Therefore, χάρις and ὀργή are heremeneutical terms, by which Paul summarizes his understanding of the death of Jesus. This was made explicit by Rom 4:23-25. With this theological and christological statement Paul identified, or rather, localized the conflict in the understanding of God. Now God is interpreted in the light of the death and resurrection of Jesus.

As Luz points out, there are similarities between Paul at this point and Luther's way of speaking of the *Deus absconditus* and the *Deus revelatus*.[2] With this terminology, Luther attempted to encompass the complete human experience of life and history, and to interpret it in the light of God. Consequently, as in Paul, it was not a doctrine about the nature of God, but rather an interpretation of the world through God. Moreover, Luther developed it from the heremeneutical use of the antithesis between the letter and the

---

[2] *Geschichtsverständnis*, e.g. 220 (Rom 5:20); 247-48 (Rom 9:19-24); 297 (Rom 11:25-32).

Spirit in his first series of lectures on the Psalms in 1513-15.[3] It is
the task of any interpretation of Paul (and of systematic theology
as well) to retain this antithetical way of speaking about God. For
one thing, this means localizing correctly the conflict which Paul
was involved in when speaking of God. In his study *Gottes Gerechtigkeit und Gottes Volk*, Ch. Müller is only partly correct in
describing the conflict as one between the God of the covenant and
the God of creation.[4] In Müller's reconstruction of this conflict,
Rom 4:17 plays an important part as his proof-text that Paul's
theology of justification is grounded in creation theology. However,
this is an oversimplification similar to the old contrast between
particularism and universalism.[5] There was no inherent conflict
between creation and covenant, which in Judaism were inextricably
bound together. Therefore, when Paul turns God's works as creator
against his acts in the covenant, the real conflict lies in the event
which made Paul contrast the two. It was only through his interpretation of creation in the light of the death and resurrection of
Jesus that Paul could use creation as a criterion against the covenant. Therefore, the real issue for Paul was whether God the
creator acted through the covenant (the law) or through Jesus
Christ. It is only when qualified by Paul's Christological interpretation that the confession of God in 4:17 can properly be
characterized as "Paul's image of God".[6]

The study by A. C. Wire to which we have frequently referred
represents another attempt to localize the conflict in Paul's understanding of God. The title of her dissertation indicates its thesis:
"Pauline Theology as an Understanding of God: the Explicit and
the Implicit". Wire sees a conflict between Paul's explicit statements about God, i.e. traditional beliefs, on the one hand, and their
implications worked out through the context, on the other.[7] She

---

[3] G. Ebeling, "Die Anfänge von Luthers Hermeneutik", *ZTK* 48 (1951)
172-230; esp. 182-203. Cf. Luther's references to 2 Cor 3:6 in these lectures,
WA 3, 89 and 4, 159.

[4] *Passim*, concerning Rom 4:17, esp. 87, 107.

[5] The section on Paul's "Gotteslehre", in F. C. Baur, *Vorlesungen über
neutestamentliche Theologie* (Leipzig, 1864) 205-7 is dominated by this
contrast. Cf. the criticism of Käsemann above, 79, n. 3.

[6] Mauser, *Gottesbild*, 188. J. Becker's use of 4:17 as an expression of "das
Gottesbild Paulus" (*Auferstehung der Toten im Urchristentum* (SBS 82,
Stuttgart, 1976) e.g. 87, 94, 110, 114, 127) is not always sufficiently qualified
in this way.

[7] 260-77.

refuses any attempt to balance the explicit views with the implicit views, and claims that only the latter reflect Paul's message. As a result the "power-language" of the traditional statements is dismissed. Wire correctly sees that God in Romans 4 deals with the weak and the powerless, and therefore, she concludes, God himself becomes weak and is not part of the power game in the world. Consequently, God is actually at the mercy of men. Here Wire has convincingly emphasized an essential aspect of Paul's theology, and described in existentialist terms the implications of the divine χάρις for God. However, the weakness in this existentialist approach is clearly exposed when Wire dismisses the "power-language" as a part of Paul's theology. Thus the antithetical structure of Paul's theology is not preserved, and it becomes impossible to speak of the wrath of God as creator.[8] Because Wire does not uphold the conflict between the explicit "power-language" and the implicit views of God in his weakness, she repeats Marcion's mistake: the God of weakness (of Paul and the New Testament) is different from the God of power (of the Old Testament).

Against this, we must emphasize that the real conflict which is present in the antithesis between wrath and grace must be endured.[9] When doing theology, we are constantly faced with the temptation to avoid the theme of the wrath of God, in order to attain a harmonious image of God. However, Paul spoke of the wrath of God primarily as an aspect of his relationship with Israel and the world. Thus we can only do away with "the wrath of God" as an anthropomorphic remnant at the cost of losing any relationship between *God and the world*. The result would be a proclamation of God utterly irrelevant to the world. This is the danger implied when all traditional beliefs in God, for example the very givenness of religious language, are given negative value only and replaced with a pure christology or Jesuology. It is this givenness in the relationship between God and mankind (be it in the law or outside) which is Paul's basis when he speaks of God. Although creation and resurrection were *given* elements they were interpreted from the Christ-event as the centre of Paul's faith. It is this new centre which

---

[8] The ultimate result of this approach is that man becomes his own creator: "Because God in his weakness does not step in to effect the power structure which man has created, he may provide some basis for a newly existing man to begin to make a world that fits him", "Pauline Theology", 276.

[9] Cf. Luz, *Geschichtsverständnis*, 224-25.

distinguishes Paul's theology from a Jewish understanding of God,
but at the same time Old Testament and intertestamental Jewish
concepts are incorporated in his theology in such a way that they
cannot be dismissed as foreign to his thought. It follows that the
common contrast between the God of the Old Testament and that
of the New Testament (Paul) is inadequate when we try to come to
terms with Paul's understanding of God.

What does it mean when we say that Paul speaks of the same
God as the Old Testament? This is one of the major issues of any
discussion of salvation-history in Paul, and is often mentioned when
commenting upon Rom 4:17 and 24. Even scholars who reject the
suggestion that the idea of salvation history played a part in Paul's
theology conclude that he saw *the same God* acting both in the
history of Israel and in Jesus.[10] However, what is a conclusion in
much of our contemporary discussion was for Paul only the beginning, a presupposition which he took for granted. We must therefore take the question one step further and ask about the implications of this presupposition in Paul's theology. His approach is very
practical, applied directly to the contemporary situation. That God
is the same, means to Paul that he is the same to Jews and Greeks,
to circumcised and uncircumcised—he relates to all groups on the
basis of faith and not of law! It is this basic conviction from his own
experience which Paul finds in God's dealings with Abraham and
Israel as well. This answer to the question whether Paul proclaims
the God of tradition has significant implications for modern discussions of God as well. It compels us to relocate the conflict: the main
issue is not that of the understanding of God in the tension between
the New and the Old Testament, but rather in the conflicts of our
own world. The "place" where Paul spoke of God was the conflict
between Jews and Greeks, high and low, insiders and outsiders.
Most of Paul's statements about God in Romans were related to
this situation in which he attempted to achieve unity through
conflict. The heremeneutical consequences of this Sitz-im-Leben
for theology have yet to be drawn, but we may tentatively say that
they point towards a unity of theory and praxis in discourse about
God.

In contrast, theological discussion in the western world has
tended to centre on theoretical and philosophical issues, such as the

---

[10] See e.g. Klein, "Römer 4", 441-42; and in more general terms, H.
Braun, "Das Alte Testament im Neuen Testament", *ZTK* 59 (1962) 30-31.

existence of God. The situation reflected in the New Testament seems to be totally different, since the existence of God is taken for granted and never brought into question. However, although Paul shared this presupposition with his contemporaries, he gave it a radically new interpretation in the light of the new act of God in Jesus. By doing this, he gave traditional beliefs a new centre. The challenge which Christians face today is not altogether different. The religious presuppositions which Christians share with others are perhaps no longer so explicitly theistic, but even so there is still a shared basis in human experiences and values. It is the interpretation of human experience through the proclamation of God which is at the centre of Christian theology, not a defence of God's existence.

This is probably why God is today spoken of most convincingly where man's situation is in desperate need of interpretation, e.g. in Africa and South America. Among Christians in these countries we sometimes meet a reversal of the traditional process of theology. The starting point is an interaction between a concrete experience and an interpretation of similarly concrete situations in the Bible, rather than an attempt to apply theological principles to a situation. Although this direct use of the Bible is open to criticism, the emphasis on the unity of theory and praxis in theology is in line with Paul's argument in Romans. More than the political implications associated with this theology, it is this understanding of God in practical terms which represents a challenge to traditional theology and a theoretical way of speaking about God.[11]

However, the most important aspect of Paul's theology arising from conflict, when we attempt to apply it to the present time, is that he seeks to overcome the conflict. This is the challenge we face as well, when we try to speak of God in the conflicts of our own time. This means that we cannot speak only of the God who reverses the unjust structures of the world—we must speak of him as mediator as well. The ultimate goal of all reversal is the creation of a unity between previously conflicting groups. In Romans Paul describes God as standing between groups, to protect the weak and the powerless. It is from this concrete situation that we realize that God cannot be spoken of in existentialist terms only, as the weak one who relinquishes his power. If God is proclaimed only as the

---

[11] See e.g. J. P. Miranda, *Marx and the Bible. A critique of the Philosophy of Oppression*, London 1977; esp. 35-108.

weak one who leaves the power game of the world to the strong, he has actually abandoned the poor and the oppressed of the world. Only an antithetical way of speaking of God in terms of weakness *and* strength, grace *and* wrath, can sufficiently interpret his presence in the world—and thereby interpret the world as well.

SELECT BIBLIOGRAPHY

1. SOURCES

A. *The Bible*

The Greek New Testament. Ed. by K. Aland, M. Black, B. M. Metzger and A. Wikgren. London. 1966.
Novum Testamentum graece. Ed. by E. Nestle. 25th edition. Stuttgart. 1963.
Biblica Hebraica. Ed. by R. Kittel *et al*. Stuttgart. (1937). Repr. 1962.
Septuaginta. Ed. by A. Rahlfs. 8th edition. 2 vols. Stuttgart. (1935). Repr. 1965.
The New Oxford Annotated Bible. With the Apocrypha. Revised Standard Version. Ed. by H. G. May and B. M. Metzger. New York. 1973.

B. *Jewish sources*

The Apocrypha and Pseudepigrapha of the Old Testament in English. Ed. by R. H. Charles. 2 vols. Oxford (1913). Repr. 1973.
Die Apokryphen und Pseudepigraphen des Alten Testaments. Ed. by E. Kautzsch. Tübingen. 1900.
Der hebräische Pentateuch der Samaritaner. Ed. by A. von Gall. vol. 1. Giessen. 1914.
Die Esra-Apokalypse (IV. Esra). Ed. by B. Violet. (GCS 18). Leipzig. 1910.
Die Apokalypsen des Esra und des Baruch in deutscher Gestalt. Ed. by B. Violet. (GCS 32). Leipzig. 1924.
The Testament of Abraham: The Greek Recensions. Transl. by M. E. Stone (SBL Texts and Translations 2, Pseudepigrapha Series 2). Missoula, Mont. 1972.
The Shemoneh Esreh:
Schechter, S. "Geniza Specimens", *JQR* 10 (1898) 654-59.
Dalman, G. *Die Worte Jesus*. Leipzig. 1898. 299-305.
Die Texte aus Qumran. Hebräisch und Deutsch. Ed. by E. Lohse. 2nd rev. edition. Darmstadt. 1974.
Fitzmyer, J. A. *The Genesis Apocryphon of Qumran Cave 1*. A Commentary (Biblica et Orientalia 18). Rome. 1966.
Pseudo-Philo's Liber Antiquitatum Biblicarum. Ed. by G. Kisch. (Publications in Medieval Studies, The Univ. of Notre Dame 10). Notre Dame, Ind. 1949.
The Biblical Antiquities of Philo. Transl. by M. R. James. London. 1917.
Pseudo-Philo: Antiquitates Biblicae. Tr. by Ch. Dietzfelbinger (Jüdische Schriften aus hell.-röm. Zeit 2/2). Gütersloh. 1975.
Philonis Alexandrini Opera quae supersunt. Ed. by L. Cohn and P. Wendland. 6 vols. Berlin. 1896-1915.
Philo. *Works*. With an English trans. Ed. by F. H. Colson and G. H. Whitaker. 10 vols. (Loeb). London. 1929-43. With supplements transl. by R. Marcus. 2 vols. London. 1953.
Philo. *Oeuvres*. Ed. by R. Arnaldez, J. Pouilloux and C. Mondésert. vols. 1ff. Paris. 1961-.
Die Werke Philos von Alexandria in deutscher Übersetzung. Ed. by L. Cohen, I. Heinemann, M. Adler and W. Theiler. 7 vols. Berlin. 1909-64.
Philonis Alexandrini Legatio ad Gaium. Ed. with introd., transl. and comm. by E. M. Smallwood. Leiden. 1961.

Mayer, G. *Index Philoneus*. Berlin. 1974.
Josephus. *Works*. Ed. by H. St. J. Thackery, R. Marcus, A. Wikgren and L. H. Feldman. 9 vols. (Loeb). London. 1926-65.
"Le livre de la Prière d'Aséneth". Ed. by P. Batiffol, *Studia Patristica* 1-2. Paris. 1889-90, 1-115.
Joseph et Aséneth. Introduction, texte critique, traduction et notes, by M. Philonenko (SPB 13). Leiden. 1968.
Joseph and Asenath. Transl. by E. W. Brooks. London. 1918.
Neophyti 1. Targum palestinense. Ms de la Biblioteca Vaticana. Ed. by A. Diez Macho. 4 vols. Madrid. 1968-74.
Pseudo-Jonathan. Thargum Jonathan ben Usiel zum Pentateuch. Ed. by M. Ginsburger. Berlin. 1903.
Das Fragmententhargum. Ed. by M. Ginsburger. Berlin. 1899.
The Bible in Aramaic. 1. *The Pentateuch according to Targum Onkelos*. Ed. by A. Sperber. Leiden. 1959.
The Targums of Onkelos and Jonathan Ben Uzziel on the Pentateuch; with the Fragments of the Jerusalem Targum. From the Chaldee. Transl. by J. W. Etheridge. 2 vols. in one. (1862-65). Repr. New York. 1968.
The Mishna. Transl. by H. Danby. Oxford (1933). Repr. 1974.
Der Babylonische Talmud. Ed. by L. Goldschmidt. 9 vols. Leipzig, Berlin, etc. 1896-1935.
The Babylonian Talmud. Transl. into English. Ed. by I. Epstein. 18 vols. London. 1935-52.
Le Talmud de Jérusalem. Transl. by M. Schwab. 9 vols. Paris. 1878-89.
Mekilta de-Rabbi Ishmael. Ed. and transl. by J. Z. Lauterbach. 3 vols. Philadelphia. (1933-35). Repr. 1976.
Bereschit Rabba. Ed. by J. Theodor and Ch. Albeck. 4 vols. Berlin. 1912-36.
Midrash Rabbah. Transl. and ed. by H. Freedman and M. Simon. 10 vols. London. 1939.
Midrasch Tanchuma. Ed. by S. Buber. 3 vols. in one. Wilna. 1885.
Pirke de Rabbi Eliezer. Transl. and annot. by G. Friedlander. London. 1916.
Beth ha-Midrasch. Ed. by A. Jellinek. 6 vols. in two. (1853-77). Repr. Jerusalem. 1967.
Bibliotheca Rabbinica. Transl. by A. Wünsche. Leipzig. 1880-85.

C. *Early Christian sources*

Die Apostolischen Väter. Neubearbeitung der Funkschen Ausgabe. By K. Bihlmeyer. 2. ed. with suppl. by W. Schneemelcher. (Sammlung ausgewählter Kirchen- und Dogmengeschichtlicher Quellenschriften 2/1, 1) Tübingen. 1956.
The Apostolic Fathers. Ed. by K. Lake. (Loeb). London (1913). Repr. 1970.
Acta apostolorum Apocrypha. Ed. by R. A. Lipsius and M. Bonnet. 2 vols. in 3. (1891-1903). Repr. Hildesheim. 1959.
Neutestamentliche Apokryphen in deutscher Übersetzung. Ed. by E. Hennecke and W. Schneemelcher. 3rd edition. 2 vols. Tübingen. 1959-64.
Die ältesten Apologeten. Ed. by E. J. Goodspeed. Göttingen. 1914.
Didascalia et Constitutiones Apostolorum. Ed. by F. X. Funk. 2 vols. Paderborn. 1905.
The Early Syrian Fathers on Genesis. From a Syrian MS on the Pentateuch in the Mingana Collection. Ed. with introd., transl. and notes by A. Levene. London. 1951.
Les anciens commentateurs grecs de l'Octateuque et des rois. Fragments tirés des chaînes. Ed. by R. Devreese. (Studi e testi 201). Rome. 1959.

2. SECONDARY LITERATURE

A. The Old Testament and Judaism

Arnaldez, R. et al. "Philon d'Alexandrie", *DBSup* 7 (1966) 1288-1351.

Attridge, H. W. *The Interpretation of Biblical History in the Antiquitates Judaicae of Flavius Josephus* (Harvard Dissertations in Religion 7) Missoula, Mont. 1976.

Aune, D. E. "Orthodoxy in First Century Judaism?" *JSJ* 7 (1976) 1-10.

Baer, R. A. Jr. *Philo's Use of the Categories Male and Female* (ALGHJ 3) Leiden. 1970.

Beer, B. *Leben Abrahams nach Auffassung der jüdischen Sage.* Leipzig. 1859.

Berger, K. "Jüdisch-hellenistische Missionsliteratur und apokryphe Apostelakten", *Kairos* 17 (1975) 232-48.

Bickermann, E. *Der Gott der Makkabäer. Untersuchungen über Sinn und Ursprung der makkabäischen Erhebung.* Berlin. 1937.

Braun, H. "Das himmlische Vaterland bei Philo und im Hebräerbrief" *Verborum Veritas. Festschrift für G. Stählin zum 70. Geburtstag.* ed. by O. Böcher and K. Haacker. Wuppertal. 1970.

——, *Wie man über Gott nicht denken soll. Dargelegt an Gedankengangen Philo's von Alexandria.* Tübingen. 1971.

Brehier, E. *Les idées philosophiques et religieuses de Philon d'Alexandrie.* 3rd edition. Paris. 1950.

Burchard, Ch. *Untersuchungen zu Joseph und Aseneth* (WUNT 8). Tübingen. 1965.

Cavallin, H. C. C. *Life After Death. Paul's Argument for the Resurrection of the Dead in 1 Cor 15. Part 1. An Enquiry into the Jewish Background* (ConBNT 7/1). Lund. 1974.

Clements, R. E. *Abraham and David: Genesis XV and its Meaning for Israelite Tradition* (SBT 2/5). London. 1967.

Delling, G. "Wunder - Allegorie - Mythus bei Philon von Alexandreia", *Studien zum Neuen Testament und zum hellenistischen Judentum.* Ed. by F. Hahn, T. Holtz and N. Walter, Göttingen, 1970, 72-129.

Elbogen, I. *Der jüdische Gottesdienst in seinen geschichtlichen Entwicklung.* 3rd rev. edition. Frankfurt. 1931.

Feldman, L. "Abraham the Greek philosopher in Josephus", *Transactions and Proceedings of the American Philological Association* 99 (1968) 143-56.

Forkman, G. *The Limits of the Religious Community* (ConBNT 5) Lund, 1972.

Ginzberg, L. *The Legends of the Jews.* 5 vols. Philadelphia. 1913-38.

Grundmann, W. "Stehen und Fallen in qumranischen und neutestamentlichen Schrifttum", H. Bardtke ed. *Qumrân-Probleme* (Deutsche Akad. d. Wiss. zu Berlin, Schr. d. Sektion f. Altertumswiss. 42). Berlin. 1963, 147-66.

Hamerton-Kelly, R. G. "Sources and Traditions in Philo Judaeus: Prolegomena to an Analysis of his Writings", *SP* 1 (1972) 3-26.

Harnisch, W. *Verhängnis und Verheissung der Geschichte: Untersuchungen zum Zeit- und Geschichtsverständnis im 4. Buch Esra und in der syr. Baruchapokalypse* (FRLANT 97). Göttingen. 1969.

Hengel, M. *Judentum und Hellenismus* (WUNT 10). Tübingen. 1969.

——, *Juden, Griechen und Barbaren. Aspekte der Hellenisierung des Judentums in vorchristlicher Zeit* (SBS 76). Stuttgart. 1976.

Hoftijzer, J. *Die Verheissungen an die drei Erzväter.* Leiden. 1956.

Jaubert, A. *La notion d'alliance dans le judaïsme aux abords de l'ère chrétienne* (Patristica Sorbonensia 6). Paris. 1963.

Kee, H. C. "The Socio-Religious Setting and Aims of 'Joseph and Aseneth' ",
  SBL Seminar Papers 10 (1976) 183-92.
Knox, W. L. "Abraham and the Quest for God", HTR 28 (1935) 55-60.
Le Déaut, R. La nuit pascale (AnBib 22). Rome. 1963.
Lohfink, N. Landesverheissung als Eid. Eine Studie zu Gen 15 (SBS 28).
  Stuttgart. 1967.
Lührmann, D. "Pistis im Judentum", ZNW 64 (1973) 19-38.
McNamara, M. "Targums", IDBSup (1976) 856-61.
Maier, J. Geschichte der jüdischen Religion. Berlin. 1972.
Mayer, G. "Aspekte des Abrahambildes in der hellenistisch-jüdischen
  Literatur", EvT 32 (1972) 118-27.
Meeks, W. A. "The Divine Agent and His Counterfeit in Philo and the
  Fourth Gospel", E. S. Fiorenza, ed. Aspects of Religious Propaganda in
  Judaism and Early Christianity (Univ. of Notre Dame Center for the
  Study of Judaism and Christianity in Antiquity 2). Notre Dame, Ind.
  1976, 43-67.
Michel, O. and Betz, O. "Von Gott gezeugt", Judentum, Urchristentum,
  Kirche. Festschrift für J. Jeremias. Ed. by W. Eltester (BZNW 26).
  Berlin. 1960, 3-23.
Moore, G. F. Judaism. 3 vols. Cambridge, Mass. 1927-30.
Nickelsburg, G. W. E. Jr. Resurrection, Immortality, and Eternal Life in
  Intertestamental Judaism (Harvard Theological Studies 26). Cambridge,
  Mass. 1972.
Nissen, A. Gott und der Nächste im antiken Judentum (WUNT 15). Tübingen,
  1974).
Petuchowski, J. J. ed. Contributions to the Scientific Study of Jewish Liturgy.
  New York. 1970.
Philon d'Alexandrie. Lyon 11-15 Septembre 1966. Paris. 1967.
Pool, D. de Sola. The Old Jewish-Aramaic Prayer the Kaddish. Leipzig. 1909.
Priessnig, A. "Die literarische Form der Patriarchenbiographien des Philon
  von Alexandrien", MGWJ 37 (1929) 143-55.
Sanders, E. P. "The Covenant as a Soteriological Category and the Nature
  of Salvation in Palestinian and Hellenistic Judaism", Jews, Greeks and
  Christians. Essays in Honor of W. D. Davies. Ed. by R. Hamerton-Kelly
  and R. Scroggs (SJLA 21). Leiden. 1976, 11-44.
Sandmel, S. "Philo's Place in Judaism: A Study of Conceptions of Abraham
  in Jewish Literature", HUCA 25 (1954) 209-37, 26 (1955) 151-332
  (reprinted, New York, 1971).
Schmid, H. H. Der sogenannte Jahwist. Beobachtungen und Fragen zur Penta-
  teuchforschung. Zürich. 1976.
Schmidt, P. "Die 'Ungläubigen' in der Bibel", Klio 43-45 (1965) 410-34.
Schmidt, W. H. Alttestamentlicher Glaube und seine Umwelt. Neukirchen. 1968.
Schreiner, J. "Segen für die Völker in der Verheissung an die Väter", BZ NF
  6 (1962) 1-31.
Seters, J. van, "Confessional Reformulation in the Exilic Period", Vetus
  Testamentum 22 (1972) 448-59.
Seybold, K. Der Gebet der Kranken im Alten Testament (BWANT 99) Stutt-
  gart. 1973.
Sjöberg, E. "Neuschöpfung in den Toten-Meer-Rollen", ST 9 (1955) 131-36.
Spiegel, S. The last Trial. New York. 1967.
Stein, E. Philo und der Midrasch (BZAW 57). Giessen. 1931.
Tcherikover, V. A. "The Decline of the Jewish Diaspora in Egypt in the
  Roman Period", Journal of Jewish Studies 14 (1963) 1-32.

——, "Jewish Apologetic literature reconsidered", *Symbolae R. Taubenschlag dedicatae* 3 (EOS. Commentarii Soc. Philol. Polonorum 48/3). Warsaw. 1957.

Thyen, H. *Der Stil der jüdisch-hellenistischen Homilie* (FRLANT 65). Göttingen. 1955.

——, "Die Probleme der neueren Philo-Forschung", *TRu* 23 (1955) 230-46.

Vermes, G. *Scripture and Tradition in Judaism* (SPB 4). Leiden. 1961.

Weiss, H.-F. *Untersuchungen zur Kosmologie des hellenistischen und palästinischen Judentums* (TU 97). Berlin. 1966.

Westermann, C. *Die Verheissungen an die Väter* (FRLANT 116). Göttingen. 1976.

White, H. C. "The Divine Oath in Genesis", *JBL* 92 (1973) 165-79.

Wolfson, H. A. *Philo. Foundations of Religious Philosophy in Judaism, Christianity, and Islam*, 2 vols. Cambridge, Mass. 1948.

B. *The New Testament and Early Christianity in general*

Andrén, O. *Rättfärdighet och frid. En studie i det första Clemensbrevet.* Uppsala. 1960.

Bauer, W. *Rechtgläubigkeit und Ketzerei im ältesten Christentum.* Ed. and with suppl. by G. Strecker. 2nd edition (BHT 10). Tübingen. 1964.

Baur, F. C. *Vorlesungen über neutestamentliche Theologie.* Leipzig. 1864.

Becker, J. "Das Gottesbild Jesu und die älteste Auslegung von Ostern", *Jesus Christus in Historie und Theologie. Neutestamentliche Festschrift für H. Conzelmann zum 60. Geburtstag.* Ed. by G. Strecker. Tübingen. 1975, 105-26.

Black, M. "Critical and Exegetical Notes on three New Testament Texts: Hebrews XI. 11, Jude 5, James I. 27", *Apophoreta. Festschrift für E. Haenchen.* Ed. by W. Eltester (BZNW 30). Berlin. 1964, 39-45.

Boers, H. *Theology out of the Ghetto. A New Testament Exegetical Study concerning Religious Exclusiveness.* Leiden. 1971.

Borgen, P. *Bread from Heaven* (NovTSup 10). Leiden. 1965.

Bousset, W. *Jüdisch-christlicher Schulbetrieb in Alexandria und Rom* (FRLANT 23) Göttingen. 1915.

Brown, R. E. "The Semitic Background of the New Testament *Mysterion*", *Bib* 39 (1958) 426-48, 40 (1959) 70-87.

Bultmann, R. *Die Geschichte der synoptischen Tradition.* 5th edition. Göttingen. 1961.

——, *Theologie des Neuen Testaments.* 6th edition. Tübingen. 1968.

——, "The Transformation of the Idea of the Church in the History of Early Christianity", *Canadian Journal of Theology* 1 (1955) 73-81.

——, "Welchen Sinn hat es, von Gott zu reden?" *Glauben und Verstehen* 1. 2nd edition. Tübingen. 1954, 26-37.

Chadwick, H. "Justification by Faith and Hospitality", *Studia Patristica* 4 (TU 79). Berlin. 1961, 281-85.

Cullmann, O. "Dissensions within the Early Church", R. Batey, ed. *New Testament Issues.* London. 1970, 119-29.

Dahl, N. A. "Eschatologie und Geschichte im Lichte der Qumrantexte", *Zeit und Geschichte. Dankesgabe an R. Bultmann.* Ed. by E. Dinkler. Tübingen. 1964, 3-18.

——, "Der Erstgeborene Satans und der Vater des Teufels (Polyk 7:1 und Joh 8:44)", *Apophoreta. Festschrift für E. Haenchen.* Ed. by W. Eltester (BZNW 30). Berlin. 1964, 70-84.

——, "Letter", *IDBSup* (1976) 538-41.
——, "Nations in the New Testament", *New Testament and Christianity for Africa and the World*: Essays in Honour of H. Sawyerr. Ed. by M. E. Glasswell and E. W. Fashole-Luke. London. 1974, 54-68.
——, "The Neglected Factor in New Testament Theology", *Reflection* 73/1 (Yale Div. School, New Haven, 1975) 5-8.
——, "The Story of Abraham in Luke-Acts", *Studies in Luke-Acts. Studies presented in honor of P. Schubert*. Ed. by L. E. Keck and J. L. Martyn. Nashville, Tenn. 1966, 139-58.
——, *Das Volk Gottes. Eine Untersuchung zum Kirchenbewusstsein des Urchristentums* (Skrifter utg. av Det Norske Vidensk. Akad. i Oslo 2. Hist.-fil. kl. 1941/2) Oslo. 1941.
Davies, W. D. *The Gospel and the Land. Early Christianity and Jewish Territorial Doctrine*. Berkeley, Calif. 1974.
Deichgräber, R. *Gotteshymnus und Christushymnus der frühen Christenheit* (Studien zur Umwelt des Neuen Testaments 5). Göttingen. 1967.
Delling, G. "Μόνος θεός", *TLZ* 77 (1952) 469-76.
Devisch, M. "Le document Q, source de Matthieu. Problématique actuelle", M. Didier, ed. *L'Evangile selon Matthieu* (BETL 29) Gembloux. 1972, 71-97.
Dibelius, M. *Aufsätze zur Apostelgeschichte*. Ed. by H. Greeven. 3rd edition. Göttingen. 1957.
——, *Der Brief des Jakobus*. Ed. by H. Greeven. (MeyerK 15 11th edition). Göttingen. 1964.
——, "Jungfrauensohn und Krippenkind", *Botschaft und Geschichte* 1. Ed. by G. Bornkamm. Tübingen. 1953, 1-78.
Dodd, C. H. "A l'arrière-plan d'un dialogue johannique", *RHPR* 37 (1957) 5-17.
Gager, G. *Kingdom and Community. The Social World of Early Christianity*. Englewood Cliffs, N.J. 1975.
Georgi, P. "Der Kampf um die reine Lehre im Urchristentum als Auseinandersetzung um das rechte Verständnis der an Israel ergangenen Offenbarung Gottes", Eckert, W. P.; Levinson, N. P.; Stöhr, M. eds. *Antijudaismus im Neuen Testament?* (Abh. z. christlich-jüdischen Dialog 2). Munich. 1967, 82-94.
Grässer, E. *Der Glaube im Hebräerbrief* (Marburger theol. Studien. 2) Marburg. 1965.
——, "Der Hebräerbrief 1938-63", *TRu* 30 (1965) 138-236.
Grant, R. M. *The Early Christian Doctrine of God*. Charlottesville, Virginia. 1966.
Haenchen, E. *Die Apostelgeschichte*. (MeyerK 3, 15th edition). Göttingen. 1968.
Hagner, D. A. *The Use of the Old and the New Testament in Clement of Rome* (NovTSup 34). Leiden. 1973.
Hahn, F. "Genesis 15:6 im Neuen Testament", *Probleme biblischer Theologie. G. von Rad zum 70. Geburtstag*. Ed. by H. W. Wolff. Munich. 1971, 90-107.
Hare, D. R. A. *The Theme of Jewish Persecution of Christians in the Gospel according to St. Matthew* (SNTSMS 6), Cambridge. 1967.
Hengel, M. "Die Ursprünge der christlichen Mission", *NTS* 18 (1971-72) 15-38.
——, "Zwischen Jesus und Paulus. Die 'Hellenisten', die 'Sieben' und Stephanus", *ZTK* 72 (1975) 151-206.
Hofius, O. "Die Unabänderlichkeit des göttlichen Heilsratschlusses", *ZNW* 64 (1973) 135-45.

Jervell, J. *Luke and the People of God*. Minneapolis. 1972.
Judge, E. A. *The Social Pattern of the Christian Groups in the First Century*. London. 1960.
Käsemann, E. *Exegetische Versuche und Besinnungen*. 2 vols. in 1. 6th and 3rd edition. Göttingen. 1970.
——, *Das wandernde Gottesvolk*. 4th edition (FRLANT 55). Göttingen. 1961.
Keck, L. E. "On the Ethos of Early Christianity", *Journal of the American Academy of Religion* 42 (1974) 435-52.
Kilgallen, J. *The Stephen Speech. A Literary and Redactional Study of Acts 7:2-53* (AnBib 67). Rome. 1976.
Köster, H. "Die Auslegung der Abraham-Verheissung in Hebräer 6", *Studien zur Theologie der alttestamentlichen Überlieferungen. Festschrift für G. von Rad*. Ed. by R. Rendtorff and K. Koch. Neukirchen. 1961, 95-109.
——, "Häretiker im Urchristentum als theologisches Problem", *Zeit und Geschichte. Dankesgabe an R. Bultmann*. Ed. by E. Dinkler. Tübingen. 1964, 65-83.
Kramer, W. *Christos, Kyrios, Gottessohn*. (ATANT 44). Zürich. 1963.
Kreissig, H. "Zur sozialen Zusammensetzung der früchristlichen Gemeinden im ersten Jahrhundert u. Z.", *Eirene* 6 (1967) 91-100.
Kümmel, W. G. *Einleitung in das Neue Testament*. 13th edition. Heidelberg. 1964.
——, "Die Gottesverkündigung Jesu und der Gottesgedanke des Spätjudentums", *Judaica* 1 (1945) 40-68.
——, *Theologie des Neuen Testaments* (NTD Ergänzungsr. 3). Göttingen. 1969.
Leivestad, R. *Christ the Conqueror. Ideas of Conflict and Victory in the New Testament*. London. 1954.
Lindars, B. *New Testament Apologetic*. 2nd. impr. London. 1973.
Lohfink, G. *Die Sammlung Israels. Eine Untersuchung zur lukanischen Ekklesiologie* (SANT 39). Munich. 1975.
Lona, H. E. *Abraham in Johannes 8. Ein Beitrag zur Methodenfrage* (EHS.T 65). Frankfurt. 1976.
Luz, U. "Einige Erwägungen zur Auslegung Gottes in der ethischen Verkündigung Jesu", *Evangelisch-katholischer Kommentar zum NT, Vorarbeiten* 2. Neukirchen. 1970, 119-30, 133-35.
McEleney, N. J. "Orthodoxy and Heterodoxy in the New Testament", *Proceedings of the Catholic Theological Society of America* 25 (1971) 54-77.
Mauser, U. W. *Gottesbild und Menschwerdung* (BHT 43). Tübingen. 1971.
Meeks, W. A. "The Man from Heaven in Johannine Sectarianism", *JBL* 91 (1972) 44-72.
Michel, O. *Der Brief an die Hebräer* (MeyerK 13. 12th edition). Göttingen. 1966.
Michel, O. "Polemik und Scheidung", *Basileia. W. Freytag zum 60. Geburtstag*. Ed. by J. Hermelink and H. J. Margull. Stuttgart. 1959, 185-98. (Also in *Judaica* 15 (1959) 193-212).
Miranda, J. P. *Der Vater, der mich gesandt hat. Religionsgeschichtliche Untersuchungen zu den johanneischen Sendungsformeln* (EHS.T 7). Frankfurt. 1972.
Osten-Sacken, P. von der, "Streitgespräch und Parabel als Formen markanischen Christologie", *Jesus Christus in Historie und Theologie. Festschrift für H. Conzelmann zum 60. Geburtstag*. Ed. by G. Strecker. Tübingen. 1975, 375-94.
Rese, M. "Formeln und Lieder im Neuen Testament", *VF* 15/2 (1970) 75-95.

Richardson, P. *Israel in the Apostolic Church* (SNTSMS 10). Cambridge. 1969.

Rigaux, B. *Dieu l'a ressuscité* (Studii biblici franciscani analecta 4). Gembloux. 1973.

Robinson, J. M. "Die Hodajot-Formel in Gebet und Hymnus des Frühchristentums", *Apophoreta. Festschrift für E. Haenchen*. Ed. by W. Eltester (BZNW 30). Berlin. 1964. 194-235.

Schelkle, K. H. *Theologie des Neuen Testaments*. 1ff. Düsseldorf. 1968ff.

Schmid, H. H. "Schöpfung, Gerechtigkeit und Heil. Schöpfungstheologie als Gesamthorizont biblischer Theologie", *ZTK* 70 (1973) 1-19.

Schneider, "Urchristliche Gottesverkündigung in hellenistischer Umwelt", *BZ* 13 (1969) 59-75.

Schütz, J. H. "Ethos of Early Christianity", *IDBSup* (1976) 289-93.

Schürmann, H. *Das Lukasevangelium* 1 (HTKNT 3/1). Freiburg. 1969.

Smith, J. Z. "The Social Description of Early Christianity", *Religious Studies Review* 1 (1975) 19-25.

Spicq, C. *L'Epître aux Hebreux*. 2 vols. Paris. 1952-53.

Stuhlmacher, P. "Das Bekenntnis zur Auferweckung Jesu von den Toten und die Biblische Theologie", *ZTK* 70 (1973) 365-403.

Theissen, G. "Theoretische Probleme religionssoziologischer Forschung und die Analyse des Urchristentums", *Neue Zeitschrift für systematische Theologie* 16 (1974) 35-56.

Thüsing, W. "Neutestamentliche Zugangswege zu einer transzendental-dialogischen Christologie", K. Rahner and W. Thüsing, eds. *Christologie — systematisch und exegetisch* (QD 55). Freiburg. 1972, 81-233.

Unnik, W. C. van, " 'Alles ist dir möglich' (Mk. 14:36)", *Verborum Veritas. Festschrift für G. Stählin zum 70. Geburtstag*. Ed. by O. Böcher and K. Haacker. Wuppertal. 1970, 27-36.

——, "Die Rücksicht auf die Reaktion der Nicht-Christen als Motif in der altchristlichen Paränese", *Judentum, Urchristentum, Kirche. Festschrift für J. Jeremias*. Ed. by W. Eltester (BZNW 26). Berlin. 1960, 221-34.

Vanhoye, A. *La structure littéraire de l'épître aux Hébreux* (Studia Neotestamentica, Studia 1). Paris. 1963.

Ward, R. B. "The Works of Abraham", *HTR* 61 (1968) 283-90.

Weiss, H.-F. "Zur Frage der historischen Voraussetzungen der Begegnung von Antike und Christentum", *Klio* 43-45 (1965) 307-28.

Wilson, S. G. *The Gentiles and the Gentile Mission in Luke-Acts* (SNTSMS 23). Cambridge. 1973.

Windisch, H. *Der Hebräerbrief*. 2nd rev. edition. (HNT 17). Tübingen. 1931.

C. Paul

Althaus, P. *Der Brief an die Römer* (NTD 6, 10th rev. edition). Göttingen. 1966.

Bammel, E. "Gottes διαθήκη (Gal III. 15-17) und das jüdische Rechtsdenken", *NTS* 6 (1959-60) 313-19.

Barrett, C. K. "The Allegory of Abraham, Sarah, and Hagar in the Argument of Galatians", *Rechtfertigung. Festschrift für E. Käsemann zum 70. Geburtstag*. Ed. by J. Friedrich, W. Pöhlmann and P. Stuhlmacher. Tübingen. 1976, 1-16.

——, *A Commentary on the Epistle to the Romans*. London. 1957.

Barth. M. "Jews and Gentiles: The Social Character of Justification in Paul", *Journal of Ecumenical Studies* 5 (1968) 241-67.

Baumgarten, J. *Paulus und die Apokalyptik. Die Auslegung apokalyptischer Überlieferungen in den echten Paulusbriefen* (WMANT 44). Neukirchen. 1976.

Berger, K. "Abraham in den paulinischen Hauptbriefen", *Münchener Theologische Zeitschrift* 17 (1966) 47-89.

Betz, H. D. "In Defense of the Spirit: Paul's letter to the Galatians as a Document of Early Christian Apologetics", E. S. Fiorenza, ed. *Aspects of Religious Propaganda in Judaism and Early Christianity* (Univ. of Notre Dame Center for the Study of Judaism and Christianity in Antiquity 2). Notre Dame, Ind. 1976, 99-114.

——, "Spirit, Freedom and Law", *SEÅ* 39 (1974) 145-60.

Binder, H. *Der Glaube bei Paulus*. Berlin. 1968.

Bjerkelund, C. J. " 'Nach menschlicher Weise rede Ich'. Funktion und Sinn des paulinischen Ausdrucks", *ST* 26 (1972) 63-100.

——, *Parakalo* (Bibliotheca Theologica Norvegica 1). Oslo. 1967.

" 'Vergeblich' als Missionsergebnis bei Paulus", *God's Christ and His People. Studies in Honour of Nils Alstrup Dahl*. Ed. by J. Jervell and W. A. Meeks. Oslo. 1977, 175-91.

Boobyer, G. H. "*Thanksgiving*" and the "*Glory of God*" in Paul. Leipzig. 1929.

Bornkamm, G. "Die Offenbarung des Zornes Gottes", *Das Ende des Gesetzes*. Gesammelte Aufsätze 1. 5th edition (BEvT 16). Munich, 1966, 1-33.

——, "Sünde, Gesetz und Tod (Röm 7)", ibid. 51-69.

——, "Der Römerbrief als Testament des Paulus", *Geschichte und Glaube* 2. Gesammelte Aufsätze 4 (BEvT 53). Munich. 1971, 120-39.

——, "Theologie als Teufelskunst", *ibid.* 140-48.

Bouttier, M. *La condition chrétienne selon Saint Paul* (Nouvelle série théologique 16). Geneva. 1964.

Bultmann, R. "Die Bedeutung des geschichtlichen Jesus für die Theologie des Paulus", *Glauben und Verstehen* 1. 2nd edition, Tübingen. 1954, 188-213.

——, "Glossen im Römerbrief", *TLZ* 72 (1947) 197-202.

——, *Der Stil der paulinischen Predigt und die kynisch-stoische Diatribe* (FRLANT 13). Göttingen. 1910.

Bussmann, C. *Themen der paulinischen Missionspredigt auf dem Hintergrund der spätjüdisch-hellenistischen Missionsliteratur* (EHS.T 3). Frankfurt. 1971.

Cerfaux, L. " 'Kyrios' dans les citations pauliniennes de l'Ancien Testament", *Recueil L. Cerfaux* 1 (BETL 6-7/1). Gembloux. 1954, 173-88.

——, *La théologie de l'Église suivant Saint Paul*. 2nd rev. edition (Unam Sanctam 10). Paris. 1948.

Conzelmann, H. *Der erste Brief an die Korinther* (MeyerK 5. 11th edition). Göttingen. 1969.

Cranfield, C. E. B. *The Epistle to the Romans* (International Critical Commentary). Edinburgh. 1975.

Dahl, N. A. "Two Notes on Romans 5", *ST* 5 (1952) 37-48.

——, *Studies in Paul*. Minneapolis. 1977.

——, "Widersprüche in der Bibel. Ein altes hermeneutisches Problem", *ST* 25 (1971) 1-19.

Davies, W. D. "Paul and the People of Israel", *NTS* 24 (1978) 4-39.

——, *Paul and Rabbinic Judaism*. Rev. edition. New York. (1955). Repr. 1967.

Delling, G. "Die Bezeichnung "Gott des Friedens" und ähnliche Wendungen in den Paulusbriefen", *Jesus und Paulus. Festschrift für W. G. Kümmel*. Ed. by E. E. Ellis and E. Grässer. Göttingen. 1975, 76-84.

——, "Partizipiale Gottesprädikationen in den Briefen des Neuen Testaments", *ST* 17 (1963) 1-59.

——, "Zusammengesetzte Gottes- und Christusbezeichnungen in den Paulus-briefen", *Studien zum Neuen Testament und zum hellenistischen Judentum.* Ed. by F. Hahn, T. Holtz and N. Walter. Göttingen. 1970. 417-24.

Demke, Ch. " 'Ein Gott und viele Herren'. Die Verkündigung des einen Gottes in den Briefen des Paulus", *EvT* 36 (1976) 473-84.

Donfried, K. P. "False Presuppositions in the Study of Romans", *CBQ* 36 (1974) 332-55.

Doty, W. G. *Letters in Primitive Christianity.* Philadelphia. 1973.

Doughty, D. J. "The Priority of χάρις. An Investigation of the Theological Language of Paul", *NTS* 19 (1972-73) 163-80.

Dreiergaard, K. "Jödernes fortrin. En undersögelse av Rom 3:1-9", *DTT* 35 (1973) 81-101.

Eckert, J. *Die urchristliche Verkündigung im Streit zwischen Paulus und seinen Gegnern nach dem Galaterbrief* (Biblische Untersuchungen 6). Regens-burg. 1971.

Eichholz, G. *Die Theologie des Paulus im Umriss.* Neukirchen. 1972.

Ellis, E. E. *Paul's Use of the Old Testament.* Edinburgh. 1957.

Feuillet, A. "Les attaches bibliques des antithèses pauliniennes dans la première partie de l'épître aux Romains (1-8)", *Mélanges bibliques en hommage au R. P. B. Rigaux.* Ed. by A. Descamps *et al.* Gembloux. 1970, 323-49.

Fischer, J. A. "Pauline Literary Forms and Thought Patterns", *CBQ* 39 (1977) 209-23.

Funk, R. W. "The Apostolic *parousia*: Form and Significance", *Christian History and Interpretation. Studies Presented to J. Knox.* Ed. by W. R. Farmer, C. F. D. Moule and R. R. Niebuhr. Cambridge. 1967, 249-68.

Georgi, D. *Die Gegner des Paulus im 2. Korintherbrief* (WMANT 11). Neu-kirchen. 1964.

——, *Die Geschichte der Kollekte des Paulus für Jerusalem* (Theologische Forschung 8). Hamburg. 1965.

Giblin, C. H. "Three Monotheistic Texts in Paul", *CBQ* 37 (1975) 527-47.

Goppelt, L. "Apokalyptik und Typologie bei Paulus", *TLZ* 89 (1964) 321-44.

Hahn, F. "Das Gesetzesverständnis im Römer- und Galaterbrief", *ZNW* 67 (1976) 29-63.

Hanson, A. T. *Studies in Paul's Technique and Theology.* London. 1974.

Heidland, H.-W. *Die Anrechnung des Glaubens zur Gerechtigkeit* (BWANT 4/18). Stuttgart. 1936.

Hester, J. D. *Paul's Concept of Inheritance* (Scottish Journal of Theology. Occasional Papers 14). Edinburgh. 1968.

Hofius, O. "Eine altjüdische Parallele zu Röm IV: 17b", *NTS* 18 (1971-72) 93-94.

Jeremias, J. "Chiasmus in den Paulusbriefen", *ZNW* 49 (1958) 145-56.

——, "Zur Gedankenführung in den paulinischen Briefen", *Studia Paulina. In honorem J. de Zwaan.* Ed. J. N. Sevenster and W. C. van Unnik. Haarlem. 1953, 146-54.

——, "Die Gedankenführung in Röm 4". *Foi et salut selon S. Paul* (AnBib 42). Rome. 1970, 51-58.

——, "Paulus als Hillelit", *Neotestamentica et semitica. Studies in Honour of M. Black.* Ed. by E. E. Ellis and M. Wilcox. Edinburgh. 1968, 88-94.

Jervell, J. "Der Brief nach Jerusalem. Über Veranlassung und Adresse des Römerbriefs", *ST* 25 (1971) 61-73.

——, *Gud og hans fiender. Et forsök på å tolke Romerbrevet.* Oslo. 1973.

——, *Imago Dei. Gen 1.26f im Spätjudentum, in der Gnosis und in den paulinischen Briefen* (FRLANT 76). Göttingen. 1959.
——, "Der schwache Charismatiker", *Rechtfertigung. Festschrift für E. Käsemann zum 70. Geburtstag*. Ed. by J. Friedrich, W. Pöhlmann and P. Stuhlmacher. Tübingen. 1976, 184-98.
——, "Das Volk des Geistes", *God's Christ and His People. Studies in Honour of Nils Alstrup Dahl*. Ed. by J. Jervell and W. A. Meeks, Oslo, 1977, 87-106.
Judge, E. A. "St. Paul and Classical Society", *Jahrbuch für Antike und Christentum* 15 (1972) 19-36.
Käsemann, E. "Geist und Buchstabe", *Paulinische Perspektiven*. Tübingen. 1969, 237-85.
——, "Der Glaube Abrahams in Römer 4", *ibid*. 140-77.
——, "Rechtfertigung und Heilsgeschichte im Römerbrief", *ibid*. 108-39.
——, *An die Römer*. 3rd rev. edition (HNT 8a). Tübingen. 1974.
Karris, R. J. "Rom 14:1-15:13 and the Occasion of Romans", *CBQ* 35 (1973) 155-78.
Kertelge, K. "Zur Deutung des Rechtfertigungsbegriffs im Galaterbrief", *BZ* 12 (1968) 211-22.
——, *"Rechtfertigung" bei Paulus* (NTAbh NF 3). Münster. 1967.
Klaiber, W. "Die Bedeutung der justificatio impii für die Ekklesiologie des Paulus". Unpubl. diss. Tübingen. 1971.
Klein, G. "Exegetische Probleme in Römer III. 21-IV. 25", *EvT* 24 (1964) 676-83.
——, "Gottes Gerechtigkeit als Thema der neuesten Paulusforschung", *VF* 12/2 (1967) 1-11.
——, "Römer IV und die Idee der Heilsgeschichte", *EvT* 23 (1963) 424-47.
Kolenkow, A. "The Ascription of Romans 4.5", *HTR* 60 (1967) 228-30.
Kuhl, E. *Der Brief des Paulus an die Römer*. Leipzig. 1913.
Kuss, O. *Der Römerbrief* 1. 2nd edition. Regensburg. 1963.
——, *Paulus. Die Rolle des Apostels in der theologischen Entwicklung der Urkirche*. Regensburg. 1971.
Lagrange, M.-J. S. *Paul. Epître aux Romains*. 6th print. Paris. 1950.
Lohmeyer, E. *Grundlagen paulinischer Theologie* (BHT 1). Tübingen, 1929.
Lohse, E. "Die Gerechtigkeit Gottes in der paulinischen Theologie", *Die Einheit des Neuen Testaments*. Göttingen. 1973, 210-27.
Luz, L. "Der alte und der neue Bund bei Paulus und im Hebräerbrief", *EvT* 27 (1967) 318-36.
——, *Das Geschichtsverständnis des Paulus* (BEvT 49). Munich. 1968.
Mauser, U. "Galater III. 20: Die Universalität des Heils", *NTS* 13 (1966-67) 258-70.
Michel, O. *Der Brief an die Römer* (MeyerK 4. 13th edition). Göttingen. 1966.
——, "Fragen zu 1 Thessalonicher 2:14-16: Antijüdische Polemik bei Paulus?" Eckert, W. P.; Levinson, N. P.; Stöhr, M. eds. *Antijudaismus im Neuen Testament?* (Abh. z. christlich-jüdischen Dialog 2). Munich. 1967, 50-59.
Minde, H. J. van der, *Schrift und Tradition bei Paulus: Ihre Bedeutung und Funktion im Römerbrief* (Paderborner Theologische Studien 3). Munich. 1976.
Minear, P. *The Obedience of faith. The Purpose of Paul in the Epistle to the Romans* (SBT 2/19) London. 1971.
Morris, L. "The Theme of Romans", *Apostolic History and the Gospel, Biblical and Historical Essays presented to F. F. Bruce*. Ed. W. W. Gasque and R. P. Martin. Exeter. 1970, 249-63.

Müller, Ch. *Gottes Gerechtigkeit und Gottes Volk* (FRLANT 86). Göttingen. 1964.
Müller, K. *Anstoss und Gericht. Eine Studie zum jüdischen Hintergrund des paulinischen Skandalonbegriffs* (SANT 19). Munich. 1969.
Munck, J. *Christus und Israel. Eine Auslegung von Röm* 9-11 (Acta Jutlandica 28/3. Theology Series 7). Aarhus. 1956.
Mussner, F. *Der Galaterbrief.* 2nd edition (HTKNT 9). Freiburg. 1974.
Nelis, J. "L'antithèse littéraire ΖΩΗ - ΘΑΝΑΤΟΣ dans les Épîtres pauliniennes", *Ephimerides theologicae lovanienses* 20 (1943) 18-53.
Neugebauer, F. *In Christus. Eine Untersuchung zum paulinischen Glaubensverständnis.* Göttingen. 1961.
Nickle, K. F. *The Collection. A Study in Paul's Strategy* (SBT 48). London. 1966.
Norden, E. *Agnostos Theos. Untersuchungen zur Formgeschichte religiöser Rede.* (1913). 4th edition. Darmstadt. 1956.
Nygren, A. *Commentary on Romans.* London. 1952.
Olson, S. N. "Confidence Expressions in Paul: Epistolary Conventions and the Purpose of 2 Corinthians". Unpubl. Ph.D. diss. Yale University. 1976.
Olsson, B. "Rom 1:3f enlight Paulus", *SEÅ* 37-38 (1973) 255-73.
Rese, M. "Die Vorzüge Israels in Rom 9, 4f und Eph 2, 12", *TZ* 31 (1975) 211-22.
Ridderbos, H. *Paul. An Outline of his Theology.* Grand Rapids, Mich. 1975.
Rohde, E. "Gottesglaube und Kyriosglaube bei Paulus", *ZNW* 22 (1923) 43-57.
Sanders, E. P. *Paul and Palestinian Judaism.* London. 1977.
Schelkle, K. H. *Paulus. Lehrer der Väter.* Düsseldorf. 1956.
Schlatter, A. *Gottes Gerechtigkeit. Ein Kommentar zum Römerbrief.* Stuttgart. 1935.
Schlier, H. *Der Brief an die Galater* (MeyerK 7. 12th edition). Göttingen. 1962.
Schmidt, H. W. *Der Brief des Paulus an die Römer* (Theol. Handkomm. z. NT 6). Berlin. 1962.
Schmithals, W. *Der Römerbrief als historisches Problem* (Studien z. NT 9). Gütersloh. 1975.
Schneider, N. *Die rhetorische Eigenart der paulinischen Antithese* (Hermeneutische Untersuchungen zur Theologie 11). Tübingen. 1970.
Schrage, W. "Theologie und Christologie bei Paulus und Jesus auf dem Hintergrund der modernen Gottesfrage", *EvT* 36 (1976) 121-54.
Schrenk, G. *Studien zu Paulus* (ATANT 26). Zürich. 1954.
Schütz, J. H. *Paul and the Anatomy of Apostolic Authority* (SNTSMS 26). Cambridge. 1975.
Schwantes, H. *Schöpfung der Endzeit* (Arbeiten zur Theologie 1/12). Stuttgart. 1962.
Scroggs, R. "Paul as Rhetorician: Two Homilies in Romans 1-11", *Jews, Greeks and Christians. Essays in Honor of W. D. Davies.* Ed. by K. Hamerton-Kelly and R. Scroggs (SJLA 21). Leiden. 1976, 271-98.
Spicq, C. "᾽Αμεταμέλητος dans Rom XI:29", *RB* 67 (1967) 210-19.
Stendahl, K. "The Apostle Paul and the Introspective Conscience of the West", *HTR* 56 (1963) 198-215.
——, *Paul among Jews and Gentiles.* Philadelphia. 1976.
Stolle, V. "Die Eins in Gal 3:15-29". *Festgabe für K. H. Rengstorf zum 70. Geburtstag.* Ed. by W. Dietrich, P. Freimark and H. Schreckenberg (Theokratia 2). Leiden. 1973, 204-13.
Stuhlmacher, P. "Erwägungen zum ontologischen Charakter der καινὴ κτίσις bei Paulus", *EvT* 27 (1967) 1-35.

——, *Gerechtigkeit Gottes bei Paulus*. 2nd rev. edition (FRLANT 87). Göttingen. 1966.
——, "Zur neueren Exegese von Röm 3:24-26", *Jesus und Paulus. Festschrift für W. G. Kümmel zum 70. Geburtstag*. Ed. by E. E. Ellis and E. Grässer. Göttingen. 1975, 315-33.
——, "Theologische Probleme des Römerbriefpräskripts", *EvT* 27 (1967) 374-89.
Theissen, G. "Soziale Schichtung in der korinthischen Gemeinde", *ZNW* 65 (1974) 232-72.
Thüsing, W. *Per Christum in Deum. Studien zur Verhältnis von Christozentrik und Theozentrik in den paulinischen Hauptbriefen* (NTAbh NF 1). Münster. 1965.
Wegenast, K. *Das Verständnis der Tradition bei Paulus und in den Deuteropaulinen* (WMANT 8). Neukirchen. 1962.
Weiss, J. "Beiträge zur paulinischen Rhetorik", *Theologische Studien B. Weiss zu seinem 70. Geburtstage dargebracht*. Göttingen. 1897, 165-247.
Wilckens, U. "Die Rechtfertigung Abrahams nach Römer 4", *Studien zur Theologie der alttestamentlichen Überlieferungen. Festschrift für G. von Rad*. Ed. by R. Rendtorff and K. Koch. Neukirchen. 1961, 11-27.
——, "Zu Römer 3:21-4:25. Antwort an G. Klein", *EvT* 24 (1964) 586-610.
Wiles, G. P. *Paul's Intercessory Prayers* (SNTSMS 24). Cambridge. 1974.
Wire, A. C. "Pauline Theology as an Understanding of God: The Explicit and the Implicit". Unpubl. Ph.D. diss. Claremont. 1974.
Wuellner, W. "Paul's Rhetoric of Argumentation in Romans", *CBQ* 38 (1976) 330-51.
Ziesler, J. A. *The Meaning of Righteousness in Paul*. (SNTSMS 20). Cambridge. 1972.
Zeller, D. *Juden und Heiden in der Mission des Paulus. Studien zum Römerbrief* (Forschung zur Bibel 8). Stuttgart. 1973.
Zuntz, G. *The Text of the Pauline Epistles*. London. 1953.

SCRIPTURE INDEX

When a larger passage is discussed in detail, individual verses within the passage are normally not listed separately.

I. OLD TESTAMENT

II. NEW TESTAMENT

IV. OTHER JEWISH WRITINGS

V. EARLY CHRISTIAN LITERATURE